Wrestling with Diversity

SANFORD LEVINSON

Wrestling with Diversity

Duke University Press DURHAM & LONDON 2003

© 2003 Duke University Press
All rights reserved
Printed in the United States
of America on acid-free paper ∞
Designed by Rebecca M. Giménez
Typeset in Sabon with Clarendon
display by Keystone Typesetting, Inc.
Library of Congress Cataloging-in-
Publication Data appear on the
last printed page of this book.

To Cynthia, a splendid

wife, mother, grandmother, and

all-around human being

Contents

Acknowledgments

One of the most satisfying things about finishing a book is the opportunity it allows to acknowledge those whose help contributed to it. Whether or not it takes a village to raise a child, it certainly took a community of friends, at least in my case, to produce the work herein. I will make no effort to thank everyone who in fact might deserve such thanks, for the names would simply go on too long. I do, however, want to select out some particular individuals without whom it is truly the case that some of these essays would not have been written.

A number of these essays began as invited lectures or presentations, and I am grateful for the opportunity to give them and the goad to write they provided. "Diversity" was first given as the Fiscus Lecture at Skidmore College and then considerably revised for presentation as the Owen J. Roberts Memorial Lecture at the University of Pennsylvania Law School. "Promoting Diversity in the Public Schools (Or, To What Extent Does the Establishment Clause of the First Amendment Hinder the Establishment of More Genuinely Multicultural Schools?)" began as part of my duties as a participant in the Allen Seminar at the University of Richmond Law School, an invitation I owe to Gary Leedes; it was rewritten for a conference organized by Robbie George and Sotirios Barber to honor my former colleague at Princeton, Walter Murphy. " 'Getting Religion': Religion, Diversity, and Community in Public and Private Schools" was written for a conference on vouchers at Boston College organized by Alan Wolfe. I appreciate not only the invitation but the alacrity with which Alan accepted my suggestion that I collaborate with Meira Levinson, who is not only an accomplished political theorist, but also, and just as relevantly, a teacher in the public school systems of Atlanta and Boston. But my gratitude to Alan goes well beyond his service as the agent of our coauthorship. He is, I believe, one of our most distinguished and truly thoughtful "public intellectuals," and I hope he will recognize in these essays some of his own spirit of intellectual engagement.

"Identifying the Jewish Lawyer: Reflections on Professional Identity" was initially presented as the Pearl and Troy Feibel Lecture on Judaism and Law at Ohio State University. Two essays are about religion and judging. The first, "The Confrontation of Religious Faith and Civil Religion: Catholics Becoming Justices," was initially presented at the Charles S. Casassa, S.J., Conference at Loyola Marymount College, The American Constitutional Republic: Triumphs and Dilemmas; the second, "Abstinence and Exclusion: What Does Liberalism Demand of the Religiously Oriented (Would-Be) Judge?" was delivered at the Religion and Contemporary Liberalism conference at Notre Dame, organized by Paul J. Weithman. "National Loyalty, Communalism, and the Professional Identity of Lawyers" began as a lecture at Williams College, thanks to an invitation from Gary Jacobsohn. The penultimate essay, "Is Liberal Nationalism an Oxymoron? An Essay for Judith Shklar," was written as a book review for the journal *Ethics*. The final essay, previously unpublished, began as a paper written by Rachel Levinson for a seminar offered by Professor Mary Anne Case at the University of Chicago. She was the very model of a helpful teacher, providing fine suggestions as Rachel worked through successive drafts to produce a very fine paper.

No acknowledgment could fail to mention Jack Balkin, my friend and frequent collaborator. The fact that his name does is not on any of these essays does not mean that he did not read and respond to many of them; they are undoubtedly better than they might have been because of his suggestions. Other colleagues and friends (and wife) who offered invaluable responses to one or another of these essays include Cynthia Estlund, Sam Issacharoff, Doug Laycock, Cynthia Levinson, Robert Post, Scot Powe, John Rosenberg, Fred Schauer, Thomas Shaffer, Mark Tushnet, and Eugene Volokh. With regard to the essay "Identifying the Jewish Lawyer," special thanks are due to Jerold Auerbach, Perry Dane, Alan Dershowitz, Moshe Halbertal, Ruti Teitel, and Avi Soifer. I also must select out for thanks my friend George Fletcher, for his kindness in asking me to teach Eastern European lawyers in a program that he was directing in Hungary. I informally refer to the essay "National Loyalty, Communalism, and the Professional Identity of Lawyers" as my "Latvian lawyer" essay, and I would never have been forced to examine some of my own presuppositions had George (and the Democracy after Communism project) not brought together many lawyers from Latvia and elsewhere in the region.

Mention should be made of a "brooding omnipresence" over this entire book, Michael Walzer. It is not simply the fact that my own grappling with problems of pluralism was immeasurably advanced by my experience thirty-five years ago as a "section man" in his political theory course at Harvard, or that I have consistently benefited from his copious writings since then, from our conversations over the years, and from our participation together in conferences at the Shalom Hartman Institute for Jewish Philosophy in Jerusalem (to which thanks are also due). In addition, and just as important, I have taken great inspiration from his own devotion to the essay as a form of intellectual life. In every way, then, his spirit pervades this book.

One of the truly great joys in both my professional and personal lives is the fact that two of the essays in this book are cowritten with my daughters, Meira and Rachel. Both were acknowledged in my first book, published when Meira was seventeen years old and Rachel fourteen, as "splendid human beings," who did not, however, make any further contribution to the book in question. They remain altogether splendid persons, but they have now become intellectual colleagues as well. The process of collaboration was both wonderful and chastening, not least because both daughters, having become fully competent adults, felt no hesitation in criticizing my own writing and formulations of ideas. There is no sense of "senior" and "junior" authorship; it truly became a collaboration of equals. One reason, I suspect, that Meira and Rachel write in a far more disciplined manner than I do—I have never learned to outline an article, for example, preferring just to plunge into the writing and then reorganize as I go along—is the model provided by their mother, Cynthia Levinson, a gifted writer herself. My own indebtedness and gratitude to Cynthia are only hinted at by the dedication.

Introduction

It is almost a cliché to describe the United States as a "multicultural society." Indeed, this cliché is deeply rooted in our history. As long ago as 1782 J. Hector St. John de Crèvecoeur memorably asked, "What then, is the American, this new man? . . . Here individuals of all nations are melted into a new race of men, whose labours and posterity will one day cause great changes in the world."[1] A fundamental topic of debate since then, and certainly continuing into the present, is whether the congeries of nations "melts" into a single new national identity or, instead, comprises a mosaic or a "rainbow" or, far more ominously, a potential source of ineradicable conflict that ultimately threatens the social order itself. This debate is not confined to the United States. A contemporary de Crèvecoeur, observing developments throughout the world, could substitute almost any traditional national term for that of "American" and create a coherent question.

We often speak of nation-states, but it should be increasingly obvious that extremely few nations are confined to a single state and, even more to the point, even fewer states are composed of only one nation. What seemed two centuries ago exceptional about America is now, of course, the norm in most of the West and, I have little doubt, elsewhere as well. Nor should one, of course, overemphasize an overly rigid sense of "nation-stateness," even at the time de Crèvecoeur wrote. After all, the United Kingdom gets its name precisely because it unites the quite distinct English, Welsh, Scots, and Irish in a single political order, with consequences that have not been completely resolved to this day.

Whether one uses the catchphrases of "pluralism," "multiculturalism," or "diversity," it grows ever harder to know exactly what one is talking about when one refers to a "German," a "Spaniard," an "Indian," or even a "Swede." Not surprisingly, a key issue in many countries concerns the abil-

1. J. Hector St. John de Crèvecoeur, *Letters from an American Farmer* 111 (1782).

ity (or desirability) of preserving what some consider the "essence" of their culture, or must one simply accept the fact that globalization indeed entails the necessary encounters of often wildly disparate cultures that inevitably change and transform one another?

My principal goal in this book is to examine the various ways that we attempt to come to terms with—to "wrestle" with—the complex issues presented by contemporary life in a decidedly diverse, multicultural, and culturally pluralistic society. Sometimes the issues have explicitly legal dimensions, as with, for example, the legitimacy of taking racial or ethnic identity into account in determining university admissions or accommodating religious objections to compliance with otherwise general laws. But any such issues, if they are truly important, almost invariably test as well our philosophical or political intuitions. They would not, indeed, generate so much public passion if they were "merely" of legal concern. The general response to most matters of strictly legal concern, save those of individual plaintiffs or defendants, is, "who cares?" That is not the likely response of someone addressing the topic of affirmative action or the duty to tolerate what appear to be strange, even bizarre, cultural practices, such as those of an Afghani father, a refugee living in Portland, Maine, who was observed kissing the penis of his eighteen-month-old son and charged with violating a Maine law regulating sexual contact.[2]

Any perusal of journals like the *New York Times* amply reveals a plethora of examples of diversity and the problems posed by its reality at home and abroad. One cannot, for instance, understand the unwillingness of many states within the European Union to admit Turkey to their ranks, while seemingly eager to let in a variety of Eastern European countries formerly under the domain of the Soviet Union, if one does not take into account the patent fears of letting a predominantly Muslim country into what is thought to remain a predominantly Christian (or secular) Europe. One could similarly look at a notably ungenerous German history toward its Turkish "guest workers" or the ability of Jean-Marie Le Pen in France to mobilize public opinion against the perceived threat presented by Arab settlement in France. And, of course, articles have been rife, particularly since 11 September 2001, about the notable intolerance of the strands of Islam

2. See *State v. Kargar*, 679 A.2d 81 (Me. 1996), discussed in Jeremy Waldron, "One Law for All? The Logic of Cultural Accommodation," 59 *Wash. & Lee L. Rev.* 3, 5–7 (2002). See also Nancy A. Wanderer and Catherine R. Connors, "Culture and Crime: *Kargar* and the Existing Framework for a Cultural Defense," 47 *Buff. L. Rev.* 829 (1999).

dominant in Saudi Arabia and the bitter opposition of many Islamicists, there and elsewhere, to the "infection" of their culture by foreign ideals (such as some semblance of equal treatment of women).

Cultures may address one another in a variety of dimensions. Language is one obvious example. The French—but not only the French—are (in)famous for trying to preserve the purity of their language from infestation by foreign elements, whereas the American form of English is in many respects a pastiche of world languages that get absorbed into a common parlance. Religion is another obvious example, with an equal spectrum of possibilities. The Puritans who first arrived in New England from Great Britain were quite literally devoted to preserving a "pure" form of their religion, and some of them did not hesitate to send into exile or even execute heretics. Other Americans developed brand new religions, such as Mormonism or Christian Science, each of which was dramatically different from an established, "mainstream" Protestantism in which, say, Baptists, Methodists, Presbyterians, and Episcopalians could coexist, however uneasily at times.

Mormons were lynched in America, and Utah was refused admission to statehood until Mormon leaders declared that they had received a revelation in effect invalidating the duty of Mormon men to engage in plural marriage. Today, of course, Mormons are fully accepted as part of the American panoply, but similar acceptance is not necessarily found abroad when the Church of Jesus Christ of Latter-Day Saints sends its adherents literally all over the world seeking converts. And Evangelical Christians have paid with their lives for attempting to spread the "good news" of their theology to certain Islamic lands where Islam is viewed as the only acceptable religion.

Conversion implies a version of "out with the old, in with the new." Many Americans, of course, amalgamate what they deem "the best" of different religious traditions, often against the opposition of those who claim to be the guardians of the "authentic" norms of the religions in question. "Jews for Jesus" are only one example of such syncretism. One might suggest, incidentally, that the American penchant for "plural identity," such as "Irish American," "Italian American," and the like, is another form of recognizing the legitimacy of syncretic identity as against what might be called complete substitution of identities.

One could go on to offer an almost endless series of examples of "diversity," precisely because there is a literally infinite set of considerations that might lead us to identify ourselves as sufficiently different from one another, thus — or so it it is claimed — justifying some measure of state recognition of these differences and concomitant reflection in relevant social policies. The most basic claim of anyone committed to "diversity" is that "one size does not fit all." Yet, of course, a fundamental principle of liberal democracy is that in at least some important respects all of us are indeed equal and therefore entitled to only one "size" of social policy. Accordingly, Columbia legal philosopher Jeremy Waldron began a recent lecture, entitled "One Law for All? The Logic of Cultural Accommodation," with the ringing sentence, "Our belief in the rule of law commits us to the principle that the law should be the same for everyone: one law for all and no exceptions."[3] Consider in this regard the slogan "one person, one vote." Or consider the equally important slogan that "no person is above the law," which some take to mean that *everyone,* regardless of specific circumstances, has a similar obligation to obey whatever the law may be. That law might, of course, be unconstitutional, but, if so, it is presumably unconstitutional for everyone and not merely for some particular people who object to following its mandate because of their own cultural imperatives.

Needless to say, the issue is not quite so simple as is suggested by this last sentence; a major consideration in both law and wider social debate is the extent to which religious freedom or cultural diversity requires a certain level of exemption from otherwise applicable laws or social norms. Even Waldron does not really suggest that the law in fact is, or should be, so relentlessly universal. He notes, for example, that "Your average statute is riddled with exemptions for all sorts of [mundane] secular circumstances," which, at the least, make it impossible simply to adopt an appeal to universality of obligation to explain to someone why her religious or cultural claim is being dismissed.[4]

Another gifted philosopher, University of Chicago professor Martha Nussbaum, devoted her presidential address to a division of the American Philosophical Association to considering the important topic of how one should decide when the state should leave people alone to conduct their own family lives however they wish and when the state, on the contrary, should intervene to protect women (or children) from what is often accurately

3. Id. at 3.

4. Id. at 4 n.4, citing Douglas Laycock, "The Remnants of Free Exercise," 1990 *Sup. Ct. Rev.* 1, 50–51, for the general argument that a government must treat secularists and the religious equally when dispensing exemptions.

described as a minityranny. This is a key question, both theoretically and practically, for anyone interested in "diversity" and its possible limits. Most relevant for purposes of this book is Nussbaum's assertion that one can scarcely hope to resolve such a difficult issue by resorting to theoretical algorithms or the slogans of grand philosophical concepts. "In general," she observed, "tension within a theory does not necessarily show that it is defective; it may simply show that it is in touch with the difficulty of life."[5]

I take great comfort from Nussbaum's comment, not simply because she is certainly a distinguished philosopher (and a member of the faculty of the University of Chicago Law School), but also because her cautionary note is so very apt to the central topic of this book: how we should approach the manifold, almost protean, notions of diversity that structure so much contemporary public debate. This book, for good and perhaps for ill, is very much about "the difficulty of life" and the tensions presented therein. Some of these tensions are, as Nussbaum suggests, theoretical, at least for those who try to present some kind of overarching approach suitable to the resolution of concrete cases. But some of the tensions arise in a more direct, unphilosophical sense, inasmuch as the topics embraced by the singular word "diversity" touch the lives — and emotions — of millions of Americans (and others) and generate concomitant argument and even anger.

What follows are efforts at examining some of life's difficulties and the problems they present for someone ostensibly committed to honoring the claims of diversity. It would be misleading to describe them as "chapters" in a tightly woven book developing a fully argued thesis reflecting a general theory of diversity. To do so would be to deny the central insight that Nussbaum captures.

My primary professional identity is that of the academic lawyer, and I should acknowledge that this may help to explain my attraction to Nussbaum's comment. Lawyers, especially within the Anglo-American legal tradition, love the myriad facts of cases, not least because they are usually so useful in deflating the pretense of some general theory to capture the complexities of the world in a single framework. "General propositions" wrote Justice Holmes in perhaps the most influential dissenting opinion in our judicial history, "do not decide concrete cases." Indeed, he continued, "The

---

5. Martha Nussbaum, "The Future of Feminist Liberalism," Presidential Address to the American Philosophical Association Central Division (22 April 2000), quoted in Jacob T. Levy, "Liberalism's Divide After Socialism — and Before," 20/1 *Social Philosophy and Policy* (2003).

decision will depend on judgment or intuition more subtle than any articulate major premise."[6] A crystallizing moment in any law-school classroom is when a student, lulled into believing that there is indeed a master norm — a "general proposition" — that resolves everything, is presented with a new set of facts that tugs in a strikingly different direction and is then informed that, indeed, competing legal doctrines have developed in a variety of directions that ultimately foreclose any neat summary.

Moreover, anyone aware of legal history knows that what might indeed have looked, at one time, like a comprehensive doctrine becomes eroded by the passage of time and is often replaced by a view that would have been found unacceptable by an earlier generation of well-trained lawyers. "The life of the law," Holmes famously asserted in the first paragraph of his classic *Common Law,* "has not been logic: it has been experience."[7] And, I am confident, this is true not only of the particular (and, for some, peculiar) domain of the law, but also of any ostensibly theoretical reflections, including, most certainly, any reflections offered about such notions as diversity.

This book is composed of nine essays, written over the past decade, that explore one or another facet of the problems linked with what is often labeled "diversity" or "multiculturalism." My general interest in the topic, though, goes back at least to my growing up as a Jew during the 1950s in a small (and highly Protestant) North Carolina town, an experience discussed at some length in the second essay in this book, and then attending and graduating from Duke University during a period in which its leadership remained firmly committed to a vision of Southern parochialism that resisted recognizing the dawning of a distinctly new day of racial integration. Needless to say, the university changed its policies at the end of the 1960s, and it is now distinguished for its commitment to a (necessarily limited) variety of diversities.

I can trace my more systematic interest in these issues at least as far back as 1964, when I took a seminar from Professor Louis Hartz, famous for his *Liberal Tradition in America,* which argued that the United States was in significant ways organized around a single set of principles derived from the liberalism of the English philosopher John Locke. Nathan Glazer and Daniel Patrick Moynihan had just published their now-classic *Beyond the Melting Pot,* which pointed to the maintenance of ethnic communities

6. *Lochner v. New York,* 198 U.S. 45, 78 (1905).
7. Oliver Wendell Holmes, *The Common Law,* lecture 1 (1881).

within American life, and I decided to write my seminar paper on the potential tensions between certain forms of liberalism and attempts to preserve what today we would call "ethnic identity," which might involve certain quite illiberal assumptions. Just as important to my intellectual development, though, was the opportunity to work at Harvard with Michael Walzer, whose central focus was then the topic of political pluralism and the attendant legitimacy of conflicts of loyalties to organizations and institutions other than the state.

My first book, *Constitutional Faith* (1988), explicitly considered, among other things, the propriety of diversity with regard to constitutional interpretation. That is, should we necessarily accept the Supreme Court as offering "definitive" interpretations of constitutional meaning, a view that I labeled as "catholic," as against a more "protestant" view that accepted the possibility of a significant plurality — or diversity — of constitutional interpretations, in which the Supreme Court would be viewed as less like the Vatican than as just one more participant in a complex network of debaters? I had no hesitation in criticizing the claims for "judicial supremacy" in favor of a far more pluralistic community of constitutional interpreters. Though the central topic was constitutional law, the metaphors themselves reveal a debt owed to the history of conflict over the legitimacy of competing notions of religion and creedal fidelity.

My next book, *Written in Stone: Public Monuments in Changing Societies,* was more directly linked to debates about diversity or multiculturalism. Its principal topic was the way that public space — the names of airports and public buildings, the statuary and monuments dominating capitol grounds, and the like — is distributed as societies accept an ever-less-homogeneous (or monotonic) definition of themselves and embrace — or at least accept — a more multicultural reality. What does a society do, for example, upon recognizing that someone who was complacently viewed as a "national" hero is in fact regarded as a villain by another part of the public that only now is emerging to take its full place within the public square? Statues may come down and airports be renamed, for starters. It is worth noting that that book was originally to be part of this present collection, but the Duke University Press kindly allowed me to turn what began as two essays into a more extended, free-standing book that considers these issues at some length.

These essays, then, can be read as part of a continuing inquiry into the problems and opportunities presented by the reality of living in a richly diverse, but sometimes (or therefore) bitterly divided, society. Much of the debate about diversity, pluralism, or multiculturalism—I discuss in the first essay below why it is that "diversity" has become for most lawyers the term of choice—has concerned race or ethnicity. National identity in an ever-more globalized world is the principal subject of two other essays in this volume. It is probably true, though, that the most recurrent topic of this book concerns some of the implications of the remarkable religious pluralism characteristic of the United States and elsewhere.

Most of these essays involve the United States, but two include substantial discussion of a variety of foreign societies. As a matter of fact, there are extremely few societies in the world that are so homogeneous as to avoid being labeled diverse (or pluralistic or multicultural). Perhaps the micro-states of San Marino or Andorra might avoid such labels; of larger states, Iceland may qualify for the "most homogeneous" award; but it is otherwise impossible to find countries that are not divided along one or another social axis, including (but not limited to) race, ethnicity, religion, and social class. That I focus disproportionately on religion should certainly not be taken as indicating that I consider these others to be unimportant or unworthy of analysis.

Perhaps because I have spent most of my adult life in educational institutions, I am especially interested in the ways that diversity arguments have played out within such institutions. Educational institutions operate, of course, to transmit cultural norms across time (and, as they become less local in their reach, space as well). It should occasion no surprise that the politics of education have often been associated with acrimony (and sometimes worse), as pitched battles, both metaphorical and real, have taken place with regard to maintaining particular cultures. The first essay, "Diversity," focuses on university admissions and expresses more than a little skepticism about the coherence of the term "diversity" as used within that domain. The third, written with Meira Levinson, who, among other things, has taught in both the Atlanta and Boston public school systems, assesses potential implications of "voucher programs" with regard to achieving diversity in secondary education, public and private.

The four essays that then follow might well be organized around the general theme of "professional and judicial identity." A question that runs through all four is what difference it makes to one's self-conception of being a lawyer or judge that one is also Jewish, Christian, or a member of a particular nation such as Latvia. The first essay in this section, "Identifying the Jewish Lawyer," I sometimes refer to as "my Sandy Koufax article" inasmuch as I structure it around the issue of to what extent, if any, it is proper to refer to Koufax as a "Jewish pitcher." This leads into a discussion of when, if ever, we could or should refer to persons as "Jewish lawyers" instead of simply as "lawyers who happen to be Jews." Although the essay focuses on Jewish identity, for some of the reasons already suggested, it is not in the least intended to be of interest only to Jews. Indeed, I have assigned it in many of my classes — and it has been used elsewhere — with regard to the far more general issue of what I call "adjectival lawyering." That is, to what extent do the modifying adjectives "female," "Jewish," "Christian," "liberal," "feminist," "lesbian," and the like, convey genuinely interesting information about the kind of lawyer one is? Will a Christian lawyer, for example, behave in interestingly different ways from a secular or a Jewish lawyer? Or, as I argue, is it part of what I term the "professional project" to "bleach out" these aspects of selfhood and promote instead a more uniform notion of what is entailed in being simply a lawyer?

The second essay in this group turns from religion to nationalism and asks if it is relevant, when deciding who can practice law, that a lawyer be an active member of the society within which the practice takes place. Although the essay, written almost a decade ago, focuses on Latvia, the general issue has become ever more pressing with the remarkable creation of a genuine European Union that, among other things, allows the cross-national practice of all occupations, including law.

The section on professional and judicial identity concludes with two essays involving judges. The first focuses on confirmation hearings involving Catholic nominees to the Supreme Court. The other essay deals with the propriety of judges drawing on their religious views, as distinguished, say, from general social norms, when making legal decisions. As George Bush increasingly selects as judicial nominees persons with strong religious faith, it takes no great imagination to extend the points made in these essays to contemporary struggles over confirmation.

The penultimate essay was originally published as a review of Yael Tamir's book *Liberal Nationalism*. In that volume she addresses, with mixed success, the problems of structuring a diverse society that consists of a "majority" together with one or another minority culture that very much desires to preserve its own integrity against what it adherents view as the dangers of assimilation or homogenization. As suggested by the title of that chapter — "Is Liberal Nationalism an Oxymoron?" — there may be an irresolvable tension between the norms of a liberal social order and one that takes nationalism with the seriousness demanded by its adherents.

The concluding essay, written with Rachel Levinson, returns to two themes enunciated in the first essay. First, it more explicitly analyzes whether it necessarily makes sense to privilege religious claims over more secular cultural claims invoked by persons who wish to live at least certain aspects of their lives in ways different from the mainstream. We conclude that the answer is no. Second, we also address, at least by example, whether one can construct theoretical algorithms that will easily resolve the tensions that we identify. Again, the answer is no. It provides a fitting conclusion to a book organized around the metaphor of wrestling with an often elusive concept that can never successfully be pinned down.

THE ESSAYS ARE reprinted, save for some very minor changes, as originally published, though several have short afterwords acknowledging relevant legal developments, or a modification of the argument that I would make today if writing on a completely blank slate. My hope is that each of the essays, including their afterwords, will serve at least to provoke and stimulate (or perhaps simply to irritate) readers who share my own beliefs both that *e pluribus unum* is a deeply inspiring national motto and that defining its meaning often generates an equally deep perplexity.

1

Diversity

Introduction

As Princeton political theorist Stephen Macedo says at the very beginning of his important book, "[d]iversity is the great issue of our time: nationalism, religious sectarianism; a heightened consciousness of gender, race, and ethnicity; a greater assertiveness with respect to sexual orientation; and a reassertion of the religious voice in the public square are but a few of the forms of particularity"[1] that we confront daily under the general rubric of diversity.

My own interest in the topic may truly be described as overdetermined. As a teacher of constitutional law for a full quarter-century, I have invariably assigned and discussed various cases and materials involving affirmative action or the toleration that is due particular religious sects whose behavioral norms are radically at odds with those of most of their fellow Americans. Indeed, I have offered seminars on multiculturalism and the Constitution. I might add that I also address some of these subjects in a second-year course that I often teach on the particular role that the Constitution plays in structuring the contemporary American welfare state, for many of the constitutional struggles about diversity are strongly interlaced with the realities of the modern welfare state. Were there, for example, no state universities providing education to their students at significantly below-market cost, then many of the most volatile debates about affirmative

This essay was originally published in *University of Pennsylvania Journal of Constitutional Law* 2, no. 3 (2000): 573. It represents a rewritten and updated version of the Owen J. Roberts Memorial Lecture presented at the University of Pennsylvania Law School, 14 October 1999.

1. Stephen Macedo, *Diversity and Distrust: Civic Education in a Multicultural Democracy* 1 (1999).

action — i.e., the use of racial or ethnic preferences to select those who shall receive such benefits — would be off the table. Similarly, as Chief Justice Rehnquist has argued, we would not be debating whether the state must pay unemployment compensation to someone who has left a job for religious reasons — another issue that tests one's views on the practical meaning of diversity and multiculturalism — if the modern state were not, in fact, supplying such compensation.[2] Thus my teaching interests alone could adequately explain my interest in the topic of diversity.

It is scarcely irrelevant, though, that my home setting, the University of Texas Law School, has the unique distinction (if that is the right word) of being the defendant in two of the three most important cases involving the particular topic that probably most often comes to mind upon hearing the word "diversity" — the use of racial classifications in higher education. What to many of my colleagues elsewhere is quite literally only an "academic interest" has, for us at the University of Texas, become extraordinarily important in shaping the circumstances of our daily lives as teachers. Whatever one's teaching interests, it is impossible for anyone at the University of Texas to avoid grappling with the implications of diversity — or its absence — as a reality of contemporary American life.

Some Relevant Cases

I begin with the three cases to which I have previously alluded, not because I intend in this discussion to break new doctrinal ground or, for that matter, even offer suitably elaborate explication of contemporary doctrine, but, rather, simply to set the stage for the more theoretical issues that are my principal focus. The first case is *Sweatt v. Painter,*[3] in which Heman Sweatt, who was denied admission to the University of Texas Law School for no reason other than his being African American, successfully challenged the school's admissions policy on constitutional grounds. Texas had, in a desperate attempt to

2. See *Thomas v. Review Bd. of the Ind. Employment Sec. Div.,* 450 U.S. 707, 721 (1981) (Rehnquist, J., dissenting) (arguing that one of the main causes of the tension between the Establishment and Free Exercise Clauses is the existence of social welfare benefits, such as unemployment compensation).

3. 339 U.S. 629 (1950). See also *Sweatt v. Painter Archival and Textual Sources* (last modified 3 April 1999), ⟨http://law.du.edu.russell/h/sweatt⟩ (providing a comprehensive set of materials on the case).

come under the "separate but equal" doctrine that had not yet been invalidated in *Brown v. Board of Education*,[4] established a so-called downtown law school that nonwhites could attend. The Supreme Court aptly cut through any arguments that this facility was in fact equal because courses were taught by University of Texas faculty in classes with a better ratio of students to teachers than existed across town at the "real" University of Texas. As Chief Justice Vinson wrote, "[t]he law school, the proving ground for legal learning and practice, cannot be effective in isolation from the individuals and institutions with which the law interacts."[5] He noted that Texas's policy excluded African Americans from contact with "the racial groups which number 85 percent of the population of the State and include most of the lawyers, witnesses, jurors, judges and other officials with whom petitioner will inevitably be dealing when he becomes a member of the Texas Bar."[6]

Although the word was not then in common use, I do not believe it is an undue stretch to interpret the Court as pointing out that legal education, practically speaking, demands that students be exposed to the *diversity* of groups within the state if they are to be effectively prepared for the various tasks of the practicing lawyer. Although Vinson made no argument that white students were significantly harmed by being deprived of access to the remaining 15 percent of the population, it seems impossible to believe that the Court then, or anyone now, would question the presence of such harm, even if it was, as a practical matter, far less damaging to white students' future effective ability to practice law than to African American law students deprived of an integrated educational setting.

The second great case is, of course, *Regents of the University of California v. Bakke*,[7] which tested the legitimacy of an admissions program established by the Regents in regard to the medical school at the University of California–Davis. The Court was bitterly divided and incapable of producing a majority opinion, as has often been true of cases involving racial preferences. Four "liberal" justices would have upheld the Davis program, which set aside sixteen places to which only members of certain racial and ethnic minorities — in particular, "Blacks, Chicanos, Asians, and American

4. 347 U.S. 483 (1954).
5. *Sweatt*, 339 U.S. at 634.
6. Id.
7. 438 U.S. 265 (1978).

Indians" — could apply.[8] Four others would have flatly rejected it, though they relied on a federal statute forbidding the taking of race into account rather than on the Constitution itself.[9] The "swing" opinion was that of Justice Powell.[10] Like the four "liberals," Powell held that the statute meant only that race could not be taken into acount in any way that would violate the Equal Protection Clause of the Fourteenth Amendment.[11] One must, therefore, determine *not* whether California had taken race or ethnicity into account, which it obviously had, but, rather, whether it had sufficiently good (and constitutional) reasons for doing so. Although Powell agreed with the "conservatives" that the particular program was indeed illegal because it operated as a hard-and-fast quota, he nonetheless agreed with the "liberals" that race and ethnicity *could* be taken into account by universities in the admissions process so long as it wasn't part of a process that included rigid quotas (as distinguished from "goals").[12]

Most important, Powell justified the possibility of racial or ethnic preferences on the grounds that they represented a reasonable way to achieve diversity within a student body, a goal that he thought legitimate.[13] Earlier in his opinion, he had explicitly rejected the legitimacy of such preferences as a way, for example, of responding to (and thus seeking to remedy) the past history of American racial discrimination[14] or of providing "role models" of achievement by members of the benefited minorities that would, presumably, both inspire others of their own group and serve to dispel invidious stereotypes on the part of the majority population.[15]

In discussing the diversity rationale, Powell quoted, with seeming endorsement, a Harvard statement about its own admissions criteria. The drive to produce "diversity" within the student body had led the Harvard admissions committee to pay special (and, presumably, favorable) attention to the

8. Id. at 274, 279 (discussing the racial criteria for the special admissions programs).

9. See id. at 412 (Stevens, J., dissenting) (relying on Title VI of the Civil Rights Act of 1964).

10. See id. at 269 (Powell, J.).

11. See id. at 287 (noting the legislative intent behind the Fourteenth Amendment was to give blacks the same rights and opportunities as whites).

12. This is not the occasion for a discussion of whether the "goals" versus "quota" distinction makes all that much sense. I am inclined to think not.

13. See id. at 311–12 ("[Diversity] clearly is a constitutionally permissible goal for an institution of higher education.").

14. See id. at 307–8.

15. See id. at 310 (rejecting the State's claim that its program would better serve underserved communities).

race of applicants. " '[T]he race of an applicant may tip the balance in his favor just as geographic origin or a life spent on a farm may tip the balance in other candidates' cases.' "[16] Furthermore, Harvard explained that the desire to "provide a truly heterogeneous environment that reflects the rich diversity of the United States" required paying some attention to the numbers of applicants admitted.[17]

> It would not make sense, for example, to have [only] 10 or 20 students out of 1,100 whose homes are west of the Mississippi. Comparably, 10 or 20 black students could not begin to bring to their classmates and to each other the variety of points of view, backgrounds and experiences of blacks in the United States.[18]

One way of interpreting Harvard's policy is simply the recognition that no sane person could in fact believe that there is a singular "black point of view" or "black experience," any more than there is a singular identity binding together persons from "west of the Mississippi." That is, even if the addition of persons from the category of African Americans, relative to a homogeneously white population, represents a net gain in diversity, along at least one dimension, it is also the case that one must pay attention to the diversity *within* any of the relevant racial or ethnic groups. Critics of affirmative action, including members of the United States Supreme Court,[19]

---

16. Id. at 316 (quoting the Harvard College Admissions program).

17. Id. at 323.

18. Id.

19. See, e.g., *Shaw v. Reno*, 509 U.S. 630 (1993) (O'Connor, J.). Justice O'Connor states:

   A reapportionment plan that includes in one district individuals who belong to the same race, but who are otherwise widely separated by geographical and political boundaries, and who may have little in common with one another but the color of their skin, bears an uncomfortable resemblance to political apartheid. It reinforces the perception that members of the same racial group — regardless of their age, education, economic status, or the community in which they live — think alike, share the same political interests, and will prefer the same candidates at the polls. We have rejected such perceptions elsewhere as impermissible racial stereotypes. (Id. at 647.)

   I have no quarrel with Justice O'Connor's reminder that "members of the same racial group" do not "think alike" or "prefer the same candidates at the polls." But, of course, she cites no one who does believe this. I do have a bit of a quarrel with her notion that members of racial groups do not even share common "political interests," though agreement or disagreement undoubtedly depends on precisely what one means by shared "political interests." It may be, for example, that both the insurance industry and medical patients have a strongly shared "interest" in the future of American health policy, though it would be surprising indeed if the industry and patients

sometimes write as if supporters of affirmative action ignore the presence of intragroup diversity, but this is clearly false. I know of no one who is so stupid as to believe that all (or even most) members of any given group necessarily have similar opinions on a variety of important issues.

In any event, because of Justice Powell's emphasis on the almost unique legitimacy of diversity as a constitutional value, it has become the favorite catchword — indeed, it would not be an exaggeration to say "mantra" — of those defending the use of racial or ethnic preferences. As Eugene Lowe has written, "[c]elebrating the value of racial and ethnic diversity has become routine in educational circles,"[20] not least, it should be obvious, because such celebrations seem licensed and, indeed, encouraged by the Supreme Court. Whatever the actual efficacy of the Supreme Court in changing the behavior of American institutions,[21] it seems indisputable that the Court sometimes fulfills the function of the French Academy in establishing the conventions of "law talk,"[22] so that all properly socialized lawyers, and many nonlawyers as well, adopt certain conventions of argument because the Court leads the way. It is a version of the old children's game of "Simon Says." If Simon says, "Stop talking about the difference between commerce and manufacture,"[23] then a mode of analysis that had been constitutive of law talk only a few years before[24] disappears almost overnight. More to the present point, if Simon says, "Start talking about diversity — and downplay any talk about rectification of past social injustice," then the conversation proceeds exactly in that direction.

Diversity is thus a ubiquitous topic of contemporary discourse. Indeed, it

---

necessarily shared specific opinions as to how best to structure the medical services industry. If Justice O'Connor's notion of a "share[d]" political interest is the latter, then, again, I know of no one who suggests that all members of given racial or ethnic groups agree with one another on how to resolve pressing political issues, so she is criticizing a nonexistent opinion. If, on the other hand, she is suggesting that there is no "share[d]" interest in the former sense, then, I respectfully suggest, as argued below, that her view would be extraordinarily foolish. See generally discussion infra at pages 37–41.

20. *Promise and Dilemma: Perspectives on Racial Diversity and Higher Education* 3 (Eugene Y. Lowe Jr., ed., 1999).

21. See, e.g., Gerald N. Rosenberg, *The Hollow Hope: Can Courts Bring about Social Change?* 39 (1991) (espousing a skeptical view on this matter).

22. See generally J. M. Balkin and Sanford Levinson, *Constitutional Grammar*, 72 *Tex. L. Rev.* 1771 (1994).

23. See, e.g., *NLRB v. Jones & Laughlin Steel Corp.*, 301 U.S. 1 (1937); *United States v. Darby*, 312 U.S. 100 (1941).

24. See, e.g., *Carter v. Carter Coal Co.*, 298 U.S. 238 (1936).

has joined family values and good medical care as something that everyone is for, as demonstrated by the fact that it is becoming ever more difficult to find anyone who is willing to say, in public, that institutional or social homogeneity is a positive good and diversity a substantive harm.[25] Opponents of affirmative action almost never attack the merits of diversity per se, but, rather, the specific means thought necessary to assure the achievement of a desired degree of diversity.[26] Were that degree attainable by nonobjectionable means, most opponents of affirmative action insist, they would be utterly delighted.

"Diversity" is, however, not a self-interpreting word. Political theorists have for several decades now posited the notion of "essentially contested concepts,"[27] i.e., notions that are extremely important but, nonetheless, without truly definite meaning. Consider the crucial American value of "freedom"; one is foolish indeed to believe that Americans have ever agreed on precisely what that term entails, although all have agreed that it is a term worth fighting (and killing) for.[28] Perhaps my favorite example of "essential contestedness" can be found in the very title of a marvelous book, *Equalities*, where Yale professor Douglas Rae and his coauthors elaborate no

25. But see Peter Brimelow, *Alien Nation: Common Sense about America's Immigration Disaster* (1995) (expressing the view that the United States is fundamentally changing for the worse because of changes in immigration law that are letting in far too many non-Anglo-Saxons). One has no doubt that Brimelow would oppose the Immigration and Naturalization Service's policy of "diversity admission" to the United States, see infra note 51.

26. See, e.g., Peter T. Kilborn, "Jeb Bush Roils Florida on Affirmative Action," *New York Times*, 4 February 2000, at A1 (detailing a tumultuous public hearing generated by the Governor's attempt to end race- and ethnic-based preferences). " 'We are embracing diversity, not rejecting it,' Mr. Bush, the first speaker at today's hearing, told the mostly black audience. 'This plan will create more opportunity for people.' " According to the article,

> There is widespread support among whites for Mr. Bush's program, which would end preferences for businesses owned by women and minorities in bidding for state contracts. And it would end college admissions preferences based on race, substituting a program guaranteeing admission to at least 1 of the 10 state universities for high school students who graduate in the top 20 percent of their class. . . .
>
> Some black leaders see promise in the One Florida plan, in that it might create opportunities for the poor, disproportionate numbers of whom are black. But they bristle at the governor's abolition of affirmative action. . . .

27. See William E. Connolly, *The Terms of Political Discourse* 225–32 (2d ed., 1983).

28. See, e.g., Eric Foner, *The Story of American Freedom* (1998) (limning the quite different, and often conflicting, meanings assigned to the notion of "freedom" throughout American history).

fewer than *128* logically coherent notions of "equality."[29] One reason why debates about, say, the Equal Protection Clause are so bitter is because one person's cogent notion of equality may differ drastically from another's equally cogent notion, though each prefers to believe, falsely, that only his or her particular notion represents "real" equality. Would that it were that easy! The same, I fear, is increasingly true of those who raise the banner of "diversity" and then argue bitterly about its meanings, especially in a context where one seeks not only, if at all, the agreement of the trained philosopher but also, and as a practical matter far more importantly, the imprimatur of a court trained to think that some legal magic resides in a program's being successfully described as contributing to diversity.

Consider now the third of the key cases — and the second one to involve the University of Texas Law School — *Hopwood v. Texas,*[30] in which Cheryl Hopwood successfully challenged the admissions program at the University of Texas Law School insofar as it took race and ethnicity into account.[31] Although the federal district judge had upheld the admissions process in operation at the time of the judgment,[32] a three-judge panel of the Fifth Circuit Court of Appeals reversed the judge and held that the law school

29. Douglas Rae et al., *Equalities* (1981). See also Peter Westen, *Speaking of Equality: An Analysis of the Rhetorical Force of 'Equality' in Moral and Legal Discourse* (1990) (arguing that equality is basically an "empty" concept, taking meaning only from a prior theory of rights or fairness that allows one to assert that certain obvious differences among human beings (skin color, height, weight, age, beauty, LSAT scores, etc.) may, or may not, be taken into account in distributing the burdens and benefits of living in American society). I am not sure whether Professor Westen, a member of the distinguished law faculty at the University of Michigan that is defending its own affirmative action program against constitutional attack on the ground of its contribution to diversity, would argue that "diversity" is a similarly "empty" concept. I note that one of Professor Westen's colleagues has also written scholarly articles on diversity that display considerable skepticism about the analytical premises behind at least some versions of the concept. See Deborah C. Malamud, "Affirmative Action, Diversity, and the Black Middle Class," 68 *U. Colo. L. Rev.* 939 (1997); see also Deborah C. Malamud, "Values, Symbols, and the Facts in the Affirmative Action Debate," 95 *Mich. L. Rev.* 1668 (1997) (book review). Again, I do not know what particular position Professor Malamud takes with regard to the law school's assertion of diversity as the primary defense of its admissions policy.

30. 78 F.3d 932 (5th Cir. 1996). See also generally Reva B. Siegel, "The Racial Rhetorics of Color-blind Constitutionalism: The Case of *Hopwood v. Texas*," in *Race and Representation: Affirmative Action* 29 (Robert Post and Michael Rogin, eds., 1998).

31. This is in fact a somewhat oversimplified description, but it does not affect the central argument.

32. See *Hopwood v. Texas,* 861 F. Supp. 551 (W.D. Tex. 1994). This process replaced the one under which Ms. Hopwood herself applied and which the University was no longer willing to defend. See id. at 560.

must design an entirely race-neutral admissions process.[33] But what about *Bakke* and its toleration of a race- and ethnic-sensitive, diversity-seeking admissions policy? A majority of the panel held that *Bakke* no longer stated the effective view of the Supreme Court and, therefore, the operative meaning of the Equal Protection Clause.[34]

The majority noted the undoubted fact that Justice Powell spoke for himself alone, as well as perhaps the even more embarrassing fact, at least in retrospect, that the four justices who would have upheld the Davis program did so not by reference to the value of a diverse student body — a notion wholly absent from their opinions — but, rather, by emphasizing the program's utility in overcoming an egregious heritage of past discrimination.[35] The majority held that subsequent decisions had so undercut Justice Powell's pro-diversity rationale that the panel, however "inferior" it might be within the structure of federal courts,[36] was no longer bound by it. Instead, it interpreted post-*Bakke* cases as holding "that the use of *ethnic diversity* simply to achieve racial heterogeneity . . . is unconstitutional."[37] The *Hopwood* panel came as close as any court has yet done to reading the Fourteenth Amendment as indeed requiring the "color-blind[ness]" of which Justice Harlan spoke in his canonical dissent in *Plessy v. Ferguson*.[38]

Does this mean that university admissions must be based on a single metric from which no deviation is allowed? Not at all. The court points to "a host of factors" that can legitimately be considered in the admissions

33. See *Hopwood,* 78 F.3d at 962.

34. See id. at 945–46.

35. See id. at 951.

36. See U.S. Const. art. III, § 1 (distinguishing between the Supreme Court and such "inferior" courts as Congress may choose to establish). I want to make it clear that I mean nothing disrespectful by reference to "inferior" courts, for I have consistently been critical of many of the claims to supremacy by the "Supreme" court. See, e.g., Sanford Levinson, *Constitutional Faith* 27–53 (1988) (describing and defending an institutionally "protestant" approach to the Constitution that rejects the claim of the Supreme Court to "ultimate" authority over constitutional meaning); see also Sanford Levinson, "On Positivism and Potted Plants: 'Inferior' Judges and the Task of Constitutional Interpretation," 25 *Conn. L. Rev.* 843 (1993) (defending the propriety of "inferior" judges thinking for themselves when engaging in constitutional interpretation); Sanford Levinson, "*Hopwood:* Some Reflections on Constitutional Interpretation by an Inferior Court," 2 *Tex. F. on Civ. Liberties & Civ. Rts.* 113–22 (1996) (refusing to criticize Fifth Circuit for departure from Supreme Court precedent).

37. *Hopwood,* 78 F.3d at 945 (emphasis added).

38. 163 U.S. 537, 559 (1896) (Harlan, J., dissenting) ("Our Constitution is color-blind, and neither knows nor tolerates classes among citizens.").

process, including "ability to play the cello, make a downfield tackle, or understand chaos theory. An admissions process may also consider an applicant's home state or relationship to school alumni."[39] Which means, for example, that the most important affirmative action program at the University of Texas Law School — the rigid setting aside, as a quota, of a full 80 percent of seats at the school for residents of Texas, whatever their "merit" may be when compared with nonresident applicants — is apparently safe from any kind of attack.[40] Moreover, law schools "specifically may look at things such as unusual or substantial extracurricular activities in college, which may be atypical factors affecting undergraduate grades."[41] Finally, schools were given permission to "consider factors such as whether an applicant's parents attended college or the applicant's economic and social background."[42] It should be obvious that the court cannot fairly be described as hostile to diversity as such (but only to the specific kind of diversity that is at the heart of the contemporary debate).

The point is best demonstrated by Judge Jerry Smith's own gratuitous comment in the majority opinion that

> Plaintiff Hopwood is a fair example of an applicant with a unique background. She is the now-thirty-two-year-old wife of a member of the Armed Forces stationed in San Antonio and, more significantly, is raising a severely handicapped child. Her circumstance would bring a different perspective to the law school.[43]

Judge Smith, then, clearly seems to endorse a self-conscious search for "different perspective[s]" within the law school's applicant pool as he offers his own completely unverified (but commonsensical and quite possibly accurate) belief that raising a severely handicapped child would generate suffi-

---

39. *Hopwood,* 78 F.3d at 946.

40. It is worth noting that such a policy would be "unconstitutional" in the new Europe that is structured by the norms of the Treaty of Rome and subsequent treaties. Nationals of any of the countries within the European Union have a right of equal access to the public universities operated by any of the members. To this extent, at least, Europe in only fifty years has become a more genuinely "united" entity than has the United States of America after 210 years. See generally David S. Clark, "Transnational Legal Practice: The Need for Global Law Schools," 46 *Am. J. Comp. L.* 261, 265 (Supp. 1998) (discussing student mobility in the European Union as a result of programs such as ERASMUS and SOCRATES).

41. *Hopwood,* 78 F.3d at 946.

42. Id.

43. Id.

ciently interesting opinions about legally relevant issues as to justify a law school in giving special weight to someone in Hopwood's position as against, presumably, a parent of a nonhandicapped child. The central point, though, is that the construction of "diverse" classes remains legitimate even for the Fifth Circuit, which scarcely wished to endorse homogeneity as such. Instead, it "simply" forbade the use of race or ethnicity as a proxy for the kinds of diverse backgrounds that can legitimately be sought by admissions committees.

Hopwood generated a national debate, as did the decision of the Regents of the University of California to order a race-neutral admissions process, which was, of course, followed by the passage of Proposition 209 via statewide initiative and referendum, which attempts to bring an end to any and all race-preferential programs within the state.[44] Whatever the status of *Hopwood* in regard to structuring the University of Texas admissions program, the Supreme Court's refusal to take the case assured that its legal reach would be limited to the three states — Texas, Louisiana, and Mississippi — covered by the Fifth Circuit,[45] and that the national debate would continue. That debate centers on the meaning of "diversity," its ostensible desirability, and whether the Constitution, properly understood, erects barriers to achieving it.[46]

44. See Lydia Chávez, *The Color Bind: California's Battle to End Affirmative Action* 2 (1998) ("[Proposition 209] promised to end the use of race and gender preferences in state employment, contracting, and education.").

45. As a matter of empirical fact, it is not clear that *Hopwood* has had anything near the impact in Louisiana and Mississippi that it has had in Texas. Possible reasons for this differential impact are beyond the scope of this essay. Moreover, the issue is currently before a United States district court within the Sixth Circuit, in which the University of Michigan Law School is attempting to defend its race- and ethnicity-sensitive admissions procedures against statutory and constitutional attack. See *Gratz v. Bollinger,* 183 F.R.D. 209 (E.D. Mich. 1998) (deciding technical procedural issues); *Grutter v. Bollinger,* 16 F. Supp. 2d 797 (E.D. Mich. 1998) (same). Not surprisingly, the essence of the university's defense is the importance of "diversity," as evidenced by the title the university gave to a compilation of reports by various experts submitted to the district court, *The Compelling Need for Diversity in Higher Education.* The compilation and all other legal documents are available at University of Michigan, Information on Admissions Lawsuits (accessed 20 January 2000), ⟨http://www.umich.edu/~urel/admissions/legal⟩. See the afterword to this essay for further comment on the *Michigan* case.

46. A bibliography search of legal journals in spring 1999 produced ninety-one articles since 1990 with the word "diversity" in the title (and this did not include articles on "biodiversity"). No doubt a search now, in January 2000, would produce many more articles and a general literature review would almost certainly produce thousands of titles.

"Diversity Talk"

How, then, do we talk about diversity? I begin by offering several examples of what might be termed "diversity talk," all quoted in an important and widely reviewed recent book defending affirmative action, by the former presidents of Harvard and Princeton.[47] It is probably not surprising to read that the presidents of the sixty-two leading universities that comprise the Association of American Universities "believe that our students benefit significantly from education that takes place within a diverse setting" that provides the opportunity to "encounter and learn from others who have backgrounds and characteristics very different from their own."[48] More surprising to many may be statements by the CEOs of Coca-Cola and Chrysler. Coca-Cola, described as "focused on taking actions that serve us best over the long run," is committed to "building . . . a diverse workforce. As a company that operates in nearly 200 countries, we see diversity in the background and talent of our associates as a competitive advantage and as a commitment that is a daily responsibility."[49] Finally, what was then only the Chrysler Corporation — though one assumes that the new Chrysler-Daimler would say much the same thing — "believe[s] that workforce diversity is a competitive advantage. Our success as a global community is as dependent on utilizing the wealth of backgrounds, skills and opinions

---

47. See William G. Bowen and Derek Bok, *The Shape of the River: Long-Term Consequences of Considering Race in College and University Admissions* (1998).

48. Id. at 252.

49. Id. at 12 (quoting M. Douglas Ivester, Chairman and CEO of the Coca-Cola Company). Given the role that Coca-Cola plays in this lecture, it is probably advisable to note a recent article, Constance L. Hays, "New Coke Chief Says Diversity Is High Priority," *New York Times*, 10 March 2000, at C2.

> In a striking move intended to counter accusations that the Coca-Cola Company has not cared enough about building a diverse work force, Coke's chairman and chief executive said yesterday that management compensation at the company, including his own, would be closely tied to diversity goals that have yet to be announced. (Id.)

Ms. Hays writes, "White men control most of the power in the company" and suggests that the announcement was in response to a recent suit filed by "eight current and former black employees who say they were unfairly treated because of their race. . . . A lawyer for the plaintiffs called the announcement 'a spectacular victory' and said it would improve conditions at the company. 'This is the first step toward moving Coca-Cola from a laggard to a leader on diversity.'" And, according to a stock analyst with Salomon Smith Barney, "[t]he most important thing Coke needs to do is mend its global public image. And if this helps in that respect, the shareholders are going to benefit."

that a diverse workforce offers as it is on raw materials, technology and processes."[50]

Thus, celebrations of racial and ethnic diversity extend well beyond the world of education.[51] Indeed, I would even hazard the guess that one could hear substantially more public opposition to "diversity-based" affirmative action on most university campuses than in most gatherings of business

50. Bowen and Bok, supra note 47, at 12.

51. Perhaps the most intriguing example that I discovered in the course of my inquiry into the topic is the presence within American immigration law of explicitly titled "diversity admissions" of immigrants who would not otherwise qualify for admission (but do not possess attributes that would *disqualify* them for admission). The apparent origin of the program is the congressional reaction to some unforeseen consequences of the demise of the national-origins-quota system of immigration in 1965, which had been justifiably criticized for trying to preserve a too-homogeneous America. See Thomas Alexander Aleinikoff et al., *Immigration and Citizenship: Process and Policy* 290–92 (4th ed., 1998) (discussing legislative attempts to increase diversity in immigration). (I am grateful to David Martin, one of the coeditors of this excellent casebook, for making me aware of this.) Among these consequences was a "steep reduction" in those granted permission to immigrate from Europe, particularly from Ireland, whose nationals had been strong beneficiaries of the national-origins system established in 1924. See id. at 291. Thus Congress in 1986 provided for 10,000 new admissions over two years "for persons from countries 'adversely affected' by the 1965 changes." Not surprisingly, "[t]he list of 36 such countries was disproportionately, but not exclusively, European." Even though the lucky admittees were selected by lottery, "Irish nationals turned out to be the biggest winners." The system was changed again in 1988, this time preferring persons from " 'underrepresented countries,' " with winners this time being natives of Bangladesh, Pakistan, Poland, Turkey, and Egypt. Congress in 1990 changed the Act again, this time settling on "an extraordinarily intricate formula" to allocate the 55,000 annual "diversity admissions"; a random lottery selects the winners from among those who are eligible. Current winners appear to be persons from Bangladesh, Ghana, Nigeria, Bulgaria, Sierra Leone, Romania, Ukraine, and Albania. See id. at 292. As can easily be seen, the most recent version of the "diversity admissions" program was adopted during the Reagan-Bush era and cannot therefore be easily ascribed, as one might have suspected, to the return to Washington of Democrats. I trust I am not alone in finding this entire program, and its political origins, fascinating, not least because the operative theory of the program indeed appears to be that national diversity, with regard to those immigrating to the United States, is itself a positive good, at least within the limited numbers. One can imagine a number of different reasons why this might be so, ranging from the assumptions that Bulgarians bring with them importantly different attributes from, say, Poles or Hungarians (who are not favored by the "diversity admissions" program) to the more self-interested view that the United States benefits from having within its borders members of all countries with which the United States interacts so that they can transmit to their friends and relatives back home a desirable picture of the United States and of its motives as an international actor. For a fine overview of the history of the "diversity visa lottery," see Anna O. Law, "The Diversity Visa Lottery: A Cycle of Unintended Consequences in United States Immigration Policy," 21 *J. Am. Ethnic Hist.* 3 (2002).

people. There seem to be few corporate analogues to Harvard's Harvey Mansfield Jr.[52] or my own colleague Lino Graglia.[53] Indeed, no one trying to understand the contemporary politics of affirmative action can fail to note that major industry has been notably unwilling to join those, like California's Ward Connerly,[54] who are leading the fight against it. Whatever explains the current backlash against the practice, it cannot plausibly be viewed as part of a campaign by big business. That being said, it is worth making the effort to understand what corporations mean by "diversity."

One meaning—I suspect a quite common one—is simply that one's workforce reflects in some important sense the demographic composition of the surrounding society. As noted by David A. Thomas and Robin J. Ely in their article in the *Harvard Business Review,* such a definition says literally nothing about the consequence of any such diversity for the way that work is carried out.[55] They note, for example, that from at least one perspective, the most successfully "diverse" organization in the United States today is the United States Army.[56] Few persons have been so bold as to suggest, though, that General Colin Powell brought a "black perspective" to his vision of military strategy. The whole point of the Army's vision of diversity is to demonstrate that all sorts of persons can be successfully assimilated into the organization without consequence for the definition of its mission or performance of its operational goals.

I have written elsewhere that one way of defining the "professional project," vividly illustrated within most American law schools, is to "bleach out" idiosyncratic personal aspects of our selves, including those that might relate to sex, race, gender, ethnicity, sexual orientation, and religion and to adopt instead a rigorously impersonal professional stance defined as appropriate

---

52. Professor of Government, Harvard University.
53. A. Dalton Cross Professor of Law, University of Texas Law School.
54. For a description of Mr. Connerly's achievements in campaigning against affirmative action see generally Edward W. Lempinen, "Connerly Widens Anti-Affirmative Action Campaign," *San Francisco Chronicle,* 16 January 1997, at A17 ("Connerly formally opened a national campaign against race- and gender-based affirmative action."); Tony Perry, "California and the West; Connerly to Lead GOP Fund-Raising," *Los Angeles Times,* 25 June 1998, at A3 ("Ward Connerly [is] the controversial leader of the drive that ended racial preferences in state hiring and college admissions.").
55. See David A. Thomas and Robin J. Ely, "Making Differences Matter: A New Paradigm for Managing Diversity," *Harv. Bus. Rev.,* September–October 1996, at 79, 79–90.
56. See id. at 81.

for one who is behaving "as a lawyer."[57] This is obviously an even more significant, and widely accepted, claim with regard to the military. Those who advocate, as I do, welcoming gays and lesbians into the military do not, at least publicly, claim that they will bring a distinct set of viewpoints that will lead to likely changes in the way that war is actually conducted. From this perspective, demographic diversity serves only to provide access to important social institutions, but it does not convey any information as to how these institutions actually operate. Thomas and Ely refer to this as a "discrimination-and-fairness paradigm," where even those who accept the validity of racial or other preferences are, nonetheless, ultimately committed to an internal organizational notion of "colorblindness" or "gender-blindness."[58] "Under this paradigm, it is not desirable for diversification of the workforce to influence the organization's work or culture."[59] There will be relatively little interest in, if not hostility to, "explor[ing] how people's differences generate a potential diversity of effective ways of working, leading, viewing the market, managing people, and learning."[60] Although there is clearly a desire to draw the applicant pool from a widely diverse population, and pride taken in the heterogeneity of background of those within the organization, it is hard to describe the overall view as one that values "diversity" as such.

I confess that I am more interested in defenses of diversity that indeed focus on the potential contribution that a diverse workforce can make to an institution by enhancing the quality of the work done within that institution.[61] One often finds arguments that the presence of some factor X enhances the quality of the product identified with the institution. The use of very good paint or of a very good microchip, it might be argued, will make one car better than its competitor, which uses an inferior paint or microchip. Similarly, the hiring of especially able engineers or product designers would similarly enhance the product. In contrast, one might freely admit that some other factor Y has nothing to do with product enhancement, but, nonetheless, assert its desirability because of its relevance to achieving other important objectives. Running a major athletic program, for example, has almost

---

57. See chapter 4.

58. Thomas and Ely, supra note 55, at 81.

59. Id.

60. Id.

61. See Samuel Issacharoff, "*Bakke* in the Admissions Office and the Courts: Can Affirmative Action Be Defended?" 59 *Ohio St. L.J.* 669, 677 (1998) (arguing that diversity as a criterion in hiring or admissions decisions must be intended to promote institutional goals, rather than aiming for "racial balance for its own sake," in order to be held constitutional).

nothing to do with enhancing the education of college students, but it may be effective as a means of generating alumni contributions or, if a public university, of attracting support from certain state legislators. Alumni "legacies" seem similarly dubious product enhancers, though one assumes that university fundraisers would bewail any significant diminution in number of such legacies as likely to harm their efforts.

For me, "product" has a very broad definition, ranging from automobiles and soft drinks to scholarly knowledge and the dispositions linked with being an "educated person." An important question, then, is how often proponents of "diversity" argue that the attainment of a suitably mixed population will lead to a higher quality of the product identified with their institutions. This question is especially important in relation to corporate proponents of "diversity."

Recall that the CEO of Coca-Cola declares that "a diverse workforce" will "serve us best over the long run."[62] One notes the no-nonsense, self-interested thrust of this argument. Coca-Cola is not doing something merely because the country (or even the world) as a whole will be better off, even, perhaps, at a cost to the economic interests of Coca-Cola's shareholders. *That* would be a rather tragic conclusion, suggesting a tension between what is good for Coke and what is good for the nation. Instead, the CEO displays a far more comedic view of the world, presenting the happy conclusion that the shareholders (and, presumably, consumers) of Coca-Cola will themselves be better off with "a diverse workforce." And why is this the case? The rationale offered has something to do with the fact that Coca-Cola "operates in nearly 200 countries." That is why Coke's management regards "diversity in the background and talent of our associates as a competitive advantage" and proclaims the achievement of diversity to be "a commitment that is a daily responsibility."[63]

Wherein comes this "competitive advantage"? First, can it plausibly be said that a diverse workforce will produce a better-tasting product or that it will even produce the same product in a better manner, e.g., more efficiently? It is obvious how the answer *might* be affirmative. Hiring people with a variety of talents in formulating potential soft drinks would certainly work to Coke's advantage, but one has to be quite imaginative to believe that such talents correlate in any robust way with the racial or ethnic de-

62. See supra note 49 and accompanying text.
63. Bowen and Bok, supra note 47, at 12 (quoting M. Douglas Ivester, chairman and CEO of the Coca-Cola Company).

mography of the workforce. I suppose it is possible that one could learn from a diverse workforce that Greeks, say, prefer sweeter drinks than do Danes, and thus formulate Coke differently in the two countries. This assumes, of course, that Coca-Cola (or any other company pronouncing a similar commitment to "diversity") chooses to formulate its drinks differently around the world, rather than adopting a marketing policy that relies on its product tasting just the same whether one buys Coke in Armenia or Zanzibar.

There is at least one circumstance where a diverse workforce would indeed be a more efficient one: if the prior, nondiverse, workforce, was generated by the presence of discriminatory barriers to employment. What "discrimination" means in this context is that a business deprives itself of what would, to a nondiscriminatory observer, be the most meritorious employees as a result of a commitment to bigotry. The lifting of discriminatory barriers will allow such employees to be hired and, therefore, bring their skills to the enhancement of the product, whether directly, as by inventing new formulas, or indirectly, as by producing it more efficiently.

As already suggested, though, this is not an argument for diversity per se; rather, it is an argument for meritocracy, with the assumption being that a nondiscriminatory hiring process will in fact generate a heterogeneous workforce. The presence of a homogeneous workforce is less an occasion for first-order criticism than for second-order suspicion as to the process by which it has been achieved. It is worth pointing out that one should be wary of confusing suspicion with proof. Assumptions that nothing other than discrimination explains any instance of variation in the demographic composition of any given segment of the workforce seem to call into question at least one tenet of "diversity," especially in its "multiculturalist" form, which emphasizes the importance of a person's "culture" as a basic shaping force. If variations in culture are as significant as they are sometimes alleged to be, then one would expect the multiculturalism of American society (and of the wider global society) to be reflected, at least to some extent, in "tastes" or propensities for different kinds of jobs and other life experiences. The key point, though, is that the highest good of an "antidiscrimination" focus is not the achievement of a diverse workforce per se, but, rather, the achievement of a bias-free selection process that guarantees to those rejected that they were not victimized by the use of illegitimate criteria and to the outside public, including shareholders, that the products are being produced in the most efficient manner possible. But if a nondiscriminatory process generates a nondiverse workforce, for whatever reason, it may still be the case that the particular product is the best it can be, and being produced as efficiently as it could be.

So what of Coke's worldwide empire? How does this become relevant? One might well surmise that persons will be more likely to order Coke from their fellow nationals, who will assuage concerns that drinking Coca-Cola is simply a way of supporting American imperialism. The Italian branch of Coca-Cola thus benefits from the presence of Italian nationals in the workforce, as bottlers, delivery-persons, and sales agents, just as the Thai branch should be eager to display Thai nationals, and so on throughout the world. Similarly, the advertising agencies preparing Coke's copy might want to include in the management team people from the targeted populations, believing that they will be especially able to think up culturally attractive jingles or, just as important, spot materials to which local audiences might take umbrage.[64] One need not go abroad, of course, to offer such justifications. One would be surprised if Coca-Cola is entirely indifferent to the ethnic composition of those it sends to solicit sales in, say, the Rio Grande Valley area of Texas or in Chinatowns in New York or San Francisco. Given the particular kind of consumer good that Coca-Cola is, one would expect the company's management to be at least as aware of, and sensitive to, the increasingly multicultural nature of American society as are most academic sociologists.

What Coca-Cola may be doing is making a version of a very traditional argument, which is simply that a company, to maximize profits, must be attentive to the preferences of its customers, including a desire to be served by "people like them."[65] Here, Thomas and Ely posit an "access-and-legitimacy

---

64. It is often reported, for example, that Coca-Cola was originally introduced into China under the phonetic pronunciation "ke-kou-ke-la," which, in Chinese, means either "bite the wax tadpole" or "female horse stuffed with wax," depending on the dialect. Upon discovering this, the company researched further into the 40,000 Chinese characters and found a close enough phonetic equivalent to the brand name with "ko-kou-ko-le," which can be loosely translated as "happiness in the mouth." See, e.g., Terri Morrison and Wayne A. Conaway, "Bite the Wax Tadpole, and Other Translation Blunders from the Annals of Bad Global Marketing," *Industry Week,* 22 December 1998, at ⟨http://www.industryweek.com/columns/ASP/columns.asp?ColumnId=400⟩ (accessed June 2003).

65. An especially important area in which this might be true is medicine. See Kenneth De Ville, "Defending Diversity: Affirmative Action and Medical Education," 89 *Am. J. Pub. Health* 1256, 1259 (1999) (citing inter alia M. Garb, "Like Doctor Like Patient: More and More Patients Choose Physicians of Same Ethnic Group, Sexual Preference," 15 *Am. Med. News* 17 (Septem-

paradigm."[66] "Where this paradigm has taken hold, organizations have pushed for access to—and legitimacy with—a more diverse clientele by matching the demographics of the organization to those of critical consumer or constituent groups."[67] Thus, "[m]any consumer-products companies that have used market segmentation based on gender, racial, and other demographic differences have also frequently created dedicated marketing positions for each segment,"[68] with attendant new opportunities for members of the given groups.[69] It is worth noting that "customer preference" arguments carry with them obvious dangers; for many years they served as justification for hiring only whites in the South on the basis that the majority of white customers (who were, of course, the majority of *all* customers) just wouldn't accept being served by members of racial or ethnic minority groups. It is refreshing—perhaps an especially appropriate word to use in regard to Coca-Cola!—to see the customer preference argument made in a way that generates a diverse workforce, though one might still issue a cautionary note that devotees of diversity accept at their peril the priority of customer preferences as a criterion for workforce hiring.

Note some other implications of Coke's policy, at least if one views it as motivated by a desire to protect its business interests in two hundred countries or even its market share in the United States. All countries or groups may be created equal in some abstract sense, but they are most certainly *not*

---

ber 1992)). DeVille writes that "[p]hysicians are less effective at treating patients who do not trust them," id. at 1260, and it appears to be the case that African Americans in particular are mistrustful of the quality of care received from white doctors.

> For example, African Americans are the patient group most likely to distrust the care they will receive at the end of life. By influencing such factors as patterns of compliance, preventive care, and patient disclosure of information and choice of therapies, such distrust can have a substantial impact on the care that minority patients receive. This suspicion is so deep-seated and widespread that, in the short term, the only remedy is to provide minority patients with physicians with whom they feel safe and comfortable. (Id.; citations omitted.)

66. Thomas and Ely, supra note 55, at 83.

67. Id.

68. Id.

69. See generally Stuart Elliott, "Ads Speak to Asian-Americans," *New York Times,* 16 March 2000, at C1. "So-called diversity marketing—pursuing customers based on differentiations like race, language, sexual orientation and age—has become a lucrative strategy for mainstream advertisers." Many companies are having difficulty penetrating a seemingly lucrative niche. "'Frankly, many marketers really don't think about this market because they don't have many Asian-Americans on their staffs,' said Alfred L. Schreiber, president at Diversity Imperatives.... 'That lack of representation in corporate America puts this group at a disadvantage.'"

created in equal numbers. It may be desirable, for example, to hire some Norwegians to take care of the relatively small Norwegian market. But if market preference is the basis of the hiring decision, then a Norwegian (or Norwegian-American) applicant might face special problems if the company already has hired relatively few Norwegians, but a sufficient number to saturate the Norwegian market. After all, few people outside of Norway would be affirmatively impressed by the presence of a Norwegian representative, unless, of course, she had talents having nothing to do with her ethnic identity.

Moreover, it is vital to recognize that Coca-Cola does not argue that its workforce in each country needs to be diverse; rather, only its overall workforce must be so. I cannot help thinking of some of the debates about school desegregation, particularly with regard to the difference it makes if one looks at the racial demographics of a given school as a whole or if one looks at individual classroom figures. It is all too easy to demonstrate that diversity (or "racial balance") exists in the former even if there is almost complete separation of the races in the latter.[70] Similarly, a multinational company could easily have a strikingly diverse international workforce while having equally striking homogeneous workforces in any given country or locale. (How many non-Thai nationals work for Coca-Cola in Thailand?)

One could, of course, say much the same about the assertion by Chrysler's then-CEO that "workforce diversity is a competitive advantage," especially insofar as he, too, points to Chrysler's presence in "a global community" and says that the company's success depends as much "on utilizing the wealth of backgrounds, skills and opinions that a diverse workforce offers as it [does] on raw materials, technology and processes."[71] I cannot forbear from noting a particular paradox in Chrysler's offering diversity of "opinions" as a corporation-embraced good. One immediately wants to ask, "Opinions about what?" I am confident that the answer for Chrysler, or any other corporation for that matter, is only opinions about the best way to build and sell cars or whatever other good is being produced by the given business. It would be astonishing, for example, if Chrysler is affirmatively interested in whether its workforce is homogeneous or heterogeneous regarding opinions about abortion, foreign policy, the merits of modern art,

70. This seems to be especially true if classes are selected by the use of certain kinds of "tracking" programs, but it can also coexist with free choice in classes.
71. Bowen and Bok, supra note 47, at 12 (quoting Robert J. Eaton, chairman and CEO of Chrysler Corporation).

or, perhaps most to the point, labor policy or general economic concerns, such as the relationship between globalization and job security or the future of the welfare state.

I do not necessarily mean to pick on business corporations. They may, indeed, be altogether typical of *any* large-scale institution. As University of California law professor Robert Post has emphasized, all "managerial" enterprises, whether private or public, define themselves in terms of specific work tasks.[72] The United States Postal Service is defined by its expertise in delivering the mail, not by its achievement of an on-the-job chautauqua featuring lively interchanges among the workforce or between the workforce and its customers. Indeed, I dare say that most of us would be appalled if our mail deliverer or postal clerk selling us stamps began inserting his or her own opinions about our choice of reading materials. Imagine a postal worker who, while delivering your mail, urged you to stop subscribing to *Playboy* or the *National Review* or pressed upon you material suggesting how you can achieve eternal salvation.

One argument for "diversity" within an academic setting (or on television talk shows) is precisely that it generates an "uninhibited, robust, and wide-open" debate[73] that an institution presumably desires (and that Justice Powell emphasized in his own embrace of "diversity" in *Bakke*[74]). For better and worse, few institutions are defined by their commitment to such debates. Certainly, this is not true of any business institution of which I am aware, and, as we shall see presently, this is scarcely an accurate description of a properly functioning university.[75]

72. See Robert C. Post, *Constitutional Domains: Democracy, Community, Management* 249–52 (1995).

73. See *New York Times Co. v. Sullivan*, 376 U.S. 254, 270 (1965).

74. See *Regents of the Univ. of Cal. v. Bakke*, 438 U.S. 265, 311 (1978).

75. Several people who responded to this lecture as delivered in Philadephia described me as (or accused me of being) very "conservative" insofar as I seemed to accept the validity of organizational imperatives against the expressive interests of the individuals who constitute the organization. There is, I suppose, a certain core of truth in the charge, though I am not sure that "conservative" is the mot juste. It seems to me that almost anyone with a sociological bent both recognizes, as a descriptive matter, that we live our lives playing certain kinds of varying social roles and accepts, normatively, the legitimacy of the role constraints on many, if not all, occasions. I am more than happy to define certain role conceptions or organizational strictures as too confining and, therefore, to support opening up space for the expression of added facets of the personalities of the organization's actors. I am much too much a child of the 1960s to believe that we ought necessarily to accept organizational roles, whether public or private, without question. That being said, I also cannot imagine what life would be like without a sense of some institu-

One's suspicion about diversity as practiced by Coca-Cola, and many other companies, is that it relates primarily to the marketing of products rather than their actual production. Not surprisingly, there is a debate about the relevance of diverse backgrounds to the quality of what is produced. One authoritative review of the evidence states:

> Under ideal conditions increased diversity may have the positive effects predicted by information and decision theories [i.e., generation of varied ideas and approaches and greater creativity]. However, . . . the preponderance of empirical evidence suggests that diversity is most likely to impede group functioning. Unless steps are taken to actively counteract these effects, the evidence suggests that, by itself, diversity is more likely to have negative than positive effects on group performance.[76]

Consider in this context a study supporting the unsurprising proposition that persons coming from different backgrounds often misread each other's social signals.[77] Different people were asked to respond to the statement: "In order to have efficient work relationships, it is often necessary to bypass the hierarchical line."[78] In one example, systematic differences emerged between Swedes and Italians. Swedish managers are described as believing

---

tional constraint, and I am certainly strongly supportive in many instances of organizational actors "knowing their place," as it were, and realizing that behavior that would be perfectly appropriate outside the organizational structure is completely inappropriate within it. Taking the example in the text, I would indeed be dismayed if postal workers attempted to convert me or otherwise engage in religious conversation when I was trying to buy stamps, though I have no dismay, only disagreement, if a Jehovah's Witness or an Evangelical Christian tries to do the same as I walk through Washington Square. I simply would not take anyone seriously who rejected in toto, descriptively or normatively, a role-oriented analysis of human behavior. And I certainly would not want to spend much time around such a person.

76. Katherine Y. Williams and Charles A. O'Reilly III, "Demography and Diversity in Organizations: A Review of 40 Years of Research," 20 *Res. in Organizational Behav.* 77, 120 (1998). (I am indebted to Cynthia Estlund for this reference.) Similar skepticism is expressed in Eugene Volokh, "Diversity, Race as Proxy, and Religion as Proxy," *UCLA L. Rev.* 2059, 2060–63 (1996) (citing, inter alia, Stephen M. Bainbridge, "Community and Statism: A Conservative Contractarian Critique of Progressive Corporate Law Scholarship," 82 *Cornell L. Rev.* 856 (1997); Robert Drago, "Share Schemes, Participatory Management and Work Norms," 23 *Rev. of Radical Pol. Econ.* 55, 58–59 (1991) (discussing gender homogeneity); Donald McCloskey, "Bourgeois Virtue," *Am. Scholar* 177, 183–84 (1994) (discussing ethnic and religious homogeneity)).

77. See Nancy J. Adler, *International Dimensions of Organizational Behavior* 39–62 (2d ed., 1991) (noting that work behaviors of individuals vary across cultures).

78. Id. at 43–45 (citing André Laurent, "The Cultural Diversity of Western Conceptions of Management," 13 *Int'l Stud. of Mgmt. & Org.* 75, 86 (1983)).

"that a perfect hierarchy — in which one's boss knows everything — is impossible."[79] It is, therefore, perfectly proper to bypass superiors and go directly "to the person most likely to have the needed information and expertise."[80] "Most Italians," however, "consider bypassing the boss as an act of insubordination," so that mutual frustration rapidly builds up between Swedish workers and Italian superiors.[81] On the other hand, Swedish superiors tend to view Italian subordinates as "lack[ing] initiative and . . . unwilling both to use personal judgment and to take risks," because the Italians engage in "constant requests for permission and information."[82]

Thomas and Ely note that "many attempts to increase diversity in the workplace have backfired, sometimes even heightening tensions among employees and hindering a company's performance."[83] By way of response, they devote their article primarily to articulating the merits of an "emerging paradigm: connecting diversity to work perspectives,"[84] by which they mean strategies for incorporating "employees' perspectives into the main work of the organization and to enhance work by rethinking primary tasks and redefining markets, products, strategies, missions, business practices, and even cultures."[85]

I want very much to believe that examples of organizational disruption caused by workforce diversity are limited only to companies that are organizationally inept at taking advantage of diversity, perhaps because they are insufficiently committed to the ostensible emerging paradigm. One might ask, though, if it matters. That is, does one's support for "diversity" turn on the answers to such empirical questions, or is it based on certain normative commitments that are, in some important senses, independent of empirical evidence? There may be good reasons to support affirmative action besides enhancement of organizational performance. One may believe, as I do, that society as a whole is likely to be better off if its workplaces are diverse, a point I shall return to shortly. But this is a different argument, patently *public-regarding,* in contrast to the purportedly *self-regarding* arguments proffered by the ceos I have discussed. Self-regarding arguments have the

79. Id. at 44.
80. Id. at 43–44.
81. Id. at 44.
82. Id.
83. Thomas and Ely, supra note 55, at 80.
84. Id. at 85.
85. Id.

advantage of appearing more hard-headed and less idealistic; they may, for better and worse, however, be subject to more stringent empirical tests than are public-regarding arguments that forthrightly admit that costs may have to be paid in order to achieve desirable social goals.

"Diversity" within Educational Settings

Let us, at last, return to educational institutions, presumably very different from Coca-Cola or Chrysler. Still, educational institutions can be said to produce certain products, including well-educated graduates and scholarship. They may also be in the business of producing good citizens, a civic task that may relate in certain complex ways to "pure" education or scholarly attainment but is, at the end of the day, quite different.

One could give an entire lecture, at the very least, about the notion of the "well-educated" person. Let me offer only two possible criteria of being well educated. One involves what might be termed "disciplinarity"; for example, chemistry courses should produce persons knowledgeable about chemistry; economics courses should, similarly, produce persons proficient in performing the tasks expected of a competent economist. As a law professor, I am interested in doing what I can to turn our students into competent analysts of law and legal structures by way of preparing them to engage effectively in the role of lawyer. A second notion might focus less on disciplinary prowess and more on other attainments. Thus, among other things, the well-educated person might be expected to possess a certain level of curiosity about the world in general, reflected perhaps in manifesting the social virtues needed to relate to a wide variety of different persons with different interests. Truly well-educated persons should be able, if sitting next to someone at a dinner party with whom they apparently have "nothing in common," to engage in conversation and even learn something from the perspectives and experiences brought to bear by the putative stranger. Beyond this is the distinctively civic virtue by which persons learn to treat social strangers as their fellow citizens, to whom they owe obligations and loyalty, even if they seemingly have little in common other than shared political identity. And beyond this is the empathic identification with "complete" strangers, such as, say, Kosovars or Chechens, who have nothing in common with most of us other than the shared status of being human and the ability to suffer. How does "diversity" work in regard to these various tasks of education?

I begin with the most obvious tasks of educational institutions: disciplinary education and the encouragement of disciplined scholarship. What does "diversity" contribute to these goals? My answer is vigorous and unequivocal: "It depends." In regard to the classes that I teach, on American constitutional development and on the American legal profession, I strongly believe that the quality of these classes is indeed a function of the classroom demographics. To take the most obvious example, I find it intensely frustrating to discuss the role of race in American history before a post-*Hopwood* class that includes few or no African Americans. It would be equally troublesome to try to discuss gender-related issues in an all-male (or, for that matter, all-female) class. Racially or gender-mixed classes can provide the same benefits provided by the presence of "a former policeman in [a] criminal procedure [class], a former business executive in corporations, and a former bank examiner in commercial law," all of whom "are sure to enrich those classes in ways that" other students, without such backgrounds, cannot.[86] To the extent that *Hopwood* functions to make much more difficult the attainment of a sufficient degree of heterogeneity in my own classrooms, I believe that the quality of legal education at the University of Texas Law School has been diminished and, therefore, the students significantly disserved.[87]

I should acknowledge, though, that my views are, to some extent, prompted by the specific courses that I teach. I am not at all certain that classroom demographics, at least with regard to race or gender, would be relevant if I taught courses, say, on the taxation of international businesses, though one can certainly imagine that it might be helpful to have students from some of the "host" countries of multinational enterprises. Looking around at the rest of the university, I am far more confident that certain

---

86. Arnold H. Loewy, "Taking *Bakke* Seriously: Distinguishing Diversity from Affirmative Action in the Law School Admissions Process," 77 *N.C. L. Rev.* 1479, 1488 (1999).

87. One must always be wary, though, of assuming that members of given minorities will conform to some preexisting stereotype that will provide the desired "diversity." Thus Deborah Malamud writes:

> The most conventional arguments for diversity are arguments that each member of a group is a representative of that group's cultural characteristics and viewpoints, and that the institution (or polity) is enriched by bringing these different cultures under the institutional umbrella. The problem with these arguments is that . . . they script the lives of diversity hires [or students admitted under "diversity preferences"]. For example, the black college student who is a jazz musician but switches to classical piano can be seen as ceasing to do his "job" for the institution. . . .

Deborah C. Malamud, "Values, Symbols, and the Facts," supra note 29, at 1691.

courses in the humanities and social sciences benefit from a "diverse" student body than do courses in the so-called hard sciences or mathematics. To the extent that I support the use of racial or gender preferences in regard, say, to admitting students to a graduate program in mathematics,[88] the reasons are necessarily other than a belief that the quality of the disciplinary education itself depends on classroom demographics.

It is worth noting some skepticism about whether classroom demographics matter in *any* course that operates only via lectures and does not include opportunity for some genuine give-and-take response to the material presented. Even among courses that depend on discussion, some subject matters more plausibly draw on students' own "personal" insights than do others. To the extent that students interact with one another outside of courses there could be real benefits from "diversity." Presumably, however, universities have more interest in (and competence to evaluate) what goes on inside their classrooms than in potential late night conversations in dormitories. And most proponents of "diversity" generally focus on that part of university education that is classroom-specific.[89]

Moreover—and here I think we come to the heart of the matter—one should acknowledge that Judge Weiner, in his concurring opinion in *Hopwood*, was entirely fair in noting that my law school in fact has a somewhat limited notion of diversity. "Focusing as it does on blacks and Mexican Americans only, the law school's . . . admissions process misconceived the

---

88. I take it that very few undergraduate admissions preferences are program specific, if for no other reason than the admissions department has only the slightest idea of what the admitted students will ultimately study. In addition, much of the most important education at the undergraduate level goes on outside the classroom, in long conversations that may have little to do with one's formal studies. The situation is quite different with graduate programs. Although one assumes that graduate students will indeed have conversations about what Justice Cardozo called "life in all its fullness," that is not what is truly bringing them to graduate study, nor is it (often) an important admissions criterion on the part of the admitting department. One is interested above all in who will make the best physicist, historian, zoologist, or logician.

89. See, e.g., University of Michigan, Expert Report of Patricia Gurin: Summary and Conclusions (last accessed 30 January 2000), ⟨http://www.umich.edu/~urel/admissions/legal/expert/summ.html⟩. Gurin states:

It is clear . . . that interaction with peers from diverse racial backgrounds, both *in the classroom* and informally, is positively associated with a host of what I call "learning outcomes." Students who experienced the most racial and ethnic *diversity in classroom settings* and in informal interactions with peers showed the greatest engagement in active thinking processes, growth in intellectual engagement and motivation, and growth in intellectual and academic skills. (Id.; emphasis added.)

concept of diversity. . . . [B]lacks and Mexican Americans are but two among any number of racial or ethnic groups that could and presumably should contribute to genuine diversity."[90] He is absolutely right. Indeed, it is his opinion, far more than the obtuse majority opinion penned by Judge Smith, that offers the greatest challenge to those who proclaim their devotion to "diversity" as a "compelling need in higher education." The reason is that he accepts the central proposition, but then goes on to show that the arguments that universities offer with regard to ostensibly diversity-oriented admissions policies are underinclusive.

I begin with a personal example: I have become especially aware of the limited nature of University of Texas's diversity because of a developing interest of mine in the constitutional implications of American expansionism, including the seizure and dominion over Puerto Rico as part of the aftermath of the Spanish-American War in 1898. Many fascinating and delicate constitutional problems were raised (and continue) as a result of our venture into imperialism. Indeed, Puerto Rico today is described by many as the world's largest remaining colony,[91] if we mean by "colony" a political entity that enjoys no formal political sovereignty and is under the ultimate control of a polity in which its own members do not have the right to participate politically. Although Puerto Ricans are American citizens, they cannot, of course, vote for the President nor do they have voting representation in Congress. And, as President Clinton's recent pardon of Puerto Rican terrorists reminded us (even if he did a notably inept job of defending his altogether defensible decision), there is a significant, albeit small, movement in Puerto Rico that is borrowing a page from America's own revolutionary past and seeking independence from those it deems its colonial oppressors.

I think it is relevant to note that my newfound interest had its genesis in 1998 at a Yale Law School conference on Puerto Rico organized by a remarkable third-year law student *from* Puerto Rico. She was determined to "bring to the mainland," as it were, the issues that so passionately concerned her. Not only were the issues brought to the mainland, she also was able to bring to New Haven a number of representatives of the decidedly different points of view, including the governor. These views ranged from the gover-

90. *Hopwood v. Texas*, 78 F.3d 932, 965–66 (5th Cir. 1996) (Wiener, J., concurring).
91. Others might name Tibet as the largest colony, though China has attempted to absorb Tibet into the legal structure of the People's Republic of China, in contrast to the decided nonabsorption of Puerto Rico into the legal entity called the United States of America.

nor's desire for statehood to those advocating for independence, with those wishing to maintain the present "commonwealth" status in between.

As a direct result of my introduction to the issue, I now assign one of the central 1901 *Insular Cases*[92] addressing the status of Puerto Rico to my introductory courses on constitutional law and have added long excerpts from that case to a casebook on constitutional law that I coedit.[93] That being said, I have no doubt whatsoever that the discussions in classes using these materials would benefit significantly if they included students from Puerto Rico. There are, to my knowledge, *no* Puerto Rican students at the University of Texas Law School, and I suspect this is true at a number of — perhaps most — American law schools. There are, no doubt, a number of explanations. Concerning Texas in particular, the state has not been a historical site of Puerto Rican migration, unlike, say, New York or New Jersey. That in itself does not, however, fully explain why Puerto Rican Americans are not sought out by the University of Texas Law School. Perhaps one might argue that one consequence of the meager migration to Texas is that, concomitantly, there is little or no history of past discrimination by Texas against Puerto Ricans, unlike the cases with African and Mexican Americans. Even if this is true, recall that it is illegitimate for the university to ground its affirmative action programs on the presence of past discrimination in the wider society. Most relevant, almost certainly, is the fact that Puerto Ricans, by being an insignificant part of the Texas population, do not count as a significant political constituency for any Texas politician. No credible political threat is posed to those who ignore the specific interests of Puerto Ricans.[94] I deeply regret this limit in our own range of diversity, for the absence of Puerto Rican students, at least on the days that we are discussing the issues raised by the *Insular Cases,* means that my course is of lesser quality than it might otherwise be.

As suggested earlier, it would by no means be enough to have *one* Puerto Rican in the classroom, given the bitter divisions among Puerto Rican proponents of statehood, independence, and maintenance of the constitutionally uncertain "commonwealth" status. It would, no doubt, be as illuminating to my students to hear heartfelt expressions of the various positions as it was to me. Of course, if the only point were *hearing* heartfelt expressions,

---

92. See *Downes v. Bidwell,* 182 U.S. 244 (1901).

93. See *Process of Constitutional Decision Making: Cases and Materials* 297 (Paul Brest et al., eds., 4th ed., 2000).

94. The same is true, incidentally, with regard to Hispanics from Central or South America.

that could be attained by playing tapes of the New Haven conference. More important, presumably, would be the opportunity to participate in a genuine encounter with the speakers, asking them questions and engaging them in real conversation. One might still ask if such encounters depend on mutual presence at the same university, as opposed to using contemporary technology to bring together remarkably diverse groups in the common ground of "distance learning" or cyberspace. I am thinking, for example, of a course on nuclear arms policy, organized well over a decade ago by Martin Sherwin at Tufts University, that consisted of his American students in Medford, Massachusetts, and a class of students at the Moscow State University who met together at frequent intervals via satellite. It would be easy enough to hook up similar connections with students at the University of Puerto Rico, and that might in fact provide a richer kind of diversity of experience than that provided by relatively atypical persons who leave their homes to attend schools thousands of miles away. We should increasingly rethink our assumptions that university education necessarily takes place in fixed geographical settings. Thus, writes Arthur Levine, the president of Teachers College, Columbia University:

> It is possible right now for a professor to give a lecture in Cairo, for me to attend that lecture at Teachers College and for another student to attend it in Tokyo. It's possible for all of us to feel we're sitting in the same classroom. . . . It's possible for the professor to point to me and my Japanese colleague and say, "I want you to prepare a project for next week's class." If we can do all of that, and the demographics of higher education are changing so greatly, why do we need the physical plant called the college?[95]

To be sure, one might still lament the lack of an opportunity to go to a coffeehouse or bar afterward and continue the arguments provoked by the relatively minimal classroom discussions, but, perhaps, intensive Internet discussions among the various students spread across the world would provide a more than adequate substitute at least with regard to the specific variable of diversity.

I most definitely do *not* believe that only Puerto Ricans are capable of thinking cogently about Puerto Rico. What I *do* believe is that persons from Puerto Rico are, as an empirical matter, far more likely to have thought

---

95. Arthur Levine, "The Soul of a New University," *New York Times,* 13 March 2000, at A21.

about issues relevant to people in Puerto Rico, such as the political status of the island, than are non–Puerto Ricans. Though I may know enough to raise the most basic issues for my students, I have no sense of the nuances that come from extended immersion within an ongoing culture, especially a culture of bitter argument. Nor, as a matter of blunt fact, do I have very great personal incentive to educate myself in-depth about the issues facing Puerto Ricans. Life is short, and the demands for my limited time and attention span are overwhelming. An intellectual interest in Puerto Rico, which I now most certainly have, is not the equivalent of truly caring deeply enough about the fate of that island to invest the ever-scarcer resources of time and energy in ways that would allow me to become truly expert. It is sad truth that most of us care most deeply about, and invest most significantly in, those things (and people) who are closest to us, both literally and metaphorically.

Race and ethnicity, therefore, at least on occasion, may act as proxies, not so much for holding specific views, but for the probability of being deeply interested (and at least somewhat knowledgeable) at all in certain issues, i.e., those issues most germane to the group in question. (One of these issues might be whether there *are* specific issues that are necessarily germane to the group!) I think it simply undeniable that African Americans are more likely to be concerned with the problems facing African Americans — and, for that matter, more aware of the complexities and divisions within the group of those comprising the community of African Americans — than are non–African Americans. This is not at all the same thing as saying that African Americans bring some privileged understanding of African American-ness or that whites are without the capacity to think cogently about African Americans (or that some whites do not care very deeply about the welfare of African Americans).

These latter assertions indeed raise the most profound difficulties and perhaps even fall victim to the Fifth Circuit's statement that "government may not allocate benefits or burdens among individuals based on the assumption that race or ethnicity *determines* how they act or think."[96] But it seems foolhardy to deny the presence of a correlation between racial and ethnic status and the *propensity* to think about related problems. To deny

---

96. *Hopwood v. Texas*, 78 F.3d 932, 946 (5th Cir. 1996) (quoting *Metro Broad., Inc. v. FCC*, 497 U.S. 547, 602 (1990) (O'Connor, J., dissenting)) (emphasis added).

this is indeed to accept the Fifth Circuit's assertion that race is no more rational a basis for decision making "than would be choices based upon the . . . blood type of applicants."[97] Most of us almost never think of our blood type; as an empirical matter, though, it is foolish beyond belief to say that we think as rarely about the implications of our racial and ethnic identities as about our blood type. And, with regard to at least certain groups that *do* spend a lot of time thinking about blood types — hemophiliacs and cancer patients interested in receiving bone-marrow transplants — one wonders if the Fifth Circuit, given its solicitude for parents of disabled children as presenters of important perspectives, would find it unthinkable to grant a preference to these particular blood-type-obsessed persons because of the insights they might contribute in courses on health policy and law.

Similarly, if I taught courses on, say, the American role abroad, I think classroom discussion, and therefore the production of educated students, would benefit from the presence of members of some of the various foreign countries that are often the objects of American policy. As I listened in 1999 to National Public Radio dispatches about the NATO bombing of Yugoslavia, I could not help but wonder how many Americans have met a single person from Kosovo or Macedonia or how, concomitantly, our views about the propriety of our policies might differ if we placed human faces on the abstractions called "Serbs," "Kosovars," or "Croats."[98] Thus Professor

97. Id. at 945.

98. During the discussion following my presentation of the Roberts Lecture, Professor Regina Austin took vigorous exception to my (then) implicit premise that students in effect serve as their professors' educational "instruments," to be used to develop points the professor believes germane to the topic of the course. I plead guilty to this charge and am happy to make the point explicit. I believe that teachers often, and properly, do attempt to draw on the experiences of their students in order to illuminate matters under discussion. If I were teaching a course on the Vietnam War, for example, I think it would certainly be beneficial to have within the classroom, say, veterans from the United States armed forces, persons from both North and South Vietnam, and an antiwar activist. Or if I were teaching a course on sports law, I think it would be useful to have as a member of the class a professional tennis or basketball player, and so on. I *do* agree with Professor Austin that, generally speaking, students come to universities to be educated *by* their professors rather than to serve as educational resources *for* their professors, but I do not see these as dichotomous alternatives. One need not believe that students should be appointed full professors in order to recognize that even the most untutored first-year student may, because of his or her own life experiences, have something valuable to contribute to a particular classroom discussion. A good professor will, of course, warn students about the fallacy of extrapolating

Loewy, in his own reflections on diversity and law school admissions, notes that "[i]n a class of 200, I would tend to choose the first Iranian or the first Sikh over the twenty-third African-American."[99] If one finds Professor Loewy's choice troublesome, then I suggest that one has not sufficiently thought through what it means to take diversity seriously. Truly to take diversity seriously might well require revolutionizing current admissions practices.

Consider only the fact that the University of Texas Law School operates under a very rigid admissions quota by which the law school may not admit more than 20 percent of non-Texans. Could a university claiming to be seriously committed to "diversity" justify such a quota? If Heman Sweatt was ill-served by being channeled to a law school that lacked any representatives of 85 percent of the population, are Texan students much better served by attending a contemporary school that may lack significant representation of the vast majority of the country that is non-Texan and, indeed, of the overwhelming majority of an increasingly globalized world that is non-American? The devastating parochialism of the "downtown law school" was absolutely obvious; other parochialisms may be less so, but no less present and, ultimately, only a little less stifling, both for the Americans charged with (or volunteering for) extraordinary influence in structuring the global order, and for the foreigners who are on the receiving end, for good and ill, of American power.

It is perhaps relevant here to mention a conversation I had this past year with the president of a major American university who mentioned his ongoing struggles with his university's own admissions office. He strongly believes that the university, which is truly "world class" by any conceivable measure, should strive to admit at least 10 percent of its entering class from abroad. The admissions office is unwilling to go beyond 5 percent, in part, one gathers, because of fears of adverse reaction from disgruntled "local" applicants, some of whom, inevitably, will be children of alumni whose continued financial support is thought vital to the university. (Recall the statement quoted by Justice Powell that emphasized Harvard's interest only in "the rich diversity of *the United States*"[100] rather than in the entire world.

---

from individual events, or "anecdotes," but a good professor will also scarcely ignore the valuable information that can be provided by looking at specific examples.

99. Loewy, supra note 86, at 1489.

100. *Regents of the Univ. of Cal. v. Bakke*, 438 U.S. 265, 323 (1977) (emphasis added).

There is no particular reason why Harvard's students need exposure only to their fellow Americans.)

But to play this kind of "diversity card" is highly unfair. *No university could* genuinely try to maximize the possible diversity of its student body. Consider the fact, for example, that the editors of the *Harvard Encyclopedia of American Ethnic Groups* in 1980 listed no fewer than 106 separate ethnic groups within the United States alone.[101] As Miranda Oshige McGowan has shown, the category of "Asian" or "Asian American" used by Davis and other schools ignores to an almost grotesque degree the profound differences among the many groups collapsed into one, empirically false, identity as "Asians." "[P]eople categorized racially as Asian often do not view themselves as such, nor do they necessarily feel a sense of identity or kinship with others categorized as Asian. Instead, many Asian Americans define themselves primarily in terms of national origin and feel an affinity with others of the same national origin."[102] Consider a school that offered preference to an invented category called "Balkans" and treated Serbs, Croats, and Albanians as a single undifferentiated group. This may be all too analogous to collapsing persons of Japanese, Chinese, Vietnamese, and Korean background into one group called "Asians."[103] Similarly, to refer blandly to "American Indians" masks the fact that there are at least 170 separate Indian tribes whose members, no doubt, would vigorously resist being assimilated into a single undifferentiated category. (Are there no significant differences between Navahos and Mohawks or, indeed, between the Navahos and their "next-door neighbors," the Hopis, with whom they seem to be engaged in almost endless dispute?) In this ever-more complex multi-

101. See *Harvard Encyclopedia of American Ethnic Groups* vi (Stephen Thernstrom, ed., 1980). Some of these groups, to be sure,

> now exist almost exclusively in the recollections of their descendants. . . . On the other hand, some groups have not yet been in the United States long enough to establish generational continuity or to develop the array of institutions conventionally associated with ethnic groups, but they seem to be in the process of formation. (Id.)

One suspects that a new edition of the *Encyclopedia* would contain entries on the Hmong, Vietnamese, Iraqis, and Palestinians, only four of the groups absent from the original edition that are present in significant numbers in one or another major American city.

102. Miranda Oshige McGowan, "Diversity of What?," *in Race and Representation: Affirmative Action,* supra note 30, at 237, 242.

103. There are other notorious problems with the category "Asian," of course, given the extension of the Asian land mass from Istanbul to Vladivostock. Are Iranians or Siberian Russians "Asian"? Any negative answer must rest on something more than a geographical notion of identity.

cultural world of ours, there are always going to be many more distinct groups making their claims for succor than there are spaces available. There is, by necessity, an "economy of diversity"; it is simply an existential reality of having to live under conditions of scarcity.

It is also worth noting, though full development of the point would certainly be worth an essay (or book) of its own, that much of the preceding discussion has assumed that we in fact know what we are talking about when we (or I) refer to people as "African American," "Mexican American," "Navajo," "Vietnamese," or whatever. But it is increasingly obvious beyond any reasonable doubt that such categories are truly social constructions, subject to remarkable instability upon close analysis. As more and more Americans (and people throughout the world) are of "mixed" parentage, deciding how to categorize people is itself a subject of major controversy.[104] Indeed, the eminent Harvard sociologist Orlando Patterson has suggested that if W. E. B. Du Bois was at least half right in suggesting that the twentieth century would be the century of the color line, then the twenty-first century will see the substantial eradication of the color (and ethnic) line, "made obsolete by migratory, sociological, and biotechnological developments that are already under way."[105] It may be that to maintain racially or ethnically oriented "diversity" programs will require, even more than is currently the case, that one engage in highly questionable, indeed demeaning, conversations about whether some person X is a "real" member of group Y given that he or she has the wrong last name, grew up in the wrong locale, etc. It is the necessity to engage in such conversations that gives weight to Justice Stevens's pointed dissent in *Fullilove v. Klutznick*,[106] when he remarks that supporters of racial preference programs should look to the Nuremberg codes (or, at the very least, the elaborate racial codes of the Old South) for guidance. (Does a "single drop of blood" suffice, or must one have at least three grandparents of the relevant ancestry, assuming, of course, that we don't ask embarrassing questions about the "purity" of the grandparents themselves?) One must note that Stevens himself has ended up a relative supporter of such programs even as the majority of the Court has

104. See generally David Hollinger, *Postethnic America: Beyond Multiculturalism* (1995); Lawrence Wright, "One Drop of Blood," *The New Yorker,* 25 July 1994, at 46; Christopher A. Ford, "Administering Identity: The Determination of 'Race' in Race-Conscious Law," 82 *Cal. L. Rev.* 1231 (1994).

105. See Orlando Patterson, "Race Over," *The New Republic,* 10 January 2000, at 6.

106. 448 U.S. 448, 532 (1980) (Stevens, J., dissenting).

adopted the position he once seemed to endorse,[107] and, of course, for all of my ambivalence amply reflected here, I still wish to praise, rather than to bury, such programs myself. Still, I think there is much merit in Patterson's position and its suggestion that the demise of "diversity" preferences will come more from the practical pressures generated by the increasing "hybridity"[108] of the American (and world) population than from the adoption of a "principled" position of color blindness.

All of this being said, I have increasingly come to believe that "diversity" is an idea of relatively limited utility with regard to understanding the actualities of such programs, even if we put to one side questions like those raised in the last paragraph. Given that any and all diversity-oriented programs will *necessarily* be limited in their scope, preferences for only certain racial and ethnic groups must be defended on the basis of some argument other than a striving for diversity as such. One must *always* assert, as a practical matter, that the diversity provided by group A is more important, along some relevant dimension, than that provided by some groups B and C. To fail to rank order will always open oneself up to the devastating riposte suggested by Judge Wiener's opinion in *Hopwood:*[109] "Why did you stop with members of groups A–G, rather than go on to seek out members of putatively absent groups H–Z?" It is *always* possible to achieve even more diversity than one has now, if only one has the will (and makes a possibly lunatic decision to prefer diversity against any competing value). So why *do* we prefer the specific groups we do? Answers must always lie in group-specific reasons, and only rarely will these reasons track those that would be suggested by someone for whom diversity per se was the primary goal.

A "tracking" reason might be something like the following: "We have examined all of the contending groups, and we believe that the most truly unusual perspectives are those associated with group A. If one purpose of 'diversity' is to provoke what some literary theorists call 'defamiliariza-

---

107. See, e.g., *Metro Broad., Inc. v. FCC,* 497 U.S. 547, 601 (1990) (Stevens, J., concurring). Stevens states:

> Specifically, the reason for the classification — the recognized interest in broadcast diversity — is clearly identified and does not imply any judgement concerning the abilities of owners of different races or the merits of different kinds of programming. . . . The public interest in broadcast diversity — like the interest in an integrated police force, diversity in the composition of a public school faculty or diversity in the student body of a professional school — is in my view unquestionably legitimate. (Id. at 601–2.)

108. See Patterson, supra note 105, at 6.

109. See *Hopwood v. Texas,* 78 F.3d 932, 962 (5th Cir. 1996) (Wiener, J., concurring).

tion'—the calling into question, or 'problematizing,' our most basic assumptions of how the world is ordered—then encounter with someone from group A will best fill the bill." It may be that there is some university or organization that does operate under such criteria, but I am not familiar with it.

Far more representative, I am confident, is the answer provided by Professor Jack Balkin, who forthrightly states that, "[i]n the context of educational affirmative action, I understand 'diversity' to be a code word for representation in enjoyment of social goods by major ethnic groups who have some claim to past mistreatment."[110] Thus, according to Balkin, inasmuch as "human capital (obtained through education) is one of the most important methods of wealth transmission in our age, it makes sense that Blacks and Hispanics should be given a larger share of this capital to make up for their relative deprivations due to social subordination."[111] He notes that "the groups that would receive a boost in cultural capital in Texas might be different from those in Washington State or Florida, for example."[112] But, if we are to "be honest about what 'diversity' is really about," he says, we should admit that "[i]t is primarily about distributive justice of human capital, and [only] secondarily about creating a civic space in which the major ethnic groups in a given society can live relatively peaceably."[113]

It is very difficult, as a practical matter, to disagree with Balkin's observations, but it should be obvious that there is also a chasm between such arguments and those that view "diversity" as a positive good per se. Balkin's arguments focus on the past traumas of our polity that in fact deprived certain groups of a "fair chance" to compete for the "human capital" represented by education or access to the employment market. Someone more genuinely committed to the positive values of diversity should be far less interested in the historical explanation for its lack and more committed to assuring a desirable mix in the future. To return to my own previous example, I do not in the least need to believe that Texas has denied Puerto Ricans any human capital to believe that the law school (and my classes) would

---

110. Letter from Jack Balkin, Professor, Yale Law School, to Sanford Levinson, Professor, University of Texas Law School (18 March 1999) (electronic mail responding to an earlier version of the present essay).

111. Id.

112. Id.

113. Id.

benefit from the presence of persons from Puerto Rico. And, if I were to support the vigorous recruitment by the University of Texas of persons from, say, Eastern Europe, I would less focus on any purported wrongs done the Eastern Europeans by Texas (or even the United States) than on the benefits of breaking down our own parochialism. To adopt the valuable language of Stanford Law School Dean Kathleen Sullivan, "diversity" should not be viewed as a penalty we pay to rectify our past sins, but, rather, a policy warmly embraced because of its service to the present and future interests of the relevant institutions.[114]

The differences among the various approaches to diversity are especially well illuminated if we consider one additional example of a group that might claim some consideration in an admissions process ostensibly committed to the premise that "diversity" is relevant to the quality of education received. I refer to people who have religious views that are out of the "mainstream," at least as defined by the basically secular culture dominant in most American colleges and universities or, at least, those usually viewed as "elite" institutions. It is an open secret that the religious identities of students at the relatively few academic institutions that do not practice de facto open admissions[115] are scarcely representative of the genuine range of views found in a remarkably pluralistic American society. Indeed, former university presidents Bowen and Bok caution that it is "easy to forget the importance of differences in religion as well as race and culture,"[116] an odd phrasing if one views religion as an important part of "culture." As someone who regularly teaches in my courses about the interaction of state and religion,[117] I believe that the classroom discussions and my students would benefit as much from the active presence of, say, fundamentalist Christians

114. See Kathleen M. Sullivan, "Sins of Discrimination: Last Term's Affirmative Action Cases," 100 *Harv. L. Rev.* 78 (1986).

115. Bowen and Bok

> estimate that only about 20 to 30 percent of all four-year colleges and universities [have enough applicants to be able to pick and choose among them]. Nationally, the vast majority of undergraduate institutions accept all qualified candidates and thus do not award special status to any group of applicants, defined by race or on the basis of any other criterion.

Bowen and Bok, supra note 47, at 15.

116. Id. at 228.

117. This topic most naturally arises in any constitutional law course, but I should note that I also raise the issue of "personal," as opposed to "professional," identity in my course on the legal profession. See chapter 4.

as do discussions about race or ethnicity benefit from the presence of African or Mexican Americans.

So why don't more elite colleges and universities take religion into account in their admissions process, at least to the extent of awarding scarce (and valuable) places to those who come from "nonmainstream" religions?[118] One quick answer, of course, is that this would be prohibited, at least for state universities, because of the First Amendment's prohibition of the "establishment of religion."[119] That answer is scarcely satisfactory, though; indeed, I am increasingly tempted to describe it as equal in obtuseness to the Fifth Circuit's decision in *Hopwood*. It is, after all, now a commonplace of legal doctrine that racial classifications, because presumptively prohibited, can be used only if justified by some "compelling interest," and most proponents of racial and ethnic preferences (including myself) purport to believe that the striving for "diversity" meets this high standard. If that is true, then it is, to say the least, difficult to see how that interest would be less "compelling" in regard to, say, Christian Pentacostalists, Hasidic Jews, Mormons, Eastern Orthodox, or Muslims, all of whom may well be "underrepresented" at America's elite institutions.[120] To be sure, there would be

118. See generally Volokh, supra note 76, at 2070–76.

119. U.S. Const. amend. I.

120. I note that Detroit has a very large concentration of Arab Americans (which may itself be an "overly inclusive" categorization collapsing important differences between, say, Iraqis and Lebanese). And, of course, not all Arab Americans are in fact Muslim. Still, one might consider a recent article by Gary Lee in the Travel section of the *Washington Post,* which had the following headline: "Not Your Father's Detroit: The Motor City Has Become the Unlikely Capital of Arab America," *Washington Post,* 9 January 2000, at E1. Lee states that:

> According to Zogby International, a national pollster, 275,000 Middle Easterners — mostly Arab Americans — have settled in Detroit, Dearborn and other surrounding towns. It's the biggest concentration of Arab Americans in the country, and is tied with the Hispanic population as the second-largest ethnic group in southern Michigan, after African Americans. (Id.)

I wonder how much effort the University of Michigan has made to assure a "representative" number of students from this group, including, of course, "representatives" of very important religious strains within it. It would obviously be anomalous if all Arab American students at the university happened to be secular and, perhaps, willing to reinforce antisectarian stereotypes directed at "Islamic fundamentalists" in the same way, for example, that "mainstream" Christians or non-Orthodox Jews may gladly demean Christian fundamentalists or Orthodox (and, certainly, Hasidic) Jews. I cannot claim to have read all of the Michigan evidence, but I note that Professor Gurin's submission emphasizes "racially/ethnically different student populations (African American, White, and Latino Students)." See University of Michigan, Expert Report of Patricia Gurin: Empirical Results from the Analyses Conducted for This Litigation (accessed 20 February 2000), ⟨http://www.umich.edu/~urel/admissions/legal/expert/empir.html⟩. Per-

many classes in which the religious identity of the student body would be absolutely irrelevant, but that, as we have already seen, is also likely to be the case with regard to racial, ethnic, or gender identity.

Balkin rejects the case for bringing religion within the diversity fold, though his explanation underscores the differences among forms of the arguments for diversity. Thus, he writes:

> If "diversity" is a code word, as I have suggested, which has little to do with ideological differences, it makes perfect sense that conservative Christians would not and should not be beneficiaries of affirmative action even if they would make the student body more diverse in an ideological sense. That is because there is no sustained history of de jure persecution and social and economic oppression of conservative Christians in the United States that compares with anything suffered by Blacks and Hispanics. To be sure, there are forms of class oppression that con-

---

haps even more relevant is the extensive statement prepared by Professor Thomas J. Sugrue, who notes in his "statement of qualifications" that his book, *The Origins of the Urban Crisis: Race and Inequality in Postwar Detroit* (1996) won four major awards, including the extremely prestigious Bancroft Prize in American History. See University of Michigan, Expert Report of Thomas J. Sugrue (accessed 20 February 2000), ⟨http://www.umich.edu/~urel/admissions/ legal/expert/sugrutoc.html⟩ ("My book and a number of my articles discuss race relations and inequality in Michigan, with close attention to metropolitan Detroit"). It is, therefore, especially startling to realize that Professor Sugrue apparently does not regard Arab Americans as an "ethnic group" that should be discussed. See, e.g., id. at Table 2: Michigan Population by Race/Ethnicity, at 21 (dividing the population into "White; Black; American Indian/Eskimo/ Aleut; Asian/Pacific Islander; Hispanic, Mexican; Puerto Rican; Cuban; Other Hispanic;" and, finally, "Other Race"). Professor Sugrue is obviously adopting the classification schema of the United States Census Bureau, which, at best, is highly problematic if not outright incoherent (or worse). See, e.g., Hollinger, supra note 104.

I note that Professor Sugrue begins his one-paragraph "conclusion" to his statement by stating, "[i]n an increasingly diverse country, deep divisions persist between whites, blacks, Hispanics, and American Indians." University of Michigan, Expert Report of Thomas J. Sugrue, at 47. Yes, this is true. But is he wholly unaware of the deep strains of anti-Arabism and anti-Islamicism that run through American society? I suspect, for example, that at least as many Arab Americans are the subjects of invasive searches and hostile questioning when attempting to engage in their "right to travel" as, say, American Indians. (Would anyone like to predict what this country would be like had Timothy McVeigh and Terry Nichols turned out to inhabit the identity originally assigned to them, i.e., "Islamic fundamentalists"?) [This note was written prior to 11 September 2001. I leave it to the reader to imagine how it might be rewritten in light of those events.]

One sometimes gets the feeling that ostensible defenders of "diversity" and "multiculturalism" have no real idea of how truly diverse and multicultural the United States has become, fixated as they are on the "traditional" racial and ethnic cleavages within this country.

servative Christians suffer, but they do not really differentiate conservative Christians from other Americans in the same class position. And
although conservative Christians may suffer from considerable stigma in
the mass media, it is hard to claim that they have been denied the ability
to amass human capital as Christians in the way that other groups have
been denied these opportunities in the past.[121]

Even if one believes that Balkin's assertions are empirically correct, one need
not deny, first, that the classrooms of many of our greatest secular universities pay a cost for the absence of distinctly religious voices and, second,
that Balkin's reasons for rejecting religious preferences sound more in rec-
tifying past injustice than in designing the optimal educational surroundings
for students lucky enough to be admitted to elite institutions.

So far I have been discussing universities as if they consist almost entirely
of students attending classes. What about faculty members who are, at least
within research-oriented universities, expected to produce scholarship? In
regard to the production of scholarship, "diversity" may be even more problematic than in regard to producing well-educated students. I start with the
point that in the overall mix of disciplinary areas found in the contemporary
college or university, there may be relatively few where one can plausibly
argue that the kinds of scholarship produced are a function of the demographics of the scholars producing it. But there is a far more basic point that
must be addressed, which involves a central paradox in regard to any and all
disciplines. As Timothy Hall contends, the very point of a given "discipline"
is to limit the number of arguments that will be taken seriously by those who
are well-educated members of it.[122] Thus, Justice Powell's emphasis on the
importance attached by the First Amendment to the notion of "robust debate,"[123] which is presumably enhanced by a diverse student body, turns out
to be interestingly problematic within an academic context.

Whatever the genuine importance of vigorous argument to a liberal education, it is also true that the academy properly places limits on arguments

---

121. Letter from Jack Balkin, Professor, Yale Law School, to Sanford Levinson, Professor,
University of Texas Law School, (18 March 1999) (electronic mail responding to an earlier
version of the present lecture).

122. Timothy L. Hall, "Educational Diversity: Viewpoints and Proxies," 59 *Ohio St. L.J.* 551
(1998).

123. See, e.g., *Dun & Bradstreet, Inc. v. Greenmoss Builders, Inc.,* 472 U.S. 749, 757 n.4 (1985)
(noting "robust debate" to be a "central First Amendment value") (citation omitted).

that would be intolerable if placed on participants in the nonacademic public square.[124] One is absolutely protected, for example, if he or she wishes to pass out leaflets on the street or in a public park denouncing Darwinian theories of evolution or endorsing the importance of an astrological understanding of the world. However, it would be a grave mistake in a college geology course to expect to be taken seriously if one proclaimed that the world was created only some six thousand years ago, as is thought by some biblical fundamentalists, and that ostensible tests indicating an older planet are misleading. A student would properly receive a failing grade if he proffered the view, on a final examination, that few Jews were killed by Nazi Germany, and that the numbers have been wildly exaggerated by a Zionist conspiracy. Every student may have a legal right to her own opinion in the public square, but there is certainly no entitlement that that opinion be granted any respect within the classroom.

Far more to the point, *no academic department seeks maximum diversity when engaging in hiring.* No political science department, for example, would hire a "political astrologer"; indeed, no reputable department would award a Ph.D. to a candidate whose dissertation sought to prove that Geminis tend to engage in interestingly different political behavior than Libras. Academic "disciplines" are just that — highly structured ways of perceiving, and then teaching about, the world — and woe unto those who try to break free of disciplinary bonds by rejecting fundamental presuppositions. The range of "diverse" arguments acceptable within a classroom, around a seminar table, or at an academic convention is always far more restricted than what is acceptable within the quite literally "undisciplined" public square, where even "craziness" has its rights. The point of disciplined education is precisely that whatever one's *legal* right to hold any opinion he or she wishes, there is no such right within an academic setting, where opinions beyond the pale are properly subject to the sanction of flunking and ultimately coerced withdrawal from the academic community. Chairman Mao made famous, in the 1960s, his ostensible desire to see "one hundred flowers bloom" within the Chinese garden of political debate. No academic department with which I am familiar would endorse Mao's call (nor, of course, did he take his own slogan seriously). Even a mythical department

124. And my examples have nothing to do with "hate speech" or other standard examples of contemporary controversy in regard to academic speech.

that *did* want to present even a dozen points of view would be limited by practical budgetary considerations, and it would always be the case that one would rank in order the particular points or perspectives one thought most important.

We cannot leave this broad tour of academic institutions without paying attention to some important goals beyond "pure" education. There are important civic values attached to participation in academic life. Bowen and Bok, for example, emphasize the importance of diverse student bodies to produce "greater 'cultural awareness across racial lines . . . ' and stronger commitments to improving racial understanding."[125] It is hard to overestimate the importance of "improving racial understanding" in contemporary American society. But is it only greater "racial understanding" that we need, or do we also need, say, greater understanding of those with what are deemed unusual religious views? Indeed, to be fair to Bowen and Bok, it is precisely on the page from which I am quoting that they remind their readers of the "importance of differences in religion."[126]

It is at this point that we can return full circle to Coca-Cola and Chrysler, for it should be obvious, in a country where even now millions of people do not go to college at all, and most go for only four years, that the reputed social benefits of "diversity" in bringing about "racial understanding" could presumably be gained from enhanced "diversity" in other institutions as well. Cynthia Estlund has recently suggested just such an argument.[127] She begins with the obvious fact that the setting within which most people spend most of their out-of-home life is the workplace. She quotes Akhil Reed Amar's and Neal Katyal's eloquent reminder that "[i]f a far-flung democratic republic as diverse — and at times divided — as late-twentieth-century America is to survive and flourish, it must cultivate some common spaces where citizens from every corner of society can come together to learn how others live, how others think, how others feel."[128] They conclude, "If not in public universities, where? If not in young adulthood, when?"[129] Although

125. Bowen and Bok, supra note 47, at 228.
126. Id.
127. See Cynthia L. Estlund, "Working Together: The Workplace in Civil Society" (17 February 2000) (unpublished manuscript, on file with the *University of Pennsylvania Journal of Constitutional Law*).
128. Id. at n. 277 (citing Akhil Reed Amar and Neal Kumar Katyal, "Bakke's Fate," 43 *UCLA L. Rev.* 1745, 1749 (1996)).
129. Id.

she gladly supports diversity within universities, she notes that the university is not the "only such space"[130] in which diversity is important. Indeed, it is almost certainly not even the most important such space, at least once we move beyond "young adulthood." It is the workplace that encourages (or forces) people to interact with others significantly different from themselves, certainly more so than, say, churches, bowling leagues, or other institutions beloved by latter-day celebrants of "civil society." That is, the principal defense of affirmative action in the Coca-Colas and Chryslers of the American economy is more the importance to America's civic health than the not-altogether-plausible argument that it necessarily enhances the quality of the products produced by these companies.[131]

Moreover, as noted earlier, Coke's genuine diversity interests, in terms of its worldwide business empire, might still yield a quite different actual workforce mix than an interest in achieving a more just, less socially and politically divided America.

To the extent that we adopt the Bowen-Bok (or Estlund) civic-education argument for diversity, we should note, at the very least, that its ramifications go well beyond institutions of higher education. Indeed, if the consequences are as important as they suggest, then policies promoting "strong diversity" should become far more pervasive than is now the case. There is no good reason to think that limiting "diversity" to a relatively few elite institutions of higher education will suffice to generate the promised benefits. Still, one must always ask about how much the instrumental goals of any given institution — whether it is producing automobiles or producing education — must be sacrificed to the political goals of civic education. And one must recognize that particular arguments for diversity offered for institution X may not at all be the same as those offered in regard to institution Y.

130. Id.

131. Estlund's manuscript offers a treasure trove of citations to the literature about the efficacy of "contact" with those different from oneself in leading to greater tolerance, cross-group friendships, etc. See, e.g., Lee Sigelman et al., "Making Contact? Black-White Social Interaction in an Urban Setting," 101 *Am. J. Sociology* 1306, 1307 (1996) ("The idea that familiarity breeds positivity has usually been sustained, particularly when people interact under conditions of relative equality."). To be sure, the evidence is mixed. As Estlund writes, "[e]vidence of the persistence of intergroup bias and friction is nonetheless instructive. It suggests that even constructive interracial contact is unlikely to eliminate prejudice, especially unconscious bias (and that the law needs to reckon with that fact)." Estlund, supra note 127, at 23.

Conclusion

My conclusions are really quite modest. First, "diversity" is one of those words, like "equality," "democracy," and "freedom," whose meaning, if not entirely a construct of the speaker, is, nonetheless, significantly ambiguous. Moreover, like those words, "diversity" as a general notion is thought to be a "good thing," though, concomitantly, someone who doesn't share one's own views about the concrete meaning of this good is often subject to dismissive contempt. This is, to put it mildly, unfortunate. One should be able to accept that there are diverse notions of "diversity," each of them likely to offer us one valuable perspective on the elephant we are trying to visualize even if none captures the whole of that complex animal. Second, because of the very diversity of the world within which we find ourselves, our devotion to diversity is necessarily limited, subject to constraints posed first of all by inevitable scarcity of resources, but imposed as well by a reasonable commitment to other goods besides maximizing the good that may well be available in diversity.

Afterword

The Sixth Circuit Court of Appeals upheld the admissions program of the University of Michigan Law School—and its use of racial and ethnic preferences—on 14 May 2002.[132] The district court below, in ruling that it was unconstitutional, refused to credit the school's "diversity" defense, in part because the actual recipients of such preferences came from such a relatively limited pool of potential "diversity" claimants. Indeed, the district judge had written that "there is no logical basis for the law school to have chosen the particular groups which receive special attention under the admissions policy."[133] It claimed, for example, that the university, without explanation, specifically preferred "mainland Puerto Ricans" to Puerto Ricans who had remained on the island.[134] My own essay, of course, argues that anyone interested in diversity might be especially interested in the latter.

132. *Grutter v. Bollinger,* 288 F.3d 732 (6th Cir. 2002).

133. *Grutter v. Bollinger,* 137 F. Supp. 2d 821, 851–82 (2001).

134. See id. at 824 n.1: "Unless indicated otherwise, the court uses the terms 'minorities,' 'minority groups,' and 'underrepresented minorities' interchangeably in this opinion to refer to African American, Native American, Mexican American and mainland Puerto Rican students,

The circuit court, in reversing the district court, responded by reference to the Harvard admissions policy that Justice Powell had endorsed in his opinion in the 1978 *Bakke* case, which remains after almost a quarter century the Court's most extensive discussion of "affirmative action" in university admissions.[135] The majority's total analysis of the point was as follows:

> The Harvard plan specifically identified "blacks and chicanos and other minority students" among the under-represented groups that Harvard sought to enroll through its admissions policy. *Bakke,* 438 U.S. at 322. The Law School's similar reference to African-Americans, Hispanics and Native Americans accordingly cannot be faulted in this respect. Moreover, the policy itself supplies the logical basis for considering the race and ethnicity of these groups — without such consideration, they would probably not be represented in the Law School's student body in "meaningful numbers." As with the formulation and consideration of race-neutral alternatives, some degree of deference must be accorded to the educational judgment of the Law School in its determination of which groups to target.[136]

To put it mildly, this scarcely counts as an adequate response to Judge Friedman's point in his initial decision, which is, of course, similar to the general argument made in my essay.

As argued in the essay, there may be excellent reasons to prefer the groups selected out by Michigan (and Texas) in their admissions policies. More than ever, however, I believe they have very little to do with any plausible theory of "diversity" and everything to do with good-faith claims to solve certain enduring aspects of what Gunnar Myrdal a half-century ago labeled "the American dilemma" of racial and ethnic discrimination. Unfortunately, the Supreme Court has made it impossible for law schools to speak candidly about what motivates their policy, which leads to the disingenuous reliance on the language of "diversity" and the intellectual poverty revealed in the circuit court's opinion. I continue to support admissions practices like those at Michigan and my own University of Texas (until invalidated by the Fifth

---

as these are identified in University of Michigan Law School documents as the groups which receive special attention in the admissions process."

135. Even though, as a matter of fact, no other justice actually joined Justice Powell's discussion of "diversity" and its merits, a point relied on by the Fifth Circuit in its own decision striking down the admissions process of the University of Texas Law School.

136. 288 F.3d 751.

Circuit), but I am increasingly dismayed at the costs to intellectual honesty of the felt need to shoehorn one's arguments into the language of "diversity."

The circuit court's opinion is scarcely the "last word," however. Indeed, the Supreme Court granted review of the Michigan cases in November 2002, heard oral argument of them in April 2003, and issued its decisions on 23 June 2003. It was one of the most anticipated decisions in many years, as evidenced by the record number of briefs amici curiae that were submitted. The Bush Administration chose to support those attacking the university's programs, though the very first sentence of the "summary of the argument" in the brief filed by the United States stated that "[e]nsuring that public institutions, especially educational institutions, are open and accessible to a broad and diverse array of individuals, including individuals of all races and ethnicities, is an important and entirely legitimate government objective."[137] Solicitor General Olson, speaking for the Bush Administration, went on to express what I believe is the entirely disingenuous notion that such accessibility for "individuals of all races and ethnicities" can be achieved without continuing to implement some form of preferential admissions. But the main point is that the Bush Administration was unwilling to say, at least publicly, that it is simply indifferent to the presence of racial and ethnic diversity in "our public institutions, especially educational institutions."

The Court in its two decisions upheld the law school's plan (by a 5–4 vote) and struck down the undergraduate program (by a 6–3 vote). The explanation for the different outcomes was the peculiarity of the undergraduate program, which used a "point system" for admissions and awarded 20 points (out of a total of 150, with 100 points guaranteeing admission) to applicants with a favored racial or ethnic background. Even Justice Breyer joined his five more conservative colleagues in rejecting the plan. Far more important, though, was Justice O'Connor's opinion upholding the law school's program. To a remarkable degree, she embraced in full the "diversity" rationale initially articulated by Justice Powell a quarter-century ago, and she quoted copiously from materials defending the importance of diversity to achieving a first-rate education.

One might be tempted to restrict her opinion to the domain of education, especially given her comment that "universities occupy a special niche in our constitutional tradition." But she also cited, when discussing the "benefits" of affirmative action, two especially significant amicus briefs that discuss

---

137. Brief for the United States as amicus curiae, *Grutter v. Bollinger*, at 9.

institutional settings well outside the university and its classrooms. One was submitted on behalf of sixty-five major national and multinational corporations. "[M]ajor American businesses have made clear," Justice O'Connor wrote, "that the skills needed in today's increasingly global marketplace can only be developed through exposure to widely diverse people, culture, ideas, and viewpoints." I have no reason to challenge the sincerity of the various CEOs who put their signatures to the well-argued brief, but the diversity argument as embraced by these business leaders (and seemingly endorsed by the Supreme Court) can, nonetheless, be subject to all of the questions posed in this essay.

The second brief, by far the most important of all of the amicus briefs that were submitted, was written on behalf of a group of retired members of the armed forces, including such well-known persons as General Wesley Clark, who has commanded NATO forces in Bosnia; General Norman Schwarzkopf, the commander of American forces in the first Iraqi war; Robert "Bud" McFarlane, who was national security adviser to President Reagan; Admiral William J. Crowe and General John M. D. Shalikashvili, both of whom headed the Joint Chiefs of Staff during, respectively, the Reagan and Clinton Administrations; William Perry and William Cohen, both of whom served as secretary of defense in the Clinton Administration; and former senators (and military heroes) J. Robert Kerrey and Max Cleland. Their argument was simple and relentless: "The military must be permitted to train and educate a diverse officer corps to further our compelling government interest in an effective military."[138] Over and over, these experienced military personnel explained to the Court that "[t]he officer corps must continue to be diverse or the cohesiveness essential to the military mission will be critically undermined."[139] The argument is based on sheer demographics. Only 61.7 percent of servicemen and -women are white; 21.7 percent are African American and 9.6 percent are Hispanic. Yet the officer corps is 81 percent white; only 8.8 percent and 4 percent of the corps are African American and Hispanic, respectively. According to the brief, "cohesion" requires an officer corps that, at least roughly, resembles the men and women it commands. Discussing the lessons learned from fighting the Vietnam War, the brief states, "Throughout the armed forces, the overwhelmingly white officer corps faced racial tension and unrest." A

138. Consolidated brief of Lt. Gen. Julius W. Becton et al., *Grutter v. Billing* and *Gratz v. Bollinger*, at 5.
139. Id. at 7.

lieutenant general is quoted as saying that "[i]n Vietnam, racial tensions reached a point where there was an inability to fight."[140] Two scholars of the military are quoted as saying that "[t]he military of the 1970s recognized that its race problem was so critical that it was on the verge of self-destruction."[141] The solution, therefore, was to take race into account in the process by which the United States determines military officers, including admission to the various military academies and ROTC programs at the country's universities.

The importance of the "military brief" was underscored at the oral argument itself, when Justices Stevens and Ginsburg, among others, asked Solicitor General Olson if the administration's position would call into doubt the racial preference programs currently in operation at West Point, Annapolis, and Colorado Springs, to name only the three most prominent places. His response was astonishingly weak, amounting to the assertion that he really hadn't given it much thought. Given that the oral argument occurred just as the war in Iraq was breaking out, that appeared to most observers a notably inept answer. (For what it is worth, there is relatively little doubt that Colin Powell, were he not a member of the Bush Administration, would have signed the brief, given his past public endorsements of affirmative action in the military and elsewhere.)

I am pleased that the Court upheld the law school's program; no doubt, the hapless undergraduate admissions officers will quickly adapt their "point-system" process to resemble the more "holistic" admissions process operated by the law school. This being said, I would not give O'Connor's opinion very high marks in theoretical acuity. She offers much praise of the concept of "diversity" without any serious effort to explicate its meaning beyond ensuring the enrollment of students from "underrepresented" groups. It is hard not to agree with Justice Thomas's acerbic statement, in dissent, that " 'diversity,' for all of its devotees, is more a fashionable catch-phrase than it is a useful term." This is exemplified by the otherwise superb military brief; the "diversity" rationale in fact boils down to the importance of making sure that there is an adequate number of African Americans and Hispanics in the officer corps. Almost all the pro-Michigan briefs were similar in their focus on a decided subset of racial or ethnic groups, as against the vast panoply that might be the attention of someone who is indeed inter-

140. Id. at 16, quoting Lt. Gen. Frank Peterson Jr.
141. Id., quoting Charles C. Moskos and John Sibley Butler, *All That We Can Be: Black Leadership and Racial Integration the Army Way* 142 (1996).

ested in diversity per se, or even adopting what might be termed a more "cosmopolitan" notion of diversity.

Similarly, Justice O'Connor quoted, without serious analysis, the fact that Michigan's commitment was to "*one particular type of diversity*," involving "special reference to the inclusion of students from groups which have been historically discriminated against, like African-Americans, Hispanics and Native Americans . . ." (emphasis added). Nonlawyers can be forgiven for believing that this "one particular type" translates rather simply into arguments for "rectification of past injustice." Yet the majority opinion continued to insist that defenses of affirmative action adopt, however misleadingly, the mantra of "diversity." The same is true, of course, with regard to what might be called "the importance to the future of our society of integrating certain marginalized groups into the economy and the polity." Both of these arguments are cogent and important; at the end of the day, though, I continue to believe that they would better be made in a language other than that of "diversity." But Simon continues to say, "talk diversity," and, no doubt, we can expect many more years of such talk.

Far more important than any given Supreme Court decision is the actual behavior of institutions responding to it, whether with enthusiastic embrace or attempts to escape what are thought to be its strictures. The main thing we know as of 23 June 2003 is that a bare majority of the Supreme Court is happy to endorse a "diversity-centered," "holistic" admissions program, even as a different majority rejected a ham-handed system that made race and ethnicity too obviously dispositive. (We also know that several states, including California and Washington, have adopted amendments to their state constitutions that go well beyond the Fourteenth Amendment in forbidding the use of racial and ethnic classifications.) So one might consider in this context a front-page article that appeared in the *New York Times* in December 2002, surely sparked by the Supreme Court's decision a month earlier to review the Michigan cases. Titled "Using Synonyms for Race, College Strives for Diversity,"[142] it examined the response by Rice University, located in Houston, Texas, and one of the country's leading private colleges, to the new regime, at least in Texas, announced by the Fifth Circuit in *Hopwood*.[143] The *Times*'s reporter detailed the procedures of Rice's ad-

---

142. Jacques Steinberg, "Using Synonyms for Race, College Strives for Diversity," *New York Times*, 8 December 2002, at A1.

143. The reason that Rice believed itself affected by the decision is that Title VI of the Civil

missions committee as it strove to select from among approximately seven thousand applicants the seven hundred students who would ultimately comprise its entering class. "Almost overnight, the admissions officers at Rice stopped saying aloud the words 'black,' 'African-American,' 'Latino,' 'Hispanic' or even 'minority' in their deliberations." The immediate consequence was that the class admitted for the following year had only one-half the number of African American students admitted the previous year, and the percentage of Hispanics declined by nearly a third.

Rice officials believed that something clearly had to be done to bring up enrollment by these specific minorities, "so in the years since, it has developed creative, even sly ways" of structuring its admissions process. Thus, writes Steinberg, "the admissions committee, with an undisguised wink, has encouraged applicants to discuss 'cultural traditions' in their essays, asked if they spoke English as a second language and taken note, albeit silently, of those identified as presidents of their black student associations." Those efforts, combined "with stepped-up recruiting at high schools with traditionally high minority populations," gave Rice for the entering class in 2001 a "near-record composition of blacks and Hispanics. Of the 700 freshmen, 7 percent are black, 11 percent Hispanic."

The reason why Rice's experience proved front-page news for the *Times* is the surmise that it "provides a preview of the subtle ways that life would most likely change inside the admissions offices of colleges like Yale, Princeton and Stanford should the Supreme Court decide to impose strict restrictions on affirmative action." As at Rice, these schools would presumably develop "a whole new vocabulary—including the overarching goal of achieving 'cultural inclusiveness' in the student body—to justify [their] admissions decisions." Steinberg describes the Rice committee as engaging in "delicate minuets," by which it can proclaim both fidelity to what it believes to be the relevant law and success in achieving its institutional goals of

---

Rights Act of 1964 bars racial discrimination by private institutions receiving federal funds. Rice receives approximately $45 million, about 15 percent of its annual budget, from the federal government. The Supreme Court in the famous *Bakke* decision of 1978 held that Title VI banned only discrimination that would be unconstitutional if engaged in by a state institution, and a five-justice majority (which could not in fact agree on a single opinion) agreed that under some circumstances race *could* constitutionally be taken into account in the university admissions process. It is this decision that was, in effect, "overruled" by the United States Court of Appeals for the Fifth Circuit, in part, as they emphasized, because no single opinion commanded a majority and, indeed, only one justice, Lewis Powell, explicitly justified racial preferences by reference to "diversity."

"inclusiveness." It should be obvious, though, that "inclusiveness" as a goal raises every one of the problems presented above with regard to "diversity." That is, it is *always* possible for any university to be more inclusive than it currently is, and any decision as to the limits of "inclusiveness" must necessarily be based on some criterion other than "inclusiveness" per se.

2

Promoting Diversity in the Public Schools

(Or, To What Extent Does the Establishment Clause

of the First Amendment Hinder the Establishment

of More Genuinely Multicultural Schools?)

Some Introductory Autobiography

I was born and grew up in Hendersonville, North Carolina, a small town of
about six thousand people in the western part of the state. There were about
thirty Jewish families in Hendersonville. I knew from a very early age that I
was Jewish and, consequently, that I was different in an important way from
almost all of my neighbors and classmates. The most evident way, especially
to a child, involved dietary prohibitions against eating pork. I also knew
that I was allowed absences from school on Rosh Hashanah and Yom Kippur while other children were not. This meant, among other things, that I
took a certain pleasure in those holidays occurring during the week, when
school met; ironically, as a law professor who cancels classes on those holidays, I very much prefer that they occur on the weekends precisely so that I
don't have to go to the inconvenience of rescheduling classes! In any event,
my Jewishness accounts for many of the memories—most of them, it is
important to say at the outset, quite pleasant—I have of growing up in
Hendersonville, and I begin this essay with two of them.

This essay was originally published as "Some Reflections on Multiculturalism, 'Equal Concern
and Respect,' and the Establishment Clause of the First Amendment," in *University of Richmond Law Review* 27 (1993): 989; a revised version appeared in *Constitutional Politics: Essays
on Constitutional Making, Maintenance And Change*, edited by Sotirios A. Barber and Robert
George (Princeton: Princeton University Press, 2001).

THESIS: LEARNING THE BIBLE AND SINGING CAROLS

As a third-grader, I won a "Bible certificate" from the State of North Carolina for memorizing a number of Bible verses, including John 3:16, which I can summon up in my mind to this very day: "For God so loved the world that he sent his only begotten Son, and whosoever believeth in him shall be granted everlasting life."[1] From the vantage point of fifty years later, I think that I recall, as a Jewish youngster, finding something at least odd, if not objectionable, about saying the verse aloud in front of my class (which is how we got credit for memorizing the verse of the week). After all, most Jewish children, at least in the United States, are initially taught about Judaism in terms of what it is *not*—i.e., Christianity—and John 3:16 is perhaps the quintessential summary of Christian belief, not to mention its being one of the central sources of the no-salvation-other-than-through-Jesus view that has been so disastrous for Jews throughout history. However difficult it may be to determine the theological tenets of traditional Judaism, it is clear that none of them recognize Jesus as divine or as the carrier of salvation.[2] Although I cannot be sure, I strongly suspect that I already knew by the third grade that, at least so far as Jews are concerned, what John was stating *I* could not affirm as the truth even as I proclaimed it aloud. But the challenge of winning the certificate (and, I suspect in retrospect, of proving myself not *so* different from my Biblically proficient classmates) prevailed over any other considerations that might have come to my very young mind.

Far more vivid in my memory are my reactions to marching each December with other public-school students to the First Methodist Church for our annual concert of Christmas carols (which, needless to say, we had rehearsed at school). This provoked a sharper conflict in regard to my own sense of Jewish identity, though, once again, I did little to set myself apart from the hegemonic majority. In retrospect, I have no idea if the concert was "compulsory." I doubt that it was; had I, or my parents, insisted on nonpar-

---

1. I have purposely left in the text what I remembered the text saying, prior to "looking it up." One "official" version is "For God so loved the world that he gave his only Son, that whoever believes in him should not perish but have eternal life." John 3:16 (Revised Standard Version). It is this version that is quoted in Michael W. McConnell, "Christ, Culture, and Courts: A Niebuhrian Examination of First Amendment Jurisprudence," 42 *DePaul L. Rev.* 191, 215 n.136 (1992) (quoting H. Richard Niebuhr, *Christ and Culture* 197 (New York: Harper, 1951)).

2. It is important to recognize, though, the existence of self-described "Jews for Jesus," or "completed Jews," who proclaim the coexistence of Jewish identity and acceptance of Jesus as their Lord and Savior. Their claims, however, have not been accepted by anyone within the "mainstream" Jewish community. See chapter 4.

ticipation, I am quite sure that would have been acceptable. The community as a whole was quite tolerant, in its own way. Jews were well integrated into the fabric of community life and were often called on to explain Passover and other Jewish holidays. So why did I march? One answer is that, if truth be known, I rather enjoyed (and enjoy to this day) the tunes of most of the various carols.

Still, I recall feeling certain tensions about some of the lyrics we were called upon to sing. My personal resolution of any such tensions that I felt was simply to avoid singing those lines that included reference to Jesus or, even more to the point, "Christ our Lord." Thus, I joined happily in calling on all of the faithful, joyful and triumphant to come to Bethlehem to adore an unnamed "him." I maintained a stony silence, however, at the last line, which seemed to suggest that I did indeed recognize "him" as "Christ our Lord." Similarly, I always enjoyed the lovely Moravian hymn "I Wonder as I Wander," but I never joined in the words "Jesus our Savior." Yet, as with John 3:16, I recall most of the words of most of the standard Christmas carols to this day.

I also believe that the elementary school day began with the Lord's Prayer. I know its text, and I remember saying it repeatedly while I was growing up. I cannot imagine where I might have learned or recited it other than the public schools. None of its overt language, of course, is offensive to a Jew—how could it be, given Jesus's own status as a Jew?—and I recall little hesitation in joining in.

Later, at Hendersonville High School, I had the opportunity to take an elective course in the Bible, taught, I believe, by volunteers supplied by local churches. It was, most definitely, *not* a course on the Bible in Western litera-ture or the like. I did not enroll in that course. Instead, I happily took typing, perhaps the most useful course I ever had in high school. I am not aware that *any* Jewish student ever took the Bible course, though the low number of such students—I was one of two in my class of seventy—limits the force of any generalization on this point.

As I got further along in school, I did begin to wonder about the legit-imacy of all of this interaction between school and church. Certainly by the time I graduated from Duke University, a Methodist school that required two semesters of religion courses in order to graduate, I had come to the firm opinion that North Carolina had behaved not simply questionably, but unconstitutionally. I had discovered in political science courses the First

Amendment and, more to the point, the "separationist" perspective identified especially with Hugo Black, Felix Frankfurter, and Robert Jackson.[3] I
am quite confident that I agreed with the latter two justices that even the
limited state aid accepted by Black in *Everson v. New Jersey*[4] was constitutionally illegitimate. There should indeed be a "wall of separation" between
church and state that would basically cordon off the institutions of the latter
from any real contact with, or encouragement of, the former. Not a penny of
public funds should go to, or otherwise indirectly help out, a religious institution. The aid upheld in *Everson* was of the latter variety inasmuch as it
provided public transportation to students attending parochial schools, and
four justices vigorously dissented from even that level of aid.

In 1962, during my senior year of college, school prayer was found
constitutionally illegitimate by the Supreme Court.[5] I rejoiced. Indeed, I can
recall quite vividly the fantasy of becoming a lawyer, returning to Hendersonville, and using my skills as a constitutional lawyer to eliminate any
reference to God from the school day.

ANTITHESIS: RELIGIOUS PLURALISM IN HENDERSONVILLE

If the first section of this chapter suggests a certain disquiet about growing
up in a highly Christian environment, perhaps this next section will indicate
why it is that I also have many happy memories of my growing up there that
I cherish to this day. Some of them, to be sure, have to do with the local
synagogue. The synagogue was too small to afford a rabbi, which meant
that services were conducted by the lay members of the community (including myself). I have little doubt that this emphasis on lay participation was
extraordinarily important in developing some of my views about the dis-
pensability of certain hierarchical roles, including "supreme" courts, that
we too often take for granted.[6]

In relation to this particular essay, however, the most important memories, and certainly among my fondest, involve what through the haze of
years appear to have been "endless" discussions with a group of friends

3. See especially the opinions of these justices in Illinois ex rel. *McCollum v. Board of Educ.* 333
U.S. 203 (1947) (invalidating in-school "released time" programs).
4. 330 U.S. 1 (1947) (upholding the provision of bus service for parochial school students).
5. *Engel v. Vitale,* 370 U.S. 421 (1962). See also *Abington Sch. Dist. v. Schempp,* 347 U.S. 203
(1963).
6. See Sanford Levinson, *Constitutional Faith* ch. 1 (1988).

about religion. A fairly typical evening, especially in summers, would be to drink beer or play poker while at the same time energetically debating the basic questions of religion, especially those involving theodicy and the presence of an afterlife. Though, as children of the 1950s, we were thoroughly segregated racially—I did not have nonwhite classmates until I began graduate school at Harvard in 1962—we were otherwise wonderfully pluralistic. My friends included a Catholic (a Massachusetts native whose father had come south when General Electric moved one of its plants to Hendersonville), several Southern Baptists, a Methodist, a Presbyterian, and myself. We argued with the particular intensity of teenagers, though never, so far as I recall, acrimoniously. (The parents of the two Southern Baptists, however, did express concern to their sons about the heretical views to which they were being exposed.)

I particularly remember my Southern Baptist friends expressing seemingly genuine regret that my failure to acknowledge Jesus as my personal Savior condemned me to eternal torment in hell. They would have preferred knowing that I would join them in heaven. This was said by them, and perceived by me, without the slightest personal hostility. My nonsaved fate was, from their perspective, simply a statement of theological fact, and their attempt to save me from what was quite literally a fate worse than death was, consequently, an act of friendship. Imagine, for example, a friend observing someone close to him or her driving while intoxicated. Surely we would not expect the friend to remain silent and accept as dispositive, following a fatal accident, the statement: "Well, it was her life, and friends don't interfere with one another." Friends *ought* to warn one another about perceived dangers facing them.

My Baptist friends were engaged in an act of such warning, even though I chose to ignore it. I did not censure them for their concern, especially given their general courtesy and willingness to tolerate my response to their entreaties that, as a Jew, I just did not see any reason to accept Jesus as divine, though I always took care to describe him as a great man eminently worth respecting even if not worshipping. Moreover, I added that I did not believe that a God worth worshipping (or even respecting) would condemn anyone to the torments of eternal punishment. My Christian friends were scarcely monolithic on any of these points, and, among other things, I got to know the differences among Christian denominations.

In looking back and trying to determine, for better or worse, what might help to account for the development of my particular persona, I often think of those friends and of our discussions. I am convinced that they had far more to do with my becoming an academic intellectual than anything that took place during the generally dreary school days, during which my primary achievement was getting so many Cs in "cooperation" that I was ineligible for the National Honor Society. It was with John, Jim, Benny Cole, and Gar that I became comfortable exploring some basic issues of life. I remain forever grateful to them.

In many ways, then, the rest of this chapter explores the possibility of synthesizing these two sets of memories generated by having grown up as a distinctly minority participant in a highly Christian culture. My interest is not simply accounting for autobiographical development, however interesting that might be to me, but also — and, I trust, more interesting to the reader — with regard to more general social and legal analysis. In any event, my own life was immeasurably aided by friendships, the result, with one exception, of mutual attendance at the local public school with other youngsters who, from a variety of perspectives, unabashedly took religious questions seriously. Less happily, my life was also affected by state-encouraged feelings of marginality and difference connected to such phenomena as the Bible memorization and Christmas carols. Is there a way of putting together these memories — and, concomitantly, engaging in cogent analysis of the issues raised by them — in some way that makes sense?

On the Difference Between Pluralism and Separatism

What I have celebrated, in the second set of memories, is the actuality of a certain model of *pluralism:* the ability of persons from a variety of subcultures to come together and encounter one another without negating those aspects that indeed make them different from each other. To use a term that was blessedly absent from the language of my youth, a kind of *multiculturalism* was present in Hendersonville, with enormous benefit. There are, of course, a host of definitions of "multiculturalism," and they tend to differ depending on whether the definer is, broadly speaking, favorably or unfavorably disposed to the concept. That being said, I find one of the most useful definitions that offered by the art and social critic Robert Hughes. Multiculturalism is the

> assert[ion] that people with different roots can coexist, that they can learn to read the image banks of others, that they can and should look

across the frontiers of race, language, gender and age [and, presumably, religion] without prejudice or illusion, and learn to think against the background of a hybridized society.[7]

Whatever the obvious limits of my small North Carolina town's multi-culturalism — the most notable certainly was a racial segregation that deprived me of any real contact with African American students — it was also a powerful reality in at least the dimension of religion, with enduring importance for my life. And what allowed these encounters across culture to take place was, in substantial part, the fact that most of us attended the same public school. (There was a Catholic elementary school, however, and some students attended a Catholic school in Asheville, twenty miles away. My friend Gar attended a local private boys' school, but very few other local students attended it.)

It is also worth saying that I hope my friends believed (and believe now in retrospect) that they benefited from having a Jewish friend. We too often automatically sneer at the phrase "some of my best friends are Jewish (or any other given religion or race)," but surely it would be a profound social good if all of us could in fact say, with conviction, that some of our best friends *are* from groups other than those with which we most centrally identify. No heterogeneous society can long survive if it becomes truly exceptional to develop the particular intimacies of friendship with anyone other than those who are exactly like oneself in most important aspects. I know that I think differently, and better, of Southern Baptists because some of my best childhood friends were members of that denomination. I would hope that the same is true for them in regard to Jews.

I also know that my life in the elite legal academy has been basically devoid of contact with committed Christians, especially evangelical Protestants. One can count literally on the fingers of one hand the number of publicly visible Protestant evangelicals who hold tenured positions at America's "leading" law schools. In this respect (and, undoubtedly, many others), no elite law school even remotely "looks like America," at least if that is meant to suggest that members of the various subcultures of American society should actively participate in each of the institutional structures that comprise that society. And, as I have written elsewhere, it is noteworthy "that almost none of the contemporary demands for greater diversity of

7. Robert Hughes, *The Culture of Complaint* 83–84 (1993).

voices within the academy include a call for a greater presence of the almost totally absent sound of a strong religious sensibility."[8]

It should be clear that the creation of a public school system that truly brings together, in a context of mutual respect and concern, persons of different backgrounds is a high social good. Concomitantly, the adoption of policies that discourage such multicultural encounters and, instead, lead to withdrawal into separate enclaves of homogeneity is, if not an unequivocal social bad, then at least something that should scarcely be applauded without grave reservations. It is in thinking about public schools that we most directly confront the questions of social reproduction and the inculcation of values that constitute us as a distinctive social order. As the Supreme Court once put it, quoting two historians: "The role and purpose of the American public school system [is to] 'prepare pupils for citizenship in the Republic.' "[9] This, one hopes, includes development of a stance of "tolerance of divergent political and religious views" and the taking into account "of the sensibilities of others."[10] My very citation of the Court's opinion in *Bethel* signifies the fact that in the United States, for better *and* worse, the kinds of questions I am raising are not merely ones of "social policy" or even political theory. Instead, what Justice Cardozo once called "[t]he great generalities of the constitution"[11] are thought to speak with sometimes surprising specificity, let the consequences be what they may. Two strands of cases are particularly important in the context of my reminiscences and subsequent reflections. The first involves the constitutionality of state aid to religious schools. The second deals with what might be termed the secularization of the public school system and consequent withdrawal of at least some Christians (and, no doubt, other sectarians as well, including Orthodox Jews) from the public schools.

8. Sanford Levinson, "Religious Language and the Public Square," 105 *Harv. L. Rev.* 2061, 2062 n.7 (1992) (book review). See also chapter 1.

9. *Bethel Sch. Dis. No. 403 v. Fraser*, 478 U.S. 675, 681 (1986) (quoting C. Beard and M. Beard, *New Basic History of the United States* 228 (1968)). This "civic-education" aspect of education is scarcely uncomplicated. See, e.g., Meira Levinson, "Culture, Choice, and Citizenship: Schooling Private Citizens in the Public Square," in *The Demands of Liberal Education* 100–113 (1999). It is safe to say, though, that no society that wishes to endure can be indifferent to the problem of socializing successor generations into the central values of the existing political order. See also chapter 8.

10. Id.

11. Benjamin Cardozo, *The Nature of the Judicial Process* 17 (1921).

There are many fine articles detailing the specific doctrinal twists and turns within these areas,[12] and this essay is not intended to compete with any of them. Instead, I want to offer some modest reflections about the interplay between current doctrinal developments and the achievement of a multicultural society whose members are nonetheless bonded by mutual respect and, if this is not too completely utopian, affection.

AID TO PAROCHIAL SCHOOLS

As already suggested, I initially had little trouble supporting the stance of "hard-core separationists" that public monies should be used little, if at all, to "support" or "subsidize" religion. People certainly had a right to be religious, but let them do so on their own time and spending their own money. They were just as certainly not entitled to even a penny of my taxes to spend in ways that furthered their religious aims. The key word in this sentence is "furthered," since, as economists teach, state provision of *any* goods, including police and fire protection, frees up funds that can now be used for other purposes, including religious indoctrination.

Though few persons are so relentlessly anticlerical as to deny policy and fire protection to a church, it is not altogether clear what distinguishes legally permitted aid (including not only police and fire protection, but also the indirect aid to religious sensibilities provided by "In God We Trust" on the coinage) from impermissible aid other than the fact that we as a culture have become inured over time to the former, whereas "new" forms of aid appear to be marked revisions of the status quo and thus, to many analysts, unacceptable. In any event, these issues were not to be settled through ordinary political debate and votes. Instead, I believed that the Court should militantly use the Establishment Clause of the First Amendment as a sword against any legislative decisions to expend public monies in ways that aided religious schools.[13] "[T]axpayers have a right," enforceable by the courts, "not to subsidize religion."[14] Religious parents *do* apparently have a consti-

---

12. I have consistently benefited from the work of my colleague Douglas Laycock, among whose more important work is "The Remnants of Free Exercise," 1990 *Sup. Ct. Rev.* 1; Douglas Laycock, "A Survey of Religious Liberty in the United States," 47 *Ohio St. L. Rev.* 409 (1986); Douglas Laycock, "Towards a General Theory of the Religion Clauses: The Case of Church Labor Relations and the Right to Church Autonomy," 81 *Columbia L. Rev.* 1373 (1981).

13. For a forthright presentation of this view, see Kathleen M. Sullivan, "Religion and Liberal Democracy," in *The Bill of Rights in the Modern State* 196 (Geoffrey R. Stone et al., eds., 1992).

14. Id. at 211.

tutional right, thanks to the 1925 case *Pierce v. Society of Sisters*,[15] to withdraw their children from public schools and educate them privately. They should not, however, expect public aid in financing this private education. Indeed, they should realize that it is illegitimate even to ask for such aid.

I have been persuaded[16] by Michael McConnell,[17] however, that this interpretation of the Constitution is profoundly wrong,[18] especially if one believes that the principle of "equal concern and respect" is a foundational predicate of our constitutional order.[19] The key here is the attitude one adopts with regard to *Pierce*. On one hand, *Pierce*'s support of a constitutional right to opt out of public education could be viewed simply as the unfortunate positive law of our Constitution, to be submitted to so long as it is not formally repealed or overruled but not to be admired. Conversely, *Pierce* could be read as a constitutional principle which should be supported and perhaps even venerated. This is the view of Mark Yudof, who has interpreted *Pierce* as standing for the proposition that governments, while "free to establish their own public schools and to make education compulsory for certain age groups," cannot use state power "to eliminate competing, private-sector educational institutions that may serve to create heterogeneity and to counter the state's dominance over the education of the young."[20]

From this perspective, *Pierce* is a powerful barrier to totalitarianism through its recognition of the legitimacy of multiculturalism. The state cannot reinforce the hegemony of the dominant culture by prohibiting parents from engaging in at least partial "secession" from that culture as a means of

---

15. 268 U.S. 510 (1925).

16. An earlier, far briefer version of this discussion can be found in my contribution to *American Jews and The Separationist Faith: The New Debate on Religion in Public Life* 74–75 (David G. Dalin, ed., 1993).

17. My colleague Douglas Laycock, who is unusual in his ability to take with utmost seriousness the claims of the religious without, so far as I know, being religious himself, also provided a great deal of help.

18. For an especially brilliant article, see Michael W. McConnell, "The Selective Funding Problem: Abortions and Religious Schools," 104 *Harv. L. Rev.* 989 (1991).

19. The term "equal concern and respect" is probably most identified with Ronald Dworkin. See, e.g., Ronald Dworkin, *Taking Rights Seriously* 180–83 (1978). However, Dworkin builds on the earlier work of John Rawls. See John Rawls, *A Theory of Justice* 511 (1971). See also John Hart Ely, *Democracy and Distrust* (1980), where the notion of "equal concern and respect" also plays a central role.

20. Mark G. Yudof, *When Government Speaks* 229 (1983).

cultivating within their children alternative ways of looking at the world.[21] *Pierce* seemingly calls for a measure of "equal concern and respect"[22] for these alternatives, certainly if parents are willing to pay the costs of the education at issue even as they pay taxes to support a public school system which they reject.

One of the key questions raised by this last sentence is, what happens if parents are formally willing, but in fact basically unable, to pay the costs of private education?[23] In other words, should the putative benefits of private education, well articulated by Yudof, be limited only to the relatively affluent or to those who receive voluntary contributions from people of greater means? It is hard, at least for those of us who profess to be egalitarian in our political sympathies, to figure out how the answer to this question might be "yes."

McConnell, for example, makes very effective use of the point that most contemporary liberals support state subsidy of abortions for poor women on the ground that their formal right to enjoy reproductive freedom, labeled "fundamental" by the Court,[24] is hollow if it is rationed by a price mechanism that effectively denies indigent women access to abortions. If we secular liberals are so solicitous about ensuring the practical right of poor women to enjoy their right of reproductive choice, why then are we not equally concerned, at least as a political matter, about the equally constitu-

---

21. The "secession" image is developed by Professor Toni Marie Massaro in *Constitutional Literacy: A Core Curriculum for a Multicultural Nation* 99–100 (1993). The "at least partial" in the text comes from the fact that not even *Pierce* places *absolute* control in the hands of parents, for the state retains the right to make sure that some "minimal" educational goods, as defined by the state, are transmitted to children. See Mark G. Yudof et al., *Educational Policy and the Law* 43–77 (3d ed., 1992). Whether these requirements actually apply to home schooling, for example, is doubtful, but as a formal question of constitutional power, there is little doubt that courts will reject a claim of sovereign right by parents to disregard any and all state commands with regard to the education of their children.

22. See Dworkin, supra note 19, at 180–83.

23. I put to one side the equally important question of whether it is legitimate to make parents pay both for public education they do not use and for private schools they patronize. My answer is that the general public benefits of (or, in the language of economics, the "externalities" generated by) public education are sufficient to support coerced taxation for public education. I offer a similar analysis with regard to taxing the childless, who make no direct use of public schools. The religious parent sending children to nonpublic schools is no different, positionally, from the childless person who is deprived of some important want because of the duty to pay education taxes.

24. *Roe v. Wade,* 410 U.S. 113, 152 (1973).

tionally protected right of less affluent parents to choose religious education for their children? Attempting to defend one's lack of equal concern by reference to the Establishment Clause simply begs the central issue of how in fact the clause should be interpreted.

McConnell argues, and I (now) agree, that arguments like Professor Kathleen Sullivan's, with their blithe reference to unacceptable "subsidies" of religious education, depend on a baseline that in effect presumes the classically liberal "night-watchman" state which leaves the provision of important services, including education, to the operation of the market.[25] It is reference to this baseline that justifies the provision of publicly funded police and fire protection to religious schools. It had simply become an accepted practice even of a relatively minimal state to provide such protection to the general public, and it would have truly appeared (and would have been) discriminatory had the state declared, in effect, that every building *except* for churches would be protected against fire or theft. Conversely, if the state had declared that it would provide some special protection *only* for churches, then I, and I think most analysts, would interpret this as clearly aiding religion in violation of any plausible interpretation of the Establishment Clause. Over the past half-century, the majority of the Supreme Court has tended to interpret aid to parochial schools (in the context of some general scheme of aid to private schools, for no one has ever defended providing aid only to religious schools) as in effect something very special, a deviation from a baseline of no aid.

Education, however, has for at least 140 years been an important aspect of governmental budgets, especially (and, until the 1960s, almost exclusively) at the local level. Even classic Western films featured the "school marm," whose state-funded task was to maintain civilization on the frontier. Like fire and police protection, education has been viewed as something the state provides, even if, from a contemporary perspective, much of the past provision was minimal. In any event, as McConnell notes, we have moved very far from the minimal state and entered the world of the contemporary welfare state. That type of state features extensive, and some would say, pervasive expenditures by the state in order to provide goods and services at less than market cost to those who could not otherwise afford

25. See McConnell, supra note 12, at 184–85. McConnell's colleague, Cass Sunstein, emphasizes the importance of baselines and their ostensible (and false) "neutrality" in setting the terms of constitutional argument in Cass Sunstein, *The Partial Constitution* (1993). See Sanford Levinson, "Unnatural Law," *The New Republic*, 19–26 July 1993, at 40 (book review of Sunstein).

them.[26] The baseline is now that of the modern welfare state, whose most substantial expenditures, particularly at the state and local levels of government, are for educating the young.

For McConnell, then, the contemporary situation is more akin to the police and fire protection example. To offer extensive aid *only* to those who will send their children to public schools or to non–religiously affiliated private schools is, in effect, to exhibit a gross lack of equal concern and respect for the non-well-off religious (and, of course, the non-well-off who desire private education for other reasons as well). Moreover, there is the reality that some parents cannot afford nonpublic education in part because taxes for public education continue to mount.

The question then becomes whether legislatures can vote to return some of this tax money through support for nonpublic education, which would, as a practical matter, be used primarily in religiously-based schools.[27] I am no longer persuaded by the argument that the Constitution deprives legislatures of the freedom to exercise such judgment. Although I generally oppose, and am often appalled by, the rightward drift of the contemporary Supreme Court, I confess to supporting the willingness of its conservative majority to reconsider what I now regard as one of the most dubious legacies of the Warren Court era — the hostility toward aid to religious schools.[28]

Although there are advances in this direction,[29] it is noteworthy that the majority has been rather cautious in rewriting doctrine. Cases upholding aid have often been intensely fact-specific: for example, in *Zobrest v. Catalina Foothills School District*,[30] a five-justice majority, through Chief Justice Re-

26. See McConnell, supra note 12.

27. A second important question, well beyond the scope of this informal essay, is whether the state has not just *permission*, but a *duty*, to return such money. I am decidedly more uncomfortable with this argument than with the more modest, though scarcely less controversial, view that the Constitution, correctly interpreted, does not deprive the state of the ability to aid private schools, including religious ones.

28. As I have said elsewhere, "I would . . . gladly overrule *Committee for Educ. v. Nyquist,* 413 U.S. 756 (1973)," one of the most important barriers standing in the way of state aid to religious schools. Levinson, supra note 8, at 2078 n.72.

29. See, e.g., *Agostini v. Felton,* 521 U.S. 203 (1997); *Zobrest v. Catalina Foothills Sch. Dist.,* 509 U.S. 1 (1993); *Witters v. Washington Dept. of Servs. for the Blind,* 474 U.S. 481 (1986). *Mitchell v. Helms,* 120 S. Ct. 2530 (2000), which will be discussed below, is an unusually interesting case, perhaps portending a far more drastic shift in doctrine, but there is no majority opinion in the case, which makes the statement in the text still accurate.

30. 509 U.S. 1 (1993).

hnquist, reversed the Court of Appeals for the Ninth Circuit, which had held that Arizona could not supply an interpreter to a Catholic high school in order to facilitate the attendance of James Zobrest, a deaf student who depended on the use of sign language. No one could accuse Rehnquist of cutting a wide swath, however.[31] After first defining Arizona's payment of the interpreter's salary as "part of a general government program that distributes benefits neutrally to any child qualifying as 'handicapped,' "[32] he went on to emphasize that the Catholic school in question was "not relieved of an expense that it otherwise would have assumed in educating its students," since it presumably was not in the practice of providing interpreters to deaf students.[33] Moreover, it was declared significant that "the task of a sign-language interpreter seems to us quite different from that of a teacher or guidance counselor," for the interpreter ostensibly exercises no discretion in communicating with his or her charge.[34] "[E]thical guidelines," stated Rehnquist, "require interpreters to transmit everything that is said in exactly the same way it was intended."[35] There is, therefore, more than enough doctrinal "wiggle-room" in the opinion to authorize the Court to strike down more expansive aid to religious schools or to their students.

Given the limited reach of Rehnquist's opinion, it is noteworthy that Justices Blackmun and Souter dissented on its merits.[36] They rejected the claim that Arizona should be able to provide funds to the private, Catholic Salpointe High School so that James Zobrest could enjoy, as a practical matter, his constitutional right to attend a religiously-based school. Instead, they accused the majority of "authoriz[ing] a public employee to participate

31. Interestingly enough, Justice Thomas's plurality opinion in *Mitchell v. Helms,* for himself and three other justices, including Chief Justice Rehnquist, offered a significantly more capacious reading of *Zobrest,* which brought forth complaint from Justice O'Connor, who, as a result, joined only in the result and not the Thomas opinion. See 120 S. Ct. 2545 (Thomas); 2558 (O'Connor).

32. 509 U.S., at 10.

33. Id. at 12.

34. Id.

35. Id. Were this an essay on theories of interpretation and postmodernism, one could certainly debate whether this guideline, in fact, is capable of being complied with (and how one might conceivably know of this). Fortunately, this is not such an essay, and I am assuming that most of us agree with Rehnquist that it is indeed cogent to view the interpreter as being in a different position from the overtly choice-making teacher.

36. Justices Blackmun, Stevens, O'Connor, and Souter dissented on technical grounds from the Court's reaching on the substantive issue.

directly in religious indoctrination," presumably by signing material with religious content that the deaf child could therefore understand.[37]

For me, especially as tutored by McConnell, this conclusion seems to tread dangerously close to an "unconstitutional condition"—that is, the forced waiver of a constitutional right as consideration for some valuable governmental benefit.[38] Here, the availability of the valuable benefit of a state-funded interpreter making it possible for a deaf child to be "mainstreamed" in regard to receiving an education requires the waiver of his right to attend a religious school. Although such conditions can be imposed on any citizen, it is obvious that the poor are especially vulnerable to the blandishments held out by the welfare state, whose "safety net" may be the only thing between the recipient and a hard fall.

It is, of course, a rich irony that the Chief Justice had been generally unsympathetic both to the plight of the poor and to the more general "unconstitutional condition" analysis,[39] while Justice Blackmun had proved himself quite sensitive both to the general needs of the poor and to the potential for abuse of governmental largesse.[40] In *Zobrest*, though, Blackmun seemed sublimely uninterested in the fact that the Zobrest family paid $7000 a year to hire an interpreter for their son following the decision of the Ninth Circuit Court of Appeals invalidating Arizona's provision of aid.[41] But what if another family in the same position as the Zobrests, but unable to afford the extra $28,000 over four years to provide an interpreter while its hearing-impaired child attended a religious school, had in effect been compelled to send her to a public school (or to a nonsectarian private school) in order to receive the necessary services of a state-funded interpreter? Why should we complacently accept this as "required" by the Estab-

---

37. 509 U.S., at 18.

38. See, e.g., Richard Epstein, "The Supreme Court, 1987 Term—Foreword: Unconstitutional Conditions, State Power, and the Limits of Consent," 102 *Harv. L. Rev.* 4 (1988); Kathleen M. Sullivan, "Unconstitutional Conditions," 102 *Harv. L. Rev.* 1413 (1989). See generally Paul Brest et al., *Processes of Constitutional Decisionmaking* 1415–92 (4th ed., 2000).

39. See, e.g., *Rust v. Sullivan*, 500 U.S. 173 (1991); *Federal Communications Comm'n v. League of Women Voters of California*, 468 U.S. 364 (1984); *Regan v. Taxation with Representation of Wash.*, 461 U.S. 540 (1983).

40. Justice Blackmun dissented, for example, in the abortion funding cases, *Harris v. McRae*, 448 U.S. 297 (1980), and *Maher v. Roe*, 432 U.S. 464 (1977), as well as in *Rust*.

41. See Linda Greenhouse, "Court Says Government May Pay for Interpreter in Religious School," *New York Times*, 19 June 1993, at 1, 8. One assumes that, as a result of the Supreme Court's decision, they were remunerated for their expenditures.

lishment Clause? I (now) see no good reason to do this. As should be obvious, I see good reason to be more understanding of the plight of families like the Zobrests.

It is possible, though, that the cracks in the classical "no-aid" view of the Establishment Clause, articulated most clearly on the current Court by Justice Souter,[42] are threatening a doctrinal dam-burst, as seen in two more recent cases. The first, *Rosenberger v. University of Virginia*,[43] involved not aid to parochial schools, but, rather, a policy of the University that, while generally funding student publications, explicitly denied funding to a Christian journal, *Wide Awake,* on the grounds that its publication was in fact a "religious activity" insofar as it "promote[d] . . . a particular belie[f] in or about a deity or an ultimate reality." A bitterly divided Court held that Virginia's policy in effect was an invidious discrimination against a particular way of viewing the world. Although the Court held that this violated the students' First Amendment interests, it is more sensible to view the case as a mixed Free Speech–Equal Protection case, insofar as the heart of the decision (and the reason for my support of the majority) was the unequal respect displayed by the state for religious perspectives even as it offered generous subsidies to a wide variety of other views. Still, Justice O'Connor, who formally joined the majority opinion, also took care to write a separate concurrence describing the case as lying "at the intersection of the principle of governmental neutrality and the prohibition of state funding of religious activities."[44]

The far more important case is *Mitchell v. Helms,* in which six justices upheld a program whereby Louisiana made a variety of resources—including "slide projectors, movie projectors, overhead projectors, television sets, tape recorders, projection screens, maps, globes, filmstrips, cassetts, [and] computers"[45]—available to nonpublic, including religious, schools. As already noted, there was no majority opinion, though Justice Thomas garnered three other votes for an extremely wide-ranging opinion that suggested that the state was free to distribute any such resources to private schools, whether secular or religious, so long as the aid is evenhandedly distributed and does not in itself contain any content that overtly endorses religion. That such aid, however, could be "diverted" to religious uses, was

42. See, e.g., his dissent in *Mitchell v. Helms,* 120 S. Ct. 2572.
43. 515 U.S. 819 (1995).
44. Id. at 847.
45. 120 S. Ct. 2592 (Souter, J., dissenting).

irrelevant for the plurality. It was this casualness about "diversion" that evoked Justice O'Connor's concurring opinion. She argued, rather implausibly, both that there was little evidence of actual diversion in Louisiana and, even more implausibly, that one should trust the assurances of local school officials that they would not in fact make use of such materials for religious purposes.

By the time this chapter is published, of course, the results of the 2000 election will be known, and with them the likely prospects to replace the justices who are almost sure to retire in the next several years. One of them is John Paul Stevens, with Justice Souter the most active adherent of the "no-aid" view, and his replacement by a Bush appointee will almost certainly mean the arrival of a fifth vote for the plurality position. Concomitantly, if a President Gore gets to replace Chief Justice Rehnquist, the most likely retirement from the conservative side, then we might look back on *Mitchell* as the "high point" (or "low," depending on one's own position) of the Court's willingness to rewrite our understanding of the Establishment Clause with regard to religious schools in the modern welfare state.

It is ever more difficult for me to understand how anyone at all supportive of one or another of the contemporary defenses of "multiculturalism" could oppose on principle the kind of legislative discretion at issue in the contemporary parochial school–funding cases. It is a deep irony that at least some of the Christian supporters of nonpublic education are vehemently opposed to "multiculturalism," which, by ostensibly promoting a kind of relativism, in their opinion attacks the one true view of the world.[46] Yet surely the strongest arguments likely to persuade secularists to tolerate (and perhaps even to support) the various Christian academies and other religious schools that dot the landscape are precisely those that emphasize the importance of nurturing a vibrant and, therefore, contentious cultural pluralism. This means, almost by definition, that we exhibit a measure of concern and respect for cultural perspectives that one not only does not identify with, but even finds abhorrent in significant aspects.[47]

---

46. See, e.g., the description of Vicki Frost's views in *Mozert v. Hawkins County Bd. of Educ.*, 827 F.2d 1058, 1060–62 (6th Cir. 1987), discussed infra.

47. No doubt there are limits to the tolerance due truly pernicious subcultures, especially if, as a matter of social fact, they potentially threaten the maintenance of liberal democracy itself. Fortunately, that is a topic beyond the scope of this particular essay. See Stanley Fish, *The Trouble with Principle* (1999), particularly chs. 4 ("Boutique Multiculturalism") and 11 ("Mission Impossible"). See also Stephen Macedo, *Diversity and Distrust: Civic Education in a Multi-*

All of this being said, though, I find myself lamenting the retreat from public education by groups who increasingly feel alienated from the culture of the public schools. That I have been persuaded by McConnell's arguments as to what the Constitution allows (and what a serious commitment to egalitarianism may require, at least as a matter of political theory) is not the same thing as saying that it is an affirmative social good that children be educated in homogeneous environments free from the taint of contact with children who may be quite different. Indeed, I have no hesitation in counting it as an overall social evil that the challenge of coming to terms with our multicultural reality is increasingly taking on a frankly separatist dimension.[48]

To this extent, I disagree with McConnell when he argues that "[t]he common school movement has run its course and no longer can establish a coherent position in the face of the conflicting demands of a diverse nation."[49] For McConnell, the American public school has in effect become estopped, either because of constitutional interpretations of the Supreme Court or simple acquiescence to the fragmented nature of American society, from "teach[ing] any god because it would have to teach all gods; it cannot teach any culture because it would have to teach all cultures. . . . The common school movement now teaches our children, unintentionally, to be value-less, culture-less, root-less, and religion-less."[50] Thus, he says, "[I]t can no longer achieve its crowning purpose of providing a unifying moral culture in the face of our many differences."[51] For McConnell, the answer is to adopt educational financing systems which would maximize the "freedom of choice" of the parents by providing them with vouchers, even if the likely consequence is the flourishing of individually homogeneous schools.[52]

At some point, the nurturance of "pluralism" requires the toleration of "separatism." This is exemplified most clearly in our constitutional law by *Wisconsin v. Yoder*,[53] where the state was required to subordinate its general

---

cultural Democracy (1999).

48. See Hughes, supra note 7 for an eloquent polemic on this point.

49. Michael W. McConnell, "Multiculturalism, Majoritiarianism, and Educational Choice: What Does Our Constitutional Tradition Have to Say?" 1991 *U. Chi. Legal F.* 123, 149.

50. Id. at 148–50.

51. Id.

52. Id. at 126.

53. 406 U.S. 205 (1972).

policy of compulsory education to the interests of a minority community in maintaining its own distinctive way of life apart from the surrounding society. In Amy Gutmann's terms, the "family state," predicated on emphasizing a common membership in an overarching political community, was subordinated to a "state of families" in which the primary unit is the particularistic community, and the wider polity more a confederation of these communities than a genuine community in its own right.[54]

All of this being said, and conceding the importance of nurturing pluralism, I think it important that we try, as much as is reasonably possible, to resist the development of the separatism to which it can too easily lead. The "resistance," it is important to say, should be based on force of argument rather than force of law. I trust I have made clear the extent to which I support the rewriting of our received doctrines interpreting the Establishment Clause in order to allow more state funding of nonpublic, including religiously-based, schools. But one can also, at the very same time, support strengthening public schools in ways designed to encourage (even if not to *require*) persons from all sorts of backgrounds, and with all sorts of views, to attend them and to interact with one another.

ON SCHOOL PRAYER AND SIMILAR MATTERS

How might one go about the task of bringing about what seems to be the increasingly utopian dream outlined in the last paragraph?[55] To answer this question adequately would obviously require an entire book. My goals here are considerably more modest. I want to address the question of what types of "concessions" (if this is the proper word) I am willing to make in order to allow self-consciously religious parents to feel more comfortable in sending their children to public schools. I am assuming, of course, that my own sensibility is not unique and that I can speak to, even if not for, others who share my own self-definition as a secularist in at least two somewhat different senses. First, I possess no "religious" beliefs, as conventionally defined. Though I continue strongly to identify myself as Jewish, this has little, if anything, to do with embracing any theological propositions myself. Second, I reject the propriety of the states' overtly articulating any theological propositions. I read the Establishment Clause as prohibiting "In God We Trust" from the coinage. I thus remain militantly opposed (as do many

---

54. See Amy Gutmann, *Democratic Education* 19–41 (1987).

55. As one reader suggested, some persons (including, presumably, the parents who brought the *Mozert* litigation discussed infra) might well regard this as a dystopian nightmare instead.

nonsecularists) to any endorsement, direct or indirect, of the United States as a "Christian" (or even "Judeo-Christian") nation.

It should be no surprise, then, that my initial delight with *Engel v. Vitale*,[56] the first Supreme Court decision striking down state-sponsored school prayer, has never entirely dissipated. Officially composed prayers, even with an opt-out provision for those who wish not to participate, easily count as a violation of my version of the Establishment Clause. I was pleased when a slender majority struck down, in *Wallace v. Jaffree*,[57] an Alabama "moment of silence" law that was passed at the behest of religious groups and involved teachers overtly informing their students that one (presumably preferred) use of the moment of silence would be "prayer." Similarly, I rejoiced when the Court, to many analysts' surprise, struck down in *Lee v. Weisman*[58] the Rhode Island school district's practice of inviting members of the clergy to deliver prayers (albeit "nonsectarian") at the official baccalaureate ceremonies that are part of graduation from high school. Again, it seemed to me that the state was in effect trying to extract an "unconstitutional condition" — the waiver of one's right not to be subjected to official state-organized prayer in order to attend the public baccalaureate ceremonies of graduation week.

On reflection, though, I am reminded of the curse of being granted what (one thinks) one wishes. Has this triumvirate of cases in fact made this a better society overall? I would like to think so, but I suspect they have made their own contribution to the perception of a *Kulturkampf* — a cultural war — between secularism and sectarianism and, concomitantly, to the further fraying of any remaining social bonds that might once have linked these elements of society.[59] Not the least contributor to the fraying is precisely the treatment of the issue of prayer in the public schools as one of high legal principle, and subject, therefore, to resolution only by the analytical techniques ostensibly mastered by constitutional lawyers. This seems increas-

56. 370 U.S. 421 (1962).
57. 472 U.S. 38 (1985).
58. 505 U.S. 577 (1992).
59. See, e.g., James D. Hunter, *Culture Wars* (1991). The most famous judicial invocation of the term is surely Justice Scalia's angry dissent in *Romer v. Evans*, 517 U.S. 620 (1996), in which the Court struck down an amendment added by popular referendum to the Colorado Constitution that seemingly denied gays and lesbians a host of legal protections. According to Scalia, "The court has mistaken a Kulturkampf for a fit of spite," id. at 636, and he left no doubt that he saw no constitutional problem in the use of the state to engage in the culture war involving the place of homosexuality in American culture.

ingly dubious as a picture of social reality, even if one accepts the perhaps even more dubious portrait of lawyers as truly skilled in the working out of principled doctrinal arguments.

As Stephen Carter wrote in a review of Ronald Dworkin's *Life's Domain*,[60] which purported to settle the questions of abortion and euthanasia by reference to consistent principles, society sometimes (perhaps often) is far more in need of compromise than of rigorous adherence to principles. As Carter points out, "[c]ompromises, by their nature, possess the internal inconsistencies and contradictions that scholars, by their nature, abhor. Scholars want arguments to *make sense;* but politicians know that arguments have to *work* — which means, in the long run, that they must form the basis for a stable consensus."[61] Therefore, what I offer now is not so much a refinement of the doctrinal arguments so ably made by others as a discussion of possible terms of compromise. That is, what am I willing to offer, by way of compromise, in order to still some of the cannon- (and canon-) fire in the Kulturkampf?

I begin with the set of issues raised in *Mozert v. Hawkins County Board of Education*,[62] in which several fundamentalist "born-again Christian"[63] parents claimed a constitutional right to have their children exempted from certain reading assignments in the local public schools because these assignments purportedly encouraged beliefs that ran contrary to the version of biblical literalism embraced by the parents. Two parents testified, in the language of the court, that they "objected to passages that expose their children to other forms of religion and to the feelings, attitudes and values of other students that contradict the plaintiffs' religious views without a statement that the other views are incorrect and that the plaintiffs' views are the correct one."[64]

---

60. Stephen L. Carter, "Strife's Dominion," *The New Yorker,* 9 August 1993, at 86 (reviewing Ronald Dworkin, *Life's Dominion* (1993)).

61. Id. at 92.

62. 827 F.2d 1058 (6th Cir. 1987). See generally the important article by Nomi Maya Stolzenberg, " 'He Drew a Circle that Shut Me Out': Assimilation, Indoctrination, and the Paradox of a Liberal Education," 106 *Harv. L. Rev.* 581 (1993). Also essential for any student of *Mozert* is Stephen Bates, *Battleground: One Mother's Crusade, the Religious Right, and the Struggle for Control of Our Classrooms* (1993).

63. By no means are all "born-again Christians" either "fundamentalists" or committed to the kinds of views articulated by the plaintiffs in this case.

64. 827 F.2d at 1062.

To put it mildly, I do not share the worldview of these parents. Taken seriously, they represent nothing less than an attack on the very notions of independent analysis and self-reflection to which I would like to think I have dedicated my own life.[65] Moreover, one notes that the readings at issue ostensibly were chosen by Tennessee to carry out the statutory duty of public schools "to help each student develop positive values and to improve student conduct as students learn to act in harmony with their positive values and learn to become good citizens in their school, community, and society."[66] For ease of argument, let it be stipulated that the readings in fact did these desirable things. Does this combination of desirable readings and questionable, perhaps even appalling, parental values conclude the discussion?

To answer this question requires returning to *Pierce* and its protection of private education. For all the emphasis placed by the court on the importance of public schools as the molder of democratic citizens, it readily embraces the legitimacy of fleeing from the public school and the presumed inculcation of quite different values. Judge Lively, for the majority in *Mozert,* sets out his view of the choices facing the parents:

> The parents in the present case want their children to acquire all the skills required to live in modern society. They also want to have them excused from exposure to some ideas they find offensive. Tennessee offers two options to accommodate this latter desire. *The plaintiff parents can either send their children to church schools or private schools, as many of them have done, or teach them at home. Tennessee law prohibits any state interference in the education process of church schools.*[67]

65. In these postmodernist times, it is necessary to note that "independence" and "self-reflection" are highly problematic notions, for we are *always* embedded within the presuppositions of a given culture, and our "self" is substantially a creation of that culture. One can, therefore, never gain a leverage point of "independence" from culture per se, nor, obviously, can one engage in out-of-self experiences in order to reflect in a thoroughly detached way on the object that goes under one's name. All of this can be conceded, I believe, without giving up all allegiance to the Enlightenment value of "thinking for oneself" that remains the core of a liberal education.

66. 827 F.2d at 1060 (quoting Tennessee Code Annotated § 49-6-1007 (Supp. 1968)).

67. Id. at 1067 (emphasis added). Judge Lively quotes Tennessee Code Annotated § 49-50-801(b) (Supp. 1968): "The state board of education and local boards of education are prohibited from regulating the selection of faculty or textbooks or the establishment of a curriculum in church-related schools." If this statute means what it appears to say on the surface, then the state does indeed seem to have ceded sovereignty to the parents (or at least to the administrators of a church school).

So the choice is (deceptively) clear: One can attend the public schools on the state's terms, or place one's children in church or home schools, which can apparently be operated entirely on the parents' (or a religious school's) terms. Are we stuck with these two alternatives?

I think not, precisely because *Pierce,* at least as interpreted by the court and substantiated by Tennessee law, seems sublimely indifferent to the universal inculcation of "positive" values. That is, once the state tolerates, either out of constitutional necessity or political ideology, what might be termed counterhegemonic schools, then it seems hard, if not impossible, for the very same state to say that it has a "compelling state interest" justifying the burden placed on religious students by disallowing them from opting out of certain aspects of the public school curriculum. If the interest is truly "compelling," then one would think that the state would act aggressively to make sure that no child is denied its enjoyment.

However, if the state allows parents to withdraw their children entirely from the public schools and to inculcate views and values that might be quite antagonistic to the interests of the liberal democratic state, then why not in addition allow these parents to enjoy the public schools on at least some of their own terms, including the opting out from offensive curricular requirements? There is an easy answer to this question, which involves the potentially high administrative costs attached to tolerating the opting out and, for example, preparing tests on reading material different from that read by most of the students. I do not in the least deny the reality of these and other costs that undoubtedly make the already hard work of the public school teacher more burdensome. I do offer two observations, though. First, there is no indication in the *Mozert* opinion of precisely what these costs, as a practical matter, would be. Second, there is a whole body of constitutional law, most of it admittedly from the Warren Court days, denigrating administrative ease and low costs as counterweights to "fundamental" constitutional interests. It seems hard to gainsay, for example, that protection of religious free exercise is at least equal in fundamentality as a constitutional value to the "right to travel" of indigents so vigorously protected by the majority in *Shapiro v. Thompson* against Connecticut's attempt to impose a one-year residency requirement, justified by reference to administrative and fiscal convenience, prior to the receipt of welfare.[68]

68. 394 U.S. 618 (1969).

Moreover, liberals who often are properly quick to label as an "unconstitutional condition" the state's attempts to "buy up" important constitutional rights through the provision of public assistance, seem all too acquiescent here.[69] Surely, at least if one is even modestly egalitarian, *Pierce* cannot stand for the proposition that the state can exact any requirement it wishes from those who attend publicly financed schools so long as individuals with enough money or ideological zeal are free to withdraw and attend nonpublic schools. It should be chastening, at the least, to realize that Justice Frankfurter, in his (in)famous dissent in *West Virginia State Board of Education v. Barnette,*[70] based his argument on the propriety of forcing children, including Jehovah's Witnesses, to begin the school day with a salute to the American flag on the proposition that, after all, the parents of the Witnesses could withdraw their children and send them to private schools if they did not want their children to commit what they viewed as idolatry by saluting the flag. "As to its public schools, West Virginia imposes conditions which it deems necessary in the development of future citizens,"[71] and, for Frankfurter, that concludes the discussion. If liberals properly reject Frankfurter's argument in *Barnette,* it is not clear what makes it so much more attractive in a case like *Mozert*.

Whatever else might be said about these parents, they were willing to reject the option of separatism that the Constitution, and the laws of Tennessee, granted them. To this extent, they should be praised rather than discouraged and made to feel ever more marginal. For better or worse, one cannot compel these students to attend public and multicultural schools; that is the meaning of *Pierce*. By definition, this means that they must be lured, and this requires offering them at least some of what it will take to keep them within the public schools. As a practical matter, *only* attending public (or what used to be called "common") schools will offer the possibility of contact being made with persons significantly different from themselves. Although one certainly should not overestimate the importance of such contact — Catholics, Eastern Orthodox, and Muslims, after all, used to live next door to one another in Bosnia — it seems to me better than the alternative of ever more separatism.

69. See Justice Douglas's dissent in *Wyman v. James,* 400 U.S. 309, 327 (1971) ("[T]he central question is whether the government by force of its largesse has the power to 'buy up' rights guaranteed by the Constitution.").

70. 319 U.S. 624 (1943).

71. Id. at 656.

Candor compels me to state that I am considerably less willing to compromise in terms of the curriculum foisted on *nonreligious* students. For example, I am certainly disinclined to support the entry into the general curriculum of "creation science." That is easy (at least for me). What is harder is deciding whether the Constitution is best interpreted as foreclosing a state legislature or local school board from requiring that "creation science" be taught as an alternative account of the origins of life to evolution.[72] I personally doubt that exposure to "creation science" arguments is all that important, and it is even possible that a gifted teacher could use the conflict between such accounts and those of more traditional evolutionary biology to teach students, including religious students, something about the way that scientific arguments are actually conducted in terms of evidence, hypotheses, the handling of anomalous data, and the like.

I suspect that the conflict, like so much legal strife, is of primarily *symbolic* importance. It has to do precisely with the determination of religious parents that the public school system pay them some formal respect by acknowledging the "thinkability" of some of their cherished views about the creation of life. To say that it is primarily a symbolic issue is not meant to denigrate it; after all, as Justice Holmes once pointed out, "[w]e live by symbols."[73] No one who has drunk from the (post)modern well of semiotics can be blind to the importance of symbolism. It is in the very nature of a Kulturkampf that the issues of maximum strife will have far less to do with the division of material resources—the basic issue of class warfare—than with the valence to be placed on certain cherished myths and symbols by which the cultural combatants give meaning to their otherwise literally meaningless lives. No less than the Godfather do most human beings yearn for "respect," and woe to the society that systematically denies respect to any large (and mobilizable) subset of its population.

The universal desire for respect, incidentally, suggests why it is important that offers of compromise be two-way, including the acceptance by the "religious right" of a substantially more secular, culturally pluralistic school system than they might otherwise prefer. There is certainly reason for secularists to believe that they are fundamentally disrespected by many of the so-called new religious right. As with tangos, it takes two to engage in a Kul-

72. See *Edwards v. Aguillard*, 482 U.S. 578 (1987) (striking down a Louisiana law that required the teaching of "creation science" together with evolution, because passage of the law was motivated by the illegitimate purpose of aiding religion).

73. Oliver Wendell Holmes, *Collected Legal Papers* 270 (1920).

turkampf. If there is no alternative to a Kulturkampf, then I have no hesitation in lining up with the opponents of religious orthodoxy. The question, though, is whether there is indeed an alternative to such a grim prospect.

All of these issues come together with regard to prayer in the public schools. To the extent that religious students continue to attend public schools, school prayer will undoubtedly continue to be a minefield. What am I willing to offer here? From one perspective, undoubtedly, the answer is not much. I still unequivocally applaud both *Engel* and *Lee;* the state has no business either composing or arranging for the offering of prayers in public events. I also have no trouble supporting the most recent decision of the Court invalidating a school district policy that allowed student-led, student-initiated prayer before football games.[74] On the other hand, I find myself much less enamored of *Wallace,* even conceding that the purpose of the Alabama legislators who passed the statute was to sneak prayer, at least somewhat, back into the schoolroom and that the teacher would state the magic word in calling the class to silence. Is it worth it, even from a secularist perspective, to prohibit such a law if the cost — and one must, of course, see this as a cost and not a benefit — is to alienate yet more religious parents (and possibly their children) from the public schools and, in some cases, to drive them from the public schools into one or another religious "academy?"

My answer, as one can readily gather, is no. The loss of such students, should it occur, deprives the public school of an important "different voice" that enhances the diversity so important to education. If one can keep some students simply by allowing a moment of silence, and allowing a teacher to say that at least some students might use this moment for prayer while others contemplate the meaning of life, last night's date, or whatever, it is a cheap price to pay. To insist on stamping out such moments in the name of the "wall of separation" is to fall victim to an ideological zeal that is little better, I am now convinced, than the zealotry exhibited by those who would wish to absorb the state as an ally in endorsing or enforcing a specific theological program. It is, therefore, my hope that *Wallace,* if not flatly overruled, will in the future be restricted to its specific facts. State-imposed moments of silence and contemplation, unaccompanied by state-composed prayers or entreaties from the teacher to engage in prayer, ought not to be viewed as presenting threats to the values underlying the Establishment Clause.

74. *Santa Fe Ind. Sch. Dist. v. Doe,* 120 S. Ct. 2266 (2000).

I conclude this section by trying to answer a series of questions directly posed to me by Professor McConnell. They both capture the kinds of controversies increasingly being litigated and, more important, present just the kinds of questions that anyone concerned with the practice (and not simply the theory) of multiculturalism must grapple with. The challenge offered by McConnell was as follows:

> [W]hat would you do if the graduating class is allowed to vote on whom to invite to give the graduation address, and the class votes for a person whose principal appeal is religious (the local bishop, perhaps—or a religious writer)? Would you allow a separate, voluntary baccalaureate service, organized by the school (or, better yet, a committee of the student government)? Would it be permissible for the student government to allow a representative sampling of the viewpoints in the class each to speak for five minutes at the graduation ceremony—and include an evangelical type? And what about non-school settings? Presumably, for the President to include prayers at his inauguration is permissible on the ground that it is done in his "private" capacity; presumably the same would be true of a joint swearing-in of a group of congressmen; why isn't the same principle applicable to graduating seniors from high school?[75]

Would I allow the graduating class to pick the speaker, even if the basis of the selection is presumably the (likely) religious content of the address? I distinguish this, incidentally, from a class vote to have a student-led prayer, which I would strike down in an instant.[76] As to selecting the speaker, one might want to know the background history that provides a "baseline" for consideration. *If* students traditionally chose the speaker, and *if,* over many years, speakers had been drawn from a variety of places on the intellectual spectrum, and *if* speakers had taken advantage of the opportunity offered them to make controversial speeches challenging conventional views (conditions that I would be absolutely astonished to find met in more than a handful

---

75. Letter from Michael W. McConnell to Sanford Levinson (7 July 1993).

76. Cf. *Jones v. Clear Creek Ind. Sch. Dist.,* 977 F.2d 963 (5th Cir. 1992), cert. denied, 113 S. Ct. 2950 (1993) (holding student-initiated prayers in graduation ceremonies acceptable). Although the Court denied review in *Jones,* the Fifth Circuit later confined its reach to graduation exercises when striking down prefootball student-delivered prayer in *Doe v. Duncanville Ind. Sch. Dist.,* 70 F.3d 402 (1995). It is impossible to believe that the majority that struck down similar process of student-initiated prayer in the recent *Santa Fe* case would not apply its analysis to graduation events, though it remains open to unsympathetic courts below to argue that *Santa Fe* is merely a "football" (or, more broadly, "athletic events") case and has no application to graduations.

of high schools), *then* I would be inclined to describe as "censorship" the refusal by a school to honor a class's choice to hear, as in McConnell's example, the local bishop and the likely invocation of religious themes.

I would analogize the example to the situation presented before the Supreme Court in *Lamb's Chapel v. Center Moriches Union Free School District,*[77] where a unanimous Court struck down the refusal of a New York school board to grant permission to Lamb's Chapel, an evangelical church in the local community, to present a film series concerning the family and encouraging the return to "traditional, Christian family values." The Board was applying its rule prohibiting the use of public school facilities, even after school hours, for "religious purposes," even though other rules allowed access to a multitude of nonreligious groups. The Court properly found this content-based distinction in violation of the First Amendment.

An obvious distinction is that the Lamb's Chapel program is not formally sponsored or otherwise endorsed by the school board, whereas the graduation ceremony, even if not compulsory, is a central public ritual, and it would be unfortunate indeed if a member of the nonhegemonic minority was reluctant to attend such an important occasion because of the anticipatory discomfort produced by the prospect of a religiously-oriented speech. But, of course, the discomfort could well be produced by inviting the local member of Congress or anyone else identified with any controversial stance on public issues.[78] Under these circumstances, then, I would support the students' choice. If, however, as I suspect is almost certainly going to be the case, student selection of the speaker is a brand-new option, adopted at least in part to evade the strictures of *Weisman* and other similar decisions, then I have little hesitancy in striking down McConnell's first example.[79]

---

77. 508 U.S. 384 (1993).

78. Consider, for example, the demonstrations mounted in June 1993 at Harvard in protest of the selection as graduation speaker of General Colin Powell, who opposed proposals by President Clinton to integrate gays and lesbians fully into the armed forces.

79. One reader of this essay objected that I am biased against "new" empowerment of students insofar as I rely for my baseline the existence of *past* events before I would allow present students to invite a religious speaker. That is probably true. One reason for my suspicion of "new" empowerment is that it often appears to occur as a fairly obvious pretext to allow (and, indeed, subtly encourage) students to do what the school district no longer can do, i.e., require prayer before school events. See, for example, the background of the student-empowerment policy adopted in *Santa Fe.* As Justice Stevens wrote for the majority, "We refuse to turn a blind eye to the context in which this policy arose, and that context quells any doubt that this policy was implemented with the purpose of endorsing school prayer." 120 S. Ct. 2282. I would be more

Would I permit a separate, voluntary baccalaureate service, organized by the school — or, better yet, a committee of the student government — at which prayer(s) would be offered? No to the school-organized service. After all, the "official" baccalaureate service is "voluntary," and that properly made no difference to the *Weisman* majority. The school system should not be in the business of organizing "separate-but-equal" services, regardless of the basis of the separation. I am inclined to give the same answer for the service organized by the student government.

Far different is a separate ceremony organized by a group of students, including, for example, the president of the student council and the captain of the football team, and held "off-campus," perhaps at a local church. I can see no argument for enjoining students from announcing their desire to offer thanks to God upon completion of their high school careers and inviting their classmates to join them. What if the "supplementary" ceremony in fact became the principal one, so that most of the students and parents showed up at the local church and relatively few bothered to come to the high school auditorium? (I assume, for ease of argument, that the two services are not scheduled at the same time.) I would regard this as most unfortunate, but again I cannot imagine any reading of the First Amendment that would bar students and parents from organizing a religious service to which the public is invited. Only if the organizing committee included school officials might there be a genuine dilemma, though even here one should be wary of forcing public employees to waive their own rights of free expression as a condition of accepting public employment.

Could the student government allow a representative sampling of the viewpoints in the class to speak for five minutes each at the graduation ceremony, and include an evangelical type? This strikes me as an easy case: The answer is yes. It becomes especially easy if the "representative sampling" includes students expressing nonreligious views likely to get under the skin of many of those in attendance, such as endorsements of gay and lesbian rights, attacks on welfare recipients, support (or denunciation) of capital punishment, and the like. *Weisman* properly bars the state from asking students to "join in" a prayer, even if they have the option to refusing the invitation. Hearing an evangelical student, one among many other students, witness his or her faith in Jesus, is simply not the same thing.

receptive to "new" empowerment were there no such evidence, but, alas, I doubt that such situations will often, if ever, arise.

Indeed, the evangelical student need not necessarily be "balanced" with nonreligious counterparts. If, for example, the valedictorian is evangelical and wishes to begin her speech with thanks to God, then that is acceptable. She earned her right to speak on grounds wholly separate from her religious identity, and, generally speaking, the state ought not be able to extract a "bleaching out"[80] of her religious identity as a condition for enjoying what all valedictorians have enjoyed before her — the right to speak to her classmates and parents. Things get far trickier, of course, if, as is common, valedictory speeches are in effect subject to censorship via submission to the principal for review. However, I confess that I find the idea of review itself to be far more constitutionally suspect than the prospect of the speaker "slipping in" some prayer. The valedictorian should have the same freedom as the president of the United States to include religious references in her speech.[81]

Conclusion: Toward Synthesis?

I have tried in this essay to offer reflections on some implications of the reality of religious multiculturalism within America. I have also tried, quite self-consciously, to present myself as a wonderfully tolerant person who genuinely wishes to reach out to persons of decidedly different sensibility from my own. Yet candor requires me to admit that one reason I would prefer the children at issue in *Mozert* to attend the public schools is precisely to increase the likelihood that they might be lured away from the views — some of them only foolish, others, alas, quite pernicious — of their parents. Perhaps *they* will meet and begin talking with, and learning from, more secular students.

Here we see the underside of terms like "tolerance," for, generally speaking, one who self-consciously "tolerates" opposing views or ways of life is

---

80. See chapter 4.

81. This being said, I must note my own personal wish that presidents would in fact choose to omit opening and closing benedictions at inaugurations. Indeed, I believe that these should come under the "unconstitutional conditions" strictures announced in *Weisman,* though I scarcely expect any court to enjoin the president from inviting ministers, priests, and rabbis — and, in the near future, Islamic and Buddhist prelates — to take part in inaugural rituals. Whatever else one might think of the selection of Joseph Lieberman to be Al Gore's running mate in the 2000 presidential election, I suspect that it set back the cause of secularism at least a decade. More than ever, it seems impossible for a major American politician to declare forthrightly that he or she has no religious beliefs and/or wishes to secularize public ceremonies by omitting religious benedictions.

unlikely to offer them "equal concern and respect." Instead, the tolerator only holds back from exercising certain kinds of force that would make the lives of the tolerated even worse. I do not mean to denigrate "toleration." There can be no doubt that the move from a society in which one is actively suppressed to one in which one is tolerated is an important gain, and most of the world would be better off if toleration were more widespread. Still, no one should confuse this with full and complete acceptance. It is this difference that is at the heart, I believe, of the contemporary debate about the public stance regarding gays and lesbians. Many straight Americans are far more willing to "tolerate" gays and lesbians than to acknowledge that there is really nothing at all objectionable about gay and lesbian behavior. Similar tensions are present when sectarians are asked to grant full legitimacy to secular perspectives and, of course, vice versa.

In any event, I find myself far more in a "tolerationist" than a genuinely "accepting" posture via-à-vis persons like Vicki Frost. Thus I confess my hope that her children, by attending public schools, will in fact meet and begin talking with (and learning from) more secular students. My anger at the Hawkins County School Board is derived as much from their driving the children away, and thus, from my perspective, contributing, albeit indirectly, to the reinforcement of their parents' worldview, as it is from the Board's exhibiting antagonism to the worldview itself. To push these students from the public schools, by refusing to make the kinds of concessions their parents demanded — which, after all, went only to *their* education and not to the materials assigned all of the other children — will assure that they will in fact be educated within institutions that are, from my perspective at least, far more limiting and, indeed, "totalitarian" than anything likely to be found within a decent public school. My desire to "lure" religious parents back to the public schools thus has at least a trace of the spider's web about it.

I recognize, of course, that in a genuinely religiously multicultural school some secular students will be led to accept the students' religious understanding. Isn't this what education is all about — to present alternative views of the world and thus potentially transform the lives of individuals who had not heretofore dreamt of these possibilities? But, as already indicated, I am, perhaps optimistically, assuming that the transformation is far more likely to run from the religious to the secular than vice versa, and I cannot honestly say I know what I would be arguing if I were persuaded that the likelihood, as a practical matter, ran in the opposite direction.

Do the last several paragraphs undercut the professed aim of this essay and thus deny the possibility of a synthesis of the initial thesis and antithesis presented at the beginning? Or, to adopt a question posed by James Boyd White,[82] do I reveal myself to be fundamentally uninterested in truly encountering the Others who do not share my own secular sensibility? And if that is the case, then why should they trust me truly to adjudicate their claims, any more than I would be inclined to trust one of them to adjudicate my own?

My professed aim is to call upon fellow secularists to think of possible grounds of compromise with religious sectarians, especially in regard to the extraordinarily complex issue of education. I would like to think that is my real aim as well. But it is altogether possible that what this essay ultimately reveals is the difficulty, if not outright impossibility, of finding a common ground on which secularists and the religiously orthodox can walk toether. After all, as the prophet Amos asked more than two millennia ago, "Do two people travel together unless they have agreed to do so?"[83] Perhaps I simply have not taken sufficient account of, and I may even illustrate, the deep chasm separating these two parts of the American social community. But we will not know this for a fact unless we at least make good faith attempts to understand the positions of the combatants in America's Kulturkampf and to see if there are indeed ways to prevent the conflicts from becoming ever more deadly to the hope of achieving some kind of *unum* among the *pluribus* of American society.

82. "I think it less important," he wrote in a very thoughtful letter commenting on an earlier draft, "how a particular judge or scholar comes out than who he manages to make himself — and his audience, and the law — in the way in which he thinks and talks about the case." Letter from White to Levinson (13 October 1993). I am not at all sure that this conclusion, rewritten as a result of White's letter, fully meets his point, but I am grateful to him for pushing me to think more deeply about what I hope to do (and to reveal) by writing this article.
83. Amos 3:3. Of course, much of the major political theory of our time is structured by the obvious reality that society has become radically pluralistic, which by definition means substantial disagreement about basic issues.

3

"Getting Religion": Religion, Diversity, and

Community in Public and Private Schools

WITH MEIRA LEVINSON

Introduction

There are many arguments for and against school vouchers or, should
"vouchers" be too politically loaded or descriptively restrictive a term, the
use of public funds, either directly or indirectly, to support private (including religious) schools. Some of these arguments are explicitly constitutional,
based on one or another reading of the Establishment and Free Exercise
Clauses of the First Amendment. Although one of us is a constitutional
lawyer, we emphasize at the outset that this paper is not in any way an
analysis of the validity of such legal arguments, even if we make occasional
descriptive reference to them. Here we are interested in the more general
normative and empirical debates surrounding such aid. If it is a good idea,
then the possibility of its being unconstitutional counts against the Constitution (or judicial doctrine), not against the proposal, and we might then turn
our attention to the best ways of changing constitutional understanding,
whether through the appointment of different judges or formal amendment
of the Constitution. Concomitantly, if such aid is a bad idea, then it is
irrelevant that it might be constitutional. The terms "constitutional" and
"unconstitutional" are not at all necessarily synonymous with "meritorious" and "unmeritorious," and it is the latter that is exclusively our focus.

There are, of course, many normative questions raised by proposals for
aid to religious schools. We focus on one particularly common — and, for

This essay was originally published in *School Choice: The Moral Debate*, edited by Alan Wolfe
(Princeton: Princeton University Press, 2003).

many, especially potent—of such arguments against vouchers and other such aid. This involves the ostensible tension between such programs and the achievement of a desirable degree of diversity within the aided schools themselves. That is, heterogeneous schools are deemed by many contemporary liberals (and, no doubt, others as well) to be better than homogeneous ones, and the dispersion of public funds to private schools, whatever the process by which this is done, is viewed as encouraging homogeneity and therefore as generating public harm rather than benefit. Thus, for example, it is often suggested that school vouchers will result in some students going to private schools that by design are segregated along one or more axes. This essay focuses on one such axis, religion, but many others deserve attention as well, including, but not limited to, nonreligious belief systems; race or ethnicity; achievement; gender; sexual orientation; raw intelligence, as ostensibly measured by aptitude or similar tests; and/or socioeconomic status. The assumption, obviously, is that in the absence of a dispersion to ideologically self-contained private schools, these students would remain in public schools, and that their very presence would promote the kinds of diversity that are desirable.

Why is diversity so desirable? Although we will offer a more elaborate answer to this question later, we can offer in outline form two especially common defenses of diversity. First, a diverse student body can help to develop the toleration of others—perhaps we should refer to "Others"—that is functional to developing the liberal democratic civic project that relies on mutual respect. This view is articulated by former university presidents William Bowen and Derek Bok in their highly influential defense of affirmative action at the university level, but the arguments hold for primary and secondary education as well: Diverse student bodies help to produce "greater 'cultural awareness across racial lines' and stronger commitments to improving racial understandings."[1] One can substitute practically any term for "racial" and the argument still works. This is the "civic-education" or "civic-toleration" justification.

A second, quite different, argument emphasizes the relevance of a diverse student body to better enabling students to develop their own autonomy by interacting with people who hold beliefs and lead lives that are different from their own. This argument can be traced back at least to John Stuart

---

1. William G. Bowen and Derek Bok, *The Shape of the River: Long-Term Consequences of Considering Race in College and University Admissions* 228 (1998).

Mill, who in *On Liberty* defended the importance of tolerating experiments in living not only because of the beneficial effects of learning to accept the existence of different approaches to life, but also because confrontation with such experiments would possibly lead the observer to evaluate one's own values and conduct and, perhaps, to change in quite dramatic ways the direction taken in one's life. Even if no change takes place, a person forced to confront significantly different ways of life would have a far sharper sense of why she remained committed to her own views. It is no coincidence that another university president, Harvard's Neil Rudenstine, when presenting his own reflections (and defenses) of the uses of diversity, quoted Mill's insistence that a person "[m]ust be able to hear [diverse opinions] from persons who actually believe them, who defend them in earnest, and do their very utmost for them. He must . . . feel the whole force of the difficulty which the true view of the subject has to encounter and dispose of . . ."[2] Presumably, if the person challenged cannot "dispose of" the difficulties presented to her own views, then she will change them and, as a result, partake in a very different form of life than might otherwise have been the case. This is the "autonomy-promotion" justification, and taken together, these are, albeit very sketchily, the "diversity arguments."

The relationship between vouchers (or other relevant forms of aid) and the diversity arguments is fairly straightforward. First, as mentioned previously, opponents of vouchers often focus on the homogeneity of the schools strengthened as the result of such aid.[3] That is, some parents are

2. Neil L. Rudenstine, "The Uses of Diversity," *Harvard Magazine,* March–April 1996, at 50. Rudenstine goes on to offer as a key example the fact that Henry Adams's graduating class of 1858 at Harvard included three Virginians, including the son of Robert E. Lee. As Adams put it, writing in the third person, "for the first time Adams's education brought him in contact with new types and taught him their values. He saw the New England type measure itself with another. . . ." Id. at 51. Rudenstine goes on to note that Adams's experience "altered Adams' consciousness, and forced him to confront and assess a type of person he had never before known. It drove him to reach new conclusions about himself and his own limitations. . . ." Id.

3. See, e.g., Jeff Spinner-Halev, "Extending Diversity: Religion in Public and Private Education," in *Citizenship in Diverse Societies* 68–95 (Will Kymlicka and Wayne Norman, eds., 2000). He suggests that "one of the basic worries" about parochial schools and their increase (especially if they receive additional public support) is that "the more parochial schools there are, the less students of different backgrounds will mix with one [an]other; the less they will learn how to cooperate with one another or realize that others with different views exist. This leaves the children in private schools isolated." Id. at 81. Spinner-Halev's interesting essay in part tracks our own concerns, especially insofar as he rightly insists that "[a] diversity that excludes religion and religious students is not very diverse." Id. at 70. Unfortunately, we became aware of his essay

assumed to want to send their children to schools whose student body will be very similar along a given metric. (Were there no such parental preferences, then one can assume that little or no advantage would be taken of policies that would allow greater homogeneity along the particular metric.) Second, they also assert that by enabling such parents, whether smart, committed, active, religious, white, what have you, to take their involvement and their children to private schools, vouchers leave public schools and the students stuck in them worse off than before. This latter argument is usually made from an egalitarian perspective, where the focus is the harm done to public schools by losing involved parents. But the "cream-off effect" argument also can derive strength from the diversity argument, insofar as the disappearance of religious, white, lower-middle-class, or other group of students from the public schools leaves the public schools less diverse along that axis, and therefore (drawing on the diversity arguments) harms the civic education and/or autonomy development of public school students left behind.

Our aim in this essay is not to rehash the pros and cons of these quite well-known arguments in the course of justifying or discrediting them. Instead, we are interested in examining the normative consequences of applying them to a question that seems to have been incongruously (and remarkably) overlooked in the general debates regarding "diversity," which have focused almost exclusively on race and ethnicity. The question is this: Does the liberal-democratic state and/or do children have a compelling interest in children going to school in a diverse *religious* setting? Positive (and negative) answers abound to the racial version of this question; the importance of "mingling together" is the foundation of most defenses of so-called diversity admissions policies by universities,[4] and it (along with important egalitarian considerations) also undergirds the attempt by many public school systems to preserve "racial balancing" policies against the recent antibusing and antidesegregation backlash.[5] Interestingly, however, the religious ver-

---

only after preparing our own and therefore do not give it the extended attention that it deserves. The same is true, alas, of another essay in *Citizenship in Diverse Societies,* Eamonn Callan, "Discrimination and Religious Schooling," pp. 45–67, which offers an especially interesting discussion of educational policy in Canada, which takes a considerably different approach to state funding of religious schools than is found in the United States.

4. See chapter 1.

5. See Gary Orfield, Susan E. Eaton, and The Harvard Project on School Desegregation, *Dismantling Desegregation: The Quiet Reversal of* Brown v. Board of Education (1996), esp. chs.

sion of this question has gone virtually unconsidered except to the extent that it applies to the autonomy-development and civic-membership interests specifically of children of religious parents who want to remove them from public education entirely.

The best-known case regarding the education of religious children, *Wisconsin v. Yoder*,[6] is discussed in terms of whether a state can force Amish children to attend schools at least through the tenth grade or whether, on the contrary, the parents of these children can terminate their formal schooling after eight years in order to further their socialization into the Amish community itself. (Interestingly enough, *Yoder* did not involve either the presence of alternative Amish schools or "home-schooling" by Amish parents.) In both the majority and minority opinions, careful attention was paid to the implications for maintaining both civic order and the Amish community, as well as for the Amish youth themselves. But although Justice Douglas, dissenting, issued a strong objection to the Court's seeming willingness to ignore the particular autonomy interests of the affected Yoder children, he wrote nary a word about any losses to the potential classmates of the Amish children whose absence from the public schools was upheld.

The same is true with regard to the much-discussed case of *Mozert v. Hawkins*,[7] which involves a clash between fundamentalist religious parents and a local school board with regard to the necessity that each and every child be exposed to the particular reading program offered by the school system, one of whose aims is precisely to expose children to different viewpoints and to teach them critical thinking skills. Much has been written about the loss (or gain) to the particular children of Vicki Frost if they cannot continue to attend public schools or "opt out" of having to confront the reading program chosen by the school board. Almost nothing has been written about the losses suffered by other children if the plaintiff's children retreat from the public schools. Finally, there are, most recently, the so-called Yale Five, who objected to having to live in Yale student dormitories that they claimed violated certain rules and behaviors attached to Orthodox Judaism. Yale defended its requirement on the ground that the Orthodox Jewish students would greatly benefit from living in dormitories consisting

---

11 and 12; Jeffrey Rosen, "The Lost Promise of School Integration," *New York Times*, 2 April 2000, at 4: 5.

6. 406 U.S. 205 (1972).

7. The key opinions are those presented in *Mozert v. Hawkins County Board of Education*, 827 F.2d 1058 (6th Cir. 1987), cert. denied, 484 U.S. 1066 (1988).

of diverse students. Less was said about the benefits to other students of having to live with—and to some degree accommodate themselves to—the Orthodox Jews.

Even when compromises, such as allowing students to opt out of reading programs or residence requirements, are suggested they most often are defended by statements to the effect that "these very specific, named children will be better off and will be exposed to a wider range of opinions if they stay in the public schools (or live in the Yale dorms), and, therefore, we must accept these compromises as unfortunate but necessary costs of allowing them to achieve such benefits." This is thought preferable to having the students withdraw, though the metric of evaluation is entirely in terms of those specific students' own interests. This assessment, of course, may be correct. Yet it is worth noting how rarely consideration is given to the consequences for *nonfundamentalist* children or *non-Orthodox* students who, by stipulation, face the possibility of remaining in public schools (or private universities) now lacking the diversity provided by their former classmates.

A similar point can be made with regard to the design of assignment zones, or what the British call "catchment areas," for public schools. Despite the vast amount of literature arguing in favor of diverse public schools and, concomitantly, the conscious use of demographic materials relating to race or ethnicity when constructing school boundaries (or deciding on the use of busing to achieve certain kinds of demographic balance), we know of no serious consideration that has ever been given to whether public schools might alter their catchment areas to achieve "religious balancing," or, less drastically and therefore potentially more intriguingly, offer incentives (e.g., a kosher or halal cafeteria, or an adjusted school schedule, including, say, no athletic events on Friday or Saturday) to attract religious-minority families to a school located in an otherwise all-Christian area of town. Thus our title—"Getting Religion"—which is intended, among other things, to suggest the possibility that it is a positive good if schools get those with religious views (and behaviors) among their student bodies and, therefore, that one should consciously design educational policy with a view to maximizing that possibility.

It is possible, of course, that the reason for such an absence of much discussion of this question is legal; many lawyers would no doubt say that it would be unconstitutional for such factors to play a part in designing public school boundaries. As indicated earlier, even if this is so, we are still entitled to ask if this is a cost, rather than a benefit, of current constitutional norms. If it is viewed as a cost, of course, then that would be a good reason for supporting changes in the interpretation of these norms.

There are many attributes beyond the religious, of course, that lend themselves to a "diversity" analysis. So a second focus of this essay is how religious diversity interests balance against other types of diversity. For example, even if the answer to the question posed above is yes, that it is a compelling interest of either the state or its children for children to be educated with children whose religious sensibilities are significantly different from their own, it is possible that a school that is not religiously diverse (e.g., a private Baptist academy or a Jewish yeshiva) will be more racially or socioeconomically diverse than other private or public schools. Indeed, as one of us has recently argued, one reality (and, perhaps, significant weakness) attached to invocations of the "diversity" argument is precisely that "diversity," if taken seriously, is truly without limit insofar as there are almost literally an infinite number of ways that sets of humans can be described as interestingly different (and thus diverse) from one another.[8] Or, as Judge Weiner put it by way of chastising the University of Texas Law School with regard to its own "diversity" defense of a program that was in fact limited to African- and Mexican Americans: "[B]lacks and Mexican Americans are but two among any number of racial or ethnic groups that could and presumably should contribute to genuine diversity."[9] Surely he is correct; moreover, as already suggested, there is no good reason to think only in terms of "racial or ethnic groups" when imagining desirable forms of diversity.[10]

8. See chapter 1.

9. *Hopwood v. Texas*, 78 F.3d 932, 965–66 (6th Cir. 1996) (Weiner, J., concurring).

10. This point is made at length in the recent decision involving the admissions program at the University of Michigan Law School, *Grutter v. Bollinger*, 137 F. Supp. 2d 821 (E.D. Mich., Southern Div., 2001), where Judge Friedman expressed strong reservations about the coherence of the Law School's claimed commitment to "diversity." He wrote, for example, that

> there is no logical basis for the law school to have chosen the particular racial groups which receive special attention under the current admissions policy. . . . During some of the years at issue in this lawsuit, the law school bulletin indicated that special attention has been given to "students who are African American, Mexican American, Native American, or Puerto Rican and raised on the U.S. mainland." The law school has failed to offer a principled explanation as to why it has singled out these particular groups for special attention. Certainly, other groups have also been subjected to discrimination, such as Arabs and southern and eastern Europeans to name but a few, yet the court heard nothing to suggest that the law school has concerned itself as to whether members of these groups are represented "in meaningful numbers." No satisfactory explanation was offered for distinguishing between Puerto Ri-

One might well believe that any given "diversity" is beneficial to all concerned. Catholic schools, for example, are notable for drawing families across many racial and socioeconomic lines. It seems quite probable that the widespread availability of vouchers or other programs of public aid would allow many other denominationally identified religious schools to draw from a much wider socioeconomic range than would a typical prep school — even one that courted diversity — or a neighborhood public school. After all, the continued (or renewed) segregation of students in public schools — whether it be all lower-income African Americans in urban Atlanta or Detroit, or mostly middle- and upper-income whites in Scarsdale — has been well documented.[11] Furthermore, as we will discuss, certain nonreligious but otherwise "special emphasis" private schools[12] (e.g., military academies, Waldorf or Rudolf Steiner schools, "free" schools, mountain or wilderness academies, etc.) are for a variety of reasons far less diverse along most axes than are many religious schools. Even self-consciously "progressive" schools, both public and private, have a hard time attracting families that are nonwhite and non-middle-class; even when access to them is easy and free, African American, Hispanic, and lower-income parents all typically favor traditional, "three Rs" schools. To the extent that voucher programs must satisfy diversity claims, therefore, it is arguable that vouchers should be provided for some religious schools but not for these other private schools. This, obviously, would be a highly unexpected twist for the application of diversity considerations to religious schools, since usually proponents of diversity (for either civic toleration–building or autonomy-promoting reasons) come down squarely against the use of vouchers for religious schools precisely on the grounds that they inappropriately segregate students.

---

cans who were raised on the U.S. mainland from Puerto Ricans who were raised in Puerto Rico or elsewhere. No satisfactory explanation was offered for singling out Mexican Americans but, by implication, excluding from special consideration Hispanics who originate from countries other than Mexico. A special "commitment" is made to African Americans, but apparently none is made to blacks from other parts of the world. This haphazard selection of certain races is a far cry from the "close fit" between the means and the ends that the Constitution demands in order for a racial classification to pass muster under strict scrutiny analysis . . . (Id. at 851–52.)

11. See generally Gary Orfield et al., supra note 5.

12. We call these schools "special emphasis" following the National Center for Education Statistics's *Private School Universe Survey, 1997–98*. See page 28 of that survey, where the various categories of schools are defined.

We should note one significant variation of a "diversity" argument, which focuses more on the overall distribution of institutional possibilities than on the demography of any particular institution. Thus, the argument might go, society in general benefits from the presence of a continuing Amish (or Seventh-Day Adventist or hippie) community, and the only way to assure the maintenance of such communities is to allow (and perhaps even encourage through public subsidy) homogeneous schools that will minimize the likelihood that the young will be tempted to leave these communities. This is, of course, the classic argument linked with pluralism or multiculturalism, which, in some variants, has a distinctly separatist tilt. Although much more could be said about the costs or benefits of a widespread pluralism within a liberal political order — and it is possible that the coauthors would disagree about the assessment of such costs or benefits — we are interested far more in the state's and children's interest in encouraging a less separatist form of education by maximizing the presence of diversity within any given educational institution. Moreover, we note Nancy Rosenblum's important insight that remarkably few partisans of educational vouchers defend their position by offering forthright advocacy of separatist pluralism or multiculturalism.[13] Instead, the primary defenses appear to emphasize less overtly controversial criteria of "achievement" and "educational quality." And, as already noted, at least some notions of "educational quality" include reference to the importance of demographic diversity.[14] We thus return to the basic arguments for diversity and attempt to spell out their implications more fully in the sections below.

The Diversity Argument Elaborated: The Importance of "Mingling"

Since their founding in America, "public" or "common" (as they were originally designated) schools have been justified by reference to the social goods that were and are thought to be produced by the process of bringing

13. See Nancy L. Rosenblum, "Separating the Siamese Twins: 'Pluralism' and 'School Choice,' " in *School Choice: The Moral Debate* (Alan Wolfe, ed., 2003).

14. This is not to say that diversity is concomitant with, or even necessary to, educational quality; although our focus in this essay is on the implications of the diversity argument for religious education, it may well be that other goals, such as achievement or equity, are more important. Be that as it may, it is not our purpose here to balance diversity claims against other educational or social norms.

together children of different backgrounds in a single setting. As Horace Bushnell wrote in 1853 of the "great institution . . . of common schools," "There needs to be some place where, in early childhood, [a child] may be brought together and made acquainted with each other; thus to wear away the sense of distance, otherwise certain to become an established animosity of orders; to form friendships; to be exercised together on a common footing of ingenuous rivalry. . . . Without this he can never be a fully qualified citizen, or prepared to act his part wisely as a citizen."[15] Similarly, Theodore Roosevelt commented some half-century later, "We stand unalterably in favor of the public school system in its entirey," because when "Americans of every origin and faith [are] brought up in them," they "inevitably in after-life have kindlier feelings toward their old school-fellows of different creeds, and look at them with a wiser and manlier charity, than could possibly be the case had they never had the chance to mingle together in their youth."[16] These high ideals carry into contemporary times. As Stephen Macedo has recently written, "The whole point of the common school is to be a primary arena where children from the different normative perspectives that compose our polity encounter one another in a respectful setting, learn about one another, and discover that their differences do not preclude cooperation and mutual respect as participants in a shared political order."[17] One might be tempted to ask, with a suitably rhetorical flourish, "If 'common' does not mean this, then what *does* it mean?"

All three of these men agreed that a diverse student body is essential for educating citizens. It is generally agreed that citizenship in a liberal democracy requires that one tolerate and even respect people who are different from oneself, who hold different beliefs and engage in actions and life practices that are unfamiliar, discomfiting, or even repugnant. The reason is eminently practical: In a contemporary society consisting of many different groups with quite conflicting ways of understanding the world, a Hobbesian world of endless conflict can be avoided only if individual citizens develop at least enough respect for one another to resist the temptation to suppress those they disagree with or, equally important, to escape the constant anxiety that they will themselves be the targets of suppression if other groups come to power. (The existence of legal "parchment barriers" against such

15. Horace Bushnell, *American Writing on Popular Education: The Nineteenth Century* 182 (Rush Welter, ed., 1971).
16. Quoted in Stephen Macedo, *Diversity and Distrust* 93 (2000).
17. Id. at 194.

suppression will scarcely suffice to control the manifold forms of hostility or oppression that can result from antagonistic views of the Other.) In order for people to come to tolerate and respect others, it is generally thought that they need to interact with these "others" in close, meaningful ways that enable them to see the commonalities among them (that serve to generate mutual respect) and at least to understand the reasons for the differences that remain between them.[18] It is also useful if these interactions occur at an early age, before prejudices have the chance to harden and block the development of mutual understanding. Schools are thus seen as being essential, possibly unique, institutions for bringing diverse individuals together under these conditions. As a result, diverse schools are lauded for their service in promoting toleration and civic virtue.

This is no small point. Both of us attribute great—and positive—significance to our experiences growing up in Southern communities with a group of close friends drawn from a variety of Christian religious denominations, ranging from Roman Catholic to Southern Baptist.[19] Not only did we (separately) spend a lot of time discussing and debating fundamental questions of religion, but we also learned, quite obviously, to tolerate the different answers that were given. Sanford Levinson has written about his experiences in Hendersonville, North Carolina, and the importance of ensuing friendships: "We too often automatically sneer at the phrase 'some of my best friends are Jewish (or any other religion or race),' but, surely, it would be a profound social good if all of us could in fact say, with conviction, that some of our best friends are from groups other than those with which we most centrally identify."[20] It is hard to believe that societies as heterogeneous as our own can flourish (or perhaps even survive) if the particular intimacies of friendship are limited to those who are exactly like oneself.[21]

18. We put it this way because it might be too heroic an aspiration that everyone accept the substantive "reasonableness" or views—and, even more so, the behavior—of others. One need not believe, for example, that it is truly "reasonable" not to mix milk and meat in order to respect the reasons that lead observant (and even some non-Orthodox) Jews to maintain adherence to this tradition of *kashruth*.

19. See chapter 2. Sanford Levinson notes also the costs of growing up in a segregated society, which meant that all of these friends were white.

20. Id. at page 68.

21. This means, among other things, that (liberal) society as a whole almost certainly benefits from the "intermarriages" that are often bewailed by leaders of particular groups. To take what some would consider an extreme example, every marriage of an Israeli Jew with an Israeli Arab, whether Christian or Muslim, would be a cause for rejoicing on the part of any liberal.

We see this same process playing out in schools today. In the eighth grade Boston classroom where Meira Levinson teaches, it has been striking to observe how the presence of even one student from a minority group can over time alter other students' attitudes toward that group. In one notable discussion, students' diatribes against the house calls made by Jehovah's Witnesses were brought to a screeching halt when they discovered that one of the most popular boys in the class was a Jehovah's Witness. Although the initial change in the tenor of the discussion was undoubtedly due to students' feeling the need to *show* respect rather than their actually *feeling* more respect, students also then started paying attention to an explanation about *why* Jehovah's Witnesses proselytized door-to-door — an explanation which they had totally ignored (although it had been brought up by the teacher) earlier in the conversation. Increases in mutual respect have also been brought about by critical confrontation in the classroom. For example, in another class, another student commented that the Chinese ate rats[22] and turned to the sole Asian student in the classroom for confirmation. When informed that she was Vietnamese, not Chinese, he responded, "Vietnamese, Chinese, whatever" — but was none too pleased a second later to hear the teacher comment, "Yeah, Dominican, Haitian, Puerto Rican, whatever." This led to a series of discussions about history (Asian, American, Caribbean, Latin American), stereotypes, prejudice, cultural differences, and (of course) eating habits, among other topics, and has noticeably increased some students' toleration of and understanding of each other, although there is still a long way to go. Furthermore, it has been blindingly clear that this author's students in a highly integrated Boston middle school are much more wordly and tolerant than her students were in an all–African American middle school in Atlanta, largely because of the relative limitedness of the latter's experience with Others.

Such anecdotal offerings are bolstered by some social scientists, such as those relied on by the University of Michigan, and in turn a federal district court, when defending the University's racial- and ethnic-preference programs against Fourteenth Amendment attack. Patricia Y. Gurin, a professor of psychology at the university, prepared a report that found that "[s]tudents . . . are better prepared to become active participants in our pluralistic,

---

22. Which is, in fact, true of at least some Chinese; see, e.g., Peter Hessler, "A Rat in My Soup," *The New Yorker,* 24 July 2000, at 38–41. However, the student's assertion was not made by way of pointing to the remarkable culinary differences among cultures but, rather, as a sign of the true "Otherness" of all Chinese.

democratic society once they leave" what the Court described as "a racially and ethnically diverse student body."[23] The judge also quoted Professor Gurin's finding that such students were also "better able to appreciate the common values and integrative forces that harness differences in pursuit of common ground."[24]

In addition to diversity's civic accomplishments, student (and sometimes teacher) diversity is also lauded for enabling individual students to develop their capacities for autonomy. This is a distinct educational goal from students' development of civic toleration and respect — although as many people have pointed out (including each of us in other contexts), probably not a distinct pedagogical process; while the goals may be logically separable, their achievement or failure seem not to be separable in practice.[25] The aim of helping students develop their autonomy, however, is a distinct justification for maintaining diverse, "common" schools. As children encounter peers and teachers who do and believe different things from themselves, and as they discuss, compare, and debate their own ways of life with others, children necessarily move from accepting their lives simply as unexamined givens to some version of an examined life. Indeed, in explaining his own intellectual development (including developing into a highly self-conscious intellectual), Sanford Levinson gives far greater weight to his friends and his intense discussions with them than to the formal courses taken at Hendersonville High School. And this is not meant as a particular knock at that particular high school; one suspects that many persons could offer similar autobiographical anecdotes even if they attended far more urbane institutions of secondary education.

The material offered by Professor Gurin (and the University of Michigan) is relevant to this strand of the argument as well. She reports that multiple sources of data demonstrate that "[s]tudents who experienced the most racial and ethnic diversity in classroom settings and in informal interactions

23. *Gratz v. Bollinger,* 122 F. Supp. 2d 811, 822 (2000), citing the Gurin report at 3. It should be obvious that this decision patently conflicts with Judge Friedman's decision several months later in *Grutter v. Bollinger,* 137 F. Supp. 2d 821 (2001). Presumably, the Sixth Circuit Court of Appeals will choose between them (and then, inevitably, the Supreme Court will be given an opportunity to weigh in). See the afterword to chapter 1.

24. Id., quoting the Gurin report, at 5.

25. Meira Levinson, *The Demands of Liberal Education* 101–6 (1999); Amy Gutmann, "Civic Education and Social Diversity," 105/3 *Ethics* 516–34 (1995); Harry Brighouse, "Is There Any Such Thing As Political Liberalism?" 75 *Pacific Philosophical Quarterly* 318–32 (1994); Eamonn Callan, *Creating Citizens* 39–42 (1997).

with peers showed the greatest engagement in active thinking processes, growth in intellectual engagement and motivation, and growth in intellectual and academic skills." They are also described as especially able to "understand and consider multiple perspectives [and] deal with the conflicts that different perspectives sometimes create."[26] Diversity thus seems an altogether winning policy, insofar as it led Gurin to conclude that on average, students who attend more diverse institutions exhibit a greater "intellectual engagement and motivation index" and a greater "citizenship engagement index."[27] In addition, an amicus brief by the United States cited "a study by Alexander Astin, Director of the Higher Education Research Institute at the University of California, in which Astin associates diversity with increased satisfaction in most areas of the college experience and an increased commitment to promoting racial understanding and participation in cultural activities, leadership, and citizenship."[28] One could, no doubt, find empirical studies of primary and secondary schools that reach similar conclusions, though, equally without doubt, one could raise all sorts of methodological questions about the ways in which one could actually test with confidence for the qualities allegedly causally linked with diversity.

In sum, diversity in schools is thought (and was historically thought) to be both civic-promoting and autonomy-promoting. Schools with diverse student bodies serve both the community, by promoting the civic virtues of toleration and respect for others, and the individual, by enabling students' development of autonomy through interaction with students who are different. As a result, for both toleration-promoting (civic) and autonomy-promoting (individualistic) reasons, "common schools" with diverse student bodies should be maintained, protected, and further developed, and school diversity should be taken into consideration when examining and evaluating school voucher programs or other school assignment options.

To say that diversity matters, of course, is to leave many questions unanswered. The most obvious is, what kinds of diversity matter? The importance of racial and ethnic diversity is what is being defended in the Michigan (and earlier University of Texas Law School) case, just as gender diversity is assumed insofar as in America (although, notably, not in Great Britain and many other countries), virtually all public schools are coeducational. For both civic and autonomy-promoting reasons, however, it would seem that

26. *Gratz v. Bollinger,* at 822, citing the Gurin report, at 5.
27. Id.
28. Id., citing Brief for the United States, at 20–21.

religious diversity would be at least as highly desirable. In the next section, therefore, we will examine two questions: (1) Should our measurement of diversity include religious diversity, and if so, what are the implications for both public and private schools? and (2) Do diversity arguments support or undermine vouchers for religious schools?

"Getting Religion"

Should our measurement of student diversity include religious diversity? On civic toleration grounds, the answer *must* be yes. In the United States, there is considerable mutual suspicion between and among conservative Christians, secularist cosmopolitans, liberal and Orthodox Jews,[29] atheists, Muslims, Mormons, Wiccans, members of the Nation of Islam, and Scientologists, to name only a few of the relevant groups. Whether or not it is accurate to describe Americans as involved in a "culture war,"[30] it is hard to believe that sustained, respectful interaction among members of different religious groups would be not be beneficial to American society. In order to promote the development of a mutually tolerant and respectful civil society, therefore, it would seem that schools should have a student body that is religiously diverse (as well as diverse along other dimensions). Indeed, immediately after university presidents Bowen and Bok speak of the importance of "greater 'cultural awareness across racial lines . . .' and stronger commitments to improving racial understandings," they go on to write as well of the "importance of differences in religion."[31] If schools are successful in their efforts to "get religion" in the sense of encouraging attendance by religious students, then their classmates might be considerably more likely to "get religion" at least in the sense of realizing that people holding even exceedingly odd religious views are nonetheless members of the same overarching community.

On autonomy-promoting grounds, it would also seem obvious that children would be well served by going to school with other children from a

29. Whose suspicions of each other is, one suspects, easily as great as any suspicion directed at Jews from outside these communities.

30. Compare, for example, James Davidson Hunter, *Culture Wars* (1991) and *Before the Shooting Begins: Searching for Democracy in America's Culture War* (1994) with Alan Wolfe's considerably more optimistic assessment in *One Nation after All: What Middle-Class Americans Really Think about God, Country, Family, Racism, Welfare, Immigration, Homosexuality, Work, the Right, the Left, and Each Other* (1998).

31. Bowen and Bok, at 228.

variety of religious backgrounds and genuinely engaging with them in respectful discussion about the ways and reasons their lives are different. Although cultural coherence arguments have some play here — we shouldn't rock a child's foundations before those foundations are even in place — certainly by middle school students should be exposed to practitioners of a variety of religious beliefs if the aim is to help them both to recognize the reasonableness of other beliefs and ways of life and critically examine their own beliefs and practices in service of developing their autonomy. This seems to be especially true for religious diversity, because at least most religions are explicitly about belief, unlike race, social class, gender, and the like. While racial diversity, for example, clearly serves civic toleration ends, it less obviously directly promotes autonomy, insofar as white students cannot choose to become black, for example, and even the questioning of one's assumptions that is the hallmark of autonomy would depend in this case on the questionable assumption itself that racial diversity necessarily implies belief diversity. Religious diversity thus not only promotes children's development of autonomy, but may be superior to other types of diversity in doing so.

This assumption that students' interaction with others will lead to engagement with others (and Otherness) is buttressed by University of Chicago law professor Emily Buss. As she notes in a recent article (and as any parent or, indeed, middle-school teacher knows without needing to read academic tomes), adolescents often withdraw in one measure or another from the intensity of the domestic setting and develop close friendships with peers, who are often those they meet at school. Citing a great deal of evidence from the literature of child development, Buss views such relationships as central to the formation by adolescents of what will, in time, become their mature adult identity. "[I]t is largely through these relationships that [adolescents] pursue the difficult and important task of identity formation — the sorting and selecting of values, beliefs, and tastes that will define their adult selves. Who those peers are and, particularly, the diversity of their convictions and attitudes, will have a significant effect on the course of that development."[32]

As a practical matter, this means that some religious children will be likely to be lured away from "home truths" because of the impact of their

32. Emily Buss, "The Adolescent's Stake in the Allocation of Educational Control Between Parent and State," 67 *Univ. Chi. L. Rev.* 1233 (2000).

more secular classmates; it also means, though, that the opposite may occur as well, that a Jewish child will in fact be persuaded that salvation requires acceptance of Jesus as her Savior or simply that a secular child raised in a relentlessly rationalistic household will develop a more "spiritual" posture toward the world than the parents might prefer. So what? It is hard to see how a liberal society can prefer, as an abstract matter, a shift from religious to secular identities, whatever might be the preferences of most people who call themselves liberals. And the fact that the various parents of the respective children might be unhappy about their "straying" from the parents' preferences is not an interest that a liberal society can regard as particularly significant. The primary goals of any such society are the reproduction of its basic commitments (i.e., to a defensible form of liberalism) in future generations and, at the same time, producing the conditions by which students can themselves become autonomous selves and not the mere reflections of their parents' desires as to how they should live their lives.[33]

If religious diversity in schools is important for promoting both civic virtue and individual autonomy, then adherents of either goal (liberal civic education or the development of an autonomous self) would have a strong incentive to oppose public vouchers for religious schools if it is true that they would serve both to increase the number of homogeneous schools and to lessen the degree of religious diversity in public schools. (Indeed, strong proponents of these goals should also oppose even private financing of religious schools, as one of us has demonstrated elsewhere,[34] but this is obviously a very controversial position. And, thanks to *Pierce v. Society of Sisters*,[35] it would also certainly violate currently accepted constitutional norms. In any event, our focus here is only on the advisability of religious school vouchers and similar aid, and not on the legitimacy of religious schools themselves.)

It is to be expected that most religious schools explicitly promote religious segregation. To take the easiest case, a Seventh-Day Adventist or fundamentalist school that is run by and uses curricula supplied by the parent church or like-minded coreligionists is unlikely, as an empirical matter, to attract students from different religious backgrounds, even assuming that the schools in fact have space remaining after serving their primary

33. These arguments are spelled out in Meira Levinson, *The Demands of Liberal Education*, supra note 25, chs. 1 and 2.
34. Id. at 144–45. See also chapter 2 of this volume.
35. 268 U.S. 510 (1925).

constituency of fellow members of the given church. The same is true for a yeshiva or, indeed, Jewish day school. We are aware of a very prominent legal academic, an evangelical Christian, who, having sent his child to a Jewish Day School because he admired its pedagogy and emphasis on values, was told that the child would not be welcome to continue his education there because it was, after all, a *Jewish* day school and the child was obviously not Jewish. (One doesn't know if the school was a bit worried that the child, as an evangelical, would engage in a witnessing of the Good News of Jesus's Messiahship, though we have never detected a propensity on the part of the father to try to convert his Jewish friends, of whom one of us is one.) Catholic schools, interestingly enough, seem quite receptive to non-Catholic students, though it would also be surprising if there were no significant selection biases held by parents who choose to send their children to such schools. (How often do atheist or even agnostic parents choose a Catholic education for their children?)

In addition to segregating by religion students who choose to attend such a school, religious schools also function to promote religious segregation in the public and nonsectarian private schools they leave behind. This is because of the "cream-off effect" mentioned at the opening of our paper. As religious students make use of school vouchers to attend religious schools, fewer religious students will remain back in the public schools, thus reducing religious diversity in these public schools. (Presumably some students using already-available vouchers at nonsectarian private schools would also choose to switch to religious schools once vouchers became available, so the argument would apply to some extent to private schools as well.) This assumes, of course, that a greater proportion of religious students than nonreligious students would choose to avail themselves of vouchers to attend religious schools, but this assumption does not seem unreasonable. This is therefore an additional diversity-based (and ultimately civic and/or autonomy-based) argument against religious school vouchers.

The same grounds that initially seem to mandate against religious school vouchers, however, also mandate in favor of new, positive, religious-diversity promotion policies in the public schools. Religious diversity should be taken into account along with racial, ethnic, socioeconomic, and gender diversity. A heavy-handed program would be to assign students to schools in a way that promotes religious diversity, via altering catchment areas and bus routes.[36] But a less heavy-handed and more realistic policy could establish schools that act as religious "magnets" to draw religious minorities voluntarily into otherwise religiously homogeneous schools. One "magnet" draw could be an adjusted school schedule that satisfies local board requirements but has longer days on Mondays through Thursdays and half-day Fridays, or plays only Thursday-night football games, or takes off Rosh Hashanah, Eid Fitr, Epiphany, or the Chinese New Year as official school holidays in exchange for extending slightly longer into the summer. Another approach would be to have a vegetarian cafeteria that is compliant with Jewish, Muslim, Buddhist, Jain, or Hindu dietary practices. Both of these strategies are entirely structural and would have no appreciable affect on the curriculum, but could significantly increase the religious diversity of the student body. This could be true as well of a third accommodation, which would be to allow "moments of silent reflection" or the installation of chapels into which, for example, Muslim students could go to say those of their five daily prayers that occur during school hours.[37] These would, presumably, alleviate at least some expressed concerns that schools are hostile to even the most minimal expression of religious commitments.[38]

A third strategy that does have curricular implications, but ones that seem quite minor, would be to broaden or change foreign language offerings at the middle or high school level to include Hebrew, Arabic, Japanese, Hindi, etc., depending on the local population. This approach again might

36. Besides being heavy-handed, one might also be tempted to describe it as unconstitutional. If, though, racial preferences, which are presumptively unconstitutional, can nonetheless be justified because of the "compelling interest" of diversity, as many of their proponents allege, then it would seem that an identical argument would legitimize the otherwise prohibited taking into account of religion when designing catchment areas. See chapter 1; see also Eugene Volokh, "Diversity, Race as Proxy, and Religion as Proxy," 43 *UCLA L. Rev.* 2059, 2070–76 (1996).

37. See Jodi Wilgoren, "On Campus and on Knees, Facing Mecca," *New York Times,* 13 February 2001, at 1 (late edition—final), which describes efforts that MIT has made with regard to the increasing number of Muslims on its campus. Indeed, it turns out that the University of Texas Law School, unlike MIT a decidedly state institution, has reserved a room within its library that serves as a chapel for students who wish to make use of it.

38. They also need not be seen as coercing other students into religion. In Meira Levinson's experience in teaching in Atlanta, at least, where Georgia law mandates forty seconds of daily silent reflection, the time is often spent by middle schoolers trying to stop for silent reflection in the most absurd physical posture possible (in midstep, for example, balanced on one foot, or perched precariously on a desk) or by teachers' snapping repeatedly, "Quiet! Close your mouths! Silent reflection!" In what at other times felt like an emphatically religious (Christian) setting, especially for a public school, "silent reflection" never seemed to acquire any religious overtones.

attract a number of families who would otherwise either stay in a neighborhood school within a minority-religious enclave, or seek out private religious schools for their children. All of these strategies would have the instrumental goal of encouraging religious diversity on the grounds that it is at least as valuable in pursuing traditional liberal goals as racial and ethnic diversity, at least insofar as the grounds for that pursuit rest on civic-education or individual-autonomy justifications. (If they rely on rectification of past injustices, then the argument takes a decidedly different form, which, interestingly enough, has almost nothing to do with the merits of diversity per se.)

Balancing Diversities

The last section concluded that religious diversity matters and is desirable, and that educational policies, including those affecting the public schools, should be designed in order to promote religious diversity. Public schools should innovate in ways to attract minority religious families, but private religious schools should not be aided in attracting those or other religious families to them, as vouchers would presumably do. The normative — even if not the constitutional — policy implications seemed pretty clear. But of course, nothing about public education policies is ever quick or easy, especially when it comes to student assignments. There were (at least) two glaring omissions in the previous section that we need now to include in our analysis. First, religious diversity is not the only desirable kind of diversity to pursue and achieve in a school community. And second, as was implied in the first section, diversity is only a means, and not even a sufficient means, to two ends: children's development of civic virtue and their development of autonomy. What are the implications of these points in practice? We will take these objections in reverse order, beginning with the recognition that diversity is not and should not be treated as an end in itself.

An extremely diverse school may, whether because its academic programs are substandard, its school culture mean-spirited, or its discipline lousy, get nowhere in promoting the development of mutual civic respect or autonomy among its students. A mostly homogeneous school, on the other hand, may successfully promote both goals because its academic programs are strong, discipline problems do not interfere with student learning, and it promotes a school culture that encourages mutual respect, critical thinking, and interaction with a diverse range of people via community service learning projects, field trips, after school programs, or Internet projects. If two of the central goals of public education, therefore, are promoting students' development of civic virtue and autonomy, then more than the potential for diversity must be taken into account when evaluating types of schools for inclusion in voucher programs. If private religious schools have better discipline and academics than public schools in the same area, then a well-designed voucher program that includes religious as well as nonsectarian private schools might be desirable.

This is especially true considering that nonsectarian schools comprise only 22 percent of the private schools in the United States.[39] To restrict school vouchers to nonsectarian schools, therefore, is automatically to exclude *78 percent* of private schools in the United States. If there is any reason to favor school vouchers, this should give us pause; no matter whether vouchers are desirable for egalitarian, libertarian, procompetitive "antimonopolistic," academic, or civic reasons, the automatic exclusion of over three-quarters of American private schools without regard to their curriculum, student body, aims and objectives, academic quality, or level of innovation ought to raise eyebrows. This gains further purchase when one considers the practical implementation of vouchers. With approximately 27,400 private schools serving almost 6 million students,[40] as compared to approximately 90,000 public schools serving over 47 million students, the private sector is already too small to absorb students participating in a large-scale voucher program. To limit vouchers to the 6,025 nonsectarian private schools that existed in 1997–98,[41] plus those that would spring up in response to demand — and how academically, pedagogically, and civically sound could we trust them to be in their first few years of existence, when schools are always struggling to define and establish themselves? — would be to invalidate the effectiveness of vouchers in providing a real range of worthwhile choices for parents before we even started.

It is also worth noting that neither Friends schools nor Episcopal schools

39. U.S. Department of Education, National Center for Education Statistics, *Private Schools Universe Study, 1997–98* 1–2 (1999) (hereinafter *PSUS*).

40. According to the National Center for Education Statistics, there were 5,971,000 students in private schools and 47,244,000 in public schools in 1999, ⟨http://nces.ed.gov/fastfacts⟩. The numbers of schools — 89,508 public and 27,402 private — are as of the 1997–98 Digest of Education Statistics (1999), ch. 2, ⟨http://nces.edu.gov⟩. The American School Directory, ASD.com, states that there are 108,000 public schools, which is, of course, a considerably higher number than that provided by the NCES.

41. *PSUS,* table 1, at 3.

generally even take religious affiliation into account in their student selection process, and also do not rate it as their most important goal. In 1993–94, 0 percent of Friends elementary schools and 2.6 percent of Episcopal elementary schools[42] (compared with 5 and 1.9 percent of Friends and Episcopal high schools, respectively[43]) included religious affiliation as an admission requirement at all. Reflecting this apparent lack of religious focus, only 1.6 percent of Episcopal schools and 11.6 percent of Friends schools rated "religious development" as their most important educational goal,[44] and well under half of these schools rated it as even one of their three most important educational goals.[45] Given that most of these schools thus neither select students according to religious affiliation nor emphasize religious belief within the curriculum, it would be fair to surmise that many Friends and Episcopal religious schools, at least, might exhibit significant religious diversity.

Even among more religiously oriented and restrictive religious schools, though, religious diversity may be the only type of diversity that is reliably lower in religious schools than in other private or public schools. Let us examine, for example, racial diversity. In terms of raw percentages, Catholic and nonsectarian schools have virtually identical racial minority enrollment — 23.4 percent and 23.3 percent, respectively — based on data from the 1997–98 school year. Only 18.8 percent of students in other religious schools (conservative Christian, affiliated, and unaffiliated) are minorities, but it is worth noting that only 19.9 percent of students in regular education nonsectarian schools are minorities; it is only because 27.1 percent of students in private special education and a whopping 38.3 percent of students in nonsectarian special education schools are minorities that nonsectarian schools as a whole achieve the 23.3 percent minority enrollment mark.[46] By way of comparison, in 1997–98, the public school system, nationally, was 36.5 percent minority.[47]

---

42. U.S. Department of Education, National Center for Education Statistics, *Private Schools in the United States: A Statistical Profile 1993–94* (2000), table 2.3a.

43. Id. at table 2.3b.

44. Id. at table 4.1.

45. Id. at table 4.2.

46. *PSUS*, table 16, at 21.

47. Digest of Education Statistics, 1999, table 45: Enrollment in Public Elementary and Secondary Schools, by Race or Ethnicity and State: Fall 1996 and Fall 1997 (http://nces.ed.gov/pubsearch).

This table offers interesting insights about American demography when it breaks down the percentages by states. Consider, for example, the beginning and end of the alphabet, Alabama

This is, of course, an almost meaningless data point given the vast demographic differences not only among given school districts but also at times within a given school system itself. Almost a half-century after *Brown v. Board of Education,* many school systems continue to look like checkerboards with identifiably "white" and "minority" schools,[48] underscoring the point that many researchers have made that more important than raw demographic percentages is the actual distribution of different groups within a system or a school.[49] If we compare the percentage of Catholic, other religious, and regular private nonsectarian schools (which seems the most appropriate comparison, since almost all religious schools offer a regular education program[50]) in which minority students make up 10 to 49 percent of the student body, therefore, we find that 27.7 percent of Catholic schools, 26 percent of other religious schools, and 44.9 percent of regular nonsectarian private schools are racially integrated by this measure.[51] By comparison, 33.4 percent of public schools in 1993–94 were similarly racially integrated (11 to 50 percent minority).[52] Thus, nonsectarian private schools are far ahead of public schools in promoting racial diversity, and religious private schools are not too far behind.

These statistics are inevitably fairly crude, and many religious schools

---

and Wyoming. In fall 1997, Alabama's public schools were 61.7 percent white and 36 percent black, together with 0.8 percent Hispanic, 0.7 percent Asian or Pacific Islander, and 0.8 percent American Indian; Wyoming, on the other hand, was 88.6 percent white, and the largest minority groups were Hispanics (6.6 percent) and American Indians (2.95 percent). Blacks accounted for only 1.1 percent of the enrollment. Texas was 45 percent white, 37.9 percent Hispanic, 14.4 percent black, 2.4 percent Asian, and 0.3 percent American Indian, while Massachusetts was 77.5 percent white, 9.7 percent Hispanic, 8.5 percent black, 4.1 percent Asian, and 0.2 percent American Indian. Perhaps most striking is California, where Hispanics in 1997 comprised 40.5 percent of all students and whites 38.8 percent; Asian/Pacific Islanders were 11.1 percent of the total, blacks, 2.5 percent, and American Indians 0.9 percent.

48. See, e.g., James Patterson, Brown v. Board of Education: *A Civil Rights Milestone and Its Troubled Legacy* 212 (2001).

49. Jay Greene, "Why School Choice Can Promote Integration," *Education Week* (12 April 2000), at 72 (also available at ⟨http://www.edweek.org/ew/ewstory.cfm?slug=31greene.h19⟩); Jay Greene, "Civic Values in Public and Private Schools," in *Learning from School Choice* (Paul E. Peterson and Bryan C. Hassel, eds., 1998); Sue Ellen Henry and Abe Feuerstein, " 'Now We Go to Their School': Desegregation and Its Contemporary Legacy," 68/2 *J. of Negro Education* 164–81 (spring 1999).

50. *PSUS,* table 8, at 12.

51. *PSUS,* table 17, at 22.

52. *Private Schools in the United States,* supra note 42, at table 2.6.

will predictably not satisfy these criteria for racial diversity. In 1993–94, Jewish schools were 98 percent white overall,[53] and fully 78 percent of Hebrew day schools had *no* minority enrollment.[54] (Solomon Schechter schools were better, insofar as only 41.5 percent had no minority enrollment, but 95 percent had less than 10 percent minority enrollment, as did 90 percent of other Jewish schools.) Other religious schools are also likely to be less diverse than the above statistics suggest: AME schools are likely all black, and nearly half of evangelical Lutheran schools are more than 50 percent minority. Nonevangelical Lutheran schools, too, are overall at least 85 to 95 percent white.[55] In addition, some types of religious schools are likely to be socioeconomically homogeneous: Episcopal schools are likely, save for relatively few scholarship students, to be predominantly middle, if not indeed upper-middle, class; and many small, nonmainstream Protestant schools may be working-class.

It should be obvious, though, that this latter concern about demographic segregation is scarcely limited to private sector schools or even to religious schools within the private sector. Military schools are, we suspect, quite unlikely to draw many poor students, and, almost by definition, they draw only such students whose parents believe in the virtues of military discipline. The same, of course, could be said of "progressive schools." Not only do schools like Dalton in New York City or Shady Hill in Cambridge, Massachusetts, cost far, far more than most non-well-off families could possibly afford; they also tempt only parents who in fact agree with the particular pedagogic (and ideological) doctrines linked with them. This means that the extent of actual "mingling" may be quite limited.[56] Although most self-

---

53. Id. at table 2.5.

54. Id. at table 2.6.

55. Id. at table 2.6.

56. It would be interesting to find out how many Dalton or Shady Hill children, in "mock elections" in 2000, voted for George W. Bush, given that such student votes are a fairly reliable proxy for the views they pick up at home. Meira Levinson can report that only 1 of her 24 students (and only 19 out of 730 students in the school overall) voted for Bush, with the remainder voting overwhelmingly for Al Gore. This presumably reflects the dominantly working-class composition of the school at which she teaches, given that Bush managed to get approximately 20 percent of the Boston vote and, within the state as a whole, approximately 30 percent. See ⟨http://www.state.ma.us/sec/ele/eleidx.htm⟩, which is the entrypoint for the web page of the Massachusetts Secretary of State and the relevant election statistics for the year 2000. In any event, few of her students have ever encountered other children who actually support (or reflect

styled "progressive" schools, no doubt, explicitly set themselves up to foster and respond to diversity, there is no reason to believe that they attract a particularly diverse clientele. If actually having "representatives" of diverse groups in the classroom is as important as suggested by, say, the University of Michigan, as distinguished from presenting materials *about* such groups, then we suspect that most progressive schools are little better than, say, a Southern Baptist religious academy. There is no evidence, for example, that racial minorities (or the poor more generally) are eager to place their children in progressive schools as against schools that emphasize traditional programs, including emphasis on the "three *Rs*" and discipline. Moreover, one doubts that many parents with strong religious viewpoints are particularly attracted to schools that are likely dominated by teachers and parents — and by verbally skilled children of these parents — with far more secular identities and viewpoints.

Many of these points could and should be made, of course, with regard to public schools as well. "Public" is not synonymous with "common." The first refers only to funding and, possibly, to overt state sponsorship; the second, on the other hand, directs our attention to a host of demographic issues having little direct connection to the source of funds. It is obvious that "neighborhood schools" have all sorts of selection biases insofar as American neighborhoods tend to discourage, as a practical matter, the maximalist "mingling" of populations. Most American neighborhoods are segregated at least by race and class, and neighborhood schools tend to reflect this segregation. Furthermore, to the extent that school districts have attempted to overcome residential segregation's affect on schools through busing, they often simply end up segregating the entire district form others, as the phenomenon of "white flight" — or its cousin "middle-class flight" — contributes to furthering the homogenization of the relevant school districts.

In recognition of this effect, and as a way of responding to increasing "market" pressures, many school districts have tried to make schools more diverse and attract families through voluntary mechanisms. Even these non-neighborhood schools may be little better, however, if they are organized along ideological or pedagogical lines that have predictable selection biases, which is true of many of these "magnet," "theme," "specialization," or

---

their parents' support) of the current occupant of the White House, as is evidenced by their frequent declarations that "nobody supports Bush." One assumes that there were schools elsewhere in the country (even if not in Massachusetts) where student opinion was equally unbalanced in favor of Governor Bush, leading to the impression that "everybody supports Bush."

"school-to-career" schools. To take one example, we mentioned private-market "progressive" schools a moment ago. Some public school systems, including Cambridge, Massachusetts, have taken to offering similarly "progressive" schools as an alternative, presumably, to more traditionally organized institutions. (One hesitates to call them "unprogressive.") At least anecdotal evidence suggests that white, upper-middle-class, academically oriented parents, many of them Cantabridgians connected with Harvard or MIT, now consider these public schools to be among the best elementary and middle schools in the community. More to the point, they may even be willing to contemplate sending their children to such public schools rather than, as had been usual, to one or another of the private-market schools that, as a practical matter, had been the standard destination of most such children. That is the good news. The bad news, though, is that the same anecdotalists report that every year these schools get fewer applications from minority and poor families, despite the "controlled choice" system that guarantees all children an equal chance of getting in. Rightly or wrongly, these latter parents prefer a different style of education for their children. Similarly, it should be obvious that an Afrocentric school sponsored by a public school system, even if formally open to any student in the district, is spectacularly unlikely to get more than a handful (if that) of non–African American students.

What these statistics and the civic and personal goals that diversity is supposed to help satisfy may suggest, then, is that receipt of public funds — in the form of direct funding of public schools, or vouchers for private schools — should be contingent either on satisfying certain diversity criteria or on adopting strategies to increase diversity at the school. In the case of public schools, therefore, schools and districts might adopt the religious "magnet" programs discussed above as a way of increasing their religious diversity, while also continuing — or, more accurately, reviving the pursuit of — racial, ethnic, socioeconomic, and other forms of diversity. Private — both religious and nonsectarian — schools that wished to receive public vouchers would need to prove they were already sufficiently diverse (and the meaning of this would obviously need to be debated and clarified in practice), or that they were taking practical, measurable steps to make themselves more so. Some schools would choose to comply; others wouldn't and therefore would not receive vouchers. And interestingly, as the data above suggests, some religious schools are more likely to be in compliance than some nonsectarian private schools.

It is worth noting that these arguments strongly weigh against any support of home-schooling. Almost by definition, home-schooling works against the kinds of diversity that we, with many others, deem important. It is, obviously, not at all the case that specific home-schooling parents might not be extremely sensitive to the kinds of concerns we are emphasizing and would, therefore, make special efforts to introduce their children to a wide array of people. But we are, to put it mildly, wary either of believing that there will be many such parents or, more important, of accepting as desirable a mode of education that limits the amount of contact that children will have with others during the "schooling" process itself. As several of our earlier anecdotes suggested, the presence of other children can be vital to appreciation of the dangers of facile stereotyping. It may be, for libertarian reasons, that parents should retain, legally, the right to home-school their children. But any such decisions should receive no affirmative public support that might, indeed, serve as an incentive for yet other parents to choose that path.

Note well, though, that the major reason to reject public subsidies for home-schooling must be the acceptance of some version of our argument about the desirability of diversity and its importance with regard both to civic education and development of an autonomous self. If education were merely instrumental, dealing, say, with the acquisition of certain knowledge capable of being tested for on standard examinations, then it is altogether possible that many home-schooled children could do just fine. Indeed, supporters of home-schooling point, with justifiable pride, to the academic success of many home-schooled children, though we have no good evidence about how representative these children are of the entire universe of home-schooled students. Interestingly enough, the voucher proposal that was submitted, and handily rejected by, the California electorate in 2000 included the possibility that home-schooling parents would be entitled to receive public funds to purchase school supplies and the like. That feature itself justified a vote against the proposal, even if someone accepting our overall argument could quite properly support at least some proposals for vouchers or other state aid to a wide variety of non-public, including religious, schools.

Conclusion

These arguments have not been balanced against other norms relevant to vouchers, such as equity or efficiency (and especially not legality). We would not argue, therefore, that our conclusions about the desirability of promoting religious diversity in public and private schools are definitive insofar as other public goals and goods may lead to other public policies that trump the ones we have put forward here. It is, nonetheless, worth emphasizing the significance — and possible counterintuitiveness — of our conclusions about the importance of religious diversity for both public and private school policy. Proceeding from explicitly liberal assumptions about the desirability of promoting children's development of civic toleration and individual autonomy, we demonstrated that many religious schools may actually be *more* deserving of vouchers that many nonsectarian private schools, and that public schools can and should do much more to attract minority religious students. Our school communities should be religiously inclusive in addition to being racially, ethnically, and socioeconomically diverse. It is not easy (and may not be possible, even with the institution of creative voluntary measures) to promote all of these at once, and we certainly wouldn't argue that we have provided any definitive guide to how to balance them. But it is a challenge worth taking on.

Afterword

Two recent cases are relevant to this essay, though neither changes the essential argument. The first is the decision of the Sixth Circuit Court of Appeals in the *Grutter* case arising from the University of Michigan Law School, which is discussed in note 10 of the present essay. The second, substantially more important, case is *Zelman v. Simmons-Harris*, which upheld the constitutionality of a school voucher program in Ohio. There is little doubt that *Zelman* "liberates" states (and the national government) to increase the level of aid to church-related schools, if they wish to do so and if that is made part of an otherwise "neutral" program that aids secular and church-related schools alike. The majority in *Zelman* deemed it irrelevant that 96 percent of the voucher recipients in that case attended church-related schools. The important thing was that that was by choice of the recipients, not the state, and that, in theory at least, they could have used the vouchers in secular schools had they wished to.

As a matter of fact, of course, vouchers remain extremely controversial politically, and there is no reason to believe that all states (or the national government) will rush to emulate the Ohio program. Moreover, a number of states have state constitutions that mandate a "stronger" separation of church and state than does the First Amendment, at least as construed by the current Supreme Court. Shortly after *Zelman,* for example, a state court in Florida struck down a voucher program on the ground that the Florida constitution prohibited any state funding of church-related education, even when occurring "indirectly" through vouchers. Governor Jeb Bush promised to appeal the decision.

It may be that the most important future litigation will concern not the constitutionality of voucher programs per se, an issued settled at least for the present by *Zelman,* but rather attacks on state constitutional prohibitions of aid on the ground that they constitute a denial of the "equal protection of the law" protected by the Fourteenth Amendment. The argument is that the distinction drawn by the state between aiding secular and religious schools is in fact forbidden discrimination. If one believes, as I certainly do, that it would be unconstitutional to offer aid only to church-related schools, then the obvious question is why it is not similarly unconstitutional to offer aid only to secular schools.[57] One answer, of course, is that the Constitution explicitly prohibits an "establishment of religion" in a way that it does prohibit an "establishment of secularism," but it takes no great effort to read the Equal Protection Clause, together with the free speech clause of the First Amendment, in ways that, at the very least, make this answer problematic and allow one to assert that, while the state need not aid private education at

57. As this book was about to go to press, the Supreme Court granted review of *Davey v. Locke,* a case involving a provision of the Washington State constitution that mandates that "[n]o public money or property shall be appropriated for or applied to any religious . . . instruction." The Washington State Supreme Court has interpreted this to forbid the grant by the state of college scholarships to otherwise eligible students who wish to pursue degrees in theology (as distinguished from students who wish to study about religion in, say, nonsectarian departments of religion, anthropology, or philosophy). One question is whether this constitutes an infringement of the religious believer's rights under the Free Exercise Clause of the First Amendment; another quite independent question is whether it might constitute a violation of the Equal Protection Clause inasmuch as it clearly differentiates between students enrolled in divinity schools, who wish to immerse themselves in the theology of their own religion, and students enrolled in religion departments, who wish to study religion from a more detached perspective. The case will be argued in the fall of 2003 and will, presumably, be decided by the United States Supreme Court in the spring of 2004. As with all legal arguments, there are "broad" and "narrow" approaches to the case, and it is possible that the Court will uphold the claim of the student in a way that has relatively little bearing on the issue of whether the state has a constitutional duty to fund parochial schools if it chooses to help fund, through vouchers or any other program, nonsectarian private schools. But it is equally possible that the Court might decide the case in a way that will resolve, for all intents and purposes, this latter question, whether affirmatively or negatively.

all, if it chooses to, it cannot differentiate between secular and religious schools.

A full consideration of this complex question would require another article. Suffice it for now to say that my current view is that the questions raised regarding both aid in general and the differentiation between public and church-related schools are matters for political resolution and that the Constitution does not speak with sufficient clarity to justify judges stepping in to offer their own solutions. Or, what is perhaps more to the point, I no longer view judges as having any special competence, derived either from their formal legal training or their experience in the world, to make decisions regarding such obviously controversial issues, a belief reinforced by the actual performance of the Court over the past thirty years. Almost no one, regardless of his or her place on the political-legal spectrum, believes that the Court during this period has offered a genuinely coherent approach with regard to aid to church-related schools. This may be, of course, because "the Court" is a fiction; it is actually composed of nine justices who may have quite different approaches to the issues presented in a given case. Thus the Court throughout this period has issued a series of 5–4 decisions in which the actual result turns on the often idiosyncratic views of the "ninth judge," whose vote is necessary to break the tie and provide a majority for a given outcome. And, as a matter of fact, there often have not been "majority opinions," indicating the agreement of five justices on a single analysis, but, rather, a number of different opinions that agree only on the specific outcome in the given case.

There is a potential contradiction in my view insofar as I would continue to support the Court's intervening to strike down a "religious-schools only" program of aid even as I would prefer that the Court accept as constitutional a "secular-schools-only" statute. The only real argument I can offer is that the Establishment Clause speaks more strongly with regard to the former than the Equal Protection Clause speaks to the latter.

4

Identifying the Jewish Lawyer:

Reflections on the Construction

of Professional Identity

Introduction: On the "Professional Project"

What follows might best be read as an extended meditation on the implications of personal participation in what I call the "professional project." I am interested in precisely what it might mean for one to adopt a "professional" identity as part of one's self-conception. This question should be of general theoretical interest to anyone interested in the phenomenon of professionalism in contemporary life. As Stephen Cohen has noted, "professions are potential communities; and, as such, they might serve as surrogates and replacements" for other kinds of communities.[1] Indeed, "some professions could conceivably rival ethnic and religious communities in many ways."[2]

I will be focusing primarily on the implications that membership in the legal profession has for one's identity as a Jew. Perhaps appropriately, this topic bridges my own professional and personal interests (and obsessions). I

This chapter was originally published in *Cardozo Law Review* 14 (1993): 1577. It was initially presented as the Pearl and Troy Feibel Lecture on Judaism and Law at Ohio State University, 1 March 1992.

1. Steven M. Cohen, *American Modernity and Jewish Identity* 84 (1983). Cohen generally argues that a strong Jewish identity has survived the entrance of American Jews into "American modernity." Id. See also Calvin Goldscheider, *Jewish Continuity and Change: Emerging Patterns in America* (1986). A far more pessimistic assessment can be found in Jerold S. Auerbach, *Rabbis and Lawyers: The Journey from Torah to Constitution* (1990) [hereinafter *Rabbis and Lawyers*]. A superb summary of Auerbach's thesis can be found in Jerold S. Auerbach, "Law and Lawyers," in *Jewish-American History and Culture: An Encyclopedia* 343, 343–47 (Jack Fischel and Sanford Pinsker, eds., 1992) [hereinafter "Law and Lawyers"].

2. Cohen, supra note 1, at 84.

am myself a lawyer and, more accurately, a legal academic. In these capacities, I have been teaching courses for almost a dozen years on "professional responsibility" and the "legal profession," in which questions of identity are at the forefront of my attention.

Lewis Coser made us aware many years ago of what he called "greedy institutions,"[3] which compete with other institutions and make insistent demands for the attentions and loyalties of their members. Part of this greed, of course, involves an effort to control the very ways that individuals conceptualize and present themselves to others in "everyday life."[4] Today we are reminded at almost every turn of the extent to which our identities are social constructions. Indeed, our psyches can be viewed as arenas of contention among competing institutions for primacy in forming a particular conception of the self. The self, from this perspective, is a "colonized" entity, representing the successful imperialistic conquest by one or another set of institutions over the basically vulnerable psyche.

Consider in this regard a comment by Monroe Freedman, which I highlight in the syllabus of my course on the legal profession. "It may be," says Freedman, "that the wisest course is to make each lawyer's conscience [or the teachings of one's religious tradition] his ultimate guide. It should be recognized, however, that this view is wholly inconsistent with *the notion of professional ethics, which, by definition, supersede personal ethics.*"[5] I think that Freedman captures one important aspect of (a particular version of) the professional project, what I call the "bleaching out"[6] of merely contingent aspects of the self, including the residue of particularistic socialization that we refer to as our "conscience." Contrast this with Thomas Shaffer's definition of religious "faithfulness" as meaning "that a lawyer imagines that she is first of all a believer," linked with a particular "community of the faithful," and is only "then a lawyer."[7] There is, I think, a chasm separating Freedman's and Shaffer's idealized conceptions of the lawyer's identity.

The triumph of what might be termed the standard version of the professional project would be, I believe, the creation, by virtue of professional education, of almost purely fungible members of the respective professional

3. See Lewis A. Coser, *Greedy Institutions: Patterns of Undivided Commitment* (1974).

4. See Erving Goffman, *The Presentation of Self in Everyday Life* (1959).

5. Monroe H. Freedman, "Professional Responsibility of the Criminal Defense Lawyer: The Three Hardest Questions," 64 *Mich. L. Rev.* 1469, 1482 n.26 (1966) (emphasis added).

6. Perhaps a Derridean would want to talk about the "erasure" of these aspects.

7. Thomas L. Shaffer, *American Lawyers and Their Communities* 198 (1991).

community. Such apparent aspects of the self as one's race, gender, religion, or ethnic background would become irrelevant to defining one's capacities as a lawyer.

A full discussion of all these aspects could well take a book of its own. My goals in this article are more modest. I want to initiate a discussion about the implications of the professional project by looking specifically at some of the problems that arise in identifying oneself (or in being identified)[8] as a "Jewish lawyer." I have already alluded to my personal interest in this topic.[9] That being said, it should be clear that the questions to be considered below can also arise if one is interested in determining what it might mean to be a "Christian lawyer";[10] indeed, one might substitute almost any similar adjective before the word "lawyer" and find oneself faced with similar problems of analysis. Still, I am most interested in the difficulties surrounding the notion of the "Jewish lawyer," and it is that topic that will take up the bulk of this Article.

SANDY KOUFAX AS A JEWISH PITCHER

Before turning to "Jewish lawyering," I want to set the stage for my inquiry into the complexities of professional identity by looking at a presumably quite different example of the intersection of religious and professional identity, Sandy Koufax. Many contemporary observers suggest that America's national pastime has become litigation, with lawyers at the center of the process. But there is, of course, another officially labeled national pastime — baseball — and it is with that activity, so important to the myths and symbols of American life and identity, that I wish to begin.

A famous episode in baseball history occurred on Wednesday, 6 October 1965, when the World Series opened in Minneapolis between the Los Angeles Dodgers and the Minnesota Twins. Pitching for the Dodgers that day normally would have been Sandy Koufax, the ace of the pitching staff who, while winning twenty-six games during the regular season, set a major league record for strike-outs. But 6 October 1965 was also Yom Kippur. Instead of digging his spikes into the pitching mound, "[t]he superstar of the

8. For a discussion of the difference it might make whether one looks to self-identification or ascription by others of the attribute of "being Jewish," see infra page 138.

9. Indeed, the question of Jewish identity was a distinct subtext of another publication of mine. See Sanford Levinson, *Constitutional Faith* 152–54 (1988).

10. See, e.g., Thomas L. Shaffer, *On Being a Christian and a Lawyer* (1981); see also Joseph Allegretti, "Christ and the Code: The Dilemma of the Christian Attorney," 34 *Cath. Law.* 131 (1988). One should also be aware of the journal *The Christian Lawyer*, which regularly includes articles such as Joel Nederhood, "Doing Christian Law," 3 *Christian Law.* 3 (1971).

Los Angeles pitching staff," the *New York Times* told us, "was in his hotel room in St. Paul observing Yom Kippur, the most solemn occasion of the Jewish year."[11]

This was not completely unprecedented. After Koufax won the decisive seventh game with only three days' rest, a "man in the news" column noted that "Koufax has never pitched on the holiday."[12] Moreover, an earlier "legendary moment" in American sports involved another baseball great, Hank Greenberg, who, after publicly anguishing about playing a key game for the Detroit Tigers on Rosh Hashanah (which he did, hitting two home runs), did not play a game that fell on Yom Kippur.[13] But no other day off

11. Joseph Durso, "Twins Turn Back Dodgers, 8 to 2, as Series Opens," *New York Times* (international edition), 7 October 1965, at 1.

12. "Master of the Mound Sanford Koufax," *New York Times*, 15 October 1965, at 45. See also Sandy Koufax, *Koufax* 258 (1966), where he writes that his refusal to pitch on Yom Kippur

> was played all out of proportion. I had tried to deflect questions about my intentions through the last couple of weeks of the season by saying that I was praying for rain. There was never any decision to make, though, because there was never any possibility that I would pitch.
>
> Yom Kippur is the holiest day of the Jewish religion. The club knows that I don't work that day.

13. Hank Greenberg described the episodes in Lawrence S. Ritter, *The Glory of Their Times: The Story of the Early Days of Baseball Told by the Men Who Played It* 330 (1984). Greenberg recounted the following:

> I realize now, more than I used to, how important a part I played in the lives of a generation of Jewish kids who grew up in the thirties. I never thought about it then. But in recent years, men I meet often tell me how much I meant to them when they were growing up. It's almost the first thing a lot of them say to me. . . .
>
> They all remember that I didn't play on Yom Kippur, the Jewish holiday. They remember it as every year, but in fact the situation arose only once, in 1934. Both Rosh Hashanah and Yom Kippur came in September that year, and since we were in the thick of the pennant race, the first for Detroit in many years, it became a national issue whether or not I should play on those days. The press made a big thing out of it.
>
> The question was put before Detroit's leading rabbi, Rabbi Leo Franklin. He consulted the Talmud, a basic source for Jewish morality, and announced that I could play on Rosh Hashanah, the Jewish New Year, because that was a happy occasion on which Jews used to play ball in the streets long ago. However, I could not play on Yom Kippur, the Day of Atonement, because that day should be spent in prayer.
>
> So I played on Rosh Hashanah and, believe it or not, I hit two home runs. . . .

Jerold Auerbach wrote of Greenberg's status as "a legendary figure to an entire generation of Jewish youngsters and their parents. . . . The Rosh Hashana episode . . . was periodically recounted, always with pride, as part of family oral tradition." Jerold Auerbach, "How Hank Greenberg Solved Pennant-Holy Day Dilemma," *Jewish Advocate*, 19 October 1989. Greenberg is also discussed at length in Peter Levine, *Ellis Island to Ebbets Field: Sport and the Jewish American Experience* 131–43 (1992).

could ever match the impact of the first game of the World Series, especially for members of the Jewish community. Over a third of a century later, Koufax's gesture remains embedded in Jewish memory.[14] I strongly suspect that it provided the basis for many Friday night sermons in Reform temples and Conservative synagogues across the land presenting Koufax as a role model for the young (and perhaps the old as well) for his unwillingness to subordinate entirely his identity as a Jew to the demands placed upon him by his role as a professional baseball player, even at such a moment as the World Series.

Sandy Koufax presented himself as a Jewish pitcher (just as the earlier Hank Greenberg had presented himself as a Jewish batter) in at least one important sense; namely, he recognized that an overarching obligation derived from his status as a Jew could, even in circumstances so weighty as the World Series, abrogate his "civilian" identity as a key member of the Los Angeles Dodgers with obligations to his teammates. If the *Times* is to be believed, though Koufax apparently did not attend services on Yom Kippur,[15] he nonetheless attended to his obligation to do no work and, perhaps, to fast and, more important, to contemplate the nature of one's life.

There obviously were many Jewish baseball players (as well as participants in other sports) before Koufax. I am sure that I am not the only bar mitzvah boy to receive books on Jewish athletes. I think it is safe to say that the message of all such books was straightforwardly assimilationist.[16] That is, persons named Greenberg, Rosen, Rosenblum, and Luckman could par-

14. I offer as evidence many conversations during the preparation of this article, as well as the report by a colleague who taught Harvard undergraduates that his Jewish students, who had, of course, not been alive in 1965, readily "remembered" Koufax's refusal to pitch.

15. Greenberg, however, "spent the entire day at Detroit's Shaarey Zedek synagogue." Levine, supra note 13, at 135.

16. Monroe Price, the former dean of Benjamin N. Cardozo School of Law, offers his own reminiscences of such books in Monroe E. Price, "Text and Intellect," 33 *Buff. L. Rev.* 562, 565 (1984). Price writes as follows:

I recall receiving, when I was young, a book called The Jew in American Sports. [Harold U. Ribalow, *The Jew in American Sports* (1963).] It was a wonderful book, with pictures of Sandy Koufax and Hank Greenberg, boxers, and baseball players. There were little descriptions of each athlete and the particular positions he played or the fights in which he had engaged. That was enough to be identity building—the notion that Jews could, in fact, be athletes, that they could use that route for advancement or for distinction. There was no suggestion then that their experience as Jews had an impact on their athletic endeavors (footnote omitted).

ticipate as equals on the playing fields or in the boxing rings. To put it mildly, what made them Jews was never discussed at any length. The point was that being Jewish really "didn't matter" in terms of one's ability to participate in key American rituals. "Merit," defined in terms entirely independent of anything having to do with being Jewish, would not be denied.[17] At one level, this is obviously true of Sandy Koufax. Yet his story, at least as I am telling it, is somewhat different. On Yom Kippur, his religion most definitely did matter in a way that went to the very heart of his role as the stalwart of Los Angeles's pitching staff.

It is crucial to recognize the limited nature of Koufax's status as a Jewish pitcher. That identity comes from his refusal to pitch on Yom Kippur. Yet what about those days he did pitch? Could anyone looking at his behavior as a pitcher — the choice of pitches, his particular pitching "style" — argue that this had anything to do with his being Jewish?

One does not want to rule out the category of national or ethnic "styles" of play too quickly. During the Olympic games, we are often reminded that there may be distinctive Italian, as opposed to Canadian or even French, styles in skiing and other major Olympic sports, and aficionados of American basketball can often be heard arguing about the effects that racial and ethnic backgrounds have on one's ability to play the game. Indeed, anyone with a sociological temperament will be interested in how the performance of any particular role, whether it be athlete, lawyer, musician, or physicist, might be affected by the social group from which a given person emerges. All of this being readily conceded, I think it is safe to say that many of us are likely to be reminded of the Nazis if anyone defines Einsteinian physics as characteristically "Jewish," and most of us are hardly more inclined to view patterns of athletic activity through a lens that focuses on religious identification.

All we can say with confidence is that Koufax's Jewishness, on occasion, would dictate when he would engage in his role as a professional baseball player, just as a Jewish physicist might not perform experiments on Yom

17. Reality was obviously more complex. Thus Marty Glickman, selected for the United States 4 × 100 meter relay team in the 1936 Olympics, was, at the last minute dropped from the team (along with another Jew and Jackie Robinson's brother), at the urging of the International Olympic Committee in order not to offend Hitler any more than was necessary. For discussion of this episode, see Levine, supra note 13, at 216–29. I own my initial familiarity with the episode to Fred Schauer.

Kippur, but not how that role would be performed. One would not expect an analyst to describe the physicist as "performing experiments like a Jew" or to say that Koufax "pitched like a Jew."

We would expect Koufax's pitching style to be unrelated to his religious background. I suspect that we would also be outraged if anyone suggested that he did throw, or ought to have thrown, different, presumably "softer," pitches to Jewish batters than those he threw to Christian batters, just as, incidentally, we would be rightly disturbed if any of the increasing number of athletes who openly identify themselves as "born-again Christians"[18] were shown to be more aggressive against Jews than against their religious compatriots. Even if Koufax might have felt a measure of "solidarity" with fellow Jews in general or even with fellow Jewish athletes in particular, it would have been inappropriate for him to have manifested this fellow-feeling on the mound. This was not likely to arise often in Koufax's ordinary working day, for there were exceedingly few Jews in the major leagues during Koufax's career. Yet, if he had faced Joe Ginsberg, a catcher for the Baltimore Orioles, during a World Series, or even during spring training, Koufax presumably would have ignored Ginsberg's status as a coreligionist and done what the "objective situation" demanded. That is, after all, what it means to be a professional, or so it generally would be argued.

With Sandy Koufax's identity as a Jewish pitcher as my background example, I turn now to the subject of lawyers. What does it mean to be a "Jewish lawyer?" Five possible models of the Jewish lawyer are sketched and elaborated upon below.

---

18. For the phenomenon of the contemporary Christian athlete, see, for example, "Prayers and the Pros — An Expanding Link; Evangelism: More and More Athletes are Practicing Something Else These Days — Public Displays of Religious Faith in the Arenas and the Locker Rooms," *Los Angeles Times,* 25 January 1992, at F17. This article mentions such groups as Campus Crusade for Christ, Athletes in Action, Young Life, the Baseball Chapel, and Athletes for Christ. It notes that "there is little mainline Protestant or Jewish influence" on contemporary athletes. See also Randy Rieland and Michael J. Weiss, "God, Gibbs and the Redskins," *The Washingtonian,* September 1992, at 58–61, 140–44 (providing an extended description of the role that evangelical Christianity played within the contemporary Washington Redskins football team led by coach Joe Gibbs); David Briggs, "Muscular Christianity Turns Fields of Dreams into Evangelism Forums," *Los Angeles Times,* 26 July 1992, at C7; George Vecsey, "Baseball: As They Look Past Their Riches, Athletes Are Turning to Religion," *New York Times,* 29 April 1991, at A1.

Five Models of the Jewish Lawyer

AN OVERVIEW

The first model is the one we would normally use if asked to give the number of Jewish baseball players. It simply asks how many persons that we identify as Jews also happen to be identifiable as baseball players or, in this instance, lawyers. Second, we can ask if these lawyers' legal practices are, in some sense, socially immersed within the Jewish community. (This question would make little sense in regard to baseball players.) Third, we might wonder how many of these lawyers identify themselves as observant Jews, at least to the extent that they would emulate Koufax by refraining entirely from the practice of their profession on certain days because of overriding duties derived from the Jewish religious calendar. A fourth model takes a quite different approach, asking if the lawyers in question practice specifically Jewish law within the context of Jewish legal institutions, such as *batei dinim* — Jewish courts. Finally, we might inquire if lawyers who practice within non-Jewish settings nonetheless find that the way they practice — and not simply when they practice — is significantly affected by duties derived from Jewish law. It should be obvious, incidentally, that these models are not exclusive. For example, anyone found in the area circumscribed by model five will also necessarily be present in the area defined by models one and three and, possibly, in models two and four as well.

It is perhaps appropriate here to mention that several readers of earlier drafts of this article suggested a sixth model, focusing on a commitment to Jewish values in the practice of law. Most often cited as exemplary of such values is the practice of civil rights or other forms of law devoted to the interests of the downtrodden. But it should be clear that such an example, however personally compatible with my own views, is quite tendentious.[19]

19. See, e.g., "Law and Lawyers," supra note 1, at 346. Auerbach writes:

It has often been claimed that the commitment of Jews to the American rule of law expresses their fidelity to venerable Jewish legal principles (law, covenant, social justice), which are also deeply embedded in American constitutionalism. That theme was first expressed more than a century ago by Oscar Straus (1850–1926), lawyer, businessman, and the first Jew to serve in the Cabinet (during Theodore Roosevelt's administration). Its frequent reiteration still reveals the yearning of American Jews to root their identity in two traditions and to merge them into a unitary Judeo-American legal tradition. But the transfer of Jewish allegiance from the Torah to the Constitution, a characteristic expression of modern Jewish secularism, also constitutes a paradigm of the acculturation process. . . . The

Are the great majority of Jewish lawyers who do not practice civil rights or similar law devoid of Jewish values? In any event, I am disinclined to offer such a model inasmuch as it requires, for cogency, a delineation of what count as specifically Jewish values. This is a subject that, even if within my competence, would also require a full book to elaborate with sufficient nuance. However, insofar as the principal purpose of this article is precisely to encourage a conversation about intersections of professional and religious identity, I welcome any contributions of other writers who would elaborate such a model.

THE MODELS EXPLICATED

The Jewish Lawyer as an "Intersection of Sets." One might be tempted to identify Jewish lawyers, at least as a group, by saying that the set of Jewish lawyers consists, no more and no less, of the intersection of two other sets: Jews and lawyers. At the very least, the first set would include anyone who is the child of a Jewish mother, plus anyone religiously converted according to the traditional understanding of Jewish law (Halakhah), guaranteed by the participation of Orthodox rabbis in the conversion procedures. The remaining task, then, would be to count the number of such people who are lawyers. The problem with this procedure is that many persons who consider themselves within the Jewish community, including myself, would object vigorously to the definition of Jewishness given above. This exemplifies what lawyers call "underinclusive" insofar as it refuses to count, for example, children of Jewish fathers (and non-Jewish mothers) raised as Jewish, as well as persons converted in non-Orthodox conversion ceremonies.

There is, of course, nothing innocent about this exclusion. It is part and parcel of an attempt by many Orthodox Jews to deny the legitimacy of both the recent declaration by the Reform movement that patrilineal descent (that is, being born to a Jewish father) is of equal importance to matrilineal descent, and the conversion procedures of the great majority of American Jews who are distinctly non-Orthodox. (Many Conservative Jews also would be unhappy about counting the children of Jewish fathers.) My point for now is certainly not to try to resolve this dispute, which raises extraor-

---

erosion of Jewish tradition, not fidelity to its norms, accounts for the fervent Jewish attachment to American law.

I believe that reality is considerably more complex than is suggested by Auerbach, but he captures very well the ideological underpinnings of any account of the tendencies of Jewish lawyers in America.

dinarily important questions as to who, within a community, has jurisdiction over the membership rules of that community.[20] Rather, my point is simply that even the presumably easiest test — based on nothing more than the intersection of numerical sets — for answering our question does not permit a single answer because there is such a sharp split within the Jewish community (or should it be "communities"?) as to who counts as Jewish in the first place.

There could, of course, also be some definitional problems in regard to lawyers. For example, it is not clear whether one must be a member of a bar and actually engaged in the practice of law to be a lawyer. (I am the first, though only rarely the second.) Yet I assume that the answers to these very real questions are unlikely to provoke the level of unhappiness — even hatred — caused by adopting one or another test for determining who is a Jew.

It should be obvious that the "intersection of sets" approach to resolving our question carries with it no implications about the actual intersection of one's Judaism with one's practice of law or, indeed, with any other aspect of one's life. It is at least conceivable that knowing that a lawyer is Jewish would provide no more information about her behavior as a lawyer than knowing that her eyes were hazel. Similarly, knowing that a physicist or a tennis player is counted as a Jew under our basically "externalist" criterion makes it actually unnecessary to ask anyone what being a Jew means to her

20. No group within Judaism in fact rejects the necessity to make exclusionary judgments in determining who is a Jew. See, e.g., Robin Pogrebin, "A Catskills Resort Fight over Who's a True Jew," *New York Observer,* 24–31 August 1992 (on file with author). This article details a boycott threatened by the Jewish Community Relations Council, an umbrella organization of about sixty Jewish groups, against the Stevensville Country Club, a kosher hotel in the Catskills, if the hotel honored a contract it had entered into with the group Jews for Jesus to host its annual convention. Although the Orthodox Agudath Israel of America had "promptly canceled its planned Thanksgiving banquet at the Stevensville," there is nothing in the article to indicate that only the Orthodox were behind the boycott. According to the prominent sociologist Leonard Fein, who is, I am quite certain, not Orthodox, "For [the Jews for Jesus] to use the word 'Jew' is an exploitative imposition. They're perfectly entitled to whatever theology they develop. [But, t]hey're not entitled to violate copyright, as it were. . . ." In response, Susan Perlman, a member of the group, declared, "There is no pope of Judaism that decrees who is and who isn't a Jew." A pope there may not be, but that does not entail that there is no need that boundaries must be declared and maintained. From the perspective of Ms. Perlman, one may see little difference between the Orthodox attack on non-Halakhic conversion and the refusal of Reform and Conservative Jews to accept her own "Judaism" that recognizes Jesus as the Messiah. It is all a turf battle over cultural jurisdiction.

as an "internal" matter.[21] I suspect that most of us currently find it implausible to believe that being Jewish provides no useful information at all about lawyering,[22] though we might explore why that is the case and then ask if we should applaud or lament the day when Jewishness was no more informative about modes of lawyering than about one's work life as a physicist or athlete.[23]

The broad question, then, is what do we think we learn when we see standard demographic measures indicating the numbers (or proportions) of any given groups in regard to any given occupation or institution. Consider, for example, our reactions even now to discovering that the number of Jews (or women, African Americans, or whatever group one wishes) entering any given occupational role or institution is increasing. One might think that one is learning a great deal about, say, the occupational preferences of Jews or of some other group. Or one might argue that the lesson has to do with the decline of prejudice and discrimination as forces that prevent members of given groups from achieving goals suitable to their talents.

One might well view the entry into a profession by a formerly discriminated-against group as a simple triumph of social justice. A group once excluded because of "prejudice" (that is, the false insistence that the group in question differs in important respects from some particular standard of behavior or ability) is now being welcomed as it becomes accepted that these differences either do not exist in any fundamental sense or, at the very least, are irrelevant to the role or institution in question (which may be a way of saying that there are no fundamental differences).

Another approach holds that, in effect, we are learning not only about the occupational preferences of Jews or about the social justice of American

21. The ability to identify Jews on the basis of external criteria, the most important of which is the status of the mother, derives from Jewish theology rather than mere sociology. To be a Jew is, in fundamental ways, an ontological status rather than one that is subject to choice. To discover who is a member of a Protestant sect may require finding out the details of one's personal biography, including the experience of God's saving grace. There are no such analogues within mainstream Judaism.

22. Though, as noted immediately below (see page 135), the information thought to be provided might be laced with touches of anti-Semitism.

23. I have little doubt, for example, that Auerbach, who poses a thoroughgoing attack on the purported declension from a distinctively Torah-centered Jewish community to one (encouraged by lawyers) centered instead on the secular Constitution (see *Rabbis and Lawyers*, supra note 1, passim), would thoroughly lament this development, even as Auerbach's analysis would lead him to expect it to occur.

institutions, but also about what might be termed the "internal" behavior of the institutions in question. That is, one might indeed acknowledge the presence of genuine differences between the formerly hegemonic groups and the new entrants, and argue that the entrance of the latter group will indeed change the nature of the institutions in question as the new sensibilities, perspectives, or ways of relating to the world are brought to bear. Those who support such changes usually do not deny the presence of fundamental difference; instead, they deny the legitimacy of prior conceptions of the practice in question and argue instead that these conceptions need to be reshaped precisely by infusing what the formerly excluded group can bring to the enterprise. Others, of course, tend to describe any such changes that they see as deviations from the appropriate way of doing things, and they may try to prevent these changes precisely as a way of purportedly preserving standards.[24]

There are, for example, both pro-Semitic and anti-Semitic stories available regarding the meaning for the legal practice of the entry of Jews into the mainstream of the profession. Robert Eli Rosen has noted that Jewish attorneys are sometimes "identified as overly aggressive, hired guns."[25] As he points out, these traits, which once operated to legitimize the exclusion of Jews from elite, ostensibly genteel, sectors of the law, became positive attributes in the aggressive market society of the 1980s,[26] though the revulsion against the excesses of that decade may lead to a more negative evaluation and at least some return to traditional anti-Semitism.[27]

Many of the contemporary debates about "multiculturalism" and the rationales of affirmative-action hiring programs for formerly-excluded minorities are importantly affected by the stance one takes on the legitimate

24. In one of his works, Auerbach describes the concerted attempt by social elites, citing the importance of maintaining standards, to prevent immigrant Jews from entering the legal profession in the early decades of this century. Jerold S. Auerbach, *Unequal Justice: Lawyers and Social Change in Modern America* 125–27 (1978).

25. Robert E. Rosen, "Jews and Corporate Legal Practice" 13 (November 1991) (prepared for November 1991 conference in Madison, Wisconsin, on Jews and the Law) (unpublished manuscript).

26. Id. at 14. It should be obvious that no reliable data exist on these behavioral differences in regard to Jewish attorneys and that we are dealing with sheer ethnic stereotypes.

27. Consider, in this regard, the controversy surrounding James Stewart, *Den of Thieves* (1991), a book describing Wall Street during the 1980s, which was accused by Alan Dershowitz of anti-Semitism for its focus on the criminal conduct of Jewish financiers such as Ivan Boesky, Dennis Levine, Michael Milken, and others.

presence of significant differences, rather than the unfairness of emphasizing more important commonalities.[28] This is seen most dramatically and
acrimoniously within the academy in regard to the importance of self-
consciously seeking out "different voices" ostensibly associated with membership in given groups. One sees it as well, however, in the debate about
whether Clarence Thomas brings an authentic African American voice to
the Supreme Court.

There is, for example, a sharp debate about the importance of the significantly larger number of female lawyers than was the case twenty years ago.
In what is admittedly an oversimplification, one can ask if this has brought a
distinctive "women's voice" to the law, reshaping the very notion of what it
means to practice law.[29] Many women, for example, have argued that traditional notions of professional roles reflect a male way of relating to the
world, with an emphasis on emotionally distanced individuals, each seeking
maximization of one's entitlements under the impersonal rules of the legal
game. Women, however, ostensibly have a far more relational stance to the
world, emphasizing the connections that create and maintain human communities.[30] One might respond, though, that the entrance of women is only a
recognition that women indeed can fill traditional legal roles just as well as
men, leaving unchanged the basic conception of what it means to be a professional. Imagine how one would justify, to a disgruntled client, the assignment of a female associate to the team of lawyers handling his case. Would
one be more likely to describe the associate as, of course, comparable in
talent to the male associates ("after all, she graduated magna cum laude from
Harvard"), or to say that the team is now stronger precisely because it does
include the special perspective that she can bring to the team? The client, of
course, might ask similar questions about any particular associate who appears to deviate from a model (or "modal") background, and the reader can
ask what would count as appropriate responses (assuming that one should
not simply denounce the client as a bigot and resign the representation).

In any event, based upon a definition of Jewish lawyers derived only from
the intersection of sets, one would presumably have no trouble counting as a
Jewish lawyer a thoroughly secular child of a Jewish mother, who has not

28. This question has been at the core of much of Martha Minow's work. See, e.g., Martha
Minow, *Making All the Difference: Inclusion, Exclusion, and American Law* (1990).
29. See, e.g., Carrie Menkel-Meadow, "Portia in a Different Voice: Speculations on a Woman's
Lawyering Process," 1 *Berkeley Women's L.J.* 39 (1985).
30. See, e.g., Carol Gilligan, *In a Different Voice* (1982).

formally left the Jewish community through conversion to another religion even as he ate a ham sandwich on Yom Kippur during a recess in the vigorous cross-examination he was conducting. Consider in this regard a recent book by Susanne Klingenstein, *Jews in the American Academy,* which refers to Joel Springarn, described as the first Jew appointed to the Department of Literature at Columbia University (in 1904), as Jewish only by "an accidental detail of his descent."[31] Indeed, Klingenstein tells us that "Jewishness played absolutely no role in Springarn's life."[32] This does not, however, prevent her use of Springarn as part of her examination of the emergence of Jews as faculty members at American universities. The attribute of being Jewish is something we consider as externally attached to Springarn rather than as a self-proclaimed aspect of his own inner identity. Perhaps it is not too harsh to say that we who are Jewish take a certain pride in Springarn,[33] despite his taking no particular pride in being one of us, and we resist his attempt to withdraw from us. (This may be a dramatic illustration of the social construction of identity, a conception central to much contemporary thought.) Such "assigned" identity is not at all an unknown phenomenon in the tortured history of individuals and groups in a dynamic society like that of the United States. We probably would have described the great Sandy Koufax as a Jewish pitcher even if he had pitched the first game of the World Series or done nothing else to affirm his identity as a Jew. It almost certainly would have earned him plaudits had he simply supported Israel (whatever precisely that means).

Jewish Lawyering as an Expression of Social and Political Solidarity. This brings me to my second category of Jewish lawyers — namely, those who feel a high degree of membership in, and presumably a loyalty to, a specifically Jewish community, regardless of whether there is an explicitly religious element to this identification. It should probably be emphasized that this kind of Jewish lawyer might well join with Felix Frankfurter in describing himself "[a]s one who had no ties with any formal religion" insofar as there is no longer any commitment to Jewish beliefs or observance of Jewish

31. Susanne Klingenstein, *Jews in the American Academy 1900–1940: The Dynamics of Intellectual Assimilation* 104 (1991).

32. Id.

33. Alternatively, this may apply to only some of us who are Jewish. In correspondence, Jerold Auerbach has asked, "Why should we who are Jewish take pride in a Springarn? I, for one, decline to take any pride in any Jew who takes no pride in being Jewish." Letter from Jerold Auerbach to Sanford Levinson (10 September 1992). This is a profound question whose resolution lies well beyond the scope of this article.

rituals.[34] Still, Frankfurter is universally viewed as a "Jewish judge,"[35] as is, most certainly, Louis Brandeis. What counts for much of the Jewish identification of Brandeis and Frankfurter is their strong commitment, at least at certain junctures of their lives, to Zionism as a solidaristic expression of Jewish communal interests.[36] I have commented, in a book review concerning Frankfurter and Brandeis, that for many of us what is most attractive about these men "is precisely that they offer ways of being Jewish without accepting any specifically Jewish theological tenets or observing any *mitzvot*."[37] (A central question of contemporary Judaism, of course, is whether this offers an authentic way "of being Jewish.") Although the appointment of each was met with a measure of anti-Semitic hostility, no one seriously argued that the danger presented by their ascendancy to the Court would be the smuggling in of Halakhic requirements drawn from Jewish law. (One might contrast this with the fears sometimes expressed that Catholic nominees to the judiciary will interpret the constitutional issues surrounding abortion in light of church teachings condemning the practice.)[38]

At one level, a model-two "Jewish lawyer" might be described by the terminology that we ordinarily use in regard to any ethnic lawyer. This requires, in the words of Professor Alan Mintz, that we "disentangle . . . Jewishness as an ethnic experience . . . from Judaism as a structure of texts and ideas."[39] Ethnic lawyers characteristically draw their client base from

34. Levinson, supra note 9, at 3. Frankfurter had, however, arranged with Louis Henkin, a former law clerk who is also an observant Jew, to recite the Kaddish, the traditional Jewish prayer for the dead, at his funeral. See Liva Baker, *Felix Frankfurter* 332 (1969).

35. It is worth noting, however, that Frankfurter described himself as "a Harvard Law Professor who happened to be a Jew" rather than a "Jewish professor at the Harvard Law School." See *Rabbis and Lawyers*, supra note 1, at 155.

36. In turn, Frankfurter especially has been subjected to withering criticism for his unwillingness to press his close friend President Franklin Roosevelt about the Roosevelt Administration's patently weak policies concerning the Holocaust and refugees from Germany. Thus, Auerbach has written that the notably cosmopolitan Frankfurter "would not utilize his position and contacts, or his irrepressible energy, in the service of Jewish needs during the most desperate years of Jewish history." Id. at 163.

37. Sanford Levinson, "Who Is a Jew(ish Justice)?" 10 *Cardozo L. Rev.* 2359, 2368 (1989) (book review). It should be clear that this present article is linked to the concern of that article, as, indeed, it is linked to an examination of the intersections of Catholicism and secular American law. See chapter 6.

38. See chapter 6, page 212.

39. Alan Mintz, "Manners, Morals, and the Academy," *The New Republic*, 9 March 1992, at 41 (reviewing Klingenstein, supra note 31).

the ethnic community and may well feel some special duties to defend fellow ethnics or coreligionists (if that is the proper term) from attack from the "outside" community. This is, of course, also seen as defending the "community's" interests as well.

In this latter sense, Alan Dershowitz is certainly a leading contemporary Jewish lawyer, especially in light of his book *Chutzpah*.[40] Dershowitz notes that a colleague describes him as Harvard Law School's first "Jewish Jew," the first member of that faculty to "wear his Jewishness on his sleeve."[41] It seems clear that Dershowitz defines at least aspects of his own personal practice of law as being part of a commitment to serve Jewish communal purposes. I am confident that he would wholly reject a 1944 statement by Lionel Trilling, already famous as the first Jew granted tenure in the Columbia English Department, that "I do not think of myself as a 'Jewish writer.' I do not have it in mind to serve by my writing any Jewish purpose."[42] Still, whatever form Dershowitz's contemptuous rejection of Trilling's assimilationism might take, a major theme of Dershowitz's book is his movement away from his Orthodox background. His book appears to be written from (and to) the stance of the contemporary secular Jew (who still continues to observe major Jewish holidays such as Passover and Yom Kippur), rather than from a position espousing a strong adherence to a specifically religious conception of Judaism.[43]

The complexities of Jewish identity are nicely captured by Dershowitz's description of his encounter, upon joining the Harvard faculty, with then-dean Erwin Griswold. This encounter concerned Griswold's assigning Dershowitz to teach a class that met on Saturday. Dershowitz responded that he would not work on Saturday, though, interestingly, the reason for this was

---

40. Alan M. Dershowitz, *Chutzpah* (1991).

41. Id. at 79 (quoting Alan Stone).

42. Klingenstein, supra note 31, at 232 n.11. It might be relevant here to note Hank Greenberg's comment that

> [w]hen I was playing, I used to resent being singled out as a Jewish ballplayer. I wanted to be known as a great ballplayer, period. I'm not sure why or when I changed, because I'm still not a particularly religious person. Lately, though, I find myself wanting to be remembered not only as a great ballplayer, but even more as a great Jewish ballplayer.

Ritter, supra note 13, at 330.

43. See, e.g., Dershowitz, supra note 40, at 11. Dershowitz describes himself as having "chose[n] a more secular road" than that walked by his parents and ancestors. "It is," he writes, "partly because I cannot leave my children the Jewish legacy that is to be found in the existing tradition . . . that I wanted to write a book that documents my journey as a Jew." Id. at 12.

not a religious one.[44] Dershowitz, who had been raised as an Orthodox Jew, had personally become nonobservant. His refusal to work on Saturday can thus better be described in terms of ethnic solidarity than religious obligation. It is worth noting that this is no small, or merely symbolic, point. A central social function of a common "day of rest," after all, is precisely to provide the opportunity for friends and family to interact with one another. One does not have to be Christian to appreciate the coordinating function served by making Sunday a common nonworking day; similarly, one does not have to be an Orthodox Jew (though it may help to have Orthodox friends or family) to appreciate a similar coordinating function for Saturday.

In effect, Dershowitz can be interpreted as claiming that forcing him to teach on Saturday would make it harder for him to retain his ties with the Jewish community, whether or not he would ever go to synagogue and pray on Saturday. In addition, Dershowitz's teaching on Saturday would make life more difficult for Jewish students at Harvard who, for whatever reason, might feel qualms about having Saturday classes. Dean Griswold acquiesced, though not without pointing out that he thought it was inequitable to exempt only Dershowitz. Thus, Harvard's traditional custom of Saturday classes was simply abolished the next year, so that the question of Dershowitz's, or any other Jew's, specialness, at least in this regard, would never again have to arise.[45]

It may be relevant to point out that the simple step of abolishing classes for all on the Jewish Sabbath has not been extended to holidays such as Yom Kippur or Rosh Hashanah, and, therefore, each year brings forth a continuing drama concerning the assertion (or acknowledgment) of Jewish identity by various faculty members. And, as with the episode of Dershowitz and Saturday teaching, the motivations for canceling classes may have as much to do with acknowledging group solidarity (and making life easier for Jewish students) than with any personal desires to attend religious services.[46]

Group solidarity, of course, can also raise important problems, as suggested earlier by the example of Koufax pitching to Joe Ginsberg.[47] Jews

44. Interview with Alan M. Dershowitz, in Cambridge, Massachusetts (24 March 1992).

45. Dershowitz, supra note 40, at 64.

46. It is, of course, a notorious truth that Christian professors are almost never put in a position of having to decide whether to cancel classes on Christian holidays and, concomitantly, need not wonder what interpretation is placed on their (un)willingness to teach on such occasions. See Douglas Laycock, "The Remnants of Free Exercise," 1990 *Sup. Ct. Rev.* 1, 51 (1991).

47. See supra page 130.

surely would have taken no pride in Koufax had it turned out that he treated Jewish opponents better than non-Jews. Indeed, it is even conceivable that, had Koufax thought of his Jewishness while on the pitcher's mound, he would have felt some need to be especially hard on other Jews precisely to still any such doubts. For this reason, Felix Frankfurter acknowledged that he exacted "higher standards from Jews" than from other Harvard law students.[48] Similarly, it has been suggested that Julius and Ethel Rosenberg were sent to their deaths by a Jewish prosecutor, Irving Saypol, and a Jewish judge, Irving Kaufman, both eager to reassure the surrounding non-Jewish community (and therefore, presumably serve the interests of the great majority of American Jews who were not Communists) that Jewish prosecutors and judges could be trusted to discipline one of their own.[49] In fact, it is precisely this aspect of what might be termed the semiotics of Jewish identity that provides the lie, at least to some extent, to Felix Frankfurter's tortured attempt to integrate his various identities in a 1943 case dealing with forcing Jehovah's Witnesses to salute the flag in school.[50] After beginning his opinion by invoking his own membership in "the most vilified and persecuted minority in history," Frankfurter immediately stated that "as judges we are neither Jew nor Gentile, neither Catholic nor agnostic. We owe equal attachment to the Constitution and are equally bound by our judicial obligations. . . ."[51]

Can the meaning of "attachment to the Constitution," owed by lawyers as well as judges, ever be completely independent of one's membership in a "vilified and persecuted minority,"[52] whether for good or for bad? Even if Irving Kaufman cannot be reduced to being only a Jewish judge, can his role in the Rosenberg case, which marked him for the rest of his life, possibly be described without recourse to that key adjective?

As it happens, Felix Frankfurter was one of the few members of the

---

48. See *Rabbis and Lawyers,* supra note 1, at 155; Dershowitz, supra note 40, at 79 n.*.

49. See *United States v. Rosenberg,* 195 F.2d 583 (2d Cir. 1952), cert. denied, 344 U.S. 838 (1952), reh'g denied, 344 U.S. 889 (1952); Ronald Radosh, *The Rosenberg File: A Search for the Truth* (1983).

50. See *West Virginia State Bd. of Educ. v. Barnette,* 319 U.S. 624, 646 (1943) (Frankfurter, J., dissenting).

51. Id. at 647. Avi Soifer has noted, however, that Frankfurter might have manifested his Jewishness by contrasting the term "Gentile" rather than "Christian." To be sure, Jews are not the only group who speak of "gentiles"; Mormons do as well. Still, it is hard to ignore Frankfurter's particular background when reading the word.

52. Id. at 646.

Supreme Court who behaved with any real integrity in regard to the Rosen-bergs,[53] though it is impossible to say with any confidence what role his Jewishness played in this. Perhaps the central question, though, is less about Frankfurter than about us: Should we hope that his Jewishness played no role at all?

Judaism Enters the Legal Workplace (But Leaves the Internal Norms of Legal Practice Untouched). From the high drama of death, we move to the mundane aspects of everyday (or at least every seventh day) behavior, and to the third model of Jewish lawyering. Can we select, from the set of all Jewish lawyers defined merely as the intersection of sets (or even that subset that feels solidarity with the Jewish community), that set that, at least occasion-ally, will subordinate its identity as "lawyer" to that of "Jew," defined in specifically religious, rather than simply ethnic, terms? It was this charac-teristic that made Sandy Koufax so special. We know that Koufax, like Greenberg, felt compelled to remain in his room rather than go to the base-ball field on that key October afternoon.

We do not find it hard to imagine Jewish lawyers refusing to appear in court or to do any work for a client on Yom Kippur, and, for Orthodox lawyers, to do the same on the Sabbath, however genuinely important it might be to the client that the work be done at that inconvenient time.[54] It would be thought odd, at the very least, to refer simply to the fact that legal professionals consider loyalty to a client as one of their central professional

53. See Michael E. Parrish, "Cold War Justice: The Supreme Court and the Rosenbergs," 82 *Am. Hist. Rev.* 805 (1977).

54. At a conference on law and religion at the Harvard Law School on 5 April 1992, I heard that Nathan Lewin, surely one of the most distinguished Jewish lawyers in the United States, say that he would rather be held in contempt of court than appear on the Sabbath. What occasioned his comment was the reference by University of Chicago professor Michael McConnell to a late eighteenth-century Pennsylvania case, *Stansbury v. Marks,* 2 U.S. (1 Dall.) 213 (1793), which had upheld a subpoena to a Jewish witness to appear in court on a Saturday, then a regular working day for state courts, which were in session from Monday through Saturday (though not, of course, on Sunday). A study of American yeshiva students noted that relatively few yeshiva alumni "entered medicine or dentistry. Aside from the long training period, the problem of Sabbath observance is probably a major factor." William B. Helmreich, *The World of the Yeshiva: An Intimate Portrait of Orthodox Jewry* 273 (1986). More yeshiva alumni, however, enter the legal professions. "Not only does [law] require logical thinking, but the style of debate and the use of specific cases to develop general principles bear a striking resemblance to the manner in which the Talmud is studied and its content." Id. at 272. See below, however, for some reservations about the analogy between the Talmudist's and the attorney's respective roles.

responsibilities, and that it would therefore ordinarily be a dereliction of their duties to allow mere personal convenience to trump the needs of the client. Many lawyers have canceled long-planned vacations or attendance at their child's school play at the last minute because of the legitimate demands based upon client loyalty. But the key term above was "mere personal convenience," and I presume that few of us would use such words to describe the desire by a lawyer to maintain a specific religious identity (or, of course, to obey what are thought to be divine commandments) by refusing to work on Yom Kippur or on Saturday.[55]

For at least some Jews, the moral of the Koufax story might well not be his unwillingness to pitch on Yom Kippur, but rather his lack of concern about pitching on the Sabbath. It should be obvious that only some Jews will be willing to celebrate Koufax's status as a Jewish pitcher, while others will point to his profanation of other holy days within the Jewish religious calendar.

Koufax did not, of course, wear a yarmulke when pitching — and not, one is confident, simply because wearing a baseball cap would have made it superfluous. Indeed, the issue of dress is of legitimate concern to many Orthodox Jews precisely because of its symbolic status in declaring their identity as Jews in the otherwise secular workplace. Although "[o]ne of the leading rabbis of the last generation ruled that one who works among gentiles and whose living would be materially harmed by wearing a yarmulke may abstain from doing so,"[56] younger Orthodox Jews entering the legal profession are justifiably reluctant to renounce what they consider to be an important expression of their unfragmented Jewish identity. They point out that, at the very least, a Jew wearing a yarmulke is recognized by almost everyone as a Jew and often treated, both by the surrounding society and by fellow Jews, as significantly different from Jews without yarmulkes.

Still, whatever the number of days taken off from ordinary secular work, or whatever one's decision about wearing a yarmulke, another question remains which moves us ever closer to the heart of this article. While one is on the job, does one's identity as a Jew in any significant sense shape one's sense of what it means to practice law?

As already suggested,[57] one way to respond to this question is to ask

55. See, e.g., Ron Coleman, "A Lawyer and His Sabbath," *Student Law.*, December 1987, at 14, 15–19.

56. Id. at 15.

57. See supra, pages 138–139.

certain kinds of sociological questions directed at such topics as client base and issue specialization. That is, it would not be at all surprising to discover that Jewish lawyers (defined by the simple intersection of sets approach), before discriminatory barriers to entry into "mainstream" law firms were lowered, would tend to have Jewish clients or be interested in certain areas of litigation of primary interest to that client base. Indeed, it would hardly be surprising if "observant" Jews would be even more likely to have such clients and specialize in such areas than "nonobservant" ones. This is, of course, what one would expect to find in regard to any sample of ethnic lawyers. The central question, though, is whether the way one practices law within the office or courtroom — as distinguished from one's client base or legal specialization — would be significantly (and legitimately) influenced by one's being Jewish.

The Jewish Lawyer as a Practitioner in Jewish Courts. The fourth model suggested above asks if the lawyer in question practices before specifically Jewish religious courts. Perhaps it would be only a play on words to suggest that the correct way to identify Jewish lawyers is to identify who practices law before a Jewish court (a *beit din*) by presenting materials and arguments drawn specifically from Jewish sources. I have already suggested that I am far more interested in examining those lawyers who are concerned with the law of the United States or the various states of the union and the potential implication of their identification as Jewish lawyers.[58] Still, it is illuminating to take note of one significant aspect of the Jewish tradition related to lawyering; namely, that the role of the lawyer, especially defined as a client-oriented advocate, is, to put it mildly, not a featured (or valued) one within the Jewish tradition.

Whatever else may explain the apparent attraction of many American Jews to practicing law, it is unlikely to be the presentation by traditional rabbinic Judaism of adversarial lawyering (as distinguished from wise judging) as a worthy way to live one's life. Observant Jewish youngsters would more likely consider great *dayanim,* or Jewish judges, as their models. Those youngsters also might imagine emulating distinguished rabbinic authors of incisive *responsa* — learned analyses of questions arising under Jewish law. This might well explain why, as American Jews became more secularized, many descendants of rabbis, such as Felix Frankfurter, seemed naturally

58. See supra, page 131.

drawn to careers in the legal academy or to service on the bench. It does little, however, to explain why they would be attracted by the particular role of the adversarial lawyer, selling his services to whatever client could afford to hire him.[59]

Rabbinic Judaism is centrally organized around Halakhah. Many Jews are said, therefore, to have a great desire to become learned about Jewish law. This, however, does not establish the existence of, let alone the importance of, the role of the advocate in Judiasm. The advocate has been recognized (and often condemned) since ancient times as far less interested in serving justice or working toward the establishment of legal truths than in simply constructing arguments to serve the interests of a client. It is this client-centered advocate who comes to mind when one recalls the standard image of the lawyer in American culture, and it is precisely such a lawyer who is criticized, if not indeed condemned, by classical Jewish thought.

Myer Galinski, writing about "the administration of justice in ancient Israel," notes that "[n]o lawyers or advocates were allowed to appear in Court on behalf of clients."[60] Although later years saw the development of "a type of special pleader, called an *orach din* (preparer of the law), who drew up pleadings, etc., indicating to a litigant how to conduct his case,"[61] this practice was frowned upon by the rabbinic sages. Such services were viewed as intended "not primarily to advance Justice, but only to promote his client's cause. The use of such a lawyer would obviously weigh in favor of the rich litigant."[62] Galinski focuses on the lawyer's presumed lack of interest in advancing "justice" rather than his lack of devotion to "truth." These goals are often connected; lawyers often are viewed as committed to neither goal.

59. It is worth noting that Frankfurter and even Brandeis, probably the most famous Jewish lawyer in history, rejected this role. Frankfurter never practiced law in the private marketplace. Brandeis did have an important legal practice in Boston, but he gained fame (and, from some quarters, opprobrium) for emphasizing his role as "attorney for the situation," seeking justice for all parties, rather than serving as the wholly committed advocate for his particular client. It was, for example, this depiction of his role as an attorney that led to at least some of the opposition to Brandeis's appointment to the Supreme Court (though other opposition was surely motivated by anti-Semitism). See Thomas L. Shaffer, *American Legal Ethics: Text, Readings, and Discussion Topics* 241–308 (1985) (providing materials on Brandeis's legal career and his conception of legal ethics).

60. Myer Galinski, *Pursue Justice: The Administration of Justice in Ancient Israel* 190 (1983).

61. Id.

62. Id.

Few indices of standard sources on Jewish law refer to "attorneys," "lawyers," or "advocates." Most existing discussions emphasize the lawyer as someone to be feared rather than embraced as a valuable participant within the decision-making system.

From the passage in Deuteronomy that "the two parties to the dispute shall appear before the Lord, before the priests or magistrates,"[63] it was inferred that all pleadings and arguments should be made directly by the litigants rather than by proxies such as attorneys.[64] Perhaps even more important than this passage from Torah is one from the *Mishnah Avot*. There we read that "Judah ben Tabbai says, 'Do not play the part of a counselor [in court].' "[65] It is this passage that is most often cited in regard to the suspicion of lawyer-counselors. Maimonides commented on this passage as follows:

> "Counselors" are those who study laws and arguments till they become specialists in their legalities, anticipating questions and answers. Thus they advise their clients, "If the judge says this, then you say that; if your adversary argues this way, then you may answer him in the following manner." It is as if the counselor orchestrates the law and the litigant, and hence he is called *orekh din* [arranger of the law]. It is this which the *Mishnah* forbids, opposing the teaching of arguments or denials which might benefit one litigant. And even if you know that this litigant has been wronged, and that his opponent is lying in order to deprive him of what is rightfully his—nonetheless it is not permissible to teach this litigant any arguments that might acquit or help him at all.[66]

It appears clear that Maimonides viewed the counselor as a legal manipulator—an artful "arranger"—concerned less with absolute fidelity to the law than with crafting ostensibly legal arguments that would enable the client to prevail against an adversary. This view of the lawyer seems very similar to that taken by Socrates in the Platonic dialogue *Gorgias*,[67] where the orator-rhetorician is denounced for his willingness to use his arts in the

---

63. Deuteronomy 19:17.

64. See Haim H. Cohen, "Attorney," in *The Principles of Jewish Law* 574 (Menachem Elon, ed., 1975) (providing a collection of articles originally written for the *Encyclopaedia Judaica*).

65. See Basil F. Herring, *Jewish Ethics and Halakhah for Our Time: Sources and Commentary* 95 (1984).

66. Id. at 97.

67. See Plato, *Gorgias* (Walter Hamilton, trans., 1960).

cause of persuasion rather than for pursuit of truth and, ultimately, to revel in making the lesser, or unjust, cause appear the greater, or just.

Whatever their other differences, the great medieval rabbi Nachmanides apparently agreed with Maimonides. Nachmanides is described as "doubting whether a third party" (that is, someone other than direct parties to a lawsuit), would "be beholden to the truth. Na[c]hmanides apparently felt that an outside agent, who might be functioning in an impersonal, somewhat 'professional' capacity, might feel able to take liberties with the truth."[68] Far from the least important word in this sentence, of course, is the word "professional." The author puts what are sometimes called "scare quotation marks" around the word. What is not clear in this context is whether the author is suggesting that taking liberties with the truth calls into account one's professionalism, so that the quotation marks indicate that one is not a "true" professional; perhaps, on the contrary, he is suggesting that one becomes a professional attorney precisely by exhibiting a willingness to take liberties with the truth. If the latter is true, we are thus warned against giving undue respect to professional lawyers, rather than merely being told to be on guard against only those inferior lawyers insufficiently respectful of truth.

In any event, Basil Herring, in his book *Jewish Ethics and Halakhah for Our Time*[69] quotes a seventeenth century rabbi who wrote of those who learned the law only for ulterior motives, "leading to argumentation and strife, deception and the adoption of false argumentation to justify the wicked and defame the righteous."[70] Another rabbi of the same period denounced the practice of Venetian "advocates" where "the greater the lies, the deceptions, and the trickeries, the more the litigants pursue their services with financial reward."[71] Thus, it should cause no surprise to read that within Jewish jurisprudence "the lawyer fills no unique role or function within the framework of the Jewish judicial process."[72] It must be noted that the views of Maimonides and Nachmanides were ultimately rejected, and that, since the Middle Ages, Jewish legal procedure has allowed lawyers to represent clients, especially in commercial litigation where it would often be exceedingly difficult to require someone, particularly a plaintiff, to be personally present in litigation rather than to be represented by a proxy at-

68. Herring, supra note 65, at 109.
69. Id. at 91.
70. Id. at 110–11 (quoting Rabbi Yair Hayyim Bachrach).
71. Id. at 111 (quoting Rabbi Hayyim Benveniste).
72. Dov I. Frimer, "The Role of the Lawyer in Jewish Law," 1 *J.L. & Religion* 297, 303 (1983).

torney.[73] The Israeli rabbinate in 1960 formally accepted "practices permitting legal counsel to argue on behalf of either litigant, on condition that such counsel be legally or halakhically licensed and competent to appear in court, and furthermore that the litigants themselves be present in court, except under extreme circumstances."[74] Thus, summarizes Dov Frimer, Halakhists have come to accept the practice of legal counsel before the court, thus overriding earlier opposition.[75] By incorporating certain safeguards and verbal warnings, they hoped to utilize the offices of the legal profession to further the goal of the attainment of the truth in court.[76]

Still, one should not be under any illusion that the Jewish legal system enthusiastically embraces adversarial, client-oriented lawyering. There is, for example, no notion that "due process" requires participation of a lawyer in the proceedings of a beit din.[77] In any event, if we were to restrict our definition of a Jewish lawyer to someone who practices as an advocate for others within the context of Jewish courts, the number would be relatively tiny, in part because of the somewhat tainted legitimacy of the notion of the advocate's role in this context.

Judaism as a Constitutive Aspect of the Practice of Law. It is time to turn to the fifth and final model which concerns self-consciously observant (and especially Orthodox) Jewish lawyers practicing in a non-Jewish legal setting. These lawyers are the ones most likely to be faced with the dilemma of deciding what it means to live within a "community of the faithful."[78] They might well resonate the following statement issued by the University of Notre Dame Campus Ministry (with the obvious substitution of the word "Jewish" for "Christian"): "The Christian life is a mediated life. That means that persons committed to growing as Christians do not make their decisions in isolation, but in consultation with the sense and insight of those they consider wise in the Christian community."[79]

73. See Aaron Kirschenbaum, "Representation in Litigation in Jewish Law," in 6 *Diné Israel* at xxv–xli (Zeér W. Falk and Aaron Kirschenbaum, eds., 1975).

74. Frimer, supra note 72, at 303.

75. Id. at 297.

76. Id. at 301–2, 305.

77. See id. at 302–3 (discussing a 1953 decision of the Rabbinical High Court of Israel rejecting the claim that a divorce proceeding before a lower (religious) court had been flawed because the court, for reasons left unexplained, refused to permit the husband representation by counsel).

78. See Shaffer, supra note 7, at 196–217.

79. Id. at 207.

As suggested earlier,[80] there is a tension between this sense of mediation and an unabashed version of the professional project. A "professional" goes through a social process, including training in law school, medical school, or a military academy, designed, as suggested earlier,[81] in some way to "bleach out" or make otherwise irrelevant what might be seen as central aspects of one's self-identity. I recall one of my teachers at Stanford saying, only half-kiddingly, that the best way to understand a Maoist thought-reform camp was to compare it to the first year of law school. There was, first, the systematic denigration of whatever one had done prior to entering law school. Just as Mao held out the promise of becoming the new socialist man or woman, so did law school promise the redemptive possibility of becoming transformed into the lawyer.

I certainly do not think that law is unique in this regard. Successful professional training to become a lawyer, doctor, or a military professional is far more significant in terms of predicting one's subsequent behavior, at least when acting within a professional role, than, for example, the fact that one is of a particular race, gender, ethnicity, or religion.

One might take justified pride, for example, that President George H. W. Bush was sufficiently indifferent toward race that he chose General Colin Powell to serve as chair of the Joint Chiefs of Staff of the armed services — or, indeed, that his son George W. Bush is similarly indifferent that he chose Powell as secretary of state. In turn, one might be bothered, indeed outraged, by the suggestion that his self-conscious identity as an African American contributed to his decisions as a military officer. This would accuse him of acting "unprofessionally." Recall, in this context, our earlier discussion of Sandy Koufax. More seriously (perhaps), there is Lionel Trilling's comment that "I should resent it if a critic of my work were to discover in it faults or virtues which he called Jewish."[82] Trilling presented himself as a trained academic ostensibly attempting to live up to the internal norms of the academy. His Judaism was, at least when he was a professor of English, merely an "external" feature of his biography, or so he proclaimed. Similarly, I would assume that any Jewish American military professional would be equally resentful if his Jewishness was considered in evaluating his military competence.

But clearly the example of military professionalism raises complications that baseball professionalism does not. Are Israeli generals Jewish in their

80. See supra page 125.
81. Id.
82. Klingenstein, supra note 31, at 232 n.11.

professionalism? One might answer yes if, for example, Israeli generals (or at least some of them) behave as if under a duty to follow Halakhically derived norms, which restrict their ability to inflict harm on enemies, even when these norms are stricter than the general norms of the Geneva Convention that limit the conduct of all military professionals of all signatory nations. Less happily, one can imagine a "Jewish general" who felt that the biblical injunction, supported by some contemporary rabbis, to exterminate all Amelikites, might support behavior clearly contravened by the Geneva Conventions. But does Ariel Sharon's wholly non-Halakhic commitment to the survival of the Israeli Jewish community make his generalship "Jewish" in any significant way?

Let me now return to the only slightly less weighty example of the lawyer, seen by some as rivaling the military professional in his capacity to inflict suffering on the morally innocent. To what extent might a specific identity, such as that of an observant Orthodox Jew, create special problems (or opportunities) for the lawyer committed to professional ideals?

Consider the *Shulḥan Arukh*, a basic compilation of Jewish law written by Rabbi Joseph Caro in the sixteenth century, which states, in no uncertain terms, that

> It is forbidden to go before non-Jewish judges and their courts, even if they apply Jewish law and even if both litigants agree to be judged by them. And one who goes to be judged by them is evil, and is regarded as having reviled, cursed, and committed violence against the Torah of Moses our teacher.[83]

To sue in secular courts, even if the principles of decision are identical to Jewish law, is a sign of disrespect for the existing Jewish court system and serves to bolster the status of the non-Jewish secular court.[84]

Now it is clear, practically speaking, that many Jews do not follow this

---

83. 1 Emanuel Quint, *A Restatement of Rabbinic Civil Law* 174 (1990), citing Joseph Caro, *Shulḥan Arukh, Hoshen Mishpat* 26(a). To this day "[a] central principle of halacha is that disputes between Jews should be adjudicated in duly-constituted rabbinical courts." Dov Bressler, "Arbitration and the Courts in Jewish Law," 9 *J. Halacha & Contemp. Soc'y* 105, 109 (1985). A similar view, of course, can be found within at least pre-Constantian Christianity. Thus Paul asks, in 1 Corinthians 6:1: "Dare any of you, having a matter against another, go to law before the unjust, and not before the saints?" It is for this reason, among others, that some explicitly Christian lawyers actively support mediation and other forms of alternative dispute resolution as alternatives to going before regular courts.

84. See Bressler, supra note 83, at 112.

Halakhic injunction and are more than willing to sue fellow Jews in secular courts. Under such circumstances, the person sued is permitted to defend himself, and a lawyer, including a Jewish lawyer (however defined), is permitted to represent the defendant. However, some rabbis have ruled that Halakhah "prohibit[s] a Jewish lawyer from representing a Jewish plaintiff in a civil suit before a secular court,"[85] at least if the plaintiff has not first attempted to summon the defendant before a rabbinical court. Although the defendant has an obligation to respond, there are, of course, no coercive measures available to the rabbinical court (or plaintiff) should the defendant fail to recognize its jurisdiction (and, therefore, of the specific system of Jewish law). Should the defendant fail to appear, the rabbis can then authorize the plaintiff to file a suit in a secular court, where a defendant has less choice about responding.[86] Under such circumstances, a Halakhically observant lawyer is also permitted to continue representating his client before the secular court.[87]

Let us consider some implications of this lesson. Imagine three nonobservant Jews each thinking of filing a lawsuit against other Jews. All describe their aim as finding "a first-rate lawyer" who will offer highly professional representation. The first potential plaintiff goes to lawyer A, about whom we know nothing in particular other than that she is a first-rate professional. A asks a series of questions of her client and offers advice about the potential costs and benefits of litigation. The second plaintiff goes to lawyer B, who we know is Jewish but nonobservant. B's behavior will, presumably, be fundamentally similar to A's. But now consider our third plaintiff, who happens to go to the office of an observant Jew.

One would doubt that either lawyer A or lawyer B would have made inquiries about the religious identities of the first two clients. They might well regard such questions (except in very special circumstances) as no more appropriate than inquiries about a client's sexual preferences. But might the observant Jew not make some effort to find out about the religious identity of the client so that there would be no risk of violating the Halakhic injunction against representing a Jewish plaintiff in a secular court without rabbinic approval?[88] Consider what would happen if the lawyer finds out that

85. Id.
86. See id. at 109–10, 112.
87. See id. at 109.
88. This might be the equivalent of asking how food is cooked in a nonkosher restaurant to make sure that one is not inadvertently ordering vegetable soup that is in fact cooked in a chicken stock.

the potential client is indeed Jewish. Rabbi Bressler writes that "it would appear that Jewish lawyers are in strategic positions to promote adherence to *halacha* by informing their Jewish clients of the legal procedures that would accord with religious requirements,"[89] including the duty to summon the potential defendant to a rabbinical court and going to a secular court only if there is no response.[90] It should be clear that we have moved far beyond defining the Jewish lawyer simply by reference to whether he will go to work on a given day. Instead, the very way that a lawyer relates to his clients seems to be affected crucially by the lawyer's self-conception as a Jew. It is central to my inquiry that this is different from the obvious fact that lawyers differ and that the various codes of professional responsibility allow fairly wide discretion to lawyers in how they will relate to their clients. The differences (and questions) are twofold. First, I am curious whether there are systematic differences between Jewish and non-Jewish lawyers. The discovery of such systematic differences, should they exist, raises questions altogether different from those based upon perceptions that differences are randomly based or otherwise unpredictable on the basis of such general attributes as race, gender, ethnicity, or, in this case, religious identification. Second, it may be misleading, at least regarding Jewish law, to view this as a question of the lawyer's discretion. A central question is whether at least some Jewish lawyers will feel themselves, because of their adherence to Jewish law, *legally* obligated to behave in a certain way about which American law is formally indifferent.

The emphasis on legal obligation is crucial. One is often tempted, in teaching courses on professional responsibility, to raise "moral" dilemmas. A teacher will commonly ask students if they would adhere, for example, to laws mandating confidentiality even where the client threatens to do significant harm to someone else. American law, in most jurisdictions, says the secret must be kept. Many students say that their moral convictions would lead them to behave otherwise. Note that what is being countered by "law" is "morals." It is usually suggested, especially within secular universities, that the proper discipline for ascertaining if any such moral demands exist is secular philosophy. Someone seeking ethical guidance is, from this perspective, well advised to read Kant, Bentham, Rawls, or Luban.[91] Rarely, if ever,

89. Bressler, supra note 83, at 112.
90. See id.
91. David Luban, *Lawyers and Justice* (1988).

does one hear suggestions that privileged guidance might be found in religious traditions and their notions of ethical duties.

One of the things that makes the problem of the Jewish lawyer interesting to me, though, is that he may feel compelled to act by genuine legal duties, derived from Jewish law rather than philosophic reflection. To be sure, one often will argue that Jewish law and morality coincide. Much traditional Judaism, however, does not make any independent inquiry into the morality of Jewish law (that is, look at the specific body of Jewish law from the perspective of a specific mode of inquiry called ethics). Instead, the law is itself deemed to be constitutive of what is moral. It becomes almost literally incomprehensible to ask whether some feature of Jewish law is moral,[92] even though this question is recognized as eminently sensible regarding any secular system of law.

It should be emphasized that there is not agreement, even among the Orthodox, as to the prohibition discussed above. At least some members of the Orthodox community would place the conduct described — assisting a Jew in bringing an unauthorized lawsuit before a secular court — as an instance of *lifnei iver,* aiding another in the commission of a sin. Although this act is forbidden by religious law, there are a number of conditions that allow exceptions to be made, the most important of which is the likelihood that the potential sinner will in fact be able to gain his object even without the help of the particular abettor.[93] To take the easiest example in this context, if someone is likely to be able to find a lawyer to press a claim anyway, then an Orthodox Jew is not estopped from taking the case even though the litigant is violating Jewish law. Under such circumstances, to abet a sin, so long as one does not actively encourage it, is not prohibited.

92. See, e.g., David Weiss Halivni, "Can a Religious Law Be Immoral?," in *Perspectives on Jews and Judaism* 167 (Arthur Chiel, ed., 1978). The answer, according to Halivni, is no. See also Aharon Lichtenstein, "Does Jewish Tradition Recognize an Ethic Independent of Halakha?," in *Modern Jewish Ethics* 62 (Marvin Fox, ed., 1975). One of the obvious differences, between at least some versions of Orthodoxy and most versions of Conservative and Reform Judaism is that the answer, for the latter, is most definitely yes. I should not claim that the answer, even for the Orthodox, is necessarily no, as I have learned over the last ten years of association with the Shalom Hartman Institute for Jewish Philosophy in Jerusalem. It seems safe, and sad, however, to say that the predominant trend in contemporary Orthodoxy is against engaging in independent analysis of the morality of Halakhah.

93. For a discussion of this exception, see Michael J. Broyde, "On the Practice of Law According to Halacha," 20 *J. Halacha & Contemp. Soc'y* 5, 12 (1990).

Much of the same kind of logic (that is, the strong distinction between the actual sinner or wrongdoer and the lawyer-agent who only offers professional assistance) underlies the standard view within the American legal profession that "[a] lawyer's representation of a client . . . does not constitute an endorsement of the client's political, economic, social or moral views or activities."[94] This idea is often described (and sometimes condemned) as "the principle of nonaccountability," by which the nefarious morality and illegal conduct of the client is not attributed to the lawyer, who is simply defending the client's legal rights within the legal system. Still, just as the American Bar Association code encourages a lawyer to bring moral issues to the client's attention, even if the client has the ultimate choice of what legal options will be pursued, it surely seems Halakhically required to encourage a Jewish client to behave according to Jewish law, even if the lawyer is permitted to accept a negative response and, thereafter, to file suit in a secular court. It still seems to be the case that a Halakhically oriented Jewish lawyer will behave quite differently from one differently oriented.

Consider an example in the area of family offered by Rabbi Michael J. Broyde. He notes, altogether accurately, "that many of the values that are at the core of halacha have been rejected by normative American society,"[95] including by many, and possibly most, non-Orthodox Jews. Nowhere, he argues, is this more evident than in regard to family law. Perhaps the clearest example is the Jewish couple seeking a civil divorce. According to Rabbi Broyde, "it would seem incumbent upon an observant attorney who is aiding a Jewish couple seeking a divorce to advise the couple that they must also seek a divorce which is proper according to halacha,"[96] that is, to obtain a *get* — an official decree authorizing the dissolution of the marriage — from a properly constituted rabbinical court. Interestingly enough, the refusal by the couple to arrange for a *get* does not preclude the lawyer's continued representation of the client, under the principle of lifnei iver.

Even more interesting, and for many of us more troublesome, is the example of a mixed-marriage couple seeking a divorce. Such a marriage is, of course, Halakhically prohibited. Thus, says Rabbi Broyde, in regard to intermarried clients, "it is incumbent upon the lawyer either to give no advice as to how to salvage the marriage or to counsel the client not to try to

---

94. *Model Rules of Professional Conduct* Rule 1.2(b) (1991).

95. Broyde, supra note 93, at 32.

96. Id. at 33.

save the marriage."[97] I am assuming, of course, that the behavior would be very different if both parties were Jewish. The lawyer in that instance would at the very least be permitted and, I strongly suspect, encouraged to suggest counseling and other techniques designed to save a marriage. Are Orthodox lawyers under a duty to disclose to the potential client that they will structure any advice they may give by the norms of Jewish law or are they permitted to remain silent and to offer "interested" advice in a more "disinterested" posture?

Enforcement of the criminal law presents other problems. One rabbi, for example, writes that Jewish law makes it

> forbidden for [an observant Jewish lawyer] . . . to help the criminal escape the consequences of his act, by relying on some technical legal points or other devices. The lawyer, just as any Jew, is directed by the Torah to "eradicate the evil from our midst" and may not actively assist someone to avoid his punishment.[98]

It is not clear whether this particular rabbi is referring to basic legal guarantees of the U.S. Constitution as examples of mere "technicalities" or to something else. If the former, and if one takes this seriously, then it would appear that no Orthodox Jew could be a criminal defense lawyer. It would certainly be interesting to find out how many Orthodox lawyers in fact practice in this branch of the law.

It is absolutely essential to note that the examples I have offered — and many other examples that could be offered — deal with what, from the perspective of American law regarding lawyers, is left to the lawyer's own discretion. That is, there is no serious argument that lawyers are legally required to take any given cases. Lawyers would be violating no one's legal rights if they simply refused to take given cases. The question is only whether they, under one of the recognized exceptions to the application of lifnei iver, are permitted to exercise a legal privilege, within American law, to take particular cases.

Nothing stated earlier in this article should suggest that there is anything questionable about being a Halakhically-oriented Jewish lawyer. I suggest only that it might comprise a distinctive way of being a Jewish lawyer that

97. Id.

98. Herschel Schachter, " 'Dina De-Malchuta Dina': Secular Law as a Religious Obligation," in *Halacha and Contemporary Society* 85, 103–4 (Alfred S. Cohen, ed., 1983).

might surprise certain clients or otherwise make it vitally important to ascertain in advance the religious sensibilities of one's lawyer before offering a retainer for representation.

We now come to a very different question, which is whether the relationship between Jewish and American law could be not only one of difference, but also of outright conflict. Could the legal systems make genuinely competing demands upon those subject to their jurisdiction? The earlier examples concerned obligations only from the perspective of one legal system. By definition, there could be no legal conflict. However, one must now broach the possibility of the existence of two legal systems each claiming to be fully legitimate and "sovereign" over the behavior of the lawyer. No problem is more complex, with more perceived dangers within the literature of political theory.

There is, to be sure, the principle within rabbinic Judaism of *dina de-malkhuta dina* ("the law of the land is the law").[99] Although one is tempted to ascribe the principle to sound prudential judgment, it is presented as a distinctly nonprudential norm: The Jew is enjoined, as a general matter, to obey the secular law even if violation would go undiscovered. This, however, does not operate as a complete subordination of the commands of Jewish law to those of the states within which Jews live. It is applied primarily in *denei mamonot,* those matters dealt with in civil commercial law.[100] It has little application in regard to *issurim,* the regulation of religious and ritual observances.[101] More generally, Aaron Kirschenbaum and John Trafimow note that "some authorities maintain [that dina de-malkhuta dina] is relative only to matters of a governmental nature; legal norms, judicial practices, and the ordinary administration of justice are not subsumed under the [principle]. . . . Otherwise, *dina de-malkhuta dina* would spell the demise of

99. See id. at 85. The literature on the concept is substantial, especially in Hebrew, a language that I do not read. For an interesting recent discussion, see Aaron Kirschenbaum and John Trafimow, "The Sovereign Power of the State: A Proposed Theory of Accommodation in Jewish Law," 12 *Cardozo L. Rev.* 925, 941 (1991); Chaim Povarsky, "Jewish Law v. the Law of the State: Theories of Accommodation," 12 *Cardozo L. Rev.* 941 (1991); Malvina Halberstam, "Interest Analysis and *Dina De-Malkhuta Dina*: A Comment on Aaron Kirschenbaum, 'The Sovereign Power of the State: A Proposed Theory of Accommodation in Jewish Law,'" 12 *Cardozo L. Rev.* 951 (1991). The concept also plays a central role in J. David Bleich, "Jewish Law and the State's Authority to Punish Crime," 12 *Cardozo L. Rev.* 829 (1991).

100. See, e.g., Kirschenbaum and Trafimow, supra note 99, at 936.

101. See id.

Jewish law."[102] Thus the principle is not at all comparable to the principle of American law that the law of the United States is (ultimately) the law of Ohio. That is, in any conflict between Ohio and the U.S. Constitution, and laws passed by Congress under its constitutional powers, the federal law prevails without exception. However deferential observant Jews might be to the legal demands of the secular state, it should be obvious that they cannot accept the obligatory force of any law that might be valid within the secular state that is contrary to Halakhah. Imagine, for example, a state that requires assent to the divinity of Jesus. No Jew could recognize this as binding law.

Fortunately, at least in the United States, we need not concern ourselves with such a law. But this does not mean that there are no imaginable true conflicts. As one might expect, the one most likey to arise (or at least the one most often discussed) within the context of the American legal profession concerns the obligation to preserve client confidences. The American Bar Association Model Rules of Professional Conduct require, with only limited exceptions, that a client's secrets be preserved.[103] The principal exception, for our purposes, involves "prevent[ing] the client from committing a criminal act that the lawyer believes is likely to result in imminent death or substantial bodily harm."[104]

What this means, in those states that have adopted the Model Rules, is that a lawyer is prohibited, for example, from disclosing a client's intent to embezzle or commit other economic crimes, regardless of the consequences to the community. Just as important is the prohibition against disclosure of past crimes. Thus, to adopt an example from the most famous (or infamous) example in the literature of the American legal profession, a lawyer who has been told by his client the location of yet undiscovered bodies of the client's murder victims is under a duty not to tell anyone else, including distraught parents who might come to the lawyer asking for any information about whether their children are even alive.

Most defenses of the confidentiality privileges are rooted in the Anglo-American individualist tradition, wherein deep (and, some would say, extreme) respect for individual autonomy is mixed with an almost equally deep mistrust of the power of the community, especially when gathered

102. Id.
103. See Model Rules of Professional Conduct Rule 1.6(b)(1) (1991).
104. Id.

together in a coercive state. It is within this context, then, that one reads Rabbi Alfred Cohen's comment, in an article on the ethics of maintaining professional confidences, that "in Jewish ethics the welfare of the community takes precedence over the needs of the individual."[105]

What is fascinating is that Rabbi Cohen does not suggest that the Halakhah provides any categorical rules for resolving the dilemma facing a professional who desires to disclose the secrets of a client in order to protect important community interests. "It may be," he writes, "that maintaining professional secrecy is so absolutely integral to the proper function of that profession and the profession so essential to the welfare of society that the halacha would decide the practitioner must maintain his professional secrets."[106] Not surprisingly, though, there is the counter possibility as well: "[T]he halacha may be that it is more important for [the lawyer] to reveal the confidential material, even if it will cause him enormous personal damage."[107]

What should observant Jews do when they feel torn about preserving a confidence that would presumptively be protected under secular law? Clearly, this is not a question that people should decide for themselves, and professional practitioners must consult with a competent Halakhic authority. "There is no way a person can overcome his own subjective motivations in deciding so sensitive and crucial a question. Sometimes the needs of society will be best served by maintaining the standards of a given profession, but sometimes that may not be the case."[108]

What is most important about Rabbi Cohen's argument is its clear rejection of the authority of the secular state to make the final decision about the values involved in a given conflict between preserving the client's secrets and disclosing them in order to protect the community. That is, he raises the possibility that a lawyer would learn from a Halakhic authority that Jewish law, correctly understood, requires, at least in a specific instance, violation of the secular legal duty to maintain a client's confidences. It is at least thinkable that dina de-malkhuta dina would not address the situation. Of course the Halakhic command cannot be made truly coercive, but, presum-

105. Alfred S. Cohen, "On Maintaining a Professional Confidence," 7 *J. Halacha & Contemp. Soc'y* 84 (1984). See also Gordon Tucker, "The Confidentiality Rule: A Philosophical Perspective with Reference to Jewish Law and Ethics," 13 *Fordham Urb. L.J.* 99 (1985).

106. Cohen, supra note 105, at 84.

107. Id.

108. Id. at 84–85.

ably, a lawyer who cared enough to seek out Halakhic guidance would feel obligated to obey its commands, even at the cost of violating the secular law.

Again I emphasize that, should this situation ever arise, it might well be analyzed as a true conflict of legal obligations, rather than as a more conventional conflict between law and morals. In deciding between rejecting the rabbi's interpretation of Halakhah and fulfilling the demand of the secular law, a lawyer would make a basic decision about which community is most truly constitutive of his identity. This might indicate, at the most fundamental level, what it might mean to be a Jewish lawyer.

One question that would immediately arise, in regard to any Orthodox Jewish lawyers who felt obliged to breach the secular legal duty of confidentiality, is whether they would properly be subject to discipline or liability to the betrayed client. That is, could one plausibly cite the First Amendment[109] on behalf of a "free exercise" permission to reject the otherwise binding law of the state? The answer is almost certainly negative, especially given the present Supreme Court's hostility to recognizing the exemption of religious minorities from state regulation even in matters that go to the heart of a minority's religious ceremonies.[110]

Conclusion

I have attempted in this article to lay out an analytical grid for use in identifying the Jewish lawyer. I have tried to show that distinctly different answers are produced depending on what model of Jewish identity is used. I most certainly do not want to argue that any one of the models is uniquely "correct." Not only do I have an intellectual predilection against making such arguments, but I would also inevitably be engaged in a kind of self-defense in urging any one argument over any others. For example, inasmuch as I classify my own Jewish identity as strongly secular, rather than religious, I could scarcely adopt either the fourth or fifth models, and I would be personally comfortable only with relatively minimal versions of the second or third.

In any event, I hope that I have shown how the question of the Jewish lawyer is not precisely analogous to questions involving other attributes like gender, race, or ethnicity. Even if one wants to argue that there are distinctive ways of looking at the world associated with these other attributes, no

---

109. U.S. Const. amend. I.

110. See *Employment Div. v. Smith,* 494 U.S. 872 (1990).

one could plausibly argue that these ways are legally mandated by membership in the group in question. If any identified group of people practice law in a distinctive manner, the explanation would, depending on your theory, lie in genetics, psychoanalytic theory, or sociology. It could not lie in the obligation felt by the group members to be faithful to a particular legal tradition with its own mandates.

My major interest is the question of identity, both in regard to being a professional and to being a Jew. Ludwig Wittgenstein[111] has taught us that "to imagine a language means to imagine a form of life."[112] One important life form that has survived from ancient times is that of religious community; for an increasing number of moderns, that has been joined by the particular language-form of life that we call professionalism. Perhaps what is distinctive about our "postmodern" society is our increasing self-consciousness that many of us are in effect multilingual insofar as we try simultaneously to inhabit quite different forms of life. This is, I think, one description of the situation of at least some Jewish lawyers. Therefore, the justification for trying to elucidate some of the tensions is implicit in the very term.

Afterword

Professor Monroe Freedman has taken severe exception to my use of his quotation at the beginning of this article about the priority of "professional ethics" over "personal ethics." He particularly objects to my suggesting that he supports what I call the "bleached-out self." He writes as follows:[113]

> . . . Professor Levinson has "identified" me, for professional purposes, as a non-Jew.
>
> He derives this offensive conclusion from a single quotation, in which I wrote: "It may be that the wisest course is to make each lawyer's conscience [or the teachings of one's religious tradition] his ultimate guide. It should be recognized, however, that this view is wholly inconsistent with *the notion of professional ethics which, by definition, supersede personal*

---

111. It may be also worth mentioning that one of the implicit messages of Ray Monk, *Ludwig Wittgenstein: The Duty of Genius* (1990), is the extraordinary complexity of ascribing a particular religious identity to Ludwig Wittgenstein, whose Viennese family had in its past been Jewish, but who lies buried in a Catholic cemetery in England.

112. Ludwig Wittgenstein, *Philosophical Investigations* 8E (3d ed., 1958).

113. Monroe H. Freedman, "Legal Ethics from a Jewish Perspective," 27 *Texas Tech L. Rev.* 1131, 1135 (1996).

ethics." Professor Levinson adds the bracketed words as well as the italics to what I actually wrote. Beyond that, the quote is taken out of context from a footnote written more than a quarter of a century ago. It was part of a response to Professor (now Judge) John T. Noonan.[114] Here is the full quote:

> Professor Noonan adds a further *petitio principii* when he argues, in the language of Canon 15, that the lawyer "obey his own conscience." It may be that the wisest course is to make each lawyer's conscience his ultimate guide. It should be recognized, however, that this view is wholly inconsistent with the notion of professional ethics which, by definition, supersede personal ethics. In addition, it should be noted that personal ethics, in the context of acting in a professional capacity for another, can require a conclusion different from that which one might reach when acting for himself. For example, the fact that a lawyer would not commit perjury on his own behalf does not in any way preclude a decision to put on the witness stand a client who intends to perjure himself in his behalf.

Thus, Judge Noonan had argued that one's duties under codified ethical rules could be determined by looking to one's conscience. I replied that this begs the question of what the rules in fact require. In context, therefore, the words Professor Levinson selected to quote were obviously intended not as an "idealized conception of the lawyer's identity," but as a truism about the nature of codified rules of ethics. There would be no need for elaborate codifications of rules of lawyers' ethics, of course, if it all came down to nothing more than "follow your own conscience." Nor would it be a defense to a violation of a disciplinary rule for a lawyer to say, "my conscience told me to disregard the rule." . . .

More important, using (and enhancing) the partial footnote as Professor Levinson does disregards what I have written in almost three decades thereafter and the way that I have lived my professional life. . . .

To put it mildly, I have no desire to challenge Professor Freedman's description of his position, not least because I admire greatly his contributions to the serious consideration of what "lawyers' ethics" might mean as well as his personal engagements as a practicing lawyer. And it would be appalling

114. John Noonan, "The Purposes of Advocacy and the Limits of Confidentiality," 64 *Mich. L. Rev.* 1485 (1966).

if I, or anyone else, called into account Professor Freedman's identity as a Jewish lawyer who takes the demands of his religion with the utmost seriousness.

Perhaps one mistake was using the term "idealized conception of the lawyer's identity." My own use of the word "idealized" was drawn from the notion made famous by the German sociologist Max Weber of the "ideal type," by which he meant not a normative ideal, but, rather, a kind of "pure" concept, whether or not fully reflected in reality, of a given social institution. I continue to believe that the notion of a "bleached-out self" remains useful as just such a Weberian "ideal," even if, blessedly, it is an "ideal" that is in fact impossible to live up (or down) to because of the inability of people entirely to subordinate other aspects of their life to the demands of the law.

The paradox, of course, is that I have no real disagreement when Professor Freedman writes that his statement is ultimately "a truism about the nature of codified rules of ethics." Or, perhaps more precisely, one might speak of "the nature of codified rules of law." One of the central issues in jurisprudence, after all, is whether there is any necessary connection between law and "ethics" or "morality." My own answer is that there is not; that it is perfectly possible, that is, to speak of evil systems of law. A contrary answer, perhaps drawn from a tradition extending from St. Augustine to Martin Luther King, is to say that a "law" requiring injustice is by virtue of that fact not really law at all, because it is a necessary condition of calling something "law" that it indeed be just or moral. It is far beyond the scope of this book to explain why I ultimately do not find the so-called just-law tradition helpful. It should be clear that this does not mean that I, or any other "legal positivist" who rejects "just law," denies the validity of moral arguments, only that we rigorously separate the realm of what might be termed "legal truths" from a realm of "moral truths" and leave open the possibility, therefore, that one is faced by genuine conflicts between legal and moral obligations.

I hope, then, that the reader (and Professor Freedman) will allow me to use the specific quotation in question, which I find a marvelously concise way of making an extremely important point, without necessarily attributing to Professor Freedman views that he would find objectionable.

5

National Loyalty, Communalism, and

the Professional Identity of Lawyers

An Encounter in Hungary

I begin with the story of an encounter in Hungary that occurred in the summer of 1992, when I was participating in a seminar for Eastern European lawyers by teaching a sequence of classes on the American view of the legal profession. The idea was that Eastern European lawyers, who were themselves participating in the design of institutional structures — including an organized bar — appropriate to the new political orders emerging in those countries, might learn something from the American experience. As we all know, however, the learning process can work two ways, and it is not always so easy to distinguish the teachers from the taught.

A central question that I wanted to explore with these lawyers concerned the conditions that could legitimately be placed by the state on entry to the practice of law. Thus I presented several cases of the United States Supreme Court dealing with constitutional limitations on state regulation of the bar. For example, could a state limit membership in the bar to "loyal Americans," defined as those untainted by contact with "subversive" ideas or by membership in organizations like the Communist Party? Several states had attempted just such limitations, which drew mixed responses from the Supreme Court. The final outcome of these cases, though, was the unconstitutionality of a state's using membership in the Communist Party per se to prevent individuals from becoming lawyers.[1] The state was entitled to *ask* applicants about membership, and to use their answers as the basis for

This essay was originally published in *Yale Journal of Law and the Humanities* 7 (1995): 49.
1. *Baird v. State Bar*, 401 U.S. 1 (1971).

further conversation about their commitment to illegal goals of the party. However, simple party membership — and even support of the desirability of radical transformation of the polity into a "proletarian dictatorship" — could not be disqualifying.

As one might imagine, these cases generated spirited discussion among the Hungarian, Ukranian, Georgian, Bulgarian, and other Eastern European lawyers gathered together in Rackeve, a small town outside of Budapest. Most of them espoused views far less tolerant than current American constitutional doctrine in regard to the rights of Communist lawyers. They tended to view American liberals like myself as almost laughably (or tragically) naive in our formal indifference to the political beliefs, including hostility to some basic norms of liberal democracy, of those who would enter the legal profession. They would scarcely entrust the bar to those whose ideological loyalties were suspect.

Overtly ideological restrictions on entry to the bar are, of course, only one example of state regulation. Another concerns one's formal status as a member of the state, a topic that also provoked considerable discussion. The most vigorous discussant in regard to this issue was a Latvian, Imma Jansone, who was employed by the Latvian equivalent of the state bar association. Although she had expressed her share of skepticism about welcoming Communists into the bar, the principal conflict between us took place over a quite different case, *In re Griffiths*,[2] a 1973 Supreme Court decision striking down a Connecticut law limiting membership in the state bar to citizens of the United States.

Ms. Jansone vigorously disagreed with my endorsement of the Court's decision, at least insofar as I used it to suggest that the Latvian and other Eastern European bars should not restrict membership to nationals of their respective countries. She defended the desire of the local bar to restrict legal practice in Latvia not only, and reasonably, to those who could pass an examination demonstrating sufficient knowledge of Latvian law, but also — more debatably — to *citizens* of the newly revived country and speakers of its language. As we began our discussion, I assumed that we simply represented the conflict between my own (highly desirable) liberal universalism and her (quite dubious) tribal parochialism, especially in light of the fact that emphasis on Latvian citizenship and linguistic abilities is often a coded way of denying full rights to longtime (and, in many cases, lifetime) Russian

2. 413 U.S. 717 (1973).

residents of Latvia who would be denied such citizenship.[3] As the discussion progressed, though, I realized that the situation may be more complex than I had first thought, that there may in fact be a defensible rationale for at least some of the limitations on admission to the bar that Ms. Jansone was proposing. My thoughts then turned to whether the rationale for her position was substantially dependent on the specific circumstances of Latvia or, indeed, if it might have implications even for our own very different political and cultural situation here in the United States. What follows is an attempt to address these questions, an exploration that involves nothing less than reflecting on the intersections, if any, of the duties of citizenship and the roles of modern lawyers.

The Lawyer as Citizen and as Friend

I want to adapt a question — "Can a good lawyer be a good person?" — that begins a famous article by Charles Fried on "the moral foundations of the lawyer-client relationship."[4] What if, for example, a lawyer worked to vindicate the legal rights of a pornographer, or of a landlord seeking eviction of a poor family for failure to pay the rent, or, as I have done, of the Ku Klux Klan to march down the main street of the capital of Texas? Fried answered his question (and countered any such examples) with a resounding affirmation of the lawyer's role. In a reasonably just society, he argued, it is *always*

---

3. See, e.g., Michael Ignatieff, *Blood and Belonging: Journeys into the New Nationalism* 168 (1994), where he notes that the attempt by Latvia to restrict citizenship to Latvian-speakers is quite likely an attempt to disenfranchise those "ethnic Russians [who] are in a majority in Riga, the capital. . . . Ethnic Russians born and brought up in Latvia lose their citizenship in the new republic unless they learn the rudiments of Latvian." It is clearly possible to have a multilingual society where some citizens speak only one of the languages, as in Switzerland, Belgium, or Canada. Perhaps the United States should be added to this list, even though it obviously has no "official" alternatives to its principal language, unlike the three countries mentioned above, which are "officially" bilingual or multilingual. In any event, would it be illegitimate for a state within the United States to restrict entrance to the bar to those who can speak (at least) English? Only if one confidently answers this question in the affirmative can one simply dismiss the Latvian language restriction, which may be not only anti-Russian (which it most certainly is), but also an attempt to assure the maintenance of Latvian as a living language in a world where its speakers are surrounded (and potentially swamped) by those proficient in other languages with no desire to learn Latvian. Ignatieff has an excellent discussion of the language issue in his analysis of Quebec. Id. at 143–77.
4. Charles Fried, "The Lawyer as Friend: The Moral Foundations of the Lawyer-Client Relation," 85 *Yale L.J.* 1060 (1976).

morally admirable to help persons achieve *whatever* the law entitles them to do, even if the lawyers in question would choose to lead their own lives in considerably different ways from those of their clients.

As has been pointed out by his many critics,[5] Fried's question is surely too broad, for only the most rabid antilawyers have argued that the lawyer *cannot* be a good person, that it would be enough to know that persons are lawyers in order to identify them as bad.[6] The more sensible question is surely something like, "To what extent, and under what circumstances, might the attributes of a good lawyer conflict with those of a good person?"

My adaptation of Fried's question is as follows: Will a good lawyer, as defined by fidelity to the norms of professional conduct, necessarily be a good *citizen?* If the answer is no, then one must assert potential distinctions between the attributes of good (i.e., professionally honorable) lawyering and of good citizenship. Someone identified by standard American professional norms as a first-rate lawyer would at the same time be potentially describable as a questionable, even "bad," citizen. A full exploration of this question would require nothing less than elaboration of the notions of both "good lawyering" and "good citizenship." The latter, in particular, would have to be distinguished from what might be termed "mere" citizenship, the possession of an "external" legal status as a citizen of a given polity that is not significantly intertwined with an "internal," phenomenological sense of strong political identity and commitment to shared political purposes. "Mere citizens" may be similar to what Michael Walzer once described as "alienated residents," individuals who may live within a formal political space but for whom that status has almost no affective meaning.[7]

I turn once more to Fried's article, in which he presented a model of the lawyer as the client's "friend." According to Fried, "like a friend [your lawyer] acts in your interests, not his own; or rather he adopts your interests

5. The classic critique is Edward A. Dauer and Arthur Allen Leff, "Correspondence: The Lawyer as Friend," 86 *Yale L.J.* 573 (1977).

6. To accept any such argument would, among other things, be especially difficult for those of us who actually teach in law schools; for then we would presumably have to recognize ourselves as *inevitable* collaborators with evil.

7. See Michael Walzer, *Obligations: Essays on Disobedience, War, and Citizenship* 113–14 (1970). "[T]he alienated residents of the modern state . . . are probably far more numerous than are the resident aliens," says Walzer, who goes on to say that whatever obligations are felt by the politically alienated, "these obligations do not involve what the ancients called political 'friendship' and do not bind [them] to share the political purposes or the political destiny of [their] fellow residents. . . . " Id. at 114.

as his own. I would call that the classic definition of friendship."[8] Whatever the problems with Fried's metaphor of the lawyer as the client's "friend" — one does not, for example, often hire one's friends — they do not preclude us from adapting it to the role of the citizen, where it may prove considerably more illuminating.

When we describe someone as a "*good* citizen," rather than a "*mere* citizen," do we not refer in some sense to a genuine friend of the polity, someone devoted to its interests and willing, if necessary, to subordinate more selfish interests to those of the polity? One name for this kind of citizenship, of course, is patriotism. As Francis Lieber wrote in the middle of the nineteenth century, "Without patriotism . . . all must dissolve into dreary, heartless egoism. But even to regret such an occurrence and strive to prevent it requires patriotism."[9] Some versions of such civil friendship are almost frightening in their monomania. I think, for example, of Rousseau's stunning invocation in *Emile* of the Spartan mother who, upon being told by a messenger that her five sons had just died in a battle, responded, "You fool. Did we win the battle or not?"[10] I presume that most of us find this exemplary not of friendship but of totalitarianism, for it seems to extinguish any noncivic loyalties and attachments. I think it too pessimistic, though, to suggest that we are forced to choose either Spartan totalitarianism or celebration of a desiccated notion of citizenship whose sole meaning becomes, in effect, the possession of rights *against* the state without any concern for *duties* owed it. Indeed, criticisms of rights-centeredness and emphasis on claims of the community are pervasive themes in both academic political theory and books written for more general audiences.[11]

In this context I am reminded of the 350-year-old oath taken by new voters in Connecticut. They must "solemnly swear" to "be true and faithful to the state of Connecticut, and to the constitution and the government,

---

8. Fried, supra note 4, at 1071.

9. 1 Francis Lieber, *Manual of Political Ethics* 89 (1881 ed.) (1855), *quoted in* Paul Carrington, "The Theme of Early American Law Teaching: The Political Ethics of Francis Lieber," 42 *J. Legal Educ.* 339, 369 (1992).

10. Jean-Jacques Rousseau, *Emile, or On Education* 40 (Allan Bloom, trans., 1979).

11. For high political theory, see, e.g., Michael Sandel, *Liberalism and the Limits of Justice* (1982). For more popular books written by academics, see Robert Bellah et al., *Habits of the Heart* (1985); Mary Ann Glendon, *Rights Talk: The Impoverishment of Political Discourse* (1991). Even some liberal critics of the new communitarianism nonetheless recognize the need for individuals to have social commitments. See, e.g., Nancy Rosenblum, *Another Liberalism: Romanticism and Reconstruction of Liberal Thought* (1987).

thereof . . . and to the constitution of the United States."[12] More to the point, the oath states that "whenever you are called upon to give your vote or choice touching any matter which concerns this state or the United States, you will do this in a manner which you shall judge contributes to the best interests of Connecticut and the nation, without respect or favor of any person," including the person of oneself.[13] We might also remember President Kennedy's famous plea in his inaugural address to the citizenry to "ask not what your country can do for you; ask what you can do for your country."[14]

"Good citizenship" is therefore far more than merely obeying the laws, just as being a good parent is, presumably, far more than simply refraining from child abuse. To earn commendation in either role requires a disposition of concern and care for others, including a willingness, when necessary, to subordinate one's own desires or interests to those of others (even as children must learn that parents have their own legitimate desires and interests which must be recognized). Of course, the purpose is to create a community, whether we call it the polity or the family, that enjoys a status quite different from a simple collection of the discrete, separated individuals counted as its members. One of the characteristics of such communities, presumably, is what Dean Anthony Kronman calls "political fraternity" — bonds of sympathy among its members "despite the difference of opinion that set them apart on questions concerning the ends, and hence the identity, of their community."[15]

I come, then, to the title of this essay, "National Loyalty, Communalism, and the Professional Identity of Lawyers." I am interested in the extent to which, in the words of the sociologist Steven Cohen, "professions are potential communities; and, as such, they might serve as surrogates and replacements" for more typical kinds of communities. Cohen even suggests that "some professions could conceivably rival ethnic and religious communities in many ways."[16] Interestingly enough, Cohen does not list political com-

---

12. See Conn. Gen. Stat. § 1–25 (1987).

13. See id. I discuss the oath in "Suffrage and Community: Who Should Vote?," 41 *Fla. L. Rev.* 545, 560–61 (1989).

14. *Bartlett's Quotations* 74 (Justin Kaplan, ed., 16th ed., 1992).

15. Anthony T. Kronman, *The Lost Lawyer: Failing Ideals of the Legal Profession* 93 (1993).

16. Steven M. Cohen, *American Modernity and Jewish Identity* 84 (1983). I explore some of these themes in chapter 4.

munities among the potential competitors for feelings of loyalty and commitment. Is it possible, however, that the professional community could even become a rival, in some significant sense, to the polity? If that should be the case, is it a cause for worry, or might we view such professional communities as just one more tile of a mosaic that celebrates cultural pluralism and the presence of mediating institutions that can resist the imperial claims of the state?

No one familiar with contemporary American culture can avoid the issue of multiculturalism and the ostensible challenges posed by cultural fragmentation to standard notions of social and political unity. Multiculturalism comes in many different disguises, though. We should be as aware of the potential conflicts generated by cultures of professionalism as we are of those caused by racial, ethnic, or religious affiliations, even if, to be sure, these latter problems are more likely to eventuate in bloodshed. Moreover, to focus on "fragmentation" may be misleading if it suggests that the only threat to national unity comes from subcommunities *within* the territorial polity. One might also note the possibility of *transnational* loyalties that go beyond the nation-state. The most obvious example is the Roman Catholic Church. For our purposes, one might ask if the internalization of the norms of the legal profession will also lead to a cross-national professional identity significantly independent of the national identity provided by the passport carried by a particular lawyer.

What Do Lawyers Do?

Before one can cogently discuss the state regulation of lawyers, including limiting membership in the profession to citizens, one obviously must have an image of what it is that lawyers do (as well as what it is that citizens do). One of the central tasks I set for myself during my sojourn in Hungary, therefore, was elaborating to the Eastern Europeans a description of how American lawyers conceptualize their own role. What, precisely, do American lawyers view themselves as doing? To begin answering this question I assigned to my students the seminal 1897 speech by Oliver Wendell Holmes, "The Path of the Law."[17] Delivered to law students at Boston University as a way of explaining to them the nature of the vocation they had chosen,

---

17. Oliver Wendell Holmes, "The Path of the Law," 10 *Harv. L. Rev.* 457 (1897).

Holmes's speech is, I believe, the most important explanation of the legal profession ever penned by an American—not least because of its decidedly unsentimental view of the lawyer's role.

What, for Holmes, is the task of the ordinary lawyer? Is it, for example, the careful study of the social good, or of norms of justice, and the conveying to clients the results of such study? Not especially: Holmes sweeps aside the traditional notion of the lawyer as a civic-republican patriot and replaces it with the image of a businessman selling a commodity, which is knowledge about the actual behavior of public officials who possess the capacity to bring public force to bear on the lawyer's clients. The "business" of the lawyer is simply the prediction of the likely behavior of public officials, particularly judges, in response to the acts of citizens. Law is ascertained through acute observation of political behavior—"experience"—rather than through dazzling "logical" analysis that might be altogether irrelevant to the actual behavior found within a particular society. Holmes's method entails a strict analytical separation between description and assessment—that is, between law and morality. He leaves no doubt that the role of the lawyer is simply to present accurate descriptive accounts to clients who will then base their behavior on a desire to avoid unfortunate encounters with, and the costs imposed by, public authority.

Holmes's positivism thus contains a decidedly skeptical view about the moral status of public authority. Although Holmes had been wounded three times during the great struggle of 1861–65 (itself the most profound clash about the meaning of American citizenship in our own history), he generally viewed life as a relentless struggle among brutally contending competitors, in which survival was its own justification. "Law" itself was simply an assertion of power, and the lawyer's role was merely the detached purveying of a certain kind of information about the likely use of public force.

What the skilled lawyer knows is the "law in action" rather than what Roscoe Pound, a contemporary of Holmes, disdainfully dismissed as the "law on the books," which was often utterly ignored even by public officials. Holmes described, and some would even say helped to create, a client who simply wishes to know, concretely, what is likely to happen upon a certain course of conduct. An important analytical construct developed by Holmes is that of the "bad man," motivated only to avoid unpleasant consequences but not concerned, for example, with doing good, however defined, for its own sake. Holmes by no means suggested that one should avoid representing such "bad men." Indeed, "bad men" comprised much of the market for the services that Holmesian lawyers sold, since their own behavior was the product not of an internal moral compass but, rather, of the simple desire to avoid actions whose costs outweighed their benefits. And the lawyer hired by such a client is basically indifferent to the use that will be made of the information by the client.

Dean Kronman has recently offered an important analysis — part jeremiad, part call to action — of the legal profession that is strikingly anti-Holmesian in its thrust. Far from the lawyer as detached predictor, Kronman's lawyer is an embedded member of a particular political community, sharing this identity with his or her clients and with the judges who will decide their cases.[18] It is this embeddedness that, among other things, generates the attribute of "statesmanship" that for Kronman defines legal practice at its best. For Kronman, "[t]he good lawyer does care about the soundness of the legal order. . . . [H]e shares the judge's public-spirited devotion to it."[19] A similar argument can be found in Robert Gordon's classic "neo-republican" essay "The Independence of Lawyers."[20]

As Kronman himself admits (and bewails), the "lawyer as statesman" is perhaps under fatal assault for reasons ranging from internal developments within American legal education to the modern culture of the large law firm. Still, there may be at least some citizen-lawyers who practice in the United States and feel some identification with the polity and its interests. Consider, though, what might be termed "multinational" lawyers who practice law outside their polities. What precisely would it mean for *them* to be "statesmen" or "republicans," neo- or otherwise? After all, what polity or social order would they identify with? One notes Secretary of Labor Robert Reich's emphasis on the relationship between national attachments and the inculcation of a necessary spirit of self-sacrifice. According to Reich, "we learn to feel responsible for others because we share with them a common history . . . a common culture . . . a common fate." He is therefore at least somewhat wary of the "darker side of [the] cosmopolitanization" represented by multinational enterprise insofar as it generates persons who iden-

---

18. See, e.g., Kronman, supra note 15, at 134 ("When a lawyer gives advice to a client based upon his prediction of the future course of judicial behavior, he is engaged in an enterprise that, broadly speaking, includes the work of judges too, namely the maintenance of the rule of law *in the political society to which lawyer, judge, and client all belong*.") (emphasis added).

19. Id. at 145.

20. Robert W. Gordon, "The Independence of Lawyers," 68 *B.U. L. Rev.* 1 (1988); see also Robert W. Gordon, "Corporate Law Practice as a Public Calling," 49 *Md. L. Rev.* 255 (1990).

tify themselves as "world citizens, but without accepting . . . any of the obligations that citizenship in a [particular] polity normally implies."[21]

How might this tension between the Holmesian and Kronmanian visions of legal practice be relevant to Eastern Europeans concerned with constructing radically new political orders? And how might it be relevant to us, who as Americans are the sons and daughters of Holmes but are, like Kronman (and many others), fearful of many of the features we see when observing our contemporary society? One answer is as follows: To the extent that members of the general society, including lawyers, restrict their operative definition of law to the actual enforcing behavior of public officials, then a state concerned to work its will must invest far more resources in enforcement procedures than might otherwise be the case.

The state cannot simply rely on its Holmesian members to exhibit, as a result of moral obligation, sufficient levels of compliance with the abstract commands of the state. Some citizens, as was presumably the case in pre-1989 Eastern Europe, might be tempted to reject the commands of the state because of a belief that the state was significantly — and illegitimately — detached from the underlying community. Others, more atomistic, might be equally disdainful of "community" and "state," viewing both as abstract reifications threatening the unrestrained realization of individual desires.

Public officials looking at the members of a Holmesian society, including presumably its lawyers, will see not "citizens" asking questions about public interest (and obligations) so much as egoists trying simply to maximize their self-interest. The commands of the state are viewed merely as expressions of desired conduct, but they are otherwise without any genuine obligatory force. Legal "duties" are transformed into simple "prices" extracted for the conduct in question. There is a striking similarity between Holmes's view and that of Georg Lukács, a Hungarian who was one of the leading Communist social theorists of this century. In describing a "total, communist fearlessness with regard to the state and the law," Lukács asserted that "the

---

21. Reich's comments are quoted in Christopher Lasch, "The Revolt of the Elites: Have They Canceled Their Allegiance to America?" *Harper's,* November 1994, at 49. Reich is also cited for his fear about the "secession of the symbolic analysts" from membership in the ordinary polity. Id. As one can readily gather from the subtitle of his essay, Lasch, who died in 1994, was extremely fearful of the consequences of any such secession. One assumes that he would have been sympathetic to Dean Kronman's attempt to revive a more citizenship-oriented conception of lawyering.

law and its calculable consequences are of no greater (if also of no smaller) importance than any other external fact of life with which it is necessary to reckon when deciding upon any definite course of action."[22] He compares the legal commands of the state with a train schedule: "The risk of breaking the law should not be regarded any differently than the risk of missing a train connection when on an important journey."[23] Thus, a lawyer's role is apparently like that of a travel agent, though instead of train schedules she offers the client accurate information concerning the actual and predicted odds of various official responses to the client's activity. The client is no more interested in the lawyer's view regarding the "best" interpretation of the law, independent of the likelihood of that view actually being enforced by officials with power, than are most customers interested in having the travel agent insist that they really ought to travel to some place different from the destination they originally chose.

I don't want to sound overly censorious of the Holmesian (or Lukácsian) attitude, for it describes the way most of us live our lives on many occasions. The easiest way of making this point is by reference to posted speed limits. I know almost no one who believes that "55 means 55" (and that disbelief is not merely the result of adherence to some fancy theory of linguistic indeterminacy). For most of us, "55" means something like "63," and I suspect it would mean "75 to 80" if we were confident that the state police would not stop anyone traveling at such speeds. And, presumably, what would lead many of us to stop increasing our speed at 80 miles per hour would be as much a calculation about the risks of accident and injury to ourselves as a focus on the increased risks borne by those sharing the highways with us.

Many of us have engaged in similar predictive analyses of the law in regard to such subjects as sex, alcohol, and drugs. A Holmesian analysis also explains why most "good Americans" feel no compunctions about participating in various World Series, Super Bowl, or Final Four office pools even though they almost certainly violate the "letter" of many states' laws prohibiting public gambling.[24] (And phone calls to out-of-state friends to make friendly bets bring one into violation of federal criminal law.) The tension between "law on the books" and "law in action" was, I think, at the

---

22. Georg Lukács, *History and Class Consciousness* 263 (1971).
23. Id.
24. See, e.g., Kimberly Garcia, "Office Wagering Not Quite So Risky," *Austin Am. Statesman,* 23 January 1993, at B1 (discussing office Super Bowl pools and unlikelihood of enforcement of law prohibiting them).

heart of the controversy generated by President Clinton's initial nomination of Zoë Baird to be attorney general. Many of her defenders plausibly viewed the laws on the books about private individuals hiring undocumented aliens as honored more in the breach than in the observance; why should even a prospective attorney general be without blemish in regard to fidelity to legal formalities?[25] Some of the same tensions may even be present in regard to the actual behavior we expect from those who administer toxic dumps or run savings and loan associations; at this point, of course, we may start worrying and begin asking about the possibility of encouraging a sense of genuinely shared destiny and membership in a social order as a way of taming more egoistic, asocial impulses.

Let us now return, at least figuratively, to Latvia.[26] In particular, I ask you to imagine a foreign investor in Latvia motivated simply by a desire to maximize profits. That is, the investor has no particular commitment to the welfare of Latvia; any contribution to general Latvian welfare will, as suggested by classical economics, be but a happy by-product of the quest for private gains. So long as these gains are sufficient, the investor is as happy to

25. See, e.g., Stuart Taylor, Jr., "Inside the Whirlwind: How Zoë Baird Was Monstrously Caricatured for the Smallest of Sins, Pounded by Press and Popular Righteousness, and Crucified by Prejudice and Hypocrisy," *Am. Lawyer,* March 1993, at 64–69. The matter of Social Security taxes is more complex, though there seems to be good evidence that Ms. Baird and her husband were in fact victims of bad legal advice rather than conscious evaders of their legal duties. In any event, even after the widespread publicity about Ms. Baird, it is unlikely that most Americans are now paying Social Security taxes for every teenager who has been paid more than $50 in a calendar quarter to baby-sit or mow the lawn, though it is probably true that many of those who contemplate future public office are changing their behavior on this matter. Spurred by the Baird and other "Nannygate" scandals, the 103d Congress and President Clinton recently enacted the Social Security Domestic Employment Reform Act of 1994. This law requires payment of the so-called nanny taxes only after an employer has paid someone $1,000 or more in a calendar year. See, e.g., Kathy M. Kristof, "New 'Nanny Tax' Rules Remove Daunting Hurdles; Law 'Decriminalizes' Baby-Sitters, Raises Filing Threshold and Reduces Paperwork," *Chicago Tribune,* 30 November 1994, at C3.

26. Perhaps I should note at this point that I know almost nothing about the Latvian legal system. I assume that, like all Continental legal systems, it is code oriented rather than common law based. It may also be the case that fifty years of Soviet hegemony within Latvia has left lawyers within that country with significantly different conceptions of their role than would have been the case had the Nazi-Soviet Pact of 1939 — which allowed the Soviet Union its unchallenged takeover of the Baltic states — not occurred. The discussion in the text concerns the general theoretical problem of the right of a state to attempt to control the ideological structure of the legal profession. To the extent that specific facts matter, I exercise the prerogative of law professors to stipulate them when convenient for my argument.

realize them in Latvia as, say, in Thailand, or even western Massachusetts or Connecticut. But the investor will not make sacrifices merely to improve the general welfare of these societies. After all, in the contemporary world, one rarely finds large business corporations devoted to the welfare of the particular communities within which they currently operate (and from which they will often relocate once better offers come along from elsewhere). Their loyalties, if any, tend to run far more to their shareholders, who are increasingly drawn from around the world.

Indeed, as already suggested, the rise of the genuinely multinational corporation with genuinely multinational leadership — and multinational lawyers — may itself be a profound commentary on the increasing irrelevance of national citizenship as a meaningful category for most people, especially if we add to this the observation that many corporations put their own "cultural" stamp on their long-term employees. Even if national citizenship will never become completely irrelevant, one should still contemplate the possibility that it may be taking on the personal meaning that state citizenship has for most of us: It might supply us with teams to root for in basketball or soccer tournaments and, more importantly, with a place from which to vote for national political offices or pay taxes in return for public services. It is, though, ever more unlikely to be of any real import in structuring our identities. There is, I suggest, a deep difference between describing oneself as "coming from North Carolina" (as I do) or even "coming from Texas" (as is the case with my daughters) and "*being* a North Carolinian," or "*being* a Texan." At some point, the same may be true of national background.[27]

Imagine, then, that our non-Latvian investor is faced with a recent law passed by the Latvian parliament requiring all factories to be equipped with a certain kind of expensive antipollution device. Despite this law, the parliament does not have a system of enforcement in place, and it is very difficult to detect from surface observation whether the device is being used. Furthermore, the fine imposed, upon discovery, is relatively insubstantial — say, for example, not more than five percent of the cost of the antipollution device. What answer should we expect a lawyer to offer when asked about Latvian "law" on the matter under discussion — that is, under what legal constraints must the profit-maximizing corporation operate? More to the point, might the answer to this question differ depending on the nationality of the law-

27. Indeed, the word "background" is interesting in this context, for one way of defining this inquiry is establishing the conditions under which one's citizenship status will be "foregrounded," either by the state or, perhaps more significantly, by a lawyer herself.

yer? (This would begin to contextualize the rather abstract notion of "a lawyer" in the preceding sentence: Would different lawyers be likely to present different answers, and which lawyers — and answers — would we prefer in which contexts?)

At the very least, the answer to our question about Latvian law would seem to depend on the comparative attention paid by the lawyer to the behavior of Latvian law enforcement agents, as opposed to the text found in Latvian law books. In this context, at least, Latvia would prefer not a Holmesian (or Lukácsian) lawyer, but a Kronmanian lawyer imbued with civic values and unequivocally committed to the welfare of Latvia as defined by the statute requiring the installation of the antipollution device.

How does Latvia (or any other country) get Kronmanian lawyers? One way might be to announce that a central premise of Latvian jurisprudence is that "law" just *is* "law on the books," and that lawyers are to pay no attention to "law in action." It should be clear, though, that this is a classic bootstrap argument. No lawyer who is persuaded by Holmesian jurisprudence and who experiences the material success that often attaches to it — at least in the United States, a success Dean Kronman laments — will be impressed by a statement that law is *not* a prediction of what officials will do (or, for that matter, a similar statement mandating that lawyers take account of social values). Indeed, no state has *ever* officially promulgated a Holmesian definition of law; *all* states pretend that their citizens are bound by the law found in law books. None of this would be particularly relevant to a Holmesian lawyer, who would ask whether *that* statement, defining law nonpredictively, is likely to have any interesting behavioral consequences. We are thus on our way to a classic infinite regress.

Latvia, then, might well doubt that the mere placing of laws on the books would be enough to ensure compliance or, more to the point, even *attempts* by lawyers to advise their clients to adhere to these laws. What might a state do to increase compliance levels beyond issuing naive pleas for compliance or engaging in the costly hiring of ever more enforcement authorities? One possibility is that Latvia would try to maximize the number of Kronmanian "statesmen-lawyers" by ensuring that lawyers are in fact members of the Latvian state, who ostensibly identify with its well-being. This will, Latvia hopes, offer some protection against the swamping of the legal system by lawyers who view themselves as simply the agents of their private-regarding clients, who may be wholly without the kinds of ties to Latvia that might otherwise lead to a commitment to its interests.

By adopting a citizenship requirement, therefore, Latvia is using the formal status of citizenship as a proxy for a certain kind of public-regarding,
communitarian sentiment. Latvian nationals, it might be argued, would be
more inclined to steer their clients into respecting the desires — and acting to
enhance the welfare — of a newly democratic Latvian state, even if that state
could not provide the enforcement mechanisms necessary to ensure desired
behavior from the Holmesian "bad man" who cares only about the costs of
given behavior. Does this make much sense, for Latvia or for the United
States? We come, finally, to the specifics of *In re Griffiths* and its rejection, at
least within the American context, of such a limitation.

On In re Griffiths

Fre le Poole Griffths, who enjoyed the legal status within the United States of
a resident alien, was a citizen of the Netherlands who had married someone
then teaching at the Yale Law School. She attended an American law school
and then applied, in 1970, to take the Connecticut bar examination. After
being refused permission to sit for the examination because of her status as a
noncitizen, she sued.

Two cases came down the same day, 25 June 1973, involving the rights of
states to restrict certain kinds of position to citizens. In *Sugarman v. Dou-
gall*,[28] the Court, through Justice Blackmun, struck down as violative of the
Equal Protection Clause of the Fourteenth Amendment a New York law
limiting entry into its civil service to United States citizens. Only then-Justice
Rehnquist dissented. Ms. Griffith's case was similarly disposed of, in a quite
brief opinion written by Justice Powell.

The Chief Justice normally would have assigned the same justice to write
the majority opinions in such similar cases, and Justice Blackmun was the
logical candidate, given an earlier opinion he had written dealing with the
rights of resident aliens.[29] I strongly suspect that the assignment of Powell to
write *Griffiths* is explained at least in part by the fact that he had been,
before being named to the Court in 1971, president of the American Bar
Association.[30] Who was better suited institutionally to explain to Connecticut, and to the onlooking bar, why states violated the Constitution in limiting bar membership to citizens?

28. 413 U.S. 634 (1973).
29. See *Graham v. Richardson,* 403 U.S. 365 (1971).
30. See John Jeffries, *Lewis Powell* 194–204, 210–11 (1994).

Justice Powell noted that membership in the bar had not traditionally been limited to citizens. Ironically enough, the major source for this observation was an 1873 decision, *Bradwell v. Illinois*,[31] (in)famous primarily because it upheld Illinois's refusal to admit Myra Bradwell to the bar solely because she was female. Along the way, however, the *Bradwell* Court noted that admission to the bar "in no sense depends on citizenship of the United States. . . . Certainly many prominent and distinguished lawyers have been admitted to practice, both in the State and Federal courts, who were not citizens of the United States or of any State."[32] Six years after *Bradwell*, though, in 1879, Connecticut limited admission to the bar to citizens, an action which Justice Powell suggested was the precursor to a host of restrictions adopted throughout the land designed "to impair significantly the efforts of aliens to earn a livelihood in their chosen occupations."[33] Whether motivated by nativism or rent-seeking desires of citizens to limit the number of potential competitors, these nationality-based restrictions were, for many years, upheld against challenge.

Beginning in 1948, however, the Court began striking down such laws.[34] The major breakthrough came in a 1971 case invalidating distinctions between citizens and resident aliens in regard to eligibility for welfare assistance. "[C]lassifications based on alienage," the Court said through Justice Blackmun, "like those based on nationality or race, are inherently suspect and subject to close judicial scrutiny."[35] As specialists know, such scrutiny imposes a very high burden of proof on the state, and few laws have managed to survive it. The Connecticut law, of course, was not such a survivor.

In *Griffiths,* Connecticut argued, in Justice Powell's words, "that the special role of the lawyer justifies excluding aliens from the practice of law."[36] As an "officer of the court," the lawyer is a quasi-public official, and, according to the Connecticut Supreme Court which had upheld the restriction, courts and the public have a right to "demand [lawyers'] loyalty, confi-

31. 83 U.S. (16 Wall.) 130 (1873).

32. Id. at 139, quoted in *In re Griffiths,* 413 U.S. 717, 719 (1973). Indeed, it may also be worth noting that many states at this time allowed at least some resident aliens to vote even in elections for national office, a practice that ended in the United States only in 1928.

33. 413 U.S. at 719.

34. See *Takahashi v. Fish & Game Comm'n,* 334 U.S. 410 (1948) (striking down California law limiting land ownership to citizens).

35. *Graham v. Richardson,* 403 U.S. 365, 372 (1971).

36. 413 U.S. at 723.

dence and respect" in order to "foster public confidence in the profession and, consequently, the judicial system."[37] The state bar, according to Justice Powell, "contrasts a citizen's undivided allegiance to this country with a resident alien's possible conflict of loyalties." The Connecticut Bar Committee had concluded "that a resident alien lawyer might in the exercise of his functions ignore his responsibilities to the courts or even his client in favor of the interest of a foreign power."[38]

The majority was unpersuaded by such arguments, not least because Connecticut offered no evidence supporting the proposition "that the practice of law offers meaningful opportunities adversely to affect the interests of the United States."[39] Justice Powell then included the following very interesting footnote:

> Lawyers frequently represent foreign countries and the nationals of such countries in litigation in the courts of the United States, as well as in other matters in this country. In such representation, the duty of the lawyer, subject to his role as an "officer of the court," is to further the interests of his clients by all lawful means, even when those interests are in conflict with the interests of the United States or of a State. But this representation involves no conflict of interest in the invidious sense. Rather, it casts the lawyer in his honored and traditional role as an authorized but independent agent acting to vindicate the legal rights of a client, whoever it may be. It is conceivable that an alien licensed to practice law in this country could find himself in a position in which he might be called upon to represent his country of citizenship against the United States in circumstances in which there may be a conflict between his obligations to the two countries. In such rare situations, an honorable person, whether an alien or not, would decline the representation.[40]

Justice Powell further suggested that Connecticut's interest in ensuring the loyalty of its lawyers could be adequately served by a requirement that members of the bar take an "attorney's oath" of integrity in the practice of law and a "commissioner's oath" to "support the constitution of the United States, and the constitution of the state of Connecticut."[41] Ms. Griffiths was com-

37. *In re Griffiths*, 294 A.2d 281, 287 (Conn. 1972).
38. 413 U.S. at 724.
39. Id.
40. Id. at 724 n.14.
41. Id. at 725–26.

pletely willing to give both oaths.[42] It is, of course, hardly clear what such pledges entail, at least in the absence of a strong theory of constitutional interpretation that resolves potentially conflicting visions of constitutional fidelity.[43] Perhaps for this reason, the Court was quick to point out that Connecticut could also "properly conduct a character investigation" and maintain "continuing scrutiny," coupled with the prospect of bar discipline, "in order to vindicate its undoubted interest in high professional standards."[44]

Chief Justice Burger, who had joined the majority in *Sugarman,* which dealt with the general civil service, dissented in *In re Griffiths,* and was joined by Justice Rehnquist. Although Burger hinted that he was ambivalent about the wisdom of the majority's relative disdain for the importance of citizenship, the primary ground for his dissent was simply the right of a state, in our federal system of government, to adopt a policy whether or not the Supreme Court believes it to be wise. It is, said Burger, "reasonable . . . for a State to conclude that persons owing first loyalty to this country will grasp [its] traditions and apply our concepts more than those who seek the benefits of American citizenship [such as the right to practice law] while declining to accept the burdens of citizenship in this country."[45] Obviously, Burger believed that being a lawyer is significantly different from being an ordinary state bureaucrat and that the state can, in effect, express more concern about who becomes the former than the latter.

When faced with a similar case, the Canadian Supreme Court came to the same decision as did the majority of the United States Supreme Court, though also over vigorous dissent. A Canadian trial judge had upheld the limitation of membership in the bar to Canadian citizens, arguing that "citizenship [is] a personal characteristic which is relevant to the practice of law on account of *the special commitment to the community which citizenship involves* and not merely because the practical familiarity with the country necessary for the occupation can generally be expected in the case of citizens."[46] On appeal, the Court rejected this reasoning. "Only those citizens who are not natural-born Canadians," said Judge McLachlin,

---

42. Id. at 726.

43. I have explored such questions in Sanford Levinson, *Constitutional Faith* 90–154 (1988).

44. 413 U.S. at 726–27.

45. Id. at 733 (Burger, C.J., dissenting).

46. See *Andrews v. Law Soc'y,* 22 D.L.R. 4th 9, 21 (1986), quoted in *Andrews v. Law Soc'y,* 56 D.L.R.4th 1, 35 (1989) (emphasis added). I am grateful to Lorraine Weinrib and Alex Aleinikoff, who informed me of the existence of *Andrews* and its obvious relevance to my project.

can be said to have made a conscious choice to establish themselves here permanently and to opt for full participation in the Canadian social process. . . . While no doubt most citizens, natural-born or otherwise, are committed to Canadian society, citizenship does not ensure that that is the case. Conversely, non-citizens may be deeply committed to our country. Moreover, the requirement of commitment to our country is arguably satisfied by the oath of allegiance which lawyers are required to take. An alien may swear that oath. In any event an alien may owe allegiance to the Crown if he is resident within this country, even if he does not take the oath of allegiance.[47]

Judge McLachlin's reasoning was essentially accepted by a majority of the Canadian Supreme Court.

Two of the five justices, however, dissented, subscribing to the view that citizenship was a rational proxy for "a commitment to the country and to the fulfillment of the important tasks" carried out by lawyers. "Citizenship," said the dissenters, "require[s] the taking on of obligations and commitments to the community, difficult sometimes to describe but felt and understood by most citizens."[48] They readily conceded that citizenship is neither a necessary nor sufficient condition to ensure the requisite commitment, but "[t]o abolish the requirement of citizenship on the basis that it would fail to insure the attainment of its objectives would . . . be akin to abolishing the law against theft, for it has certainly not insured the elimination of that crime."[49]

The general issue of public-employment rights of noncitizens has generated extensive case law within the United States, of which *Sugarman* and *In re Griffiths* were only the beginning. The Supreme Court has, for example, upheld the limitation of employment to citizens in the case of members of a state police force,[50] and of probation officers within the criminal justice system.[51] It has also struck down citizenship requirements such as a Texas law attempting to prohibit resident aliens from becoming notaries public.[52] The Court has adopted a " 'political function' exception"[53] to the rules

47. 27 D.L.R.4th 600, 612–13 (1986), quoted in 56 D.L.R.4th at 43.
48. See 56 D.L.R.4th at 29 (McIntire, J., dissenting).
49. Id.
50. *Foley v. Connelie,* 435 U.S. 291 (1978).
51. *Cabell v. Chavey-Salido,* 454 U.S. 432 (1982).
52. *Bernal v. Fainter,* 467 U.S. 216 (1984).
53. Id. at 220.

announced in *Sugarman* and *In re Griffiths,* which has been invoked in regard "to laws that exclude aliens from positions intimately related to the process of democratic self-governance."[54]

Perhaps the most interesting application, in regard to the issues raised by this essay, of this "political function" test was in *Ambach v. Norwich,*[55] which upheld New York's ban on having "aliens who have not declared their intent to become citizens" teach in public schools. Justifying its decision, the Court described public-school teachers as "possess[ing] a high degree of responsibility and discretion in the fulfillment of a basic governmental obligation." Teachers not only "have direct, day-to-day contact with students [and] exercise unsupervised discretion over them," but also "act as role models, and influence their students about the government and the political process."[56] For all of these reasons, a state may choose to limit public-school teaching, and other similar roles, to "full-fledged members" of the political community, at least as that is measured by the formal status of citizenship.

One could, of course, devote an entire essay to the relevance of citizenship to public-school teaching. Suffice it to say for now that I find it difficult to distinguish lawyering from school teaching or working in the criminal justice system. Lawyers often exercise a significant degree of discretion in relating to their clients; far more to the point, one might well argue that a central role of lawyers should be to influence their clients in regard to legal obligations. That is, one might desire that the lawyer be something more than the basically amoral Holmesian predictor and instead adopt a more Kronmanian role, actively remonstrating with the client to adhere to legal duties even if the prospects of enforcement are relatively low. It is also worth mentioning that a patriot-lawyer might remonstrate with the client, under some circumstances, to *forgo* enjoying certain legal rights because of their impact on important social values, including the general health of the polity. Under this conception, lawyers identifying themselves as committed citizens of the polity and friends of *its* claims as well as the client's, would view their role as including conversation with clients about the meaning of engaged citizenship.

Such a conception can be found even within the norms of professional conduct promulgated by the American Bar Association and adopted by

54. Id.
55. 441 U.S. 68 (1979).
56. *Bernal,* 467 U.S. at 220.

many states. Thus the ABA has indicated that "[a]dvice of a lawyer to his client need not be confined to purely legal considerations. . . . In assisting his client to reach a proper decision, it is often desirable for a lawyer to point out those factors which may lead to a decision that is morally just as well as legally permissible."[57]

There is, it should be said, no reason to believe that the desires of the state are themselves necessarily moral, which calls into question the organized bar's flat prohibition on "counsel[ing] a client to engage . . . in conduct that the lawyer knows is criminal."[58] There is no reason for a lawyer (or anyone else) to be a thoughtless cheerleader for the law; I accept a notion of good citizenship that includes willingness not only to forgo voluntarily one's legal rights, but also, under some circumstances, to defy the law. But this notion of engaged lawyering (or engaged citizenship) is light-years away from the Holmesian view of the lawyer as austere instrument of the client, which now prevails.

The Lawyer as Transmitter of Core Political Values

Let me turn once more to asking what it is that lawyers — or, for that matter, school teachers — do. This time I would like to contrast the conception of the lawyer (or teacher) as simply the possessor of certain *cognitive* skills or bodies of information with a quite different conception that emphasizes the role played by the lawyer (or teacher) as a transmitter of cultural norms and, indeed, as a model of what it might mean to conceive of oneself as a member of an overarching political community. It may be, of course, that the actuality of felt membership is so weak, when all is said and done, as to make a mockery of the kinds of analyses described above that give great weight to the status of citizenship.

I suggest that what has come to be called the "standard view" of the lawyer's role presents a remarkably thin conception of political member-

---

57. Model Code of Professional Responsibility EC 7-8 (1969); see also Model Rules of Professional Conduct Rule 2.1 (1983) ("In rendering advice, a lawyer may refer not only to law but to other considerations such as moral, economic, social, and political factors, that may be relevant to the client's situation."). I can testify that few law students seem to find such a potential role as moral counselor attractive or even plausible. Most view any such role as an incursion into the autonomy of the client, who is presumed either to have thought through in advance any moral or political dilemmas or to be impervious to the lawyer's own potential suggestions. Full analysis of the actual impact of the ABA's delineation of the lawyer's role is far beyond the scope of this essay. 58. Model Rules of Professional Conduct Rule 1.2(b) (1983).

ship, including that formalization of membership called citizenship. Consider, for example, what may be the most famous articulation of the lawyer's duty of zealous loyalty to a client. Although the author is Lord Henry Brougham, an English lawyer of the early nineteenth century, the sentiment can be found in almost any contemporary American examination of professional responsibility:

> An advocate, in the discharge of his duty, knows but one person in all the world, and that person is his client. To save this client by all means and expedients, and at all hazards and costs to other persons, and, amongst them, to himself, is his first and only duty; and in performing this duty he must not regard the alarm, the torments, the destruction which he may bring upon others. Separating the duty of a patriot from that of an advocate, he must go on reckless of consequences, though it should be his unhappy fate to involve his country in confusion.[59]

In that particular instance, Lord Brougham was threatening to defend his client, Queen Caroline, against King George IV's accusations of adultery, by revealing the King's secret marriage to a Catholic, which violated the Act of Settlement of 1689 and would presumably have cost George his crown and, more important, caused a significant political crisis. Lord Brougham's comment is often quoted for its tone of professed indifference to the "torments" and "destruction" that the lawyer, in the course of vigorous advocacy, might be visiting upon adversaries or, even worse, innocent third parties. That indifference obviously raises important questions about the morality of the advocate's enterprise, which has generated hostile response at least since Plato's scathing critique of oratory in the *Gorgias*.[60] But I want to focus more on the "separat[ion of] the duty of the patriot from that of the advocate," for this seems to suggest that the lawyer can, at some level, cast off the constraints of citizenship (assuming that this is a proxy for patriotism) when such constraints would interfere with the lawyer's primary duty of zealous commitment to the interests of the client. To be sure, a lawyer is never

---

59. Quoted in David Luban, *Lawyers and Justice* 54–55 (1988). Luban's book is obviously relevant to the general issues presented in this essay, especially insofar as he offers a vigorous critique of Holmesian lawyering. Id. at 20–30. I focus on Dean Kronman's book instead because it is more self-consciously written within the civic republican critique of the kind of egoistic liberalism linked with Holmes.

60. See Plato, *Gorgias* (Walter Hamilton, trans., 1971).

entitled, at least from the perspective of those in control of the legal system, to act "illegally" on behalf of a client (though this observation only underscores the importance of having a cogent theory of what constitutes "the law"); but a lawyer is permitted, indeed encouraged, according to a common understanding of the professional role, to assert with vigor any and all nonfrivolous claims that a client might make, regardless of the social cost they might entail.

What are we to think of such a conception of professional responsibility? Is it fair to suggest that our answer will depend, at least in part, on the extent to which we ourselves feel relatively little patriotism or are otherwise suspicious of strong notions of national loyalty? Also important, I suspect, is the extent to which we adopt a strongly individualistic view of the world that regards institutions, including the nation-state, primarily as threats to individual liberty, identity, or even the possibility of a moral life. It is quite possible, then, that "citizenship" need not carry as one of its meanings any particular feelings of friendship toward the political order.

Indeed, that view characterizes much of American political thought. Many of our political forebears were influenced by antistatist versions of eighteenth-century political thought that have survived into our twenty-first-century world. Furthermore, it must also surely be relevant that so much of our population is composed of emigrants (and their offspring) from other countries and cultures who, by definition, were sufficiently "unencumbered" to find tolerable and even attractive the abandonment of old loyalties and identities and the move to what indeed would become a very new world. To be sure, it is difficult to understand American culture without paying attention to aspects of American nationalism and, some would say, chauvinism. That said, however, I wonder how much the view that "No one is going to push *us* around!" or that "We're number one!" translates into a notion of community that leads one to identify with the travails of strangers who share "only" common membership in our polity.

It seems ever harder in the United States to envision a sense of shared enterprise and loyalties that might, for example, lead a lawyer to press, in conversation with the client, the claims of citizens likely to be hurt by the client's proposed course of action, let alone to refuse work from that client. One wonders how much this is increasingly true of Europe as well. Even as Eastern Europe, in particular, offers daily examples of the most virulent forms of nationalism, we must recall that the diminution of traditional borders — and, therefore, of identity — continues in Western Europe. To the extent that national barriers will fall in the legal marketplace, as well as others, one would expect a diminishing concern on the part of many legal professionals with the consequences of their clients' activities — unless, of course, it turns out that a London lawyer will indeed feel sufficiently "European" to care deeply about the fate of, say, Italy, or that an Italian lawyer will feel sufficiently "northern" to care about the fate of, say, the Netherlands.

A Digression on "Residence"

I have been emphasizing the (ir)relevance of formal membership in a polity, as symbolized by the passport one carries. But perhaps one can argue that the relevant inquiry is really more "informal" and empirical; that is, we might choose to focus on the realities of residence rather than the legal formalities of citizenship. One can readily believe that someone who lives in Latvia or Texas, regardless of his or her formal citizenship, would in fact be more concerned about Latvian or Texan welfare than a "Latvian" or "Texan" choosing to live elsewhere. The reason for this belief has nothing to do with the perhaps implausible sociopsychological assumptions underlying an emphasis on altruism or civic republicanism and everything to do with what most of us regard as altogether "normal" incentives to look after one's own personal interests. After all, should the quality of life in Latvia or Texas be diminished, through pollution or whatever else, residents themselves (including, of course, the lawyer) will pay the cost.

Resident lawyers would have every incentive to limit blind commitment to the client's interests if the realization of those interests would in fact be costly to themselves and their families. One assumes that only the most "disciplined" lawyers will accept without question the imposition of increased risks on their children, even if they are all too willing to foist such risks on the children of others. At the very least, one might count on such lawyers to bring to their clients' attention the potential social costs of the policies under contemplation, even if one expects the lawyer to go loyally ahead and attempt to attain the clients' goals upon a declaration that the clients are utterly indifferent to the costs and are interested only in maximizing profits.

Interestingly enough, the United States Supreme Court has invalidated most state attempts to limit bar membership to state residents.[61] And, I confess, I support all such invalidations, for the state policies strike me as far more describable as objectionable barriers to entry mounted by a bar monopoly than as public-regarding regulations designed to protect important civil interests. Similarly, no one alive during the 1960s can forget the importance of "outside" lawyers who were willing to brave the courthouses of the Deep South in the struggle for civil rights and basic justice. Indeed, reference to the preformed Deep South makes one aware as well of the potential costs of a too-quick acceptance of Kronman's elegiac evocation of membership in a common community by client, lawyer, and judge, as well as his emphasis on incremental prudentialism as the keystone to lawyerly statesmanship. There is almost no place in his scheme for the "outside troublemaker" who views the community as fundamentally flawed and in need of radical transformation.

But this may simply be to recognize that life is complex and policies can never be analyzed outside of the specific contexts from which they spring. It is possible, therefore, that the factors leading me to express at least a modicum of sympathy for the exclusion of noncitizens from the practice of law might lead me to reconsider at least in part my opposition to limitation on the basis of residency.

Conclusion

So where now do I stand in regard to *In re Griffith* and the limitation of entrance to the legal profession to American nationals? At the very least, I am now considerably more ambivalent than I was before my trip to Hungary and my encounter with Ms. Jansone and her resistance to the idea of a "cosmopolitan" bar. It no longer strikes me as bigoted or unthinkingly tribalistic to desire that those who join the legal profession, and subject themselves to the norms of professional culture, feel as well the pull of other loyalties — the most important one, for our purposes, being the constellation of emotions and identifications often linked with citizenship.

That being said, I must also say that I do not see in the contemporary United States a culture that takes citizenship sufficiently seriously to justify

---

61. See, e.g., *Barnard v. Thorstenn*, 489 U.S. 546 (1989); *District of Columbia Court of Appeals v. Feldman*, 460 U.S. 462 (1983).

the distinction that Connecticut wanted to draw. Connecticut's limitation of bar membership to American citizens — interestingly enough, Connecticut did not care if its lawyers were citizens of Connecticut itself — seems more meanspirited, not to mention economically protectionist, than expressive of a rich conception of political community.

I see no meaningful way of turning back toward a richer conception, even if one finds it attractive rather than potentially frightening. I am inclined, though, to think that this is far more a statement about life in the contemporary United States than it is a general truth about how societies should conduct themselves. Small, vulnerable societies, concerned with preserving (or restoring) a particularistic culture against the perceived threat of being overwhelmed by cultural outsiders, might legitimately reach different conclusions from our own about the attributes deemed desirable in those who would practice law. At bottom, I suppose the question raised by countries like Latvia is whether we respect them — and their desire *not* to become cosmopolitan and "multicultural" — enough to allow them, without criticism, to limit such socially complex occupations as lawyering (or school teaching) to their own citizens.

Perhaps Latvia — not to mention its neighbors to the south in the Balkans — simply illustrates the dreadful ambiguity of the Wilsonian focus on national self-determination. After all, that legacy, so central to American politics in the ensuing seventy-five years, seems to emphasize the legitimacy of groups defined by nationality (or ethnicity) gaining political control over given territory and, therefore, being able to use the coercive power of the state to maintain their national identity. As Daniel Patrick Moynihan eloquently notes, there are good reasons to lament aspects of the Wilsonian heritage.[62] Nationalism that is unleavened by liberalism is frightening indeed.[63]

I confess that I myself have no wish to live in a political order defined by ethnicity. I count it as one of the glories of the United States that it is *not* a true *nation*-state, but, rather, a political state composed of many nations. Even if I sometimes think that the American conception of citizenship is too thin, I have no desire to make it *very* thick. I much prefer the integrative and antinationalist developments in Western Europe over the rediscovery of nationalist roots that seems to pervade contemporary Eastern Europe.

62. See Daniel Patrick Moynihan, *Pandaemonium* 63–106 (1993).
63. See Yael Tamir, *Liberal Nationalism* (1993); see also chapter 8.

Still, one meaning of "multiculturalism" is a respect for particularistic cultures, including their desire to maintain their distinctiveness in a cosmopolitan world. And a central question posed by multiculturalism is whether those who are not members of (or who do not otherwise identify with) a given culture can sufficiently appreciate challenges to it or accept the necessity of certain measures to maintain it. I cannot reject as "irrational" a belief that citizenship may be a significant marker of commitment in small (and vulnerable) polities, even though it may not be in larger (and less vulnerable) ones like our own. I am still not at the point of *supporting* the Latvian prohibition of noncitizen lawyers, but, perhaps more importantly, I can no longer bring myself to condemn it. As Justice Holmes famously put it, "General propositions do not decide concrete cases."[64] Whether discussing Connecticut, Canada, or Latvia, one must pay close attention to context in determining the relevance of citizenship (or residence) to such social roles as lawyering.

Afterword

In distinguishing between Latvian and non-Latvian lawyers, this essay generally refers, with regard to the latter, to lawyers who come from outside Latvia (such as myself) and suggests that persons without any sense of felt membership in the society might behave in systematically (and interestingly) different ways than persons who indeed identify with (or are "encumbered" within) a given social order. This is simply another way of saying that there may be genuine differences between "cosmoplitans" and persons with more "local" (or, somewhat more pejoratively, "parochial") identities (and loyalties). "Universalist" commitments, whether expressed in the language of Kant or utilitarianism, make it necessarily difficult to figure out why one should prefer the interests of one's neighbors — or even one's family. Most persons find such universalism unacceptable, not least because of the psychological implausibility of being so indifferent to local interests, including that particular form of localism that we call patriotism.

There is, however, an important subtext in any specific discussion involving Latvian lawyers, the subject that generated the foregoing article. Latvia, after all, was for a half-century an involuntary member of the Union of Soviet Socialist Republics and, therefore, extensively settled by persons

64. *Lochner v. New York*, 198 U.S. 45, 76 (1905).

from Russia and other members of the USSR. An important issue since the renewed independence of Latvia in 1989 is whether Russian settlers, many of whom by now include persons born and raised in Latvia, will be recognized as Latvians or kept within some permanently subordinated status. A recent article in the *New York Times* is aptly titled "Latvia Struggles to Include People of Its Soviet Past,"[65] and notes that those who now control Latvia remain uncertain (at best) of what the status should be of its large Russian (or Ukranian or Belarussian) minority. Indeed, approximately 500,000 permanent residents have still not been recognized as "citizens" of Latvia, in substantial part because of an inability to pass stringent tests of an ability to speak the Latvian language. "The easiest thing to do," concedes the Foreign Minister of Latvia, "would be to create a process that gives citizenship automatically" to these residents of Latvia. "But," he insists, "you have to create a mentality of citizenship. What we need are Latvian patriots," which, apparently, requires tests in which, according to the article, one can demonstrate "at least basic proficiency in Latvian, recite the Latvian national anthem and pass a test on Latvian history."

Among other things, this argument requires us to recognize the difference between "residence" and full community membership. It certainly seems plausible to believe that the former alone would be enough to guarantee some (or, more to the point, enough) of the kind of lawyering that I discuss in the essay. After all, one need not be a citizen of a given state to be worried about pollution or traffic safety if one actually lives within the state. What concerns me in the essay is what might be termed the truly "outside" lawyer who has no linkage at all with the community in question. It would seem to me that ethnic Russians who have lived in Latvia their entire lives have more than enough linkage. The sympathy expressed in the essay for a certain mistrust of someone like myself, a quintessential "outsider" who has no identification at all with Latvia, should not be read as extending to quite deliberate attempts to prevent "hyphenated" Latvians from enjoying the same rights to practice law as the ostensibly "purer" Latvians.

The question of the legitimacy of linguistic diversity is, of course, a major issue in itself, though it receives relatively little discussion in this book. To put this within an American context, one can imagine a Puerto Rican lawyer, who, like most Puerto Ricans, speaks only Spanish. (Spanish is, indeed,

65. Steven Lee Myers, "Latvia Struggles to Include People of Its Soviet Past," *New York Times,* 4 August 2002, at 3.

the language of government in Puerto Rico.) Imagine that she moves to New York and demands the right to practice law without demonstrating a competence in the English language. The United States in fact requires proficiency in English in order to become a naturalized citizen; Puerto Ricans are, however, citizens of the United States and, therefore, have a constitutional right to settle wherever they wish in the continental United States. One might well predict that a Spanish-only speaker would be at a distinct disadvantage in practicing law on the mainland. The question, though, is whether it is legitimate to bar a non-English speaker from even participating in the legal marketplace. Concomitantly, if one is truly concerned about the "patriotism" of lawyers (or school teachers or other public officials), it is certainly not clear why an ability to speak the majority's language should be thought sufficient to demonstrate any such attribute.

6

The Confrontation of Religious Faith and

Civil Religion: Catholics Becoming Justices

Roman Catholicism represents a beautiful anachronism in
our age of crazed nationalism; virtually every devout Catholic
preserves in his heart some remnants of his denomination's
transnational loyalty and the duty of Catholics to defy immoral
laws. — Istvan Deak, "The Incomprehensible Holocaust"

Introduction

Consider some possible reactions to this comment by Istvan Deak, found,
not at all coincidentally, in an article on the range of response to state-
sponsored evil during the Holocaust.[1] One might challenge its empirical
accuracy on two separate grounds. First, one might question the assertion that Roman Catholicism in fact continues, assuming it ever did, to
promote some kind of "transnational loyalty" that can stand firm against
the "crazed" excesses of nationalism. Or, to the extent that one concedes
the reality of this "transnational loyalty," one might argue that Catholicism is simply a subset of the much more general and important set of
religious institutions. All of these institutions — or at least those we are
most familiar with in the West — tend, by asserting the existence of a living sovereign God, to challenge the idolatrous claims of the nation-state.
One might also be interested, of course, in the perceived social meanings,

This essay was originally published in *DePaul Law Review* 39 (1990): 1047. It was initially
presented as a lecture at the Charles S. Casassa, S.J., conference, 10 March 1989.
1. Deak, "The Incomprehensible Holocaust," *New York Review of Books,* 28 September 1989,
at 66.

both within the Catholic community and outside, of membership in the Roman Catholic Church (the "Church"). That is, independent of empirical demonstrations—however we might imagine such things—of a willingness to oppose state demands, do committed Catholics describe themselves in such a fashion?

Putting these empirical questions to one side, one could also respond to the value claims quite obviously contained within Deak's description of the Church. Here again there are two possibilities: one is to be thrilled by the recourse to moral claims transcending the often amoral and sometimes immoral claims of the nation-state. But another, drawn from a devotion to the claims of the nation-state as a Hobbesian barrier against the ravages of anarchy, is to be dismayed by the possibility of such recourse. Indeed, a person with this latter view may well feel impelled to limit, if not eliminate, the existence of this threat to state sovereignty.

Indeed, Deak's formulation raises in its own way the classic eighteenth-century problem of *imperium in imperio,* the so-called dual sovereignty dilemma that was resolved, for American constitutional theory, by the fiction of the sole sovereignty of "we the people" who happened to subdivide the structures of government into various competing components. With popular sovereignty presumably comes an obligation to obey the will of the sovereign as manifested in legal commands, or so it is often suggested. But what if "the people" turn out, even in theory,[2] not to be indisputably sovereign after all, if their decisions are in fact subject to challenge, or even negation, by a competing sovereign? At the very least, it should be obvious that Deak's beautifully compressed sentence carries within it implications for those of us who purport to analyze social life, whether as empirically-oriented social scientists, latter-day Geertzian interpreters of social meaning, or traditional political theorists concerned about such subjects as political sovereignty or theories of obligation. The purpose of this article is to explore some of these implications.

I want in particular to examine some of the implications of the subsuming of religious identities within the more secular—or at least nonsectarian—culture of American constitutionalism. My explorations will focus, by and large, on exchanges occurring during confirmation hearings held in regard to Catholic nominees for the United States Supreme Court. (A sub-

2. It is, of course, clear that popular sovereignty as an empirical matter is either false or empirically untestable. For a valuable study of the subject, see Edmund S. Morgan, *Inventing the People: The Rise of Popular Sovereignty in England and America* (1988).

ject of this article is to ask what we mean by referring to someone as a "Catholic nominee").

I should emphasize in advance that this article is in no way an attempt to predict judicial behavior or even the judicial language that will be used by a member of the Supreme Court offering justifications for decisions. Instead, I am trying to do something else, to examine the American civil religion in operation by focusing on a specific, highly stylized ceremony of that religion—the investiture of new justices as high priests of the sacred constitutional text. This discourse, I believe, encompasses a fear that the "private" realm of religion—and, more particularly, given our particular national past as a highly anti-Catholic, Protestant social order, of Catholicism—will illegitimately invade the public space of judicial decision making. As a result, this concern about the "private" invasion of the "public" ends up subtly forcing upon those who would become public officials a revision of their "private" identities as religions beings.

This influence on private identity is evident in the context of judicial appointments. I believe that justices identified with Catholicism have been forced to proclaim the practical meaninglessness of that identification. To refer to one of my specific examples, William Brennan in effect claimed that his Catholicism is formally irrelevant as he reassured the Senate, and therefore the rest of the nation, that it would play no role whatsoever in his understanding of the judicial role.[3] This suggests, among other things, that identifying someone as a Catholic justice provides only the same illumination—effectively none at all—as might be provided by identifying him as a blue-eyed justice. How plausible is this suggestion? If true, it surely disconfirms any of Deak's assertions about the social meaning of Catholicism. If, though, we do believe that religion matters (or, more modestly, might matter), then we must confront a very troublesome question: should we countenance legislative probes into the meaning of a nominee's Catholicism to him- or herself and, ultimately, to the nation that he or she helps to lead? Whatever else may be true about this article, I hope that it will demonstrate that the question is a serious one demanding more serious treatment than it has tended to receive.

My goal in this article is not so much making an argument as attempting to provoke a conversation about the cultural structures of American life and

---

3. Like, for that matter, Antonin Scalia after him: the last thing I want to do in this article is to suggest that I have any interest in counterposing "liberal" to "conservative" justices.

some of the ramifications of the peculiarly American solution to the role of religion in public life. This is especially the case in regard to the topic under discussion, for I freely confess my own uncertainty about the views under consideration. This particular article should be conceived, therefore, as a "work in progress" as I try to unravel the various conundrums that my profession so far has enabled me to discern.

I will proceed first by laying out some basically empirical observations about patterns of assimilation in the United States. The heart of the article, though, will focus on public discourse linked with the appointments to the Supreme Court of members of the Roman Catholic Church, particularly Justices Brennan, Scalia, and, to a lesser extent, Kennedy.

Civil Religion and Judicial Oaths

The relationship between religious faith and adherence to the Constitution has been the topic of much discussion. Much of my scholarly work has been an attempt to conceptualize the American constitutional order as a "civil religion."[4] One of the formal tenets of that religion, I argue, is that it professes to know neither Christian nor Jew but only "Americans" constituted in significant measure by their common adherence to the Constitution. This notion is most passionately captured in Justice Frankfurter's anguished statement, coming immediately after the identification of himself as a member of "the most vilified and persecuted minority in history," that, nonetheless, "as judges we are neither Jew nor Gentile, neither Catholic nor agnostic. We owe equal attachment to the Constitution and are equally bound by our judicial obligations."[5]

This obligation, of course, is immediately derived from the judicial oath, which had much earlier served as a predicate for judicial review itself in *Marbury v. Madison*.[6] To a degree that we can no longer appreciate, eighteenth-century Americans took oaths with extreme seriousness.[7] We should thus pay special attention to Article VI of the Constitution, where a prohibition of any religious tests as a condition for public office is coupled

---

4. See Sanford Levinson, *Constitutional Faith* (1988).

5. *Board of Education v. Barnette*, 319 U.S. 624, 646–47 (1943) (Frankfurter, J., dissenting).

6. 5 U.S. (1 Cranch) 137, 180 (1803).

7. There is something richly symbolic about the fact that literally the first law passed by the new government of the United States established a framework of oaths of office. See An Act to regulate the Time and Manner of administering certain Oaths, ch. 1, 1 Stat. 23 (1845).

with a requirement that all public officials of state and nation take an oath of fidelity to the Constitution.[8]

As a Jew, I have a special reason to be grateful for the prohibition of religious test oaths, though in fact the list of those owing gratitude goes far beyond the relatively few members of the Jewish community or those who do not adhere to any religion at all. It was certainly not inevitable that the United States would choose to march along a path of religious toleration in deciding who was eligible to serve as a public official. Neither Jews nor Catholics, among many others, had any special reason two hundred years ago to believe that they would be truly welcomed into the political fellowship of the new nation that had wrested its independence from Great Britain. After all, such complete toleration was not to be found in such luminaries as Locke or John Milton. And, as Thomas Curry has noted in *The First Freedoms,* his extremely valuable study of church and state before the passage of the First Amendment in 1791, initial American notions of the relationship between pulpit and government were carried on "within a framework wherein *Protestant* Christianity and American culture intertwined."[9]

As Professor Bradley has observed, the No Test Oath Clause "is the *only* occasion on which the Constitution's makers actually addressed" the rela-

---

8. The pertinent part of Article VI reads,

> The Senators and Representatives before mentioned, and the Members of the several State Legislatures, and all executive and judicial Officers, both of the United States and of the several States, shall be bound by Oath or Affirmation, to support this Constitution; but no religious Test shall ever be required as a Qualification to any Office or public Trust under the United States.

U.S. Const. art. VI, cl. 3. See Gerard Bradley, "No Religious Test Clause and the Constitution of Religious Liberty: A Machine That Would Go of Itself," 37 *Case W. Res. L. Rev.* 674 (1987) (general discussion of Article VI).

9. Thomas J. Curry, *The First Freedoms: Church and State in America to the Passage of the First Amendment* 218 (1986) (emphasis added). Curry goes on to note that at the time of the Northwest Ordinance, in 1787, "a country wherein eleven of thirteen states restricted officeholding to Christians or Protestants hardly envisaged Catholicism or Judaism, not to mention Mohammedism or any non-Christian group," as within the cultural consensus. Id. at 221. See also Morton Borden, *Jews, Turks and Infidels* (1984) (discussion of the development of religious liberty within a Christian nation). Finally, Professor Bradley, commenting that "the Founders' anti-Catholicism would be difficult to overestimate," notes that John Jay, our first chief justice (and coauthor of *The Federalist*), "frankly estimated Catholicism and American citizenship to be fundamentally incompatible." See Bradley, supra note 8, at 699.

tionship between law and religion.[10] Not the least remarkable aspect of the clause is that it was placed in the Constitution at a time when at least twelve of the states, and perhaps Virginia as well, employed religious tests as a prerequisite for holding public office.[11]

It is not clear why the No Test Oath Clause made its way into the Constitution. I suspect that the most plausible explanation is simply the fear of each particular sect that it might become the victim of any test actually chosen, so that it was safer to prohibit all oaths. Professor Bradley has demonstrated beyond doubt, though, the rank implausibility of any notion that they were motivated by an affirmative desire on the part of most Americans to welcome Catholics, Jews, or, perhaps most unthinkable of all, atheists, into positions of leadership.[12] Although developments since 1787 have scarcely been unmixed, it is clear that formal religious tests have indeed played no role, at least at the national level, and even informal ones have become ever weaker throughout our history.[13]

I believe that we can only applaud these developments and praise the drafters of Article VI, whatever their motivations. One's appreciation for the formal elimination of sectarian affiliation as a precondition for public office increases as one looks around at certain other societies, whether dominantly Christian, as in Northern Ireland; Jewish, as in Israel; or Islamic, as in Lebanon. All of these countries are riven by continuing political and social cleavages predicated on sectarian differentiation even within these apparently overarching religious categories.[14] Still, I think we have all become

---

10. Id. at 677 (emphasis in original). The First Amendment, of course, was added after the drafting and ratification of the Constitution.

11. Id. at 679, 681–87.

12. Id. at 710–11.

13. But see Frederick J. Crosson, "Religion and Natural Law," 8 *CCIA Annual: Liberty and Law: Civil and Religious* 75 (1989). "We have, despite our Constitution, a de facto religious test for office." Id. at 94. By this I presume that Professor Crosson is suggesting the unlikelihood of a professed atheist succeeding to high office, and possibly even the necessity of public officials' suggesting that they adhere to something called "the Judeo-Christian tradition." At the formal level, though, *Torcaso v. Watkins,* 367 U.S. 488 (1961), invalidating a Maryland test oath, certainly remains an accurate statement of positive constitutional law, with its evocation of "the historically and constitutionally discredited policy of probing religious beliefs by test oaths or limiting public offices to persons who have, or perhaps more properly profess to have, a belief in some particular kind of religious concept." Id. at 494.

14. This is clearest in Northern Ireland, where the conflict is between Catholic and Protestant. But if there were no Arabs, either Christian or Muslim, in Israel, there would still be bitter

aware that political life often presents paradoxes, so that even the most beneficial policies almost inevitably turn out to have hidden costs. One cost inherent in our government may be the diminution of individual religious identity in the lives of public servants.

Sameness, Difference, Religion, and Politics

SAMENESS AND DIFFERENCE

One way of conceptualizing the problem is to place it within the context of the much-discussed issue of "sameness and difference" in social life. That is, whether one is referring to race, gender, or practically anything else, many of the arguments boil down to two contradictory assertions. At least some of the time proponents of members of group A (blacks, women, Jews, for example) will argue that they are really the "same" as some group B (whites, men, or Christians) that is socially favored. The equality principle that like should be treated alike thus reveals the unfairness of treating "similar" groups differently. However, one sometimes finds the very same proponents arguing that there are really significant differences between the As and the Bs. Here, the problem is alleged to be the violation of what might be termed the "inequality" principle. This principle advances the idea that it is legitimate, and sometimes necessary, to treat different groups differently, so that the unfairness is the application of a single criterion to the As and Bs that collapses the differences between them. Thus, for example, an Orthodox Jew serving in the Air Force claimed, unsuccessfully, that the Constitution protected his right to wear a yarmulke. This was in contradiction to a rule promoting sameness by prohibiting the wearing of any hat besides the one that is part of the Air Force uniform (and that, of course, can be worn only when appropriate).[15]

The question before us in this instance is the meaning of religious identity. To what extent does the identification of oneself as "religious" entail as well a suggestion of significant differences existing between the religious and the irreligious? Does such an identification also imply a distinction between the specific denomination with which one identifies, and all others, whether

---

tensions among elements of the Jewish community, just as there are equally strong tensions within the Islamic communities in Lebanon and, as we are now aware, in Iraq.

15. See *Goldman v. Weinberger*, 475 U.S. 503, 509–10 (1986) (no First Amendment violation in Air Force regulation that prohibited a serviceman from wearing a yarmulke).

of different religious commitment or irreligious? And are there occasions when these differences can — or must — be taken into account in the making of public policy? To what extent, on the other hand, are such ostensible differences irrelevant, to be dismissed as we emphasize instead the more important "sameness" of each of us? Andrew Greeley has argued that "[m]odern sociology emerged in substantial part from a discussion of the differences between Catholics and Protestants."[16] Others have placed the emergence of sociology more in the "attempt[] to formulate and nurture secular and civil sources of morality to replace those of religion."[17] In any event, it is clear that a classical concern of sociology is the place of a religious dimension in the social order, whether religion be defined traditionally or in terms of "civil religious" replacements for more God-centered institutions. The implications for the general social order of religious identification, or the likelihood of achieving a robust civil religion, is, of course, of interest to far more than the sociological community.

One reason for the interest in "difference," alas, is the propensity Lucinda Finley has noted, discussing gender classification: "to be considered different can mean being stigmatized or penalized."[18] She links stigmatization to an "assimilationist idea" that links an entitlement to equal treatment with the recognition on the part of power holders of the essential "sameness" of those seeking such treatment with themselves. Thus, argues Finley, "the recognition of difference threatens our conception of equality, and the proclamation or identification of difference can serve as a justification for existing inequities."[19] One option, of course, is for members of the subordinated group to proclaim its essential similarity to the dominant group, but this may simply mean that the former must behave like the famous Marrano Jews of Spain, who hid their difference from the Christian majority that demanded sameness as the price of social inclusion. A further possibility, of course, is that the subordinated group actually does change in important ways and takes on the attributes of the favored majority.

16. Andrew Greeley, "Protestant and Catholic: Is the Analogical Imagination Extinct?" 54 *Am. Soc. Rev.* 485, 485 (1989).

17. Letter from Professor Allen Silver, Department of Sociology, Columbia University to Sanford Levinson 2 (10 December 1989).

18. Lucinda Finley, "Transcending Equality Theory: A Way Out of the Maternity and the Workplace Debate," 86 *Colum. L. Rev.* 1118, 1154 (1986).

19. Id.

THE INFLUENCE OF SAMENESS ON RELIGIOUS IDENTITY

This discussion of sameness and difference is, of course, all very abstract. It is time to become more concrete. Before moving on to the issues raised by Catholic appointees, I want briefly to note how I have recently addressed some of these problems in regard to a study by Professor Robert Burt, *Two Jewish Justices*, about Justices Brandeis and Frankfurter.[20] Though it is clear that all of us identify these two as "Jewish justices," I think it important that neither Brandeis nor Frankfurter exhibited any real interest in their adult lives in what might be termed traditional Judaism. I titled a review of Burt's book "Who Is a Jew(ish Justice)?"[21] In it I commented, "What is attractive about Brandeis and Frankfurter is precisely that they offer ways of being Jewish without accepting any specifically Jewish theological tenets or observing any *mitzvot* [commandments of Jewish law]."[22] One discovers the paradox, that their concrete beliefs "consisted of commitment to a mixture of Athenian and Enlightenment ideals, as opposed to the words of a living God who might command behavior contrary to some of those ideals."[23] The attractiveness I was writing about, I should make clear, is from the perspective of basically secular Jews like myself. "Judaism," in the case of Brandeis and Frankfurter, is far more a sociological than a religious category, at least where "religion" has anything to do with the affirmation of propositional notions about God and the world or the acceptance of specific behavioral duties imposed by the tenets of the religious community. Although both of them suffered from anti-Semitic opposition, I doubt that even the most overheated opponent of either man ever seriously suggested that either justice would be likely to subordinate the commands of the Constitution to those of the Halakha, the Jewish law.

One point of my review was to question whether nonsecular Jews could feel quite the same sense of pleasure in Frankfurter's and Brandeis's careers as can secular Jews, given the fact that their success came in part because of their rejection of the particular disciplines imposed by traditional Judaism. A committed traditional Jew might be excused, though, for refusing to

20. Robert Burt, *Two Jewish Justices: Outcasts in the Promised Land* (1987).
21. Sanford Levinson, "Who Is a Jew(ish Justice)?" 10 *Cardozo L. Rev.* 2359 (1989) (book review). One of my purposes in choosing that title is obviously to play on the contemporary controversy taking place in both Israel and the United States concerning the criteria that must be met for a convert to Judaism to be regarded as "genuinely" Jewish for purposes of Israeli law. No issue more sharply divides the American and Israeli Jewish communities.
22. Id. at 2368.
23. Id.

identify Brandeis and Frankfurter as the kinds of "Jewish justices" that would truly resonate with their own sense of Jewish identity or provide inspirational role models. Instead, they would be symbols primarily of the necessity to give up any truly distinct — or different — religious identity in order to accommodate, and thus indicate the similarity to, the sensibilities of the wider community.

Writing that review, coupled with an invitation to participate in a symposium on the Constitution at Loyola Marymount College, a distinguished Catholic institution, led me to wonder if similar tensions might be revealed in the history of America's Catholic justices. I doubt that a parallel title — "Who is a Catholic (Justice)?" — would work. But the precise title is surely less important than the underlying problem, which is whether the pattern suggested by Brandeis and Frankfurter might be found as well in the stories of similarly eminent Catholic jurists.

As I noted at the outset, one social reality shared by Jews and Catholics is living within an historically Protestant culture that has been suspicious of both, though for obviously different reasons. Jews were thought untrustworthy for our failure to accept the tenets of Christianity, whereas all but the most rabid anti-Catholics presumably recognized that Catholics were indeed Christian. Still, that common Christianity was itself riven apart in the storm of the Reformation. Even four hundred years later it has not completely subsided. This is in light of the historical fact that animus against Catholics was substantially predicated on the particular institutional role played by the Roman magisterium as what we might today describe as the "privileged" interpreter of the demands of the truly Christian life.

I am old enough to remember John Kennedy's trip to Houston, where he had to reassure Protestant ministers that he would, if elected, behave as a loyal American and not, as feared by his fundamentalist audience, in fact take orders from the pope. "I believe in an America," said the man who would become our first Catholic president, "where the separation of church and state is absolute."[24] He rejected the propriety of any "religious body

24. Arthur M. Schlesinger Jr., "O'Connor, Vaughan, Cuomo, Al Smith, J.F.K.," *New York Times*, 2 February 1990, at A31. The article notes the declaration some thirty years before Kennedy's, by New York Governor Alfred E. Smith, the first Catholic to be nominated for the presidency, that "I recognize no power in the institutions of my Church to interfere with the operations of the Constitution of the United States or the enforcement of the law of the land. I believe in absolute freedom of conscience . . . in the absolute separation of church and state. . . ." The occasion for Professor Schlesinger's "op-ed" article was the declaration by Cardinal O'Con-

seek[ing] to impose its will directly or indirectly upon the general populace or the public acts of its officials."[25] Thus, he assured his audience,

> Whatever issue may come before me as President — on birth control, divorce, censorship, gambling or any other subject — I will make my decision . . . in accordance with what my conscience tells me to be the national interest, and without regard to outside religious pressures or dictates. And no power or threat of punishment could cause me to decide otherwise.[26]

Put to one side that the Protestant ministers were almost certainly misinterpreting the authority in fact assigned by Catholic theology to the pope and that Kennedy was merely correcting them. More to the point is that, in a variety of subtle ways, the views of outright anti-Catholics have become incorporated into the self-understanding at least of American Catholics forced, by the demands of the political process, to appeal to them for support. Perhaps this helps to explain the finding, in a cross-national survey analyzed by Andrew Greeley, that "differences between Protestants and Catholics," in a variety of attitudinal variables, "are more modest in the United States than in the other four countries" studied: Great Britain, Ireland, Canada, and Australia.[27] In fact, though, even here statistically significant differences emerge from the data he has analyzed.[28]

The problem of survey data, of course, even aside from methodological considerations, is that at best it reveals only tendencies. There are obviously wide overlaps between any of the groups being analyzed; furthermore, it is always the case that there will be Xs (perhaps in fact numbering in the millions) who will have more of the traits that "tend" to cluster in Ys than

---

nor of New York City that Bishop Austin Vaughan was correct in "warn[ing] *any* Catholic that his soul is at risk if he should die while deliberately pursuing any gravely evil course of action, and that such would certainly include advocating publicly, as the Bishop puts it, 'the right of a woman to kill a child.'" Sam Howe Verhovek, "Cardinal Defends a Jailed Bishop Who Warned Cuomo on Abortion," *New York Times,* 1 February 1990, at A1. See infra note 66 for further discussion of this controversy.

25. Schlesinger, supra note 24.

26. Id.

27. Greeley, supra note 16 at 493.

28. For example, "in all countries Catholics are more likely to emphasize 'fairness' and 'equality' while Protestants are more likely to emphasize 'freedom' and 'individualism' in the workplace. With the exception of Great Britain, Catholics are also more likely to advocate strengthening of authority and of the family." Id.

will be the case with many Ys (perhaps in fact also numbering in the millions), who will have the traits one associates with the Xs. This is the basis for the reminder that one should never be confident about one's inferences about individuals on the basis of knowledge only of even the most impeccable macrolevel data. Still, however well advised we are not to draw conclusive presumptions from them, human life could scarcely proceed if we did not use such data for some kinds of filtering purposes, even if only to serve as the basis for further conversation designed to find out more about the particular individual we are interested in. There is a reason that we ask the questions we do at cocktail parties or mixers, where gross categories, such as occupation, regional background, education, and, indeed, religion are all used as predictors about likely attitudes or interests. Those predictions may well be disconfirmed by the further conversation. Still, we would probably stop asking the questions entirely if past experience had shown only random correlation between the answers and the deeper attributes about which we were "really" seeking information. To this extent we all rely on "stereotypes" even as we should feel wary about this.

Catholic Justices: A Historical Perspective

Let me now turn to some of the implications of these points for the topic under consideration — the assessment of Catholic nominees for the Supreme Court. How does the issue of sameness and difference work itself out in this context? Likewise, how might the presentation of their faith by American Catholics be influenced by the experience of living as a minority within a society that has often been characterized by at least a certain skepticism, if not virulent hostility, toward the legitimacy of the Roman Catholic Church?

ANTI-CATHOLICISM AND THE JUDICIARY

Even a cursory look at the historical record involving Catholic Justices certainly reveals the presence of overt anti-Catholicism. President Warren Harding, for example, was castigated by the members of the Women's Auxiliary of the Ohio State Good Government Association when he nominated Pierce Butler for membership on the Supreme Court. They described the Roman Catholic Church as "un-American" and did not understand how Harding could appoint one of its members to our highest court.[29] Still, the

---

29. David Danelski, *A Supreme Court Justice Is Appointed* 92 (1964).

major attack on Butler was because of his conservatism, and he was easily confirmed by the Senate. In addition, Butler was by no means the first Catholic to gain membership on the Supreme Court. That achievement was Roger Brooke Taney's, who succeeded John Marshall as our fifth chief justice in 1836. He had, to be sure, been rejected once before, but no one seriously argues that his Catholicism, rather than his devoted service to his patron Andrew Jackson, explains the episode.[30] Edward White, a Louisiana Catholic, filled Taney's office in 1910, after reaching the Court in 1894, and three other Catholic justices served over the next forty years. Joseph McKenna, a notably obscure jurist, served from 1898 to 1925. His last three years overlapped with the term of the aforementioned Pierce Butler, who fought the good fight against President Roosevelt's New Deal and died while on the Court in 1939. He was succeeded by another Catholic, Frank Murphy, who died prematurely in 1949. President Eisenhower named William Brennan to the bench in 1956, shortly before the Presidential election, in a move viewed as shoring up his support among Northeastern Catholics.[31] Finally, Justice Brennan was joined, as he neared his retirement, by his coreligionists Antonin Scalia and Anthony Kennedy.

One doesn't exactly know what to do with these figures: the approx-

30. See Barbara Perry, "The Life and Death of the 'Catholic Seat' on the United States Supreme Court," 6 *J.L. & Pol.* 55, 60 (1989). Perry offers a very useful overview of the nominations of each of the eight "Catholic justices." Her thesis is summarized in the following paragraph:

[I]n none of the eight Catholic appointments (nine counting White's promotion to Chief Justice) was religion the overriding factor in the President's selection. Nevertheless . . . Catholicism [evolved] from a coincidental factor or actual handicap to be overcome (Taney and White's first appointment), to what I label an "over-the-top" consideration (McKenna and White's promotion), to an explicit concern of advisers to the President (Butler), to its high point as one of the President's top two or three concerns (Murphy). The gap between Murphy's and Brennan's tenures on the Court, and the lessening emphasis on the latter's religion, weakened the tradition of the "Catholic seat." More recently, Scalia's Catholicism arguably was not an unwelcome characteristic for President Reagan and his advisers to consider, but it is apparent that his ideology, jurisprudence, age, and even ethnic ties were all more decisive factors in his selection. Finally, Kennedy's appointment has brought Catholic religious affiliation full circle to its previous status as a purely coincidental factor in nominations to the Supreme Court. (Id. at 91.)

31. This triggered a denunciation by Fred Rodell of the Yale Law School of Brennan as "a technical Democrat of such conservative stripe" as to be described best as "a charming Catholic Republican." See Rodell, "The Joker of Judicial Experience," *The Progressive*, January 1957, at 9. This was, to put it mildly, not one of Professor Rodell's best moments, either as a predictor or as an exemplar of religious tolerance. For a more scholarly discussion of the importance of Brennan's Catholicism as an explanation for his nomination, see Perry, supra note 30, at 83–85.

imately 7 percent appointment rate for Catholic justices is significantly smaller than the population of Catholics in the United States, at least since the great migrations of the 1820s and 1830s. On the other hand, three out of nine, the current figure, is scarcely evidence of underrepresentation, assuming that one wants to use such language at all.[32] For many decades, though, Roman Catholics have been able to look at the United States Supreme Court and see evidence of their legitimate membership within the wider ambit of the American polity.

As Judge Noonan has written, the praise visited upon Chief Justice White by Justice Holmes and the support given Butler by established, and largely Protestant, businessmen demonstrated to Protestants "that they did not need to fear Catholics in high position in the federal government," and to Catholics that they were indeed accepted.[33] Anti-Catholic bigotry might blight the political landscape, as anti-Semitism certainly did in regard to the Brandeis and Frankfurter nominations, but the more important point is that the bigots were unsuccessful, and all of these nominees were accepted as fit members of the bench.

Judge Noonan, who is of course himself both a committed Catholic and a distinguished federal judge, cautions, though, that this acceptance came at a certain price: "silence" as to what might truly be "distinctive" about being a member of the Roman Catholic religious community. But, says Noonan, no one was inclined to notice this "when the difference in beliefs between Catholics and other Americans appeared in practice to be small."[34] For Jews and Catholics alike, then, it seems plausible to argue that there is a price attached to entry into leadership positions within the polity. This price has been the modulation, if not outright suppression, of much awareness of anything within their respective religious traditions that might be significantly different from — let alone pose a challenge to — the wider American (and Protestant?) culture. Is it significant, for example, that Justices Brennan, Scalia, and Kennedy, like Justices Brandeis and Frankfurter, went to the decidedly secular Harvard Law School, which could validate their identity

32. The so-called Jewish seat, occupied by Justices Brandeis, Frankfurter, Goldberg, and Fortas, was vacant for more than two decades, until President Clinton in 1993 appointed Ruth Bader Ginsburg. Stephen Breyer, appointed the following year, is also Jewish, which means, given Justice Thomas's conversion to Catholicism, that a majority of the Court is, for the first time, non-Protestant.

33. John Noonan, "The Catholic Justices of the United States Supreme Court," 67 *Cath. Hist. Rev.* 369, 378 (1981).

34. Id. at 379.

as assimilated Americans? Indeed, only Justice Scalia went to a Catholic school for his undergraduate education (Georgetown); Justices Brennan and Kennedy went to the University of Pennsylvania and Stanford, respectively. The "differences" some might have seen as following from disparate religious sensibilities were minimized, in favor of the "sameness" of socialization within the subsuming American political order.

THE INFLUENCE OF SECULARISM

To a significant extent, of course, religious traditions themselves have lost their hold on many members of the wider culture—thus the emergence of the "secular Jew" as a distinct social, rather than religious, category. I do not know whether the category of "cultural Catholic," used sometimes to refer to those still significantly marked by a background in the Church even if they have formally left it, is truly similar. I am unaware that the notion of "secular Protestant" has any contemporary meaning at all in our society. In any event, it is clear that many people born and raised in these respective religious communities have left them behind as they have moved self-consciously into a more secular understanding of the world.

It is important to note, though, that "secularism" has a far different meaning within American culture than it bears elsewhere, for here there has been far less of the outright antireligious animus that is such an important part of European history. No serious American political party, for example, has ever defined itself as proudly secular and overtly hostile to the expression of any religious sensibility in public life.[35] I am not, however, primarily interested in such persons who present themselves self-consciously as "secular," whether in its European or more gentle American definitions. Instead, I am interested in the self-presentation of persons who continue to affirm the meaningfulness to them of membership in religious communities even as they also take on responsibilities of public office at the highest levels of government.

This necessarily raises an important question: has there been a significant redefinition in our culture of what it means to adhere to religion? I am inclined to answer yes, with the most important development being what I would call the "privatization of religious identity." Protestant theology has in fact significantly affected almost all of us within the United States, whatever our formal identification. It is to certain strands of Protestant thought, especially as interpreted by more secular liberal political theorists, that we

---

35. I owe recognition of this point to Allen Silver.

owe our almost instinctive identification of religion as essentially "private," that is, basically unrelated to our common lives as citizens in a collective enterprise.[36] Although there is bitter dispute over what the nature of those common lives or collective enterprise might be, there is, partly as a result of Article VI, wide agreement that its definition must be nonreligious.

It should be obvious that this privatizing of religion and the concomitant separation of the public from the private is scarcely inevitable or uncontroversial. Traditional Judaism was historically totalistic in its scope, as the commands of the Jewish law, the Halakha, reached from the bedroom to the public square. Indeed, a source of tension within contemporary Israel is precisely what it means to take seriously the task of being a "Jewish state"; there are many (too many, from my perspective) who argue that it requires that the state enforce Halakhic norms, including, for example, observance of the Sabbath even against those Jews who are not observant. Similar controversies are raging within Islamic societies.

The Roman Catholic Church certainly has not, at least historically, been identified with a strong separation between a religious, private realm and a secular, public one.[37] Protestants per se have surely not proved unwilling to use state power in behalf of religious ends. However, there is in Protestant-

36. See Gerard Bradley, "Dogmatomachy: A 'Privatization' Theory of the Religion Clause Cases," 30 *St. Louis U.L.J.* 275 (1986) (discussing the Supreme Court's treatment of the religion clauses, which has eliminated the influence of religious factions and shaped religion into a private matter).

37. As is true almost of any statement about the institutional Catholic Church, the reality is more complicated than the text suggests. Pope Gelasius I, in addressing the Roman Emperor Anastasius in 494 C.E., articulated a distinction between "sacred authority" (auctoritas) of the priesthood and the "royal power" (potestas) of the emperor and indicated that "the bishops themselves, recognizing that the imperial office was conferred on you by divine disposition, obey your laws so far as the sphere of public order is concerned." See Gelasius I, "Letter to Emperor Anastasius," quoted in Brian Tierney, *The Crisis of Church and State, 1050–1300*, at 13–14 (1964). This quote was also mentioned by William Luckey at the annual meeting of the American Political Science Association in 1989. See Luckey, "The Role of Religion in Modern Democracy in the Political Thought of John Courtney Murray, S.J." 3 (August–September 1989) (unpublished manuscript). Professor Luckey noted that this Gelasian understanding of separate spheres was supplanted in the Middle Ages by "political Augustinism" culminating in the Bull *Unam Sancta* of Pope Boniface VIII in 1302, which stated "that the temporal sword is in the power of Peter" and his papal successors. Id. at 5. In reaction, some medieval writers, including Dante and Machievelli, wrote in behalf of secular rule "completely free from the spiritual *auctoritas.*" Id. at 6. Luckey went on to analyze the important thought of John Courtney Murray, who sought a middle way between these two positions and whose thought was enormously influential in the decisions made by Vatican II in the 1960s. Id. at 6–23.

ism much more of an analytical separation between the realms of God and Caesar, particularly in the pietistic traditions associated with the Lutheran Reformation and subsequent developments.[38] Thus one[39] is inclined to identify the Roman Catholic Church, far more than any Protestant church, with calls for the organization of the public realm in many respects on the basis of the decidedly nonrelative, transcultural moral norms of natural law, as distinguished from norms that are the product of more specific religious revelation. Indeed, is not this the heritage that Deak is making reference to in the comment quoted at the outset of these remarks? No doubt, as I have been reminded by a friend, himself a secular Jew teaching at Georgetown University, there have been major changes in Catholic doctrine on this point following Vatican II, and the Church may today be far less "militant" in its proclaimed reach than was earlier the case.[40] One way of framing my remarks, though, is in asking how important it is that we (non-Catholics interested in American politics) become more knowledgeable about changes within the Catholic community. The answer depends, of course, on the potential relevance of the information to our political decisions, which brings us back full circle.

Interrogating Catholic Nominees

Professor Kent Greenawalt, who describes himself as religious, tells his readers that "[m]y convictions tell me that no aspect of life should be wholly untouched by the transcendent reality in which I believe, yet a basic premise

38. I have been reminded by Laura Underkuffler that in fact "[m]any Protestant groups . . . see no separation between the religious and secular parts of their lives." In addition to certain "fundamentalist" sects, she includes as opponents of "compartmentalization of their lives" such groups as the Society of Friends (Quakers) and the Amish, Mennonites, and Schwenkfelders. Although she agrees that "the separation of the individual and collective" is certainly "a strong strain in Protestantism," it is just as certainly "not universal." Letter from Laura Underkuffler to Sanford Levinson (22 November 1989). See also Laura Underkuffler, " 'Discrimination' on the Basis of Religion: An Examination of Attempted Value Neutrality in Employment," 30 *Wm. & Mary L. Rev.* 581 (1989) (discussing the effects of employers' religious beliefs in the work place and the extent of legal intervention to prevent discrimination on the basis of religious beliefs).

39. The better word here may well be "I," standing perhaps for the non-Catholic community in general.

40. But see Vatican Council II, Declaration on Religious Freedom, no. 2, which notes that religious people should be free "to show the special value of their doctrine in what concerns the organization of society and the inspiration of the whole of human activity." Quoted in David Hollenbach, "The Common Good Revisited," 50 *Theological Stud.* 70, 90 (1989).

of common legal argument is that any reference to such a perspective is out of bounds."[41] He has devoted a recent book to considering the tensions implicit in these two assumptions. I will be borrowing from his analysis even as I try to develop its ramifications in a context that he leaves basically undiscussed, the confirmation process of persons nominated to serve on the United States Supreme Court.[42]

THE JUDICIAL CONFIRMATION PROCESS

Many functions are served by the judicial confirmation process. For those of us interested in political culture, the process serves mainly[43] to demonstrate the creedal demands that nominees are expected to affirm. This affirmation provides symbolic reassurance that the nominees can be entrusted with the power of high office, which in the case of the Supreme Court of course includes lifetime tenure. The appearance of nominees themselves before the Senate Judiciary Committee is a comparatively recent development in our public ritual life. Not until the nomination of Harlan Fiske Stone to become an associate justice of the United States Supreme Court did a judicial nominee testify personally in front of the Senate Judiciary Committee.[44] Before that the nominee remained well in the background, even as friends and

41. Kent Greenawalt, *Religious Convictions and Political Choice* 5 (1988) [hereinafter Greenawalt, *Religious Convictions*]. Among the most thoughtful reviews of the book are: Robert Audi, "Religion and the Ethics of Political Participation," 100 *Ethics* 386 (1990) (book review); David A. J. Richards, Book Review, 23 *Ga. L. Rev.* 1189 (1989) (also reviewing Kent Greenawalt, *Conflicts of Law and Morality* (1987)); Mark V. Tushnet, Book Review, 89 *Colum. L. Rev.* 1131 (1989). Professor Greenawalt elaborates his views and assesses the arguments of his critics in Greenawalt, "Religious Convictions and Political Choice: Some Further Thoughts," 39 *De Paul L. Rev.* 1019 (1990) [hereinafter Greenawalt, "Some Further Thoughts"].

42. But see Greenawalt, *Religious Convictions*, supra note 41, at 239–41, where Greenawalt offers a brief discussion of the propriety of judges making recourse to their religious convictions.

43. It can obviously be argued that confirmation hearings serve "mainly" to confirm or deny confirmation to nominees, as witnessed most recently by the Bork hearings. It is certainly true that confirmation hearings carry with them a "bottom line" of a yea or nay vote on capacity to serve on the Supreme Court, and to this extent the statement in the text may be overstated. Yet it is clear that most hearings do not carry with them a serious possibility of rejecting the nominee, and that they therefore take on the more purely "ritualistic" aspect noted in the text. (And, of course, even the Bork episode was highly ritualistic, whatever else it was as well.)

44. Ethan Bronner, *Battle for Justice: How the Bork Nomination Shook America* 220 (1989). On confirmation hearings in general, see the excellent article by Grover Rees III, "Questions for Supreme Court Nominees at Confirmation Hearings: Excluding the Constitution," 17 *Ga. L. Rev.* 913 (1983); see also Lucas A. Powe, "The Senate and the Court: Questioning a Nominee" (book review), 54 *Texas L. Rev.* 891 (1976).

opponents might appear before the Senate urging confirmation or rejection. It was with Felix Frankfurter's nomination in 1939 that our norms in this regard appear to have more significantly changed, and it has now become expected that nominees will indeed appear before the Senate (and, via C-SPAN and the networks, before the American people) to answer a wide range of questions purportedly relevant to their fitness to serve. One of the key concerns is that nominees affirm that aspect of the American creed that requires them to subordinate any merely "personal" aspects of their selves to the demands placed on them by their public role.

RECENT CATHOLIC NOMINEES

Let us turn now to the Senate hearings considering the nominations of William Brennan, Antonin Scalia, and Anthony Kennedy to the Supreme Court. I begin with a specific exchange that occurred on February 27, 1957, during the hearings on the nomination of William J. Brennan to join the Court. Senator Joseph O'Mahoney of Wyoming asked special permission to direct a question at the nominee.[45] O'Mahoney was himself a Catholic, as he emphasized when taking personal responsibility for asking Justice Brennan a question propounded by the members of the National Liberal League, an organization purportedly devoted to the separation of church and state. I say "purportedly" because the League indicated its opposition to the appointment on the ground that the United States, as "a predominantly Protestant country," should not have Catholics on its highest court. In any event, the League requested that Justice Brennan be asked the following question:

> You are bound by your religion to follow the pronouncements of the Pope on all matters of faith and morals. There may be some controversies which involve matters of faith and morals and also matters of law and justice. But in matters of law and justice, you are bound by your oath to follow not papal decrees and doctrines, but the laws and precedents of this Nation. If you should be faced with such a mixed issue, would you be able to follow the requirements of your oath or would you be bound by your religious obligations?[46]

45. Nomination of William Joseph Brennan: Hearings Before the Committee on the Judiciary, United States Senate, 85th Cong., 1st Sess. 32–34 (1957).
46. Id. at 32.

Justice Brennan then answered as follows:

Senator, I think the oath that I took is the same one that you and all of the Congress, every member of the executive department up and down all levels of government take to support the Constitution and laws of the United States. I took that oath just as unreservedly as I know you did, and every member and everyone else of our faith in whatever office elected or appointive he may hold. And I say not that I recognize that there is any obligation superior to that, rather that there isn't any obligation of our faith superior to that. And my answer to the question is categorically that in everything I have ever done, in every office I have held in my life or that I shall ever do in the future, what shall control me is the oath that I took to support the Constitution and laws of the United States and so act upon the cases that come before me for decision that it is that oath and that alone which governs.[47]

Justice Brennan in effect returned to this theme during an interview with a former law clerk on the thirtieth anniversary of his appointment to the Court. He was asked if he "ever had difficulty dealing with [his] own religious beliefs in terms of cases," and the justice responded that he had, in 1956, "settled in my mind that I had an obligation under the Constitution which could not be influenced by any of my religious principles."[48] Although he would "as a private citizen" do "what a Roman Catholic does . . . to the extent that that conflicts with what I think the Constitution means or requires, then my religious beliefs have to give way."[49]

A considerably tamer, though I think possibly even more interesting, version of the O'Mahoney-Brennan dialogue occurred during the August 1986 Senate confirmation hearings on the nomination of then–Circuit Court Judge Antonin Scalia to be an associate justice of the United States Supreme Court.[50] Interestingly enough, at no time during the hearing does explicit notice appear to have been taken of Justice Scalia's Catholicism.

47. Id. at 34.

48. Levinson, supra note 4, at 56 (quoting Leeds, "A Life on the Court," *New York Times Magazine*, 5 October 1986, at 79).

49. Id.

50. Nomination of Judge Antonin Scalia: Hearings Before the Committee on the Judiciary, United States Senate, 99th Cong., 2d Sess. 43–47 (1986) [hereinafter Scalia Hearings].

Instead, everyone emphasized the splendid fact that he would be the first Italian American member of the Court.

Republican Senator Charles Mathias noted that Scalia had "expressed doubts about [*Roe v. Wade,* the Supreme Court's 1973 abortion decision,] both on moral as well as jurisprudential grounds."[51] For reasons I shall suggest presently, I think that Catholic nominees might especially be the recipients of questions directed at their "moral" views, so that such inquiries are in some way only slightly concealed ways of inquiring into their religious beliefs. But there is also an obvious special interest in the views of Catholic nominees regarding the substantive issue of abortion, given the leading role taken by the Catholic Church in attacking the moral legitimacy of abortion and of its legal tolerance.[52] It is within this context, then, that one must understand both the question directed at Judge Scalia and his answer.

Judge Scalia replied that although he may well have criticized *Roe,* "I do not recall passing moral judgment on the issue." He immediately went on to reassure Senator Mathias that "I agree . . . that one of the primary qualifications for a judge is to set aside personal views."[53]

Senator Mathias probed further: "What does a judge do about a very deeply held personal position, a personal moral conviction, which may be pertinent to a matter before the Court?" The answer, according to Scalia, is to recognize the moral obligation that comes with living "in a democratic society and to be bound by the determinations of that democratic society. If he feels that he cannot be, then he should not be sitting as a judge."[54] Even if he as a justice were faced with laws "that I might even think in the largest sense are immoral in the results they produce . . . [i]n no way would I let that influence my determination of how they apply."[55] Should he feel unable to separate his personal moral feelings from his duties as a servant of the law, he would recuse himself from the case.[56]

51. Id. at 43.

52. Of course, some Catholic political leaders, including Mario Cuomo and Geraldine Ferraro, have been specifically criticized by officials of the Church for their failure to support the Church's stands. See infra note 66.

53. Scalia Hearings, supra note 50, at 43.

54. Id.

55. Id.

56. Id. John Leubsdorf, while discussing an earlier presentation of this article at Columbia on 11 December 1989, brought to my attention the structural linkage between the problem addressed in the article — judicial confirmation — and the issue of judicial recusal (or involuntary disqualification) based on the purported "partiality" of a judge because of his or her having

Finally, at his confirmation hearing, Anthony Kennedy was asked by Senator Biden about a column written by Cal Thomas, a former official of Jerry Falwell's "Moral Majority," in which Thomas purported to describe a conversation between Kennedy and Senator Jesse Helms of North Carolina.[57] Helms was quoted as saying, "I think you know where I stand on abortion." According to Thomas, "Judge Kennedy smiled and answered, 'Indeed I do and I admire it. I am a practicing Catholic.' "[58] In response to Senator Biden's inquiry about the accuracy of the column, Judge Kennedy noted that "I admire anyone with strong moral beliefs. Now it would be highly improper for a judge to allow his or her own personal or religious views to enter into a decision respecting a constitutional matter."[59]

PERSONAL IDENTITIES AND SOCIETAL IMPLICATIONS

An analysis of these nomination hearings, thirty years apart in time, may help to explain the way the American political culture tries to come to terms with the problem of personal identities. Here, of course, I am interested in one particular — and volatile — mixture: on the one hand, there is one's self-understanding as what Michael Sandel, one of our leading "communitarian" political theorists, might call an "encumbered" member of a religious community. Such a community might make demands on its members ranging from what appear to be relatively non–morally freighted rituals

---

certain attributes, including that of membership in given religious bodies. Thus he noted that lawyers on occasion have filed recusal motions in regard to Catholic judges on the grounds that they could not dispassionately assess certain issues presented by the case before them, such as the meaning of the establishment clause as it relates to state aid to parochial schools. Such motions, he said, have rarely, if ever, been successful. Though recusals are beyond the scope of this particular article, they are obviously relevant to the overall topic, both in terms of the perceived difference (or sameness) of Catholic and non-Catholic judges and the response of the operational judicial system to these perceptions. In addition to Leubsdorf, I am indebted as well to Arthur J. Jacobson of Cardozo Law School who has shared with me materials on judicial disqualification that will form part of a casebook, *Justice and the Legal System: A Coursebook,* that he is preparing with Anthony D'Amato. See also Judge Jerome Frank's opinion in *In re J.P. Linahan,* 138 F.2d 650, 652–53 (2d Cir. 1943) ("Much harm is done by the myth that, merely by putting on a black robe and taking the oath of office as a judge, a man ceases to be human and strips himself of all predilections, becomes a passionless thinking machine.").
57. "The Questions Begin: 'Who Is Anthony Kennedy?' " *New York Times,* 15 December 1987, at B16 (transcript of exchanges between members of Senate Judiciary Committee and Judge Anthony Kennedy).
58. Id.
59. Id.

(for example, fasting on particular days) to adherence to what is generally thought the "essence" of morality (for example, nonparticipation in murder, whether capital punishment, for some, or abortion, for others). Professor Greenawalt describes, apparently with approval, the view that "it is scarcely possible for anyone who takes religion seriously to acquiesce in its being treated as a private matter. Unless there are good reasons for religious believers to discount the evident relevance of religious convictions for political choice, these convictions will affect some political decision they make."[60] On the other hand, there is one's self-understanding as a member of a pluralistic civil community, which calls for the suspension, or at least bracketing, of one's religious identity when entering the public arena. This bracketing may seem especially important if one chooses to accept a public office requiring that one act as an agent of others rather than as a first-order decision maker, as is the case presumably with the standard view of the judge.[61]

Identification as a Public Official. As I have suggested in my book *Constitutional Faith,* many readers probably take the subordination of religion, or "personal morality," to the Constitution as a sine qua non of what it means to be a public official. The "many" in this case would almost certainly include all who define themselves as secularist, for they by definition find intellectually implausible religion-based claims about the world. But others might feel distinctly less comfortable at the privileging of the demands of the secular state over one's religious duties. The "others" in this instance might include many who reject, at one level or another, a secular stance toward the world. Consider, for example, the remark of Professor Paul Simmons, a Southern Baptist: "For Christians and Jews, loyalty to God must transcend any earthly loyalties."[62] Stanley Hauerwas, a Protestant theologian who has taught at Notre Dame, has criticized the diminution within contemporary religious culture of a willingness on the part of believers to present "the Gospel as truth." He is particularly fearful that this has led as well to a significant weakening of "a Church that has a people capable of saying 'no to the state' "

60. Greenawalt, *Religious Convictions,* supra note 41, at 35.

61. See Frederick Schauer, "May Officials Think Religiously?" 27 *Wm. & Mary L. Rev.* 1075 (1986) (discussing Greenawalt's position that public officials may base decisions on religious beliefs and suggesting, rather, that they may be precluded from doing so).

62. Quoted in Levinson, supra note 4, at 57.

or, indeed, "capable of challenging the state."[63] From this perspective, what the secularist positively describes as adherence to one's constitutional duty can be given the much more negative description of idolatry.[64]

Whatever the obvious differences we might perceive between the politically liberal Justice Brennan and the conservative Justices Scalia and Kennedy, their self-descriptions as judges within the civil realm seem remarkably similar. The ultimate question is whether we are genuinely reassured by these descriptions. It should be obvious, incidentally, that a linked task is to discover whether in fact there is a real "we" that shares a common perception of these justices' comments. It has become a truism of cultural criticism that the rhetorical use of the word "we" often is designed to suppress any awareness of the presence of significant division that, if taken seriously, makes impossible any facile assumption of shared identities and perceptions.

The question asked of Justice Brennan presumably grew out of the same soil as did a letter from a Minneapolis citizen who saw in Pierce Butler's nomination by President Harding not an occasion for pride in the success of a fellow Minnesotan but rather the specter of "tighten[ing] the papal noose

---

63. Id. at 118 (quoting Stanley Hauerwas, "Freedom of Religion: A Subtle Temptation" 2, 19 (unpublished manuscript)).

64. Indeed, Professor Thomas Shaffer, the former dean and now law professor at Notre Dame Law School, has told me that he opposed honoring Justice Brennan because he "understand[s] Brennan to be an idolater, plain and simple, and I (and many Catholics) are as solemn about idolatry as the Rabbis were." In a later letter, Professor Shaffer has added that he finds Kennedy's answer "evasive," and he states that I "underestimate" an important aspect of Scalia's answer: "He said if the law required a result at odds with conscience, he would resign from the bench." What Shaffer emphasizes is that for him "the issue is idolatry." Insight into what might be meant by idolatry in this context is provided by Professor Yovel in his recent study of Spinoza: "If this world has no transcendent dimension, then some particular entity within the world can possibly gain metaphysical significance, and even be sanctified by some person as the foundation of his or life. This is not merely 'paganism' but outright idolatry." See Yirmiahu Yovel, 1 *Spinoza and Other Heretics: The Marrano of Reason* 123 (1989). One might note in this overall context the controversy that developed in 1989 when Spalding University, a small Catholic university in Louisville, Kentucky, announced the award of an honorary degree to Justice Brennan. The archbishop of the Louisville diocese, Thomas Kelly, announced that he would refuse to attend Spalding's commencement, and a local priest, claiming the support of Kelly, attempted to organize further protest. Although the university remained firm in its intention to honor Justice Brennan for his thirty years of service as a member of the Supreme Court, he ultimately chose not to attend the ceremonies. The university, however, awarded the degree to Brennan in absentia. Tony Mauro, "Brennan Gets an Education in 'Intolerance,' " *Legal Times*, 29 May 1989, at 10.

around the neck of America almost to the strangulation point."[65] To what extent is a Catholic bound to follow the strictures of a foreign potentate housed in the Vatican? Anti-Catholics, of course, have always found it far too easy to assume of Catholics that they are indeed bound to follow the pronouncements of the pope on all matters of faith and morality. The image is presumably that of the automaton, who has ceded his or her capacity for judgment to some external agent. This is obviously grotesquely simple-minded. Anyone even dimly aware of the history of the Church knows of the heated arguments that indeed occurred, and are occurring, within it over matters of faith and morals.

Still, it is scarcely anti-Catholic to note the institutionalized nature of the Roman Catholic Church and, more particularly, the claims that have on occasion been made in behalf of its magisterium. Indeed, even as I was writing the most recent draft of this article, the *New York Times* headlined that "Bishops Warn Politicians on Abortion," going on to describe a resolution passed at the annual National Conference of Catholic Bishops stating that "no Catholic can responsibly take a 'pro-choice' stand when the 'choice' in question" involves abortion. Some individual bishops apparently are suggesting that the Church might need "to look at" the possibility of excommunicating or otherwise sanctioning Catholic public officials who reject the Church's position.[66]

---

65. Danelski, supra note 29, at 92. There is also a similarity to the views enunciated by New York's Governor Mario Cuomo in an unusually thoughtful speech, "Religious Belief and Public Morality: A Catholic Governor's Perspective," at Notre Dame on 13 September 1984, in part given as a direct response to the criticisms he had received from officials in the Catholic hierarchy for his position on abortion. In that speech, Governor Cuomo accepted the premise:

> [T]hat I have a salvific mission as a Catholic. Does this mean I am in conscience required to do everything I can as Governor to translate all my religious values into the laws and regulations of the State of New York or the United States? Or be branded as a hypocrite if I don't?

Timothy L. Fort, *Law and Religion* 108 (1987) (quoting Mario Cuomo, "Religious Belief and Public Morality: A Catholic Governor's Perspective" 6 (13 September 1984) (unpublished manuscript)). As one might expect, the answer to both of these questions is no. Cuomo emphasized that:

> Our public morality, then — the moral standards we maintain for everyone, not just the ones we insist on in our private lives — depends on a consensus view of right and wrong. The values derived from religious belief will not — and should not — be accepted as part of the public morality unless they are shared by the pluralistic community at large, by consensus. (Id. at 107.)

66. Peter Steinfels, "Bishops Warn Politicians on Abortion," *New York Times,* 8 November 1989, at A18. *See* Ari Goldman, "Legislator Barred From Catholic Rite," *New York Times,* 17

One way that we might understand (though I should immediately emphasize, not necessarily justify) the question directed at Justice Brennan is by placing it within the American concern, going back to 1795, that its citizens—of at least the naturalized variety—publicly renounce commitments that are viewed as competing with the loyalties to the United States

------

November 1989, at A18. The article describes the order by San Diego Bishop Leo T. Maher that California State Assemblywoman Lucy Killea refrain from receiving communion so long as she continues to support abortion rights as part of her campaign in a special election for the California Senate. In a letter to Killea, Bishop Maher stated that "by your media advertisements advocating the 'pro-choice' abortion position in the public forum, you are placing yourself in complete contradiction to the moral teachings of the Catholic Church." He cited Canon 915 of the Code of Canon Law, giving him the right to deny communion to those who "obstinately persist in manifest grave sin." See also Peter Steinfels, "Question for Catholics," *New York Times,* 20 November 1989, at A16 (analyzing Bishop Maher's action). Steinfels points out that "[b]ishops . . . have wide latitude to act in their own dioceses, which is often forgotten by many, including Catholics, who view the Catholic Church as a tightly organized body that speaks with a single voice."

The *New York Times* commented on the subject further with an editorial "lament[ing]" Bishop Maher's action, even as the editorial stated that "[o]utsiders have no business challenging [his] religious authority to take such action." "The Bishop and the Truce of Tolerance," *New York Times,* 26 November 1989, at 4: 12. But the editorial writer, referring to Kennedy's "memorable pledge" at Houston that "I do not speak for the church and the church does not speak for me," strongly suggested that Bishop Maher's action threatens the "truce of tolerance by which Americans maintain civility and enlarge religious liberty." According to the editorial, should other bishops join Maher:

[M]any non-Catholic Americans may once again be moved to withhold their trust from Catholic candidates who could no longer credibly promise to follow the Kennedy and Cuomo examples. . . .

Above all, to force religious discipline on public officials risks destroying the fragile accommodations that Americans of all faiths and no faith have built with the bricks of the Constituton and the mortar of tolerance.

This in turn was answered by a *Times* reader, who described the paper's notion of "truce" as:

Timespeak to describe the situation in which a Roman Catholic may piously mouth his beliefs so long as he in no way acts on them. . . .

Bishop Maher is not forcing obedience to a religious political agenda, but simply reminding one of his flock that if she wants publicly to call herself a Catholic, she must abide by the church's teaching on the sanctity of human life. If she values her job above the tenets of her faith, she is free to make that choice. . . .

Spare us your crocodile tears over the impoverishment of American public life if "Catholic" politicians like the Kennedys and Cuomos lose the confidence of the electorate because of their so-called Catholicism. They are Catholic in name only—precisely the kind of Catholics you welcome or allow into the public arena. Real Catholics who live their faith need not venture out; their place is in the catacombs. (Moreland, Letter to the Editor, *New York Times,* 17 December 1989, at E20.)

and to the Constitution that are at the heart of what limited national politi-cal identity we share. Thus to this day the United States requires of anyone who would become a naturalized member of the American polity not only an affirmative promise of fidelity to the Constitution but also a declaration that one is willing to "renounce and abjure absolutely and entirely all alle-giance and fidelity to any foreign prince, potentate, state, or sovereignty of whom or which the petitioner was before a subject or citizen."[67] I suspect that anti-Catholics in effect view the pope as the "potentate" of a sovereign community, so that the question directed at Brennan is the equivalent of a demand for explicit renunciation and abjuration of what anti-Catholics perceive as a possibly competing loyalty.[68] Of course, what is bothersome about this suggestion is precisely the application of what have become en-

The controversy continued upon the suggestion, by Bishop Austin Vaughan, that Governor Cuomo's soul might be endangered by his unwillingness to renounce *Roe v. Wade*. See supra note 24. Upon the seeming endorsement of this view by John Cardinal O'Connor of New York, Professor Arthur Schlesinger immediately wrote an op-ed piece in the *New York Times* arguing that "Bishop Vaughan and Cardinal O'Connor are in danger of vindicating those who have been saying that Catholics in politics must obey the ukases of Rome. The prelates seem to imply that Al Smith and John Kennedy were wrong in contending that Catholics in politics are as free as communicants of other faiths." Schlesinger, supra note 24. I strongly suspect that this debate has continued even as this article was published (and, of course, well afterward).

In terms of the central focus of this article, judicial nominations, one might want to dis-tinguish legislators from judges in terms of the far greater "free will" of the former relative to the "constrained" agency role of the latter as simple enforcers of legal command. A Supreme Court Justice supporting *Roe* can claim that he or she is simply fulfilling the command of the Constitu-tion rather than engaging in any kind of discretionary choice about what counts as a preferable public policy. Two questions immediately arise, however. First, to what extent does this distinc-tion between discretion and agency survive legal realism, especially in areas like abortion and so-called privacy rights? Second, even if one accepts the distinction, at what point must a moral judge at least recuse him- or herself from decisions involving the enforcement of unjust law, not to mention the possible duty to resign entirely from the bench? For discussions of this point, see Robert Cover, *Justice Accused* (1975); see also the afterword to chapter 7.

67. Levinson, supra note 4, at 103 (quoting the oath required by the Immigration and Nationality Act). Thus Justice Taney's biographer Carl Swisher notes that his nomination "was widely criticized on the ground that he was a Catholic, and therefore subservient to a 'foreign poten-tate.' " Carl Brent Swisher, *Roger B. Taney* 37 (1935), quoted in Perry, supra note 30, at 60.

68. Or consider the campaign for governor of Pennsylvania waged in 1857 by Republican candidate David Wilmot, who appealed to the nativist members of the American Party by emphasizing to naturalized citizens that they must acknowledge "no earthly power superior to the Constitution and the sovereignty of the American people" and then denouncing the presence in American politics of a "priestly order . . . acknowledging as their head a foreign potentate." Wilmot's campaign is discussed in Kenneth Stampp, *America in 1857: A Nation on the Brink* 248 (1990).

tirely secular categories to a body that envisions itself, after all, as the instantiation of Jesus Christ and the God whose son he is claimed to have
been. But this is simply to repeat once again the essential problem that
underlies this article.

Moral Judgment and Natural Law. I want to suggest, moreover, that this
emphasis on the role of the institutionalized Church as authoritative artic-
ulator of moral and theological truths may deflect us from recognizing the
centrality of an even more fundamental issue, which is the role of moral
judgment as an aspect of law. I don't want to suggest that the issue of
institutional authority is unimportant. It is, for example, surely behind the
current controversy over the status of Father Curran as a Catholic theologian, not to mention the criticism sometimes visited by Church officials
upon Catholic politicians for their apparent deviation from Church positions in regard to abortion. But the question of institutional authority, however important, is joined to an even more substantial issue: can human
beings discern — and feel bound by — transcendent moral norms?

Professor Greenawalt presents as "the traditional Roman Catholic perspective" a "belief in natural law" joined "with a vitally important role for
authoritative statements of the church hierarchy."[69] From my perspective

69. Greenawalt, *Religious Convictions,* supra note 41, at 41. See also the study of John Courtney
Murray by Professor Luckey, supra note 37, who emphasizes the grounding of Murray's thought
in natural law theory. Thus Murray, who emphasized the "relative autonomy" of the political
order, nevertheless wrote that "[t]he limits of [the ruler's] direct power are set by natural law." Id.
at 9, quoting John Courtney Murray, "Governmental Repression of Heresy," in *Proceedings of
the Catholic Theological Society of America* 56 (1948). For Murray, the possibilities inherent in
free government "can be realized only when the people as a whole are inwardly governed by the
recognized imperatives of the universal moral law." Luckey, supra note 37, at 11, quoting
Murray, *We Hold These Truths: Catholic Reflections on the American Proposition* 24 (1960)
(emphasis added). Luckey describes Murray as offering a notion of the U.S. Constitution that
viewed it as having two aspects. "Firstly, it is a charter of freedom, recognizing human dignity
and the right to choose what one ought. Secondly, it is a plan for political order, a plan based on
these recognized principles of a universal moral law." Luckey, supra note 37, at 11.

Notre Dame Professor Richard P. McBrien offered an analysis of Murray in his own presentation at the Casassa Conference where I presented the initial version of the present article. He
cited Murray as rather sharply distinguishing between the realms of the moral law, which, in
Murray's words, "governs the entire order of human conduct, personal and social; it extends
even to motivations and interior acts." McBrien, "Religion and Politics in America: A Catholic
Reflection" 19 (9–10 March 1989) (unpublished manuscript). On the other hand, the civil law
"looks only to the public order of human society; it touches only external acts, and regards only

outside the Church, I share what I take to be Professor Greenawalt's view that one of the defining tenets of the Roman Catholic community is the existence of moral claims upon us, the content of which can be known through the disciplined application of human reason.[70] Thus arises the traditional Catholic emphasis on natural law and natural justice and the propensity to judge the commands of positive law against the purported claims of natural law. And, as Professor Deak suggested, one consequence of such judgment may be to delegitimize, or invalidate, the authority of positive law. It is probably an overstatement to assert that Catholic doctrine holds that "an unjust law is not law at all."[71] Although St. Augustine did in fact state that "a law that was unjust wouldn't seem to be the law," John Finnis argues that Thomas Aquinas presents a much more nuanced analysis. Aquinas's analysis allows the possibility of recognizing as valid — even though clearly not the "best" law — a legal command that violates the norms of natural law. Indeed, Finnis states that "[t]he tradition goes so far as to say that there may be an obligation to conform to some . . . unjust laws in order to uphold respect for the legal system as a whole."[72] In any event, it seems clear that

---

values that are formally social." Id. For McBrien, the implication is that "the scope of civil law is limited and its moral aspirations are minimal. To have made the moral argument against abortion, therefore, is not necessarily to have made the legal argument as well." Id. at 20 (emphasis omitted).

70. I should note that the analysis of the binding nature of natural law in Catholic thought is considerably more complex than suggested in the text. Thus, Professor Frederick J. Crosson argues that for Aquinas, the duty to adhere to natural law did not come from simple rational cognition of its teachings, but rather from the fact that it is commanded by God "that good is to be done." Otherwise, the natural law is merely "a rule or standard by which human actions were to be measured," though not necessarily, to use a quintessential American term, invalidated. Crosson, supra note 13, at 87–88. Father McBrien agrees. See McBrien, supra note 69, at 19. He quotes Aquinas's comment, in *Summa Theologica,* II-I, quest. 96, art. 2, as saying that the civil law "does not lay upon the multitude of imperfect people the burdens of those who are already virtuous, namely, that they should abstain from all evil. Otherwise these imperfect ones, being unable to bear such precepts, would break out into yet greater evils."

71. See John Finnis, *Natural Law and Natural Right* 363 (1980) (section on "Lex injusta non est lex").

72. Id. at 365. See Questions 90–96, "First Part of the Second Part of the Summa Theologicam," in *The Political Ideas of St. Thomas Aquinas* (Dino Bigongiari, ed., 1953) (unjust laws "do not bind in conscience, except perhaps to avoid scandal or disturbance"). As noted by Professor Wright, the quoted passage puts to lie any easy notion that adherents to Thomistic natural law are "counseled to . . . disobey [unjust] law, whatever the cost in disruption and scandal." George Wright, "Legal Obligation and the Natural Law," 23 *Ga. L. Rev.* 997, 1009 (1989). However, this basically instrumental defense for obeying what one believes to be an unjust law may not

immersion in traditional Catholic teachings about natural law at the very least would lead to a sensitivity about the justice of the alleged commands of the positive law. These are two different claims, of course. The first is epistemological, that it is possible to know what morality demands of us. The second is jurisprudential, that nothing should be accorded the dignity of being regarded as binding law if it manifests injustice. Both are obviously questions of the highest importance.

THE LAW, MORALITY, AND CATHOLIC JUSTICES

At this point arises the central question of this discussion: Is it legitimate to be especially concerned about the views held regarding these epistemological and jurisprudential issues by someone who comes out of the Roman Catholic community? One might be more likely to ask Roman Catholic nominees such questions than, say, Lutherans, because the Catholic Church has historically insisted on the reality of natural law in a way that the Lutheran community has not.

The Constitution clearly prohibits religious tests for office. This means, presumably, that it would be illegitimate to make dispositive a nominee's belief — or lack thereof — in God, since a conscientious senator should be unable to take into account any given answer to that question. That being said, should we interpret the no test oath clause as equally prohibiting any inquiries motivated by the interlocutor's interest in the nominee's adherence to claims associated with the particular church or sect to which he or she is known to belong, especially those claims that have undoubted relevance to the conceptualization of one's role as an actor within the world? Consider, for example, Senator Howell Heflin's comment, in his opening statement during the Bork hearings, that "[t]here are those who charge that Judge Bork is an agnostic or a non-believer. These critics contend that such beliefs will affect the opinions of the courts and hence, our churches, our synagogues and, ultimately, our lives."[73] Senator Heflin made this comment by way ostensibly of "remind[ing his] colleagues" about the no test oath provision of Article VI and emphasizing that "it should be observed in pursuing any inquiry, whether it be legitimate or not, as to one's personal religious feelings,"[74] though the context makes one doubt how genuine the

---

satisfy the state, which is looking for the kind of enthusiastic commitment that stills any embarrassing questions about the possibility and implications of unjust laws.

73. Bronner, supra note 44, at 294–95.

74. Id.

senator was in his protestations. The doubts are multiplied when one discovers that the senator justified his ultimate vote against confirmation in part on religious grounds, telling his constituents, for example, that "I was . . . disturbed by his refusal to discuss his belief in God or the lack thereof."[75]

Ethan Bronner, in his book on the Bork nomination, describes Heflin's opening statement as "inexcusable" and says that he "shamelessly" returned to the issue of Bork's religious beliefs.[76] In an earlier draft of this article, I described the statement as outrageous, given the inability of a constitutionally conscientious senator to base her vote on the religious beliefs of a nominee. I confess, with genuine trepidation, that I now think that the question might be more complicated, even if I remain willing to condemn Senator Heflin in the specific instance for his Nixonian hypocrisy in raising the issue by way of insisting that it whould be excluded from the discussion.

The evaluation of Senator Heflin's remarks may be different if he had forthrightly stated the view that the presence or absence of "belief in God" might be relevant to one's fitness for public office. One might wish to deny this *tout court* by asserting a lack of empirical evidence that suggests that the gross attribute of "believer" or "nonbeliever" predicts anything interesting about the likely behavior of a person, but this assertion itself might be highly controversial.[77] The traditional rationale given for disqualification of atheists is their presumed propensity to violate their oaths, given their lack of fear of a hereafter in which punishment would be visited upon sinners, but I assume that no one, at least in academic circles, would defend such a proposition. More seriously, one might believe that an atheist, as distinguished from an agnostic, might be less accepting of certain kinds of free exercise claims insofar as atheism is a more militant, Enlightenment-based rejection of religious "superstition" than the more tolerantly skeptical agnosticism. But this rationale brings one perilously close to the exaction of a test oath that is barred by Article VI. Still, agreement that one could not legitimately base a vote on the bare answer to the question "Are you an atheist?" does not prove that one cannot ask it at all.

75. Id. at 295.
76. Id. at 294.
77. Thus Professor Silver has informed me that there is a sizable body of empirical material that suggests that believers and secularists tend to differ in their behavior. Letter from Allen Silver to Sanford Levinson 2 (10 December 1989).

Permissible Inquiries and the Danger of Prejudice. The appropriate American constitutional referent to the issue of atheism might be the cases decided by the Supreme Court during the 1950s and 1960s dealing with the validity of asking candidates for the bar if they had been members of the Communist Party.[78] To put it mildly, I am ambivalent about crediting them with any validity at all inasmuch as they were part and parcel of one of the least attractive eras of American public life. Still, with all the wariness that their backgrounds should compel, we might nonetheless examine their logic for any help they provide on the issue under discussion. Concomitantly, if one decides that religious commitments are absolutely ruled out as a subject of senatorial questioning, then that should certainly call into doubt the cogency of the cases mentioned.

As I understand these cases, the Court, even while rejecting the proposition that Communist Party membership per se would be enough to warrant rejection of an applicant for membership in the bar, indicated that Committees on Character and Fitness could nonetheless inquire about membership. The rationale was that affirmative information as to membership could serve as a reasonable basis for a more probing conversation about questions arguably relevant to one's fitness to practice law or otherwise inhabit public office.[79] The cognate question then might be whether, in spite of the clear prohibition of making any religious affirmation dispositive as to one's fitness for office, the equivalent of a committee on character and fitness — for instance, the Senate Judiciary Committee engaging in its constitutional power to advise and consent to appointments to the federal judiciary — may properly even seek information about one's religious views as the basis of further conversation about their implications relative to public office.

One might, of course, concede the relevance of a given question, but, at the same instant, make a policy decision to prohibit its being asked on the grounds that whatever quantum of relevant information will be garnered

---

78. E.g., *Schware v. Board of Bar Examiners,* 353 U.S. 232 (1957); *Konigsberg v. State Bar,* 353 U.S. 252 (1957), aff'g lower court decision on remand to deny petitioner bar admission, 366 U.S. 36 (1961).

79. See *Konigsberg,* 353 U.S. at 273–74 (fact of past membership in Communist Party, by itself, is an insufficient basis for finding an applicant disloyal or of bad character). The Court limited the use of these inquiries later, however, in holding that a state could not ask broad questions about all organizations to which an applicant has been a member. E.g., *Baird v. State Bar,* 401 U.S. 1, 6 (1971); *In re Stolar,* 401 U.S. 23, 30 (1971).

will be distorted in its application by the likely prejudice of the information seeker. This, of course, is precisely the analysis we use in the law of evidence, where the justified assertion of a question's relevance is in fact not always sufficient to overcome an objection predicated on its prejudicial potential.[80] Here, too, one might even be willing to concede that information about a nominee's religious stance would be relevant, but nonetheless prohibit inquiries about that stance either because of the likely unfairness for the particular nominee or, more generally, because of the adverse consequences for the general tone of American public life. Still, the general thrust of the evidentiary system involves the desirability of presenting truthful information about relevant matters, and the burden of persuasion is usually placed on the person seeking to limit the scope of inquiry.[81]

The Relevance of Morality. The analysis of the standards of evaluating a public official's personal identity necessarily involves moral issues. Returning to the specific interrogations of our three Catholic nominees, I think that they can be subsumed under (something like) the following general questions:

> You belong to a religious community that claims of human beings that they are able to discern, through a mixture of revelation and reason and presumably the help of authoritative Church officials, the requirements of morality and justice. That is, the Church has set itself resolutely against the various doctrines that can loosely be brought together under the rubric "moral skepticism," which suggest that nothing can be known about moral duties or, what is functionally similar, that moral positions are hopelessly idiosyncratic. First, do you accept the Church's teaching that genuine knowledge exists (and is knowable) as to what is required to us if we wish to be moral beings? Second, if you accept these ontological and epistemological claims, do you feel bound to accept the Church's teachings, whether delivered through Papal encyclical or the oral general magisterium, concerning the specific content of natural law? Finally, do you accept the proposition asserted by distinguished theorists associated with the Church, including St. Augustine and, according to some,

---

80. The Federal Rules of Evidence provide that relevant evidence "may be excluded if its probative value is substantially outweighed by the danger of unfair prejudice." Fed. R. Evid. 403.

81. See Fed. R. Evid. 301 ("[A] presumption imposes on the party against whom it is directed the burden of going forward with evidence to rebut or meet the presumption").

Thomas Aquinas, that any command by a putative sovereign that requires violation of natural law is not itself to be described as "law"?

Justice Brennan responded to the question about institutional authority, and he reassured his audience that the Constitution, rather than the pope, would be the source of guidance as to his duties as a judge. But this way of putting the question — and answer — eludes what is surely the central question, which is whether constitutional adjudication in any important respect includes reference to moral norms of the kind claimed by the Church to exist — in other words, transcendental truths ascertainable through right reason. Justice Scalia indeed addressed this question, albeit slightly obliquely, and I want to explore some of the ramifications of his answer.

Recall that Scalia described the judge in a democratic society as "be[ing] bound by the determinations of that democratic society." That obligation extends even to laws "that I might even think in the largest sense are immoral in the results they produce. In no way would I let that influence my determination of how they apply." I think it is worth closely analyzing Scalia's venture in political theory. At the very least, he is clearly and unequivocally rejecting what I have described as the classic Catholic analysis of law, for Scalia strips law of any necessary connection to morality. The Constitution may require or prohibit many things, but it cannot be said that the Constitution either requires justice or prohibits immorality. Justice Scalia instead accepts in toto the notion that the authority of the Constitution — indeed its very meaning — comes from the sovereignty of the people. To say that the voice of the people is the voice of God is no idle metaphor, for the very point is that the voice of the people can supplant the voice of God.

The question whether popular sovereignty is limited by normative constraints, of course, goes back to the very beginning of our constitutional debates. Against Justice Chase's argument in *Calder v. Bull*[82] that "certain vital principles," even if not overtly expressed in the constitutional text, would justify "overrul[ing] an apparent and flagrant abuse of legislative power," Justice Iredell answered that the Court was without authority to pronounce a law "void, merely because it is, in their judgment, contrary to the principles of natural justice."[83] In any event, I find elements of paradox in this attempt by a Catholic judge to reassure his interlocutor that he will

82. 3 U.S. (3 Dall.) 386 (1798).

83. Levinson, supra note 4, at 35–36 (quoting *Calder v. Bull,* 3 U.S. (3 Dall.) 386, 387–89 (1798)).

behave properly as a judge. Scalia offers such reassurance by embracing a kind of legal positivism associated in American thought particularly with Justice Holmes, with its relentless repudiation of natural justice in favor of the judge's duty to acquiesce to the commands of those with political power. Wherein lies the paradox? It comes from the fact that Holmes was strongly reacting against the claims of natural law identified with the Catholic Church.[84] Yet it has now become a standard part of our public rituals that Catholic nominees for the Supreme Court demonstrate their adherence to Holmesian positivism and, in effect, renounce, albeit *sub silentio,* certain doctrines identified with their church.[85]

84. See Holmes, "Natural Law," in *Collected Legal Papers* 310 (1920).

85. Professor Robert George of Princeton has taken issue with this sentence:

As I understand him, Scalia does not deny that there are objective moral truths; nor does he deny that these truths are accessible to reason; nor does he deny the authority of the *magisterium* to teach these truths; nor does he deny that positive law (including constitutional law) can be evaluated by reference to these truths; nor does he deny that one must avoid complicity in the wrongdoing of others. He does, I think, deny that moral truths determine the meaning of positive laws (including constitutional provision). Thus, in his view, there really can be immoral positive laws; the positive law really can stand in conflict with the natural law. In cases of such conflict, Scalia apparently believes that his duty as a judge is to determine the meaning of the positive law and to render judgment accordingly. Now, it is this belief about judicial duty, I think, that generates your critique. How can a judge who believes in natural law hold that he has a duty to render judgment in accord with positive law even when the positive law in question is unjust (or otherwise immoral)?

According to natural law theorists, judges are under the same obligations of truth telling that the rest of us are under. If the law is in conflict with the natural law, the judge may not lie about it. If his duty is to give judgment according to the positive law, then he must either (i) do so or (ii) recuse himself. If he can give judgment according to immoral positive law without rendering himself formally or unfairly material[ly] complicit in its immorality, and without giving scandal, then he may licitly do so (though he may also licitly recuse himself). If not, then he must recuse himself. (A great deal of traditional casuistry has to do with problems of formal and material complicity in wrongdoing.)

But doesn't natural law theory say that a judge's duty is to give judgment according to the natural law in cases of conflict between natural and positive law? No. In my opinion, the question of how much legislative authority a judge has to translate the natural law into positive law by nullifying positive law which he believes to be unjust is a question of positive law, not natural law. Different political systems reasonably differ (both in theory and practice) as to how much legislative authority they confer upon judges. . . . If his views about judicial duty make him a "positivist," his positivism does not, I think, place him in conflict with his Church's teachings about natural law.

Letter from Robert George to Sanford Levinson (3 April 1990).

If one assumes that Scalia's position, as reconstructed by Professor George, is a *possible* position within Catholic natural law theory, one might still wonder if an equally serious Catholic

Justice Scalia's response to Senator Mathias is especially dramatic insofar as it appears to be an unusually broad abnegation of the role of moral analysis in constitutional decision making. Consider two possible versions of Justice Scalia's argument. The first would be something like this: although one should strive to interpret the Constitution in a way that maximizes the congruence between the demands of morality, there are occasions when this will simply be impossible. The only plausible meaning of the Constitution will be one that recognizes its requirement of immorality or prohibition of what justice might require. The easiest historical example within American constitutional history is clearly slavery. No less a personage than John Marshall expressed his belief that slavery is contrary to the law of nature, even as he proceeded to rule that the trade was nonetheless legitimated by the conventions of public international law.[86] Similarly, Marshall's colleague Joseph Story both denounced slavery as "repugnant to the great principles of Christian duty, the dictates of natural religion, the obligations of good faith and morality, and the eternal maxims of social justice"[87] and, nevertheless, in *Prigg v. Pennsylvania,*[88] upheld the constitutionality of the tyrannical fugitive slave clause because the maintenance of the rights of slave owners was necessary in order to guarantee the preservation of the Union.[89]

Justice Scalia seems, however, to be making an even stronger argument than the one I have just described, which says "only" that morality does not necessarily trump immoral commands of the Constitution. But this way of

---

could read authoritative Church material as requiring a more privileged position for the teachings of natural law when they are in conflict with (at least some readings) of positive law. If the latter is the case, then we would still be faced with the question as to the legitimacy of senators inquiring into the view of Catholic theology held by Catholic nominees. In any event, I am extremely grateful to Professor George for taking the time to analyze the point so thoughtfully, particularly given his expertise on the intricacies of natural law theory. See, e.g, Robert George, "Recent Criticism of Natural Law Theory," 55 *U. Chi. L. Rev.* 1371 (1988) (book review); George, "Moral Particularism, Thomism, and Traditions," 42 *Rev. of Metaphysics* 593 (1989). I also direct the reader's attention to George Kannar, "The Constitutional Catechism of Antonin Scalia," 99 *Yale L.J.* 1927 (1990), especially pp. 1310–20, where Kannar discusses Scalia's relation to Catholic thought.

86. Levinson, supra note 4, at 67 (quoting *The Antelope,* 23 U.S. (10 Wheat) 66, 120 (1825)).

87. Id. at 67 (quoting *United States v. La Juene Eugenie,* 26 F. Cas. 832 (C.C. Mass. 1822) (No. 15,551)).

88. 41 U.S. (16 Pet.) 536 (1842).

89. See Levinson, supra note 4, at 67. These dilemmas served as the basis of Robert Cover's *Justice Accused,* which examined the patent conflict between law and morality that was resolved by so many judges in the name of the law. See Cover, supra note 66.

putting it does not necessarily stand for the proposition that morality is irrelevant to legal analysis. Imagine, for example, that one is presented with a genuinely "hard case." One may not be sure whether or not the fugitive slave clause applies, for example, or whether a previous precedent extends to the new case. Is it proper in resolving such hard cases to take account of the moral costs or benefits of deciding one way or the other? Would it be legitimate, for example, for the judge to say, "I will enforce the immoral fugitive slave clause when I am convinced beyond doubt that it applies, but in the absence of such overwhelming evidence, I will hold that it doesn't apply, because all applications involve the subordination of morality to mere popular sovereignty." We often find judges construing statutes in a way that does not raise constitutional problems because of a judicial policy in favor of minimizing the occasions for judicial invalidation of legislative activity. Would it be improper for a judge to announce that he or she will construe statutes in a way that minimizes their moral problems? This, presumably, would be the jurisprudence proffered by a "Dworkinian" nominee to the Supreme Court, who accepts the proposition that the Constitution must be construed, if at all possible, to be as morally attractive as possible in terms of some extraconstitutional theory of morality. Would we accept this as proper at the same time we would deny confirmation to an overtly religious nominee who indicated that she would construe the Constitution to cohere, if at all possible, with what God (or right reason) commands to humankind?[90]

90. Both nominees would presumably accept the proposition that such coherence might not always be possible, so that they would then either have to lie about what they believed the law to require or to resign, perhaps to take up arms against a sufficiently iniquitous state. In this context, Professor Stephen Siegel has asked in conversation, if we, members of the elite legal academy, respond differently to someone claiming a secular basis, say the philosophy of John Rawls, for the morality that she wishes to inject into legal analysis than to someone who presents an unabashedly religious background for the morality he sees as linked to resolution of the legal problem. From other presentations of this paper, I know that there are some who object not to the law-morality linkage as such, but rather to the possible penetration of law by religion-founded morality. The most worked-out versions of such an argument are found in Audi, "The Separation of Church and State and the Obligations of Citizenship," 18 *Phil. & Pub. Aff.* 259 (1989), and Thomas Nagel, "Moral Conflict and Political Legitimacy," 16 *Phil. & Pub. Aff.* 215 (1987).

If one prefers a secular David Richards (see Richards, supra note 41, at 1189) to a religious Kent Greenawalt, is this anything more than an expression of the Enlightenment-based animus within the intellectual community to religion as such? Though understandably respectful of Greenawalt's abilities, Richards leaves no doubt that for him public discourse—and, of course,

Consider in this context Professor Greenawalt's suggestion that a judge, faced with a moral-legal issue where the standard resources of analysis present "indeterminate" solutions, should feel authorized to look to the guidance that might be provided by her (necessarily particularistic) religious tradition to help provide an answer. Greenawalt offers the example of a

---

the decisions of state officials — should be as removed from religious articulations as possible. "The requirement of Lockean legitimacy is that all political power (both that exercised by leaders and by citizens) be justifiable in terms of secular interests, and citizens (like their leaders) have the responsibility to limit their political claims to such interests." Id. at 1200. In form, though, Richards professes respect for religious sensibilities, even as he wishes to limit their domain. For a more old-fashioned, though one suspects not completely atypical view, see Suzanna Sherry, "Outlaw Blues," 87 *Mich. L. Rev.* 1418, 1427 (1989) (reviewing Mark V. Tushnet, *Red, White, and Blue* (1988)). "[S]uch things as divine revelation and biblical literalism are irrational superstitious nonsense" and should fall within "the liberal tradition of excluding nonrational modes of discourse." Id. One can wonder, of course, precisely how we decide what is "irrational superstitious nonsense" or a "nonrational mode[] of discourse," especially if one is even a partial devotee of "poststructuralism" or any of the other critiques of confident rationalism that are so much a part of the contemporary intellectual culture.

For an interesting meditation on this problem, see Stephen L. Carter, "The Religiously Devout Judge," 64 *Notre Dame L. Rev.* 932, 944 (1989) ("[O]nce a judge's moral understanding is permitted to play a role, the liberal argument cannot distinguish religiously based knowledge from other moral knowledge, or at least, cannot do so without arguments that require a bit too much cognitive dissonance."). Professor Greenawalt ultimately distinguishes between the development of political views based at least in part on religious foundations and their articulation in the overt terms of one's religious convictions. Thus he writes that "I believe argument for political positions in the wider polity is more like legal argument than a candid account of all one finds relevant. One makes arguments likely to persuade and reassure the audience, and one makes arguments in terms that affirm more general political values. I do think people should *acknowledge* the place of religious convictions in their own positions, but I still believe it is counterproductive for debates on particular political issues to be formulated explicitly in terms of religious convictions." Greenawalt, "Some Further Thoughts," supra note 41, at 1046 (emphasis in original). Professor Alan Hyde, responding to an earlier presentation of this article, proffered the distinction between the "thinking about it" and the "writing it up" stage of adjudication: "[I]f the religious influence is only in the 'thinking about it' state, that influence is inevitable," though the judge, when "writing it up," should strive "to be consistent with any recognized theory of adjudication (positivism, Dworkin, original intent [etc.])," the assumption being, of course, than none of the "recognized" theories allow overt reference to religious norms. See Letter from Alan Hyde to Sanford Levinson (12 December 1989).

Quite different problems, of course, are raised by those who might want to reject all nominees bold enough to assert the relevance of rights not enumerated and to reject one variety or another of an allegedly pure textual or historical positivism. See, e.g., Robet Bork, *The Tempting of America: The Political Seduction of the Law* (1990). Much of the book is a vigorous (some would say dogmatic) attack on everyone — ranging from Samuel Chase and William Brennan to Oliver Wendell Holmes and John Marshall Harlan — who has ever suggested that judges might

judge interpreting an environmental statute and finding the statutory language void of direction. "Resolution of the issue seems finally to turn on how much respect is owed by humans to the natural world. . . . I see no escape from the proposition that the judge . . . may in such settings find it necessary to rely on his religiously informed answers to what is right."[91] To be sure, Greenawalt cautions a judge to "be extremely wary of relying on religious convictions, especially when he recognizes that his premises or the positions they yield are not widely shared." Still, "when such judgments are genuinely unavoidable, the judge within the constraints of the judicial role, should be able to rely on religious premises" to at least a limited extent.[92]

Justice Scalia, I believe, can be read as rejecting either of these last two formulations, at least if one takes his colloquy with Senator Mathias seriously. Is this not the implication of his saying that "[i]n no way" would he let his perception of a statute or a constitutional clause as fundamentally immoral "influence my determination of how they apply"?[93] This is a far more radical thesis than the announcement that on occasion one would have to recognize the legitimacy of an immoral law, for he seems to be arguing that legal analysis does not include reference to moral norms.[94] There would, of course, be nothing astonishing about such a thesis if one were a moral skeptic, fundamentally dubious about the existence of what Michael Moore has called "moral reality."[95] And I am in no way arguing that moral skeptics are wrong; in some of my other writings, I have defended positions identified with skepticism, though it would require another article to do justice to these debates.

There are good reasons to believe that Justice Scalia, whatever his state-

---

make any reference to norms not enumerated that could limit the power of political majorities as represented in legislatures. But Bork also describes as one of his purposes "to persuade Americans that no person should be nominated or confirmed who does not display both a grasp of and devotion to the philosophy of original understanding." Id. at 9.

91. Greenawalt, *Religious Convictions*, supra note 41, at 241.

92. Id.

93. See supra note 50 and accompanying text (transcript of confirmation hearing).

94. One might dispute this argument from the materials of conventional constitutional jurisprudence, for it certainly seems plausible to read both the Ninth Amendment and the privileges and immunities clause of the Fourteenth Amendment as directing the judge to take account of rights not enumerated that are retained by the people against governmental limitation. I have addressed the ninth amendment in Levinson, "Constitutional Rhetoric and the Ninth Amendment," 64 *Chi. [-]Kent L. Rev.* 131 (1988).

95. Michael Moore, "Moral Reality," 1982 *Wis. L. Rev.* 1061; Moore, "A Natural Law Theory of Interpretation," 58 *S. Cal. L. Rev.* 278 (1985).

ment to Senator Mathias, does not actually place a wall of separation between law and morality. Consider, for example, his use, in his eloquent concurring opinion in *City of Richmond v. J.A. Croson Co.*,[96] of the following passage from Alexander Bickel's *The Morality of Consent*: "The lesson of the great decisions of the Supreme Court and the lesson of contemporary history have been the same for at least a generation: discrimination on the basis of race is illegal, immoral, unconstitutional, inherently wrong, and destructive of democratic society."[97] The question raised by this litany is whether it is a merely contingent, happy fact that law, morality, and prudence (that is, what is instrumentally useful to maintaining a democratic society) are joined together in this instance or whether the immorality and destructiveness are part of what identifies racial discrimination as illegal. One might also be curious about one other joinder, that of the positive morality of the general social order with Scalia's own notions of morality. It is clearly possible, as demonstrated in *The Adventures of Huckleberry Finn* among other places, for one's own morality to run counter to what the best folks in one's society deem fitting and proper. In any event, though he does not indicate the source of his moral convictions, there can be no doubt that Justice Scalia has them.

Conclusion

It should be clear that although I disagree with Justice Scalia on the merits of *Croson*—I do not see racial preferences as the particular kind of racial discrimination embraced in his and Bickel's analysis—I am not at all critical of his reference to morality. I do not see how the enterprise of constitutional analysis could be carried out if words like "just," "moral," "unjust," or "immoral" were excised from the judicial vocabulary. This is especially true because a systematic elimination of these words would tend as well to eliminate any reason for the reflective citizen to feel committed to the legal system, at least on any other than rawly instrumental prudential grounds, or to venerate the Constitution that ostensibly serves as the basis of the legal system. What is interesting is not whether law and morality are inevitably and inextricably connected in the practical doing of constitutional analysis, for surely the answer is yes, but how we come to terms with this fact on

96. 109 S. Ct. 706, 735 (1989).
97. Id. at 735 (Scalia, J., concurring) (quoting Alexander M. Bickel, *The Morality of Consent* 133 (1975)).

those occasions when it is most important to state the fundamental creed of our constitutional order, such as confirmation ceremonies. Generally speaking, I think we do a fairly terrible job of it. A process that leads men and women of undoubted intelligence and integrity to say things that they cannot possibly wish to have represented as their genuine reflections on complex and important matters scarcely provokes admiration.

I leave you, though, with one final question: If I have persuaded you that these events can be profitably described as representing the triumph of American civil religion, is this tale hopeful or cautionary? Or, in keeping with an earlier theme, for *whom* of us is it the one, for whom, the other?

7

Abstinence and Exclusion:

What Does Liberalism Demand of the

Religiously Oriented (Would-Be) Judge?

I

Few subjects interest me more than the relationship between religion and liberalism. I confess, though, that almost none seems to be more difficult in terms of figuring out acceptable solutions. It is not simply the case that there is quite obviously no scholarly consensus as to what is the proper relationship. Rather, I discover that even when examining my own views, I am scarcely satisfied with my conclusions. Indeed, one reason I eagerly accepted an invitation to investigate the subject in this essay was precisely the opportunity it presented to see where I now stand regarding the intersection of religion and liberalism. During the New York newspaper strike in 1966, James Reston was quoted as asking, "How do I know what I think until I read what I write?" It is easy to identify with Reston's plaintive question. One writes not only to spell out arguments but also, and perhaps ultimately more importantly, to try to figure out what arguments one really is comfortable making and, of course, whether one is still comfortable with arguments presented in the past.

    I thus begin by referring to a prior essay of mine that examined religious language and the public square.[1] In this essay, a review of Michael J. Perry's

This essay was originally published in *Religion and Contemporary Liberalism,* edited by Paul J. Weithman (Notre Dame: University of Notre Dame Press, 1997).

1. See Sanford Levinson, "Religious Language and the Public Square," 105 *Harv. L. Rev.* 2061 (1992) (review of Michael J. Perry, *Love and Power: The Role of Religion and Morality in American Politics* (1991)).

book *Love and Power: The Role of Religion and Morality in American Life,* I noted that a prominent strain of liberal thought (about which I shall have a bit more to say presently) had developed the argument that entry into the public square should in effect be conditioned on a willingness to speak only in the language of an areligious secularity. Among other things, this means that cosmopolitan academics, who probably oppose the "English-only" movement in the United States as insufficiently respectful of the multi-cultural nature of our society, often have little hesitation in endorsing a "secular-only" version of public discourse that, from the perspective of those who speak other languages, seems at least as dismissive of those from different cultures as is the view that English is the only acceptable mode of discourse within American life. One question is whether this is a genuine paradox that self-styled cosmopolitans ought to address.

In any event, I suggested in my review that liberal democracy, at least in its American version, should be interpreted as "giv[ing] everyone an equal right, without engaging in any version of epistemic abstinence, to make his or her arguments, subject . . . to the prerogative of listeners to reject the arguments should they be unpersuasive." From the perspective of those who, like myself, define themselves as secular, "[i]t seems enough . . . to disagree vigorously with persons presenting theologically oriented views of politics. To suggest as well that they are estopped even from presenting such arguments seems gratuitously censorial."[2] The elegant phrase "epistemic abstinence" is not my own; I borrowed it from an important article by Joseph Raz[3] that was itself a critique of an earlier argument by Thomas Nagel that the effective functioning of a liberal society, defined in part as a society including a variety of (conflicting) fundamental perspectives or, in Rawls's language, "comprehensive views," "requires that a limit somehow be drawn to appeals *to the truth* in political argument."[4]

As I understand the argument, it is as follows: Even if a reasonable person might believe that some argument is true, resting, presumably, on onto-logical and epistemological predicates that might well establish satisfac-tory truth conditions, that person should, nonetheless, refrain from offering

2. Id. at 2077.

3. Joseph Raz, "Facing Diversity: The Case of Epistemic Abstinence," 19 *Phil. & Pub. Aff.* 3 (1990).

4. Thomas Nagel, "Moral Conflict and Political Legitimacy," 16 *Phil. & Pub. Aff.* 218 (1987) (emphasis in original).

it (or, under some formulations, from even privately being motivated by it) if the argument is religious rather than secular, precisely because many of one's fellow citizens do not share the assumptions necessary to establish the truth conditions of a religion-based argument. (I am assuming, for purposes of argument, that one finds notions like "truth conditions" meaningful, as Nagel appears to do; other problems are presented if one follows, say, Richard Rorty instead of Nagel and adopts one or another version of "postmodernist antifoundationalism" that tries to dispense with such language.)

One cannot, I think, overemphasize the importance of the point that arguments such as Nagel's are, in form at least, totally different from what might be termed classic antireligious arguments. Those arguments were based on a basically high-Enlightenment dismissal of religious notions as either superstitious poppycock, ontologically, or, slightly more moderately, as resting on insupportable epistemological assumptions about the ability to know God's will. In any case, antireligionists in the past were prone to assert that religion-based argument—especially the kind found in Protestant America, which is often based more on some notion of revealed truth rather than, say, on the working out of natural law premises as in Roman Catholicism—could not possibly serve as a predicate for offering truthful sentences about how we should live our lives. This was true even though, on occasion, there was an overlap between the conclusion of a religion-based argument and the findings of more authoritative secular systems of argument; any such overlap, however, was completely contingent, a happy accident rather than anything that might count as verification of religious premises. To oppose religious language in the public square, from this perspective, is exactly like rejecting, say, astrological argument or other "irrational" views.

However, the most interesting contemporary arguments, at least within the academy, are less overtly dismissive of religion. Indeed, relatively few are heard today who forthrightly adhere to classical antireligionism. It may be that the willingness of many leftish academics to defend, in the name of "multiculturalism," a variety of less than wholly plausible views of reality when articulated by some suitably sympathetic group, such as Native Americans, has in effect disabled them from engaging in classic religion-bashing. There are, to be sure, writers like the literary theorist Jonathan Culler[5] or

5. See Jonathan Culler, *Framing the Sign: Criticism and Its Institutions*, ch. 4 (1988).

University of Minnesota law professor Suzanna Sherry,[6] who are willing to assert unabashedly antireligious positions, but I believe that they are relative outliers in contemporary American culture. Even Stephen Carter, in his denunciation of what he termed "the culture of disbelief,"[7] took care to subtitle his book *How American Law and Politics Trivialize Religious Devotion*. "Trivialization" may be objectionable, but it is far different from an out-and-out attack on such devotion as, say, representing submission to delusional fantasy.

More typical of the contemporary debate, I think, is the comment of New York University law professor David A. J. Richards, who writes that "religiously based values . . . may be valid and true,"[8] but, nonetheless, goes on to argue that a precondition of a liberal political order is that religious believers voluntarily refrain from offering religious arguments in recognition of the fact that many of their co-citizens do not share their perspectives and, therefore, do not recognize religious materials as an authoritative source of true arguments. This "abstinence" obviously does not mean that the abstainer disbelieves the arguments that he or she is agreeing to suppress. Rather, these "true" arguments (from the perspective of the religious believer and "possibly true" even from the perspective of the now-generous religious skeptic) are in effect sacrificed by the believer as the price for maintaining the liberal (and pluralistic) political order.

As Michael Perry pointed out, there is an important asymmetry in regard to the "terms of trade" that secularists and religionists must offer one another in order to participate in a liberal polity. Secularists are in effect free to make whatever truthful arguments they believe to be relevant to any important issue of the day; this freedom holds even if, as a matter of fact, almost no one within the polity is educated enough to be able to follow the arguments, as in the case, say, of arguments that rest on the resolution of complex scientific controversies. But what of those who view their "basic moral/religious convictions [as] (partly) self-constitutive" and, therefore, "a principal ground . . . of political deliberation and choice"? According to Perry, to

6. See Suzanna Sherry, "Outlaw Blues," 87 *Mich. L. Rev.* 1418, 1427 (1989) (describing "such things as divine revelation and biblical literalism [as] irrational superstitious nonsense"). One doubts that my friend Professor Sherry is significantly more admiring of nonliteral biblicism.

7. Stephen L. Carter, *The Culture of Disbelief: How American Law and Politics Trivialize Religious Devotion* (1993), reviewed in Sanford Levinson, "The Multicultures of Belief and Disbelief," 92 *Mich. L. Rev.* 1873 (1994).

8. David A. J. Richards, Book Review, 25 *Ga. L. Rev.* 1189, 1197 (reviewing Kent Greenawalt, *Conflicts of Law and Morality* (1987) and *Religious Convictions and Political Choice* (1988)).

ask those who view the world through the prism of religious convictions to " 'bracket' such convictions" as the price of engagement in liberal politics is to ask them "to bracket — to annihilate — essential aspects of one's very self."[9] Perry regards this demand as intolerable. And, as already suggested, the theme of my review-essay on Perry, although critical about certain aspects of his argument, nonetheless agreed with him on this basic point. But, to put it mildly, many questions remain, and I turn now to consideration of some of those questions.

II

I am certainly not the only lawyer to have considered the demands of liberalism on religiously oriented justices. And even if I were inclined to ignore a desire to draw on some aspect of my legal training in this analysis, sheer prudence would dictate that I not try to compete with the truly distinguished philosophers and political theorists who have written elsewhere on this subject. If I have a comparative advantage, it is surely not my ability to explicate Rawls, Nagel, or Raz or to offer any new philosophical insights to the genuinely knotty problems that confront anyone trying to figure out the relationship between religion and liberalism. One comparative advantage that I do have, though, is almost certainly having read more legal cases than many of them have.

One temptation is to do what lawyers are presumably skilled at, which is to try to explicate the current doctrines of the United States Supreme Court in regard to religiously motivated legislation or other governmental decisions. For better or worse, though, I will not succumb to any such temptation, not least because these doctrines are, by common consensus, hopelessly confused. If truth be known, I detest reading most of the relevant Supreme Court cases, which tend to be a series of 5–4 decisions in which highly idiosyncratic views of one or another justice lead to results in a given instance that seem either patently inconsistent or simply absurd when one decision is placed next to another.

But there is another advantage to reading cases beyond becoming aware of the doctrines that courts purport to be applying. That advantage is simply the confrontation with fascinating facts that supply a concreteness sometimes lacking in the writings of philosophers. It is, I think, through respond-

9. Michael Perry, *Morality, Politics and Law: A Bicentennial Essay* 181–82 (1988).

ing to concrete examples that one's intuitions are best examined. I thus invite you to look with me at some very specific examples of the use of religious language in the public square and to put them within the context of a particular question: To what extent, if at all, do the rules of what might be termed the "liberal-polity game" require the exclusion of certain kinds of religion-based arguments, even from the perspective of one like myself who would profess to be maximally inclusive (or, more precisely, as inclusive as is reasonably possible)?

I draw my primary example from Professor Kent Greenawalt's most recent book.[10] Greenawalt is surely among the most distinguished contributors, as both philosopher and lawyer, to the general debate about liberalism and religion and, more specifically, about the extent to which membership in a liberal polity presupposes the exclusion of certain kinds of arguments from the public realm. One of the things that makes his writings especially interesting is that he speaks as a professed religious believer. Although Greenawalt is willing to tolerate a wide range of arguments from ordinary citizens and the use of religious perspectives in deciding, for example, how to vote in elections, he goes on to argue that many public officials operate under different, and more constrained, standards. Thus, to take what for him is the easiest example, judges ought to suppress any explicit reference to their own personal religious perspectives — and, concomitantly, avoid using them as purported *justifications* for particular outcomes — even if their religious views in fact constitute part of the *explanation* for the judge's reaching a particular decision.[11] He would, I believe, substantially agree with the statement of a Wisconsin judge that, "[w]hile the law may have had part of its origin in the same customs and necessities as did traditional religion, it is a distinct entity from religion, functioning in a different manner and *being guided by different principles*."[12]

As a presumed negative example, Greenawalt cites a case from the South Dakota Supreme Court involving a bitter dispute between former spouses over visitation rights regarding their two children.[13] In particular, the con-

10. Kent Greenawalt, *Private Consciences and Public Reasons* (1995).

11. Id. at chapter 13. Probably the best known critic of positions like Greenawalt's is Stephen L. Carter. See "The Religiously Devout Judge," 64 *Notre Dame L. Rev.* 932 (1989). The most extensive scholarly article in the law review literature is Scott C. Idleman, "The Role of Religious Values in Judicial Decision Making," 27 *Ind. L. Rev.* 433 (1993).

12. *City of Milwaukee v. Wilson,* No. 77-670 (Wis. Ct. App. Jan. 19, 1979) (LEXIS, States library, Wisc. file), aff'd, 291 N.W.2d 452 (Wis. 1980), quoted in Idleman, supra note 11, at 433 n.2.

13. *Chicoine v. Chicoine,* 479 N.W.2d 891 (S.D. 1992).

flict concerned the noncustodial mother's lesbianism, and the custodial father's objection to an order by the court below that allowed the mother to
have unsupervised overnight visitations with her daughter. The Supreme
Court reversed the court, demanding that the court below engage in a
"home study, to be assured that the children are not placed in an unsafe or
unstable environment."[14] What is of central interest to me, given the central
topic of this essay, is a concurring opinion filed by Justice Henderson. The
crux of that opinion is the following sentence: "Until such time that she can
establish, after years of therapy and demonstrated conduct, that she is no
longer a lesbian living a life of abomination (*see* Leviticus 18:22), she should
be totally estopped from contaminating these children."[15]

Such language is relatively rare in our judicial reports, but, as Scott Idleman well shows, Judge Henderson is certainly not unique.[16] And, of course,
as with white ravens and black swans, all we really need is one actual
occurrence of such language to raise the question of whether it violates what
might be termed the "essence" of the adjudicatory role within a liberal
society. Or, on the contrary, is simply a legitimate, albeit statistically unusual, variation of that role?

Needless to say, I am not interested in exploring whether or not what
Justice Henderson says is true, though I suspect that no reader will be surprised at learning that I do not agree with him and find his homophobia
appalling. But for our purposes that is beside the point, for one must assume
that he believes his statements to be true, in precisely the same way that, say,
Vice President Al Gore believes himself to be stating other than nonsense
when he writes of the "moral principles defining our relationship to both
God and God's creation"[17] and goes on to suggest that his own particular
environmental views are importantly linked to a religious "faith [that] is
rooted in the unshakeable belief in God as creator and sustainer, a deeply
personal interpretation of and relationship with Christ."[18] The question is
whether Judge Henderson (or the vice president) should feel under a duty to

14. Id. at 894.

15. Id. at 896.

16. See Idleman, supra note 11, at 476–77, nn. 147–56. One of Idleman's examples is another
opinion of Henderson's, this time in dissent: "[C]hildren are entrusted to parents as part of God's
great plan," and "the Law should be ever so cautious in interfering with that edict," citing,
according to Idleman, "numerous passages from the Old and New Testaments." Id. at n.155,
quoting from *In re S.L. and L.L.*, 419 N.W.2d 689, 697–98 (1988).

17. Al Gore, *Earth in the Balance: Ecology and the Human Spirit* 256 (1992).

18. Id. at 368.

maintain a public silence about the religious roots of their views or whether we should properly censure them for not excluding them from the public square. (And, of course, public silence might not be enough; as Robert Audi argues, we might also want to require them to be genuinely motivated by secular concerns and not merely to suppress the "real" grounds for their political or judicial positions.)

Let us look more closely at Justice Henderson's harsh, Leviticus-based attack on Ms. Chicoine's lesbianism. Child custody and visitation decisions are based, at least in theory, on the "best interests of the child." Application of this standard presumably requires the conscientious judge to believe that there are, in fact, such interests that are cognizable through testimony by child psychologists, moral philosophers, or whomever. Indeed, one important question almost inevitably raised in child-custody disputes is precisely who counts as an "expert" on the child's best interest, and one need not be overly postmodernist to recognize in the question an echo of Foucault's emphasis on the endless battle over discourse legitimacy.

Can, for example, a minister testify as an "expert" on what constitutes a child's best interest? Is one such interest living a maximally sin-free life and thus escaping, among other things, the risk of eternal damnation?[19] Surely, if one accepts the ontological reality of eternal damnation, then it would seem to follow that it would be in one's best interest to avoid it, assuming that there is anything that might count as reliable knowledge about methods of damnation avoidance. And what if one simply accepts the possibility that there *might* be such a possibility or that there *might* be such knowledge? Should society make a Pascalian wager on its actuality? Or are such considerations necessarily inadmissible in an American court of law?

One strongly suspects that Judge Henderson is neither an ontological nor an epistemological skeptic about damnation. He obviously believes that it violates the best-interest standard to place a child in a context suggesting, in any way, that nonheterosexuality is a morally available option in living one's life, rather than an "abomination." Whether one agrees with them or not, millions of Americans not only endorse his substantive view, but also the propriety of looking to the Bible for guidance in the resolution of such questions. Is this relevant? Or should a condition of his being a judge be a

19. On the role of religion in child custody disputes, see Donald L. Beschle, "God Bless the Child? The Use of Religion as a Factor in Child Custody and Adoption Proceedings," 58 *Fordham L. Rev.* 383 (1989); Note, "The Establishment Clause and Religion in Child Custody Disputes: Factoring Religion into the Best Interests Equation," 82 *Mich. L. Rev.* 1701 (1984).

duty to ignore — to exclude — what he regards as the best evidence of moral truth or falsity, including valuable guidance as to how children should be raised, if that evidence is religion-based rather than secular? That is, is his opinion *worse,* because it evokes Leviticus, than would be an opinion that offered only secular reasons for the adoption of similarly homophobic views? Concomitantly, would Gore's environmentally protective views be even more attractive, to those of us who indeed find them so, if he refrained from justifying them by reference to his religious beliefs?

Indeed, let me ask perhaps the question in the strongest possible way: Would Henderson (or Gore, were he a federal judge offering such comments as I have quoted in the course of an opinion explaining his perhaps tortuous construction of a statute in the most environmentally protective manner) merit impeachment if he refused to cease from looking to, and then publicly articulating, the religious bases of his decisions? Would such refusals constitute the deviation from "good behavior" that properly merits exclusion from public office? Only slightly less strong is the question whether Judge Henderson's citation of Leviticus would be sufficient to justify a senator's voting against his confirmation to the federal judiciary after being nominated by a president who, obviously, did not find the language disqualifying. One suspects, for example, that Henderson might be extremely attractive to a president supported by the so-called Christian Coalition, but then, so was Gore's open religiosity presumably attractive to President Clinton.

In spite of my inclusiveness, which would allow citizens Henderson and Gore to write religion-saturated letters to the editor and perhaps even candidate Gore to make similar speeches to the public while seeking their votes, I am certainly inclined to agree with Professor Greenawalt that "[o]f all officials, judges are the most carefully disciplined in restraining their frames of reference. Asking them to try to decide exclusively, or nearly exclusively, on the basis of authoritative materials and publicly accessible [i.e., non-religious] reasons is not too great an imposition."[20] But how, precisely, does one enforce such an "imposition," especially if it is the case that Greenawalt's view is itself controversial rather than a truly accepted convention that, by being accepted, is made uncontroversial?

Consider, for example, the following statement: "Sometimes I think the environment in which we operate is entirely too secular. . . . [T]hose of us who have faith should frankly admit that we are animated by that faith, that

---

20. Greenawalt, supra note 10, at 149.

we try to live by it—and that it does affect what we feel, what we think, and what we do."[21] This was said by President Clinton, who has also ostentatiously endorsed Professor Carter's book and *its* call for greater respect of those who are serious rather than "trivial" in integrating their religious perspectives into the performance of their public duties. Carter in turn has noted his respect for those who engage in "prayerful consideration" aimed toward "discerning and then enacting the will of God."[22] So let us assume that we are indeed presented with a judge who refuses to cordon off his or her religious beliefs. What ought to be our response, especially if we share Professor Greenawalt's view that this refusal indeed is problematic? Can we do anything beyond writing critical, albeit almost certainly ineffective, criticisms?

As already suggested, one way to enforce such a *cordon sanitaire* is impeachment; as a practical matter, though, that is a spectacularly inefficacious procedure within American government. One might also hesitate to pay the costs of the full scale Kulturkampf that would undoubtedly attend an impeachment effort based on a judge's religiosity. A far better solution, practically speaking, is to prevent the appointment in the first place by denying Senate confirmation to a presidential appointee (assuming, of course, we are talking about the federal level of the polity). As demonstrated by the nomination of Clarence Thomas, this is no easy process, either. Still, the example of Robert Bork stands as evidence that "difficult" does not mean "impossible." Thus one can well imagine vigorous senatorial interrogation of Henderson and other nominees before voting on their confirmations.[23] The question, obviously, is whether we are pleased or dismayed by the prospect that senators would believe that they could legitimately inquire into a nominee's religious views and then take the answers to these inquiries into account when deciding whether or not to confirm the nomination.

There is, to be sure, precedent for such inquiries, though many would scarcely place them among the happier aspects of the American past. Thus William J. Brennan, in his own confirmation hearings in 1957, was asked, by Wyoming's Senator Joseph O'Mahoney (who was himself Catholic), whether Brennan "would . . . be able to follow the requirements of your oath

21. Remarks by President Clinton in a photo opportunity during White House interfaith breakfast, U.S. newswire, 30 August 1993, quoted by Fred Barnes in "Rev. Bill," *The New Republic*, 3 January 1994, at 11.
22. Carter, supra note 7, at 77.
23. What follows is drawn, in part, from chapter 6.

[to enforce the Constitution] or would you be bound by your religious obligations?"[24] O'Mahoney asked his question at the behest of the National Liberal League, though the "liberalism" of the league is open to at least some doubt insofar as its opposition to Brennan was based less on its commitment to separation between religion and state than to the purported unseemliness of the United States, "a predominantly Protestant country," having to suffer the presence of a Catholic on its Supreme Court. Brennan knew his role in this subtle degradation ceremony. Expressing no objection to the question per se, he told the Senate first that he did not recognize within Catholicism any obligations "superior" to his constitutional oath and, secondly, that "what shall control me is the oath that I took to support the Constitution and laws of the United States."[25] This may simply reflect his belief that *all* laws passing muster under the Constitution were also sufficiently moral to pass muster under Catholic doctrine. To put it mildly, that itself is a highly controversial—many would say wildly implausible—doctrine of constitutional interpretation.

In any event, with Justice Brennan providing our precedent, we might ask Judge Henderson and other nominees if they would ever allow their religious views to "interfere" with their task of judgment. Stephen Carter offers his own version of what he calls "the separation question": "If we confirm you and you become a judge, will you be able to separate your religious beliefs from the task of judging?"[26] Would, for example, they promise to refrain from seeking guidance as to legal meaning in biblical materials or other obviously religious sources? Perhaps they would promise to avoid seeking even "prayerful guidance" as to God's will before deciding a controversy brought before them for authoritative legal adjudication. Indeed, as with Brennan's public testimony that the judicial oath dominated over any potentially conflicting loyalties, we might seek acknowledgment from any nominee that "epistemic abstinence" is a requirement of conscientious judging at least within our society and properly refuse to confirm any nominee who felt unwilling to pledge such abstinence.

The immediate question before us is whether it is *permissible* to reject a nominee solely because of an unwillingness to promise "abstinence." I find it hard to see how one can offer a strongly negative answer to this question, at

24. Nomination of William Joseph Brennan: Hearings Before the Committee on the Judiciary, United States Senate, 85th Cong., 1st. Sess. 32.
25. Id. at 34.
26. Carter, supra note 11, at 932 (emphasis omitted).

least if one accepts Greenawalt's premises. To reject the notion that it is even *permissible* would be, I think, to accept Stephen Carter's position that "reliance by judges on their personal religious convictions is as proper as reliance on their personal moral convictions of any other kind."[27] So perhaps the question is whether judges should be asked to pledge abstinence from *any* materials believed to be true if they do not fit within some quite narrow version of acceptable sources of positive law.

This question itself raises profound jurisprudential questions that are well beyond the scope of this particular essay. Very briefly, though, one might note the differences among quite different arguments. First, one could assert that a judge ought have recourse to *nothing* beyond a limited set of strictly denominated legal materials, which entails, among other things, that the judge qua judge must always distinguish, in John Marshall's words, between the tasks of "the jurist" and "the moralist."[28] This position requires formal indifference to the possibility that the "best" meaning of a given law, based on these limited materials, is immoral. A competing position says that a judge *can* properly look to the guidance of secular morality at least in all cases when there is some genuine dispute about the meaning of a patch of legal text. The decision rule might be, "always construe disputed passages in such a way as to achieve the most attractive moral result" — but that the judge can *never* look to sectarian sources for guidance as to what counts as "the most attractive moral result." One could, of course, accept the decision rule set out under this position but go on to argue, as Stephen Carter seems to, that the judge ought to feel free to consult *any* sources she personally deems authoritative as to the meaning of morality, including, of course, religious ones. A final position, of course, is the classic "just law" argument that nothing violating the substantive dictates of justice can count as law, whatever the formal provenance (as, for example, in majority will, presidential command, or whatever). Once again, one could distinguish between secular and religious sources of insight as to the meaning of justice.

Assume that one adopts some version of the second principal, such as that of Greenawalt's as described above. That is, even what Carter calls "the religiously devout judge" ought to operate under a self-denying ordinance in

27. Id. at 933.
28. *The Antelope*, 23 U.S. (10 Wheat.) 66, 121 (1825). Not at all coincidentally, the case involved slavery. In an opinion upholding the rights of slaveholders, Marshall insisted that "this court must not yield to feelings which might seduce it from the path of duty, and must obey the mandate of the law." Id. at 114.

all but the most exceptional of circumstances. We must then confront an even stronger question, going well beyond the *permission* that Greenawalt presumably gives one to vote against a nominee who gave the wrong answer to the "separationist question." Should a "Greenawaltian" be *required* to vote against the nominee? After all, isn't this the way that operative conventions are in fact preserved, by sanctioning those who would deviate from them? Assume that the Senate is willing to confirm a nominee who forthrightly indicated that "prayerful guidance," mixed with study of scripture, would constitute one standard source for the decisions that she would render, and opinions that she would write, as a judge. Would that confirmation not serve as powerful evidence for the proposition that, contrary to Greenawalt, we as a society now believe that it *is* "too great an imposition" on judges to require that they exercise restraint in "their frame of reference"?

Interestingly enough, Greenawalt offers several caveats to his own argument: Thus it might be acceptable for a judge to rely on his or her religious views if otherwise authoritative materials generated a perfect equilibrium or were otherwise radically indeterminate; reliance might also be acceptable in the presumably extraordinary situation where "the judge finds 'the law' to be so abominable she feels a duty to subvert it in some way . . . "[29] Otherwise, though, Greenawalt appears to accept the desirability of restraint, which would seemingly entail the possibility that a senator would indeed be under a duty to reject an otherwise attractive nominee who failed to agree to abstain in all but the most extreme situations.

It should be obvious that the suggestion of such a duty (which I emphasize is my own rather than Greenawalt's) could be read by those who disagree as indicative of liberals' own participation in the Kulturkampf. I take it that most of us would be outraged if a senator were to inquire into the possibly atheistic beliefs of a nominee and to announce that such atheism would itself serve as a basis for rejection. Perhaps the senator would revive eighteenth-century arguments as to the potential untrustworthiness of those who did not fear divine punishment for misbehavior. But would any argument justify rejecting a "secular humanist" simply on the grounds of lack of sufficient religious commitment? I take it that the question is truly "rhetorical," admitting of only one answer.

There is, of course, one way to avoid the comparison between our Gospel-oriented, prayerful nominee, on the one hand, and the secular hu-

29. Greenawalt, supra note 10, at 149.

manist nominee, on the other, and that is to evoke the Establishment Clause of the First Amendment. Would it not be precisely an illegitimate "establishment" if religious belief were made a prerequisite for public office? Indeed, one scarcely needs the Establishment Clause to make this argument. After all, Article VI of the original unamended Constitution explicitly stated that "no religious Test shall ever be required as a Qualification to any Office or public Trust under the United States."[30] This seems clearly to rule out requiring any belief in God and, perhaps, even asking any questions about whether one believes in God. But is the Test Oath Clause symmetrical in preventing any inquiry about religious belief even of someone who has indicated, whether in speeches and books like those of President Clinton and Vice President Gore or published judicial opinions like those of Judge Henderson, that religious views (and sources) will indeed be viewed as relevant to one's behavior in office? I can see no good reason for avoiding inquiry into an aspect of a nominee's life that he or she has publicly indicated might be relevant to later conduct while in office.

Perhaps the more fundamental question, though, is if such a "symmetrical" Test Oath Clause, read to preclude any taking account of a person's religious views into a determination of fitness to serve in public office, is normatively attractive. After all, even if one agrees that that is what the Oath Clause means, one might still go on to bewail its presence in the Constitution and advocate its repeal by amendment. I confess myself troubled by a reading of the clause that would render legally impossible the interrogation of Judge Henderson as to the linkage between either the book of Leviticus and the U.S. Constitution or the book of Leviticus and the determination of what counts as the best interest of a child. And I confess as well that I would hold Judge Henderson's use of Leviticus against him. If the Test Oath Clause prohibits this, then, I suggest, so much the worse for the clause.

One must ask, of course, whether one would be so opposed to Judge Henderson if one were attracted by his substantive values. So what ought the response to a "Judge Gore" be? It seems like a patent double standard to hold Henderson's citation of Leviticus against him if one is not also perturbed by the hypothetical Judge Gore's reference to his reading of biblical passages (and values) as the source for his environmentally protective views.

---

30. See Gerard Bradley, "No Religious Test Clause and the Constitution of Religious Liberty: A Machine That Would Go of Itself," 37 *Case W. Res. L. Rev.* 674 (1987).

To be sure, it is easy for most of us to offer religion-independent defenses of environmentalism, whereas almost all antihomosexual arguments seem, at bottom, to rest on religious grounds. But should the availability of non-religious arguments for a given position make irrelevant the offering by a particular judge of religions ones? It is hard for me to see why the answer should be yes. Presumably the point is whether a given judge will honor the duty to confine his or her attention only to what is stipulated to be a properly confined range of materials. On the other hand, if one is resistant to disqualifying the putative "Judge Gore" from a position on the federal judiciary, then perhaps one should reconsider the basis of opposition to Judge Henderson. Perhaps one should simply say that one is appalled by his substantive views, whatever their derivation. If he held an acceptable set of views, again regardless of their derivation, then one would vote for him. But this does not seem a satisfactory resolution, either. It is almost impossible to escape the belief that law and what Ronald Dworkin has famously called "legal integrity" rest at least in part — and what percentage that part constitutes is perhaps the most pervasive debate in jurisprudence — on the process by which a judge decides, independent of the result achieved. So we necessarily return to the place within legal process of recourse to explicitly religious norms.

What makes Justice Henderson's opinion so interesting is its unabashed tone of religion-based moralism. Indeed, in another part of his opinion, dealing with the lower court's division of the marital property, Justice Henderson denounces the award to the former wife of some $42,000 in cash. "This compounded and perpetuated an existing wrong," thundered Henderson, "for it rewards a rejection of the good things in the sacrament of marriage. I would pray that God help the decent hard working young farmers and ranchers of this state."[31] One rarely reads language like this in the opinions of more "sophisticated" judges.

Consider, though, another example of religious reference in a judicial opinion, this one drawn from an opinion written by one of the most sophisticated judges in American history, Justice William O. Douglas. The case involved the criminal prosecution, under the Mann Act prohibiting so-called white slavery, of a Mormon "fundamentalist" who had refused to accept his church's 1890 repudiation of polygamy — itself the result of the most systematic religious persecution in American history — and, therefore,

31. 479 N.W.2d 898.

continued to adhere to Brigham Young's teachings about the necessity of plural marriage.[32] Justice Douglas, writing for the majority of the Court, had shockingly little trouble upholding the conviction of Harlan Cleveland for transporting one of his wives across a state line "for immoral purposes." (He had, presumably, traveled from Southern Utah to Northern Arizona, which continue to this day to be havens for groups of old-line Mormons.) Douglas, who would later face censure for his own marital circumstances, quoted language from earlier decisions that denounced polygamy as, among other things, "contrary to the spirit of Christianity and of the civilization which Christianity has produced in the western world."[33] (One might compare this to Chief Justice Burger's evocation forty years later of "Judaeo-Christian moral and ethical standards" to justify Georgia's criminalization of what he termed "homosexual sodomy.")[34] To be sure, Douglas also goes on to state, in his own language, that "[t]he establishment or maintenance of polygamous households is a notorious example of promiscuity,"[35] and the moral revulsion presumably felt by most right-minded Americans amply justified, as a constitutional matter, Congress's using its power to regulate interstate commerce to punish the hapless Mormons. An eloquent (and lonely) dissent was written by Frank Murphy, the one Catholic member of the Court during that era. Although he carefully noted that it is "not my purpose to defend the practice of polygamy or to claim that it is morally the equivalent of monogamy,"[36] he went on to describe it as "one of the basic forms of marriage," offering as evidence for this proposition "the writers of the Old Testament" and its perpetuation even in the twentieth century "among certain pagan and non-Christian peoples of the world."[37]

Douglas's language is far more ambiguous than is Henderson's. There is not a scintilla of doubt that Henderson is writing in his own voice. It would be an extraordinary law clerk indeed who would dare write the language that appears in the *Chicoine* opinion. Douglas, on the other hand, is writing in more indirect discourse. That an earlier Court had denounced polygamy as un-Christian is not necessarily evidence for the proposition that Douglas

32. *Cleveland v. United States,* 329 U.S. 14 (1946).
33. Id. at 19, quoting *The Late Corporation of the Church of Jesus Christ of Latter-Day Saints v. United States,* 136 U.S. 1, 49 (1890).
34. See *Bowers v. Hardwick,* 478 U.S. 118, 196, 197 (1986).
35. 329 U.S. 19.
36. Id. at 25.
37. Id. at 26.

believes its violation of Christian doctrine is a good reason for him to suppress it. One might think that *his* reason had to do with the "promiscuity" purportedly linked with polygamy. As I have discovered in many conversations about *Reyolds v. United States*,[38] the (in)famous case in which the Supreme Court upheld the prosecution of a Mormon bigamist against claims that this violated his free exercise of religion protected by the First Amendment, there are many academics today who readily denounce bigamy on secular grounds, such as its purported entrenchment of patriarchy. They therefore need make no reference to any religious norms against the practice.

Still, one can ask whether Justice Douglas should have quoted the language cited. And even if one gives him the benefit of a "that's the way they talked in the unenlightened old days" defense, should any person who finds unproblematic the presence in 2003 of such language in judicial opinions be readily confirmed for the bench? Things can become even more complicated, though. Consider, for example, a nominee who (sincerely) says that she herself has no religious commitments but that she views the judicial role as enforcing our "fundamental social norms"? And, the nominee goes on, given the particular history of the United States, identification of such "fundamental norms" requires that due attention be paid to the religious roots of basic American values and practices. From this perspective, an essential role of the judge is that of the cultural anthropologist. It is truly difficult to understand most societies, and impossible to understand the United States, without paying due heed to the role of religion. If one treats Christianity (or that peculiarly American amalgam "Judeo-Christianity") simply as a culture, it is hard to see why its norms should be ignored by any anthropologically sensitive judge in favor of some other set of cultural norms, unless, of course, one were willing to make the argument that nonreligious cultures necessarily offer greater access to certain important social and moral "truths" than is the case with religiously based cultures. Perhaps there is good reason to believe that. Is it relevant, though, that the public articulation of any such view would surely be enough to doom one's career in public life, including, one strongly suspects, prospects for Senate confirmation to the judiciary?

I offer one final example of the kinds of issues that both interest and perplex me. Armstrong Williams, in an interview with Clarence Thomas,

38. 98 U.S. 145 (1878).

asked him whether he thought he should use his position on the Court to advance the interests of the black community.[39] Thomas answered as follows:

> You cannot embrace racism to deal with racism. It's not Christian. [Thomas went on to compare using the law to favor blacks as similar to the hypocrisy of] the self-righteous religious leaders who wanted to stone the prostitute [in the Bible]. Jesus said go and sin no more. That is what I have to do.
>
> At stake is the principle of equality, including equality before law that is, or ought be, the domain of the Supreme Court. Behind that precept is a high moral imperative: to do unto others as you would have them do unto you. I cannot do to white people what an elite group of whites did to black people, because if I do, I am just as bad as they are . . . I can't break from God's law just because they did. . . .
>
> From the minute they put the first slave on the first ship, they violated God's law. From the first drop of the venom of racism to the slave codes to the Jim Crow law, they broke God's law. If I type one word at my word processor in one opinion against them, I break God's law. . . . If I write racism into law, then I am in God's eye no better than they are.

Whatever one's position on the merits of affirmative action (or on the merits of his appointment), I think it is difficult indeed not to be moved by the intensity of Justice Thomas's comments and his commitment to maintain fidelity to his highest loyalties. That being said, is one *only* moved, or is there also a proper element of disquiet, at the extent to which Thomas either believes that he knows what "God's law" in fact is, or interweaves into his role as a judge the apparent duty of fidelity to it? Forget Anita Hill. Should these comments alone, had they been made to the Senate, have disqualified Thomas? Is it possible, on the contrary, that they would actually count as a reason for supporting his nomination?

My general posture in considering issues is ambivalence, and I scarcely feel, at the conclusion of this essay, genuinely closer to a resolution than I was at the outset. Yet part of my contract with those who invited me to participate in this collective discussion — and with the reader who has stuck

39. The quotations below come from a version of the article published in the *Charlestown Post and Courier,* 17 August 1995, that is available on LEXIS. It was sent to me by Professor Richard Duncan, a fellow participant in a marvelous e-mail discussion group on law and religion that features a remarkable (and courteously expressed) range of opinions.

with me this far — is presumably to offer conclusions, however tentative. If forced, then, I am willing to defend the following three propositions:

1. Greenawalt is right in suggesting that judges must be especially resistant of the temptation to treat religious sources as containing any privileged statements of moral truth; and
2. this justifies, first, interrogation, and then a negative vote in regard to any nominee whose statements lead one to doubt whether this temptation will in fact be resisted. However,
3. it is tolerable to treat religious cultures as providing insight into what might be described as the positive morality of our social order, so long as one recognizes that religious cultures are indeed only a part of the American mosaic, and that nonreligious cultures must be given "equal concern and respect."

Hanging over this entire discussion, of course, is whether any public officials other than judges have a duty to make the pledge of abstinence when performing their public roles. I confess that I find it harder than do some to draw bright lines between judges and legislators or executive officers. My skepticism comes in part from the basic perspective of legal realism, which I share, that one cannot necessarily distinguish between "law" and "politics" and, therefore, that the judicial function often in fact overlaps with the legislative insofar as both judge and legislator "make policy" even if the method by which this is done is quite dramatically different. This being said, I am, like Greenawalt, unwilling to be censorious of ordinary citizens or even political candidates who present religious sources as the basis, at least in part, for their advocacy of certain political positions. But, again like Greenawalt, I am truly uncertain as to what successful candidates, who now inhabit public office, should be allowed, within the limits of an adequate liberal theory, to articulate as the basis for using the coercive power of the state to require or prohibit certain activity. Fortunately, my contract did not require that I answer *all* of the issues raised by our subject, and, like a restrained judge, I reserve fuller discussion for another occasion.

Afterword

The topic of the religious views of judges was raised in an op-ed essay in the 8 July 2002, *New York Times* by Princeton professor of history Sean

Wilentz titled "From Justice Scalia, a Chilling Vision of Religion's Authority in America." It referred to a speech given earlier in the year at the University of Chicago Divinity School by Justice Scalia that focused especially on the death penalty.[40] In it Justice Scalia conceded the legitimacy of the late Justice Blackmun's description of his judicial role as being part of "the machinery of death." Where he disagreed with Blackmun is with regard to its immorality. Justice Scalia has no moral problems with the death penalty. Indeed, he stated, "I could not take part in that process if I believed what was being done to be immoral." Even more notably, Scalia suggested that "in my view the choice for the judge who believes the death penalty to be immoral is resignation. . . ."

This naturally led to a discussion of the basis of moral judgment. "It is a matter of great consequence to me," Scalia writes, "whether the death penalty is morally acceptable. As a Roman Catholic — and being unable to jump out of skin — I cannot discuss that issue without reference to Christian tradition and the Church's Magisterium."[41] Scalia assesses that tradition with particular reference to the views of Saint Paul, most notably in Romans 13, where he refers to "rulers" as "ministers of God."[42] Thus, says Scalia, "the *core* of his message is that government — however you want to limit that concept — derives its moral authority from God," and its power includes the power to "revenge" and "to 'execute wrath,' including even wrath by the sword (which is unmistakably a reference to the death penalty)." Justice Scalia states that "[t]hese passages from Romans represent the consensus of Western thought until very recent times," a "consensus that has been upset, I think, by the emergence of democracy." The reason is that we are far less prone to look at leaders who emerge out of a democratic political process as God's ministers than we are with regard to "rulers whose forebears, in the dim mists of history, were supposedly anointed by God, or who at least obtained their thrones in awful and unpredictable battles whose outcome was determined by the Lord of Hosts, that is, the Lord of Armies."[43] In any event, Scalia indicates that he personally shares what he terms the more "traditional" view, which is to view "rulers," even those produced by a democratic political process, as sufficiently the instantiation of God's authority to be allowed to impose capital punishment.

40. The speech is reprinted as "God's Justice and Ours," *First Things*, May 2002, at 17–21.
41. Id. at 18.
42. Id. at 18–19.
43. Id. at 19.

He moves on to consider whether the contemporary Catholic Church has in fact adopted a sufficiently anti–capital punishment position to require that he, as a loyal Catholic, must accept its teachings and therefore, presumably, resign from the judiciary. He concludes his brief inquiry by writing that "I am . . . happy to learn from the canonical experts I have consulted that the position set forth in *Evangelicum Vitae* [which expresses doubts about the morality of capital punishment] and in the latest versions of the Catholic catechism does not purport to be binding teaching—that is, it need not be accepted by practicing Catholics, thought they must give it thoughtful and respectful consideration." He notes that he has indeed "given this new position thoughtful and careful consideration—and I disagree."[44]

There are many things one might say about Justice Scalia's talk. One of them is that he both takes discussions within the Roman Catholic Church extremely seriously *and* is thoroughly capable, both intellectually and as a member of the Catholic community, of coming to his own conclusion, though he does concede that things might be different if the Vatican had pronounced its teaching to be "binding."

Consider, though, the analysis offered by Professor Wilentz, who writes that "Mr. Scalia seems to believe strongly that a person's religious faith is something that he or she (as a Roman Catholic like Mr. Scalia) must take whole from church doctrine and obey." He inferred this from Scalia's noting, with what Wilentz termed "relief," that the Catholic Church's increasingly vocal opposition to the death penalty was not "binding" on adherents to the Church. "If it had been, Mr. Scalia said, this teaching would have led the church to 'effectively urge the retirement of Catholics from public life,' given that the federal government and 38 states 'believe the death penalty is sometimes just.' " From this statement Professor Wilentz inferred that "Mr. Scalia apparently believes that Catholics, at least, would be unable to uphold, as citizens, views that contradict church doctrine," noting that "[t]his is exactly the stereotype of Catholicism as papist mind control that Catholics have struggled against throughout the modern era and that John F. Kennedy did so much too overcome. But Mr. Scalia sees submission as desirable—and possibly the very definition of faith. He quotes Saint Paul, 'For there is no power but of God: the powers that be are ordained of God.' "

As noted, Scalia pointed to a tension between democracy and traditional

44. Id. at 21.

religion. Thus, Scalia said, "The reaction of people of faith to this tendency of democracy to obscure the divine authority behind government should not be resignation to it, but the resolution to combat it as effectively as possible."[45] Wilentz denounced this assertion, stating that "the framers in Philadelphia . . . rejected the idea that political authority lay with anyone or anything other than the sovereign people."

Wilentz states that Justice Scalia's view has "no appreciable place in our constitutional history because the framers rejected it. . . . They had an idea that sovereignty rested with a free people, even if some among those people didn't believe in God, or in the same God, or in the same way."

Wilentz concludes his analysis as follows:

> In Chicago Mr. Scalia asserted, not for the first time, that he is a strict constructionist, taking the Constitution as it is, not as he might want it to be. Yet he wants to give it a religious sense that is directly counter to the abundantly expressed wishes of the men who wrote the Constitution. That is not properly called strict constructionism; it is opportunism, and it threatens democracy. His defense of his private prejudices, even if they may occasionally overlap the opinions of others, should not be mislabeled conservatism. Justice Scalia seeks to abandon the intent of the Constitution's framers and impose views about government and divinity that no previous justice, no matter how conservative, has ever embraced.

I have no particular desire to defend Justice Scalia, whose jurisprudential views I generally abhor and whose religious commitment I do not share. But, as argued at some length in the essays in this volume, it seems to me that one should think long and hard before sacralizing "democracy" or "popular sovereignty" the way that Wilentz does. It is no small matter to say, in the words of a slogan that goes back to medieval times, that "the voice of the people is the voice of God": One idolizes the demos and gives it the same authority that others give to God. If one seriously believes in a divine authority that issues binding commands on humankind (and if one's conception of divinity includes the proposition that God is necessarily good), then it is nothing less than idolatry to suggest that one should substitute the "voice of the people" for the "voice of God" — unless, of course, one is using the mantra not as a metaphor, but as an analytic proposition. In other words, the preferences of the majority just *are* what God wishes inasmuch as God

45. See id. at 19.

has chosen temporal majorities as the agent of divine revelation. To make such an argument, of course, would be as saturated in theology as anything Scalia put forth. Moreover, it seems especially difficult to present a coherent philosophical notion that the "voice of the people" is indeed the "voice of God" (and not merely a metaphor indicating that it should be given the same weight as earlier generations gave to what they considered the "voice of God") insofar as God would seem to speak in remarkably different, indeed contradictory, ways to different bodies of "sovereign peoples."

At the end of the day, I find Professor Wilentz's views every bit as problematic as those he attributes, fairly or not, to Justice Scalia. It is a serious thing to take God seriously. I describe myself as a "secular Jew," which means, among other things, that I find it difficult to accept the notion of a divine presence in our lives. But, obviously, that is a highly particular, and controversial, point of view, and there is no reason at all to expect persons who do not share my own (and, I assume, Professor Wilentz's) theological skepticisms to find them compelling. This is especially true inasmuch as a serious theological position like that of Justice Scalia — that one disagrees with him is no warrant for labeling him a fool — is dismissed so tendentiously. After all, Justice Scalia quite explicitly does *not* call for religious judges to impose their own views on the constitutional order inasmuch as he suggests that conscientious Catholic judges would be forced to resign (or refuse to accept appointment in the first place) were the Church's opposition to the death penalty "binding" on professing Catholics, given Scalia's view that the best understanding of the Constitution is that it in fact licenses the death penalty. Indeed, Justice Scalia's position is almost exactly opposite of the view attributed by Professor Wilentz.

In any event, the truly serious issues raised by Justice Scalia merit more than the cursory and conclusory arguments offered by Professor Wilentz. I obviously hope that my own essays are more subtle and nuanced. That is, of course, for the reader to decide. It is all too possible that the deep divide between the secular and (at least some of) the religious is too wide to allow acceptance of adversaries' arguments as "subtle or nuanced," however great an author's effort to "play fair" with opposing views. The existence of such divides may be precisely what constitutes a "diverse" society, though this scarcely seems a cause for celebration.

8

Is Liberal Nationalism an Oxymoron?

An Essay for Judith Shklar

I

More than mere sentiment leads me to dedicate this essay to the memory of Judith Shklar, for my last encounter with her was as a member of the audience listening to her scathing comments, as a discussant on a 1992 American Political Science Association panel on the political theory of nationalism, regarding an argument offered by one of the paper givers that any viable liberal political theory should integrate within it at least some element of nationalism. Combining the erudition and passion that made her a uniquely formidable (and unforgettable) figure, she exhibited almost palpable outrage at the suggestion. Shklar did endorse the merits of what I believe she called "restrained patriotism," but that was, one inferred, altogether different from nationalism, which she seemed to view as being essentially irrational and almost inevitably dangerous, characterized first by excessive attention to bloodties and then, all too often, by bloodshed of those not within the requisite tribal connection.[1]

I have no doubt that she would have agreed with Michael Ignatieff's laconic observation that "if a nation gives people a reason to sacrifice them-

This review of Yael Tamir's *Liberal Nationalism* (1993) was originally published in *Ethics* 105 (1995): 626.

1. Ironically or not, there seems to be a deep affinity between Shklar's view and that recently expressed by Pope John Paul II on his visit to Croatia, where he said, "It is necessary to promote a culture of peace which does not reject a healthy patriotism but keeps far away from the exasperations and exclusions of nationalism." See Roger Cohen, "In Croatia, a Frail Pope John Paul II calls for a 'Culture of Peace,'" *New York Times* (11 September 1994), 9 (sec. 1, National Sunday edition). One suspects that Shklar would have used a much stronger term than "exasperation," but the basic sentiments seem similar enough.

selves, it also gives them a reason to kill."[2] Nationalism therefore is particularly likely to generate the cruelty whose prevention she saw as the primary virtue of liberalism. "Liberal nationalism" thus served as the perfect example of an oxymoron, and to countenance its possibility—even at a panel of the American Political Science Association—might lead to potentially pernicious political consequences by lowering our guard against the ravages of any and all nationalisms. And, in a period dominated by headlines from Bosnia (and, since her death, Rwanda as well), it is harder than ever to gainsay the potentially catastrophic implications of nationalism and, therefore, the possibility that Shklar's warnings are dismissed at our peril.

It is thus no small matter that Yael Tamir, buttressed by enthusiastic book-jacket comments from such eminent theorists as Michael Walzer, Sir Isaiah Berlin, Michael Sandel, and Amy Gutmann, has thrown down the gauntlet to those political theorists who share Shklar's contemptuous stance toward any and all nationalism.[3] Instead, Tamir argues, "the liberal tradition, with its respect for personal autonomy, reflection, and choice, and the national tradition, with its emphasis on belonging, loyalty, and solidarity, although generally seen as mutually exclusive, can indeed accommodate one another" (p. 6). Thus for Tamir "liberal nationalism" is most definitely not an oxymoron; on the contrary, it is the most attractive theoretical approach to political life inasmuch as it combines attention to the liberties of the individual—the traditional strength of liberalism—with equal solicitude for "the importance of belonging, membership, and cultural affiliations as well as the particular moral commitments that follow from them" (p. 6). A basic condition for human flourishing, she seems to suggest, is that individuals be "able to share their lives with some particular others they care about and see as their partners in a life-project" (p. 94); surely among the most important of such life projects, for millions of human beings, are those identified with the maintenance through time and space of those particularistic communities denominated nations. Tamir defines nationhood by reference to "both a sufficient number of shared, objective characteristics—

2. Michael Ignatieff, *Blood and Belonging: Journeys into the New Nationalism* 247 (1993).
3. David Miller has also been willing to defend (some aspects of) nationalism; see Miller, "The Ethical Significance of Nationality," 98 *Ethics* 647 (1988) and "In Defence of Nationality," 10 *J. Applied Phil.* 3 (1993). One might also mention Will Kymlicka's influential collection of essays, *Liberalism, Community and Culture* (1989), though it is worth noting that Kymlicka almost resolutely avoids the term "nationalism" (which does not appear in the index) in favor of "community."

such as language, history, or territory — and self-awareness of its distinctiveness" (p. 66).

As should be obvious, there is a strongly cultural component to this definition. It differs significantly, for example, from Sieyès's earlier answer to the question, What is a nation? His answer—"[a] body of associates living under a common law and represented by the same legislature"[4]— leads to political formalism. One need not underrate the importance of political formalism; its categories, after all, provide the basis for membership in the United Nations. Still, we also know the difference between a "bi-" or "multinational" state, like Canada, Israel, Belgium, and the United States,[5] and what I suppose should be called a "uninational state" in which everyone within the political territory shares a single cultural identity as a member of a given nation. My failure to offer an example of such a state — perhaps a "ministate" like Andorra or Lichtenstein might count—is a sign that there may be no true "uninational" states in the contemporary world. Therein lies what some see as the problem and what is certainly the background for Tamir's analysis.

Tamir argues that liberals should acknowledge a basic "right to culture," which is defined as a "public sphere in which individuals can share a language, memorise their past, cherish their heroes, [and] live a fulfilling national life" (p. 8) that is different in important respects from simply sharing a bloodless legal identity as a member of a political state. Tamir herself draws attention to the fact that her interest in these questions is not merely "academic." She is a Jewish Israeli,[6] and her "attempt to introduce national values into the liberal discourse is motivated by an ongoing personal commitment to pursue a national vision while remaining faithful to a set of liberal beliefs" (p. 5).

Two obvious subtextual questions therefore run through the book, even if they only rarely take center stage. One, of course, is whether Zionism, which as an ideology arises out of the context of explicitly antiliberal

---

4. Quoted in Rogers Brubaker, *Citizenship and Nationhood in France and Germany* 7 (1992).
5. One need only cite the presence of the various nations of American Indians within the United States to make the point, though it is worth adding that one of the essentially contested questions of much contemporary debate concerning "multiculturalism" is whether, say, Mexican Americans should be viewed not only as an "ethnic group," but also as a "nation" within the polity called the United States. There was, e.g., in New Mexico in the 1970s the *la raza* movement that called for secession from the United States, though it never became a serious political movement.
6. It is absolutely necessary, in keeping with what is, after all, the central theme of her book, not to assume that all Israelis are Jewish even if Israel proclaims itself as an explicitly Jewish state.

nineteenth-century organic nationalism,[7] is compatible with the set of commitments identified with liberalism. Or must a "Jewish state," like any other true "nation-state," necessarily be caught in a (perhaps fatal) tension between the universalistic thrust of liberalism and the particularistic claims of the nation? The second subtextual question involves Jewish-Arab relations or, more specifically, the legitimacy of Palestinian claims to a state of their own. If Zionism supports the idea that there should be a Jewish state (and not merely a Jewish homeland, which could conceivably be under the ultimate political control of non-Jews), then what prevents similar arguments being made in behalf of stateless (and, of course, in many cases homeless) Palestinians? It is clear that Tamir is addressing absolutely basic questions, of both theory and practice. It presumably occasions no surprise that her answers are entirely unlikely to still the debate even as they provide illumination as to what is at stake.[8]

II

It should be said at the outset that Tamir is considerably more liberal than she is nationalistic, which, no doubt, will make her book more attractive to cosmopolitans who tend to populate the academy even as it will be subject to dismissal by the kinds of nationalists Shklar most despised. Tamir "places reflection, choice, and internal criticism at [the] center" of her notion of liberal nationalism; she concomitantly "rejects the notion that nationalism must necessarily 'exalt the idea of the nation above all other ideas'" (p. 79; see also pp. 83–84). She therefore calls on us to see "national self-determination . . . as an *individual* right, contingent on a *willed* decision of *individuals* to affiliate themselves with a particular national group and to give public expression to this affiliation" (p. 73, emphases added). Her emphasis on assertions of individual will, as is true for any of the classical liberal theories emphasizing consent, coexists most uneasily with any theo-

---

7. See Carl E. Schorske, *Fin-de-Siècle Vienna: Politics and Culture* 146–75 (1979). Two readers objected that I am overemphasizing a particular wing of Zionist thought and that important early Zionists, including Herzl and Ahad-Ha'am, could easily be described as liberal nationalists. This is a fair point, though it is obviously part of the debate over the "essentially contested concept." See, for a good basic review of the positions, Shlomo Avineri, *The Making of Modern Zionism: Intellectual Origins of the Jewish State* (1981).

8. See Tony Judt, "The New Old Nationalism," 41 *New York Review of Books,* 26 May 1994, at 44, for a thoughtful review of a half-dozen recent books on nationalism, including Tamir's and Ignatieff's.

ries, be they Heideggerian or even Sandelian, that emphasize instead the extent to which we are "thrown into" an "embedded" national identity that is both most definitely unchosen and truly constitutive of the person whose "individuality" can be described only in terms of the group(s) that form her (and which she must honor in much the same basically unreflective way as the Fifth Commandment might be read as bidding us to honor our mothers and fathers, regardless of any "desert" to be honored). Consider, for example, Sandel's suggestion that we are not "bound only by the ends and roles we choose for ourselves" but, rather, we can "sometimes be obligated to fulfill certain ends we have not chosen—ends given . . . by our identities as members of families, peoples, cultures, or traditions."[9]

To be sure, Tamir is sufficiently postmodern herself to "portray an autonomous person who can reflect on, evaluate, and choose his conception of the good, his ends, and his cultural and natural affiliations" precisely "*because* he is situated in a particular social and cultural environment that offers evaluative criteria" (p. 33, emphasis added).[10] For Tamir the concrete person—the "contextual individual" (p. 33)—and not some entirely presocial or prepolitical self—is the basic unit of the sociopolitical order. There is no "nowhere" from which to view politics; we are all embedded in our particular "somewheres." Still, however much she claims to recognize "the binding, constitutive character of cultural and social memberships," it is hard to ignore her own embeddedness in a liberal tradition that focuses on "free and autonomous participants in a communal framework, who conceive of national membership in Renan's terms, as a daily plebiscite" (p. 33) subject to affirmation or rejection.

What would it mean to vote no in such a plebiscite? Surely one answer can be derived from Albert Hirschman's classic formulation: one should always have available the option of exit from, as a necessary supplement to voice within, the community. In the language of the oath that the United States requires of its naturalized citizens, one can always imagine "renounc[ing,] abjur[ing], and repudiat[ing]" prior loyalties even as one pledges new ones

9. Michael Sandel, "Political Liberalism," 107 *Harv. L. Rev.* 1765, 1768 (1994) (review of John Rawls, *Political Liberalism*). One notes, as with Kymlicka, Sandel's seeming aversion to including "nation" within the group of obligation-generating entities. One does not know if this is an explicit rejection of nationalist claims or, instead, a retreat to euphemism lest one be tarred with the negative associations linked to nationalism (that are presumably absent in regard to family, etc.).

10. See Kymlicka, supra note 3, at ch. 8, for a similar suggestion.

(as, in this example, to the United States itself).[11] Political and cultural identities, even like contemporary marriages, are not necessarily forever; should they not be fulfilling, divorce is an ever present, in fact theoretically desirable, option.

Whether one is interested primarily in preserving the nation or the family, one apparently need not worry about the implications of allowing relatively free exit. "Not only," says Tamir, "are our communal affiliations — or, for that matter, our marriages — not weakened by the constant exercise of choice, they are in fact strengthened by it" (p. 22). This strengthening is presumably the joint product of the recognition reached by one spouse, while considering exit, that the marriage really is desirable and the pleasure taken by the spouse's partner in the affirmation of the relationship. This is, of course, an empirical rather than a conceptual point; to put it mildly, I am more than a little curious how one would try to demonstrate its validity to a skeptic worried about the contribution of such attitudes to either national or marital disintegration.

Finally, as already suggested, Tamir distinguishes between the socio-cultural nation and political state. Consider in contrast the definition of nationalism recently proferred by Michael Ignatieff: "Nationalism is a doctrine which holds (1) that the world's peoples are divided into nations, (2) that these nations should have the right of self-determination, and (3) that full self-determination requires statehood."[12] Whether or not full self-determination requires a state, Tamir makes clear her belief that a *sufficient* degree of self-determination can be found even in a state dominated by other nationalities, at least if respect is paid to the principle of cultural rights. Like many other sensible people, she refuses to privilege the "nation-state," based on a unity of the two, at least insofar as any such privileging would suggest that the contemporary world map should be redrawn (and peoples resettled) to accord with some notion of "one nation, one state."

One might well come to this position from a strictly theoretical route by focusing on the goods attached to membership in a polity composed of interestingly diverse national subgroups instead of being trapped in a boringly homogeneous country. But probably the more compelling reason to reject this version of a Wilsonian commitment to national self-determination is simply the pragmatic point that there are far too many nations to make any

11. See Sanford Levinson, *Constitutional Faith* 103 (1988).
12. Ignatieff, supra note 2, at 145.

such notion feasible, at least without bloodshed that would make Bosnia look almost mild. The phrase "self-determination," especially when it is interpreted as a call for political independence, is, as said by Wilson's own secretary of state, "simply loaded with dynamite. It will raise hopes which can never be realized. It will, I fear cost thousands of lives."[13] Lansing's only error, of course, was the almost literally incredible underestimation of costs.

Tamir does not despair, though, in terms of safeguarding what is valuable about nationalism. "Although it cannot be ensured that each nation will have its own state, all nations are entitled to a public sphere in which they constitute the majority. The ideal of the nation-state should therefore be abandoned in favor of another, more practicable and just" (p. 150). One might, of course, wonder precisely how a nation with "a public sphere in which they constitute the majority" is different from a state, unless this majority is willing to put the fate of its "public sphere" in the hands of a presumably quite different nation. I shall have more to say about this issue later.

It should be clear that Tamir's "ideal" state rejects integral nationalism. It does not, however, reject nationalism per se; this is, after all, what makes her a liberal nationalist instead of a pure liberal. Thus she distinguishes her notion of the preferred liberal nationalist state from that adopted by many contemporary liberals attracted by notions of "neutrality" toward any particular culture or conception of the good life. For Tamir, on the other hand, "the political system *will* reflect a particular national culture" — what she describes as "a distinct cultural foundation" (p. 163, emphasis added). Among other things, this means that a liberal nationalist state will be permitted to prefer as immigrants those who share that national culture, at least "if all nations have an equal chance of establishing a national entity, in which its members will be given a fair chance of pursuing their personal and collective goals" (p. 161).

Thus, paradoxically, the best legitimator of Israel's Law of Return, which privileges Jewish as against all other immigration,[14] would seem to be an independent Palestinian state that could, presumably, pass its own Law of

13. See Daniel Patrick Moynihan, *Pandaemonium: Ethnicity in International Politics* 83 (1993) (quoting Robert Lansing's diary entry of 30 December 1918).

14. Israel is not the only state with a Law of Return. Perhaps the most notable other example is Germany. See, e.g., Brubaker, supra note 4, at 14, who notes that Germany is at once niggardly in awarding citizenship to "non-German immigrants," including their children and grandchildren even if born in Germany, while at the same time it is "remarkably expansive toward ethnic Germans from Eastern Europe and the Soviet Union, [which] reflects the pronounced ethnocultural inflection in German self-understanding."

Return to encourage a gathering together of the Palestinian diaspora. Tamir appears to endorse the desirability (and, presumably, the feasibility) of an independent Palestinian state (see, e.g., p. 160). Yet she presumably makes the judgment on a prudential basis of what is practically possible at what cost. Given her rejection of an entitlement by every nation to a state, her argument cannot be a "principled" one, for that would suggest that every national group would indeed be entitled to carve out a political state in which it would be the dominant majority. As already indicated, that way, practically speaking, lies madness.

One wonders about the implications of Tamir's condition—that each nation be guaranteed "a national entity, in which its members will be given a fair chance of pursuing their personal and collective goals"—before countries can legitimately prefer adherents of their own distinctive culture. The very multiplicity of nations without states of their own, or even protected "public spheres" would seem as a practical matter to negate Tamir's acceptance of culturally restrictive immigration.

Still, even if a Tamirian liberal state can manifest a specific national culture (reflected, possibly, in its immigration policy), it must nonetheless take care to assure that subcommunities of citizens within the polity "will be free to practice different cultures and follow a variety of life-plans and conceptions of the good" that might, of course, differ quite radically from those of the dominant majority (p. 163). Though national in some sense involving cultural practices and civic-religious ceremonies and rituals, Tamir's state nonetheless accepts broad diversity and commits itself to a de facto multiculturalism that pays genuine respect to a variety of national communities. As she herself recognizes, though, even life within such a tolerant state comes at a cost for the minority community. "Members of minority groups will *unavoidably feel alienated* to some extent" (p. 163, emphasis added) from the dominant culture; they will always, presumably, retain some sense of being guests in someone else's national home. Still, alienation is better than suppression (or worse), and the affected groups can presumably flourish—possess a protected "public space" of some kind—even in what presumably is from their own perspective a less-than-ideal condition of political subordinacy to a dominant (albeit tolerant) majority.

It should be clear that zealous political nationalists will find relatively little attractive in *Liberal Nationalism*. For them her book is a counsel of compromise and the giving up of dreams (or at least demands) for political sovereignty in any traditional sense. What she would guarantee is not at all trivial or unimportant, and I would be thrilled if governments would endorse her program and nationalist groups would settle for it. But one doubts that either will occur with sufficient dispatch to save the world from ever-increasing nationalist-inspired carnage (whether the inspiration comes from the dissatisfied minority or a rapaciously hegemonic majority).

III

Many aspects of Tamir's book deserve extended discussion in their own right. I have already alluded to her discussion of Israel's Law of Return and the wider issue of immigration policy of which it is an illustration. Similarly, anyone interested in the modern crisis of the welfare state is aware of the ever-increasing tensions associated with claims by nonnationals, even those resident within the state, to the provision of the goods of the welfare state. It is easy enough even for those who recognize duties to their metaphorical "brothers and sisters" to deny any obligations to those outside the national family. If one rejects universalism — a rejection that is entailed by any robust notion of nationalism — it is hard indeed to figure out why any such obligations might exist.[15] Tamir offers insight into both of these problems, as well as many others. Limitations of space, though, dictate that choices must be made, and I choose to focus on what for me is ultimately the most important tension facing the liberal nationalist (and perhaps any liberal theorist), that involving education of the young.

As already noted, liberal nationalism as a concept joins together (and some would say is torn apart by) the liberal emphasis on autonomy and the nationalist emphasis on the constituted nature of one's identity as an embedded member of an existing community.[16] Only the most extreme nationalist believes that self-conscious identity is a product of genes; most recognize that identity is the product of community practices that socialize, or educate, its young. These youngsters are all equally capable, as a biological matter, of speaking (and having the cultural attributes usually associated with being) Japanese, Hungarian, or Parsi. This point, presumably, becomes more complicated if one associates particular physical characteristics, most

15. See, e.g., the very thoughtful essay by Joseph Carens, "Immigration and the Welfare State," in *Democracy and the Welfare State* 207–30 (Amy Gutmann, ed., 1988).
16. I have benefited, in regard to what follows, from a paper presented by Meira Levinson to a political theory seminar at Oxford University on 8 June 1994, and the ensuing discussion, on the relationship of autonomy and education.

notably race, with national identity, but this association may be less common than one thinks. Even if, in the list above, it might raise problems for the white child socialized "to be Japanese," it would have nothing to do with regard to such volatile differences as, say, being constituted as Serb or Croat, Arab or Sephardic Jew. The crucial question facing any heterogeneous political community, that is, the non-nation-state, is the practical freedom that will be given to minority communities to maintain themselves through time by being given significant control over the education of "their" young. Without some measure of real independence from the state, the promise of a protected public sphere even for the culturally deviant rings hollow. But too much independence may, of course, threaten the state itself, including, most certainly, the quite attractive version articulated by Tamir.

Such questions, of course, are chestnuts of liberal debate, but they are often put in terms of conflict between the state and individual. Although Tamir's analysis is couched in the language of individualism, it is hard to escape the conclusion that what is often really at stake is the right of a group—in the context of her argument, a nation that is resident within a state controlled by some other national entity. The cultural rights at issue are ultimately held, if at all, by a group for whom a particular individual is, at best, merely a synecdoche. Education is initiation into a preexisting, collective, way of life, and it is those who are already committed to that way who are most insistent that it be protected against the inevitable death that comes with the failure of renewal through proper initiation.

Tamir's most notable bibliographic omission is Amy Gutmann's *Democratic Education;* similarly, when turning to the index, one will find "economic wellbeing" followed immediately by "egoism." One is tempted to suggest that "education" is the word that dare not speak its name, lest the entire project of liberal nationalism come crashing down. It is telling, I think, that one of the extremely few uses of the word "education" in the entire book is found in a quotation from Michael Walzer, who writes that "when [regional organizations] freely celebrate their histories, remember their dead, and shape (*in part*) the education of their children, they are more likely to be harmless than when they are unfree" (p. 153, emphasis added). The "in part," of course, raises the most profound theoretical issues.

To be sure, Walzer's quotation is not the only reference to education. Thus Tamir notes that "one of the implications of the *right* to culture . . . [is] that different cultural groups have a *right* to establish schools that cater to their specific needs," and it is fair "for these schools to favour children who belong to the group they are meant to serve" (p. 111, emphasis added). The reference to rights is an interesting counterpoint to Walzer's own adoption of the far more utilitarian criterion of "harmlessness." As Ronald Dworkin has taught us, a state that is committed to "taking rights seriously" must accept the ability of a rights holder to use the right in question as a "trump" that can be played even when it is very harmful to the larger political order.

Some of the tensions raised by education are further revealed in Tamir's almost offhand comment that "children may quite clearly be placed under pressure to conform with their parents' wishes, but it is of educational value to stress the relation between their choice and their right, teaching them not only to respect their culture but also their own individuality" (p. 54). It should be obvious that assessment of the "educational values" of emphasizing to the young their right to reject a culture if it is found too oppressive of "individual" flourishing is itself entirely dependent on a particular theory of the purpose of education. Liberals have little trouble adopting Tamir's scheme of valuation; deeply committed nationalists, I suspect, would find it far more questionable.

Tamir herself concedes that "every nation" wishes to "assur[e] its continued existence" and "the continuous re-creation of its culture," which includes "learning and respecting its traditions" (p. 88). To the extent that national communities are, in Benedict Anderson's famous notion, above all "imagined,"[17] it is obvious why a nationalist would be concerned to make sure that the primary imaginings—and dreams—of the young are those of the nation. But to what degree can one simultaneously be taught, on the one hand, to imagine and "respect" and, on the other, to question? And, more to the point, which goal should have priority, particularly if one is indeed part of a minority culture that rationally fears the hegemonic ambitions of the surrounding culture, even one that adopts Tamir's version of liberal nationalism? In any event, one wants from Tamir a far more extensive limning of the "right to culture," especially as it relates to education, before one can be confident of the genuine meaning of her project.

The tensions within Tamir's theory can be most easily observed by placing it in the context of other liberal proponents of autonomy and the exercise of meaningful choice among competing ways of life. Consider, for example, James S. Fishkin, who in his *Dialogue of Justice* presents the case for what he calls a "self-reflective political culture" constituted by the will-

---

17. See Benedict Anderson, *Imagined Communities* (rev. ed., 1991).

ingness of its members to participate in "continuing critical examination through unmanipulated debate" of the practices and presuppositions of the social order.[18] Similarly, Amy Gutmann, who focuses on the difficulties presented by raising the young within a regime devoted to liberal democratic values, argues that "children must learn not just to *behave* in accordance with authority but to *think* critically about authority if they are to live up to the democratic ideal of sharing political sovereignty as citizens."[19] There is in both Fishkin and Gutmann more than a trace of what Scott Brewer has called "the principle of interpretive candor." Drawing on Mill and Socrates for this principle, Brewer emphasizes the necessity of interpreters "constantly to *alienate* themselves from accustomed patterns of interpretive inference, for only by such an interpretive practice can interpreters fulfill the Socratic injunction to lead the examined life, to know themselves, and thereby to open up to high-level critical scrutiny both the institutions that restrain legal meaning and the interpretive values by which they do so."[20]

Would Tamir reject such visions? It is hard to see how she could, given the emphasis throughout *Liberal Nationalism* on autonomy and choice. Presumably the best state assures the presentation to its citizenry, including its young, of a variety of possible ways to live one's life, even if it is not necessarily "neutral," in a strong sense, among these possibilities. But doesn't this mean that parents, not to mention the larger subcommunities that constitute the parents' identities, would have to be (relatively) indifferent to whether their children share their particularistic visions of the good life and, therefore, the desire to maintain a possibly beleaguered national culture? Indeed, it would also appear that at some level governmental authorities in turn would have to be equally indifferent whether the young were being trained to maintain allegiance to the existing multicultural constitutional order or instead being encouraged to replace it with some more homogeneously organic alternative.

Simply to state this is to indicate how truly radical these notions are—

---

18. James Fishkin, *The Dialogue of Justice* 124 (1991). Mention should also be made of Jeff Spinner, *The Boundaries of Citizenship: Race, Ethnicity, and Nationality in the Liberal State* (1994), which also emphasizes the link between liberalism and "self-critical reflectiveness," (p. 94).

19. Amy Gutmann, *Democratic Education* 51 (1987) (emphasis in original).

20. Scott Brewer, "Figuring the Law: Holism and Tropological Inference in Legal Interpretation," 97 *Yale L.J.* 823, 843 (1988).

except, perhaps, among those of us with only the most tenuously felt membership in national communities. But consider only some of the contemporary divisions within our own polity in the United States. For example, some fundamentalist Christian parents quite literally view themselves as members of a distinctly Christian nation within an increasingly infidel state and wish to educate their children free of any supervision by pagan state bureaucrats. And racial nationalists want to inculcate in their young a vision of the world strikingly different from that held by the majority.[21] It should be patently obvious that formal indifference to the views of the next generation — or, what is substantially the same thing, commitment only to a process of self-reflection that privileges no particular set of substantive values — is not a universally, or perhaps even widely, shared point of view even within the United States, let alone throughout the world. And distinguished political theorists certainly challenge the notions of autonomy put forth by Fishkin and Gutmann.

William Galston, for example, argues that even a theoretical commitment to preparing children to participate in public life "does not warrant the conclusion that the state must (or may) structure public education" — let alone, presumably, regulate private education — "to foster in children skeptical reflection on ways of life inherited from parents or local communities."[22] A liberal society, that is, need not be committed to the virtue of the examined life, at least if parents prefer that their children accept without serious question traditional ways.

One might well believe, in terms of actual behavior, that parental control of education is a value honored more in the breach than the observance. Most of us are delighted to cede jurisdiction over the lives of our children to

21. See, e.g., the controversy over introduction of a so-called Afrocentric curriculum into the public schools. See Molefi K. Asante, *Kemet, Afrocentricity and Knowledge* (1990) and *The Afrocentric Idea* (1987); Kevin Brown, "Do African-Americans Need Immersion Schools? The Paradox Created by Legal Conceptualization of Race and Public Education," 78 *Iowa L. Rev.* 813 (1993).

22. William Galston, *Liberal Purposes: Goods, Virtues, and Duties in the Liberal State* 253 (1991). This passage is quoted in a very fine survey article by Will Kymlicka and Wayne Norman, "Return of the Citizen: A Survey of Recent Work on Citizenship Theory," 105 *Ethics* 352, 367 (1994). They point to the fact that, whereas "civil society theorists" "face the question of when to intervene in private groups in order to make them more effective schools of civic virtue, liberal virtue theorists, on the other hand, face the question of when to modify civic education in the schools in order to limit its impact on private association." They go on to say that "neither group has, to date, fully come to grips with these questions" (pp. 367–68). This seems, alas, to be true of Tamir as well.

the state, and many people seem to believe, and behave as if, the earlier the better. But it is obvious that there remains, within a pluralist culture as broad as that of the United States, a sizable body of parents who are less complacent about the virtues of public, or even what might be termed "conventional" college-prep private, schooling and the imposition of state- or secular-elite-decided points of view. Most of these parents, at least at the present time, are religious, and the legal reporters increasingly feature litigation testing their rights, though the issues raised, at least for the political theorist, obviously go beyond religion-based rejection of the surrounding culture.

It is, no doubt, unfair to expect Tamir, who is neither American nor a lawyer, to be familiar with any of these cases. One of the primary contributions the legal system makes, though, is the instantiation of otherwise abstract controversies in all-too-concrete cases, and it is certainly helpful, even for the most nonlawyerly political theorist, to test one's general principles against such cases. Certainly the most famous single case is *Wisconsin v. Yoder,* which involved the rights of the Amish community in Wisconsin to be exempt from compliance with that state's compulsory education law.[23]

The Amish demanded the right to bring formal education to an end after the eighth grade, whereas Wisconsin at that time demanded ten years of education. Chief Justice Burger, writing for the majority, described the basis of Amish resistance to additional formal education as rooted in their perception that "the values" taught in high school "are in marked variance with Amish values and the Amish way of life; they view secondary school education as an impermissible exposure of their children to a 'worldly' influence in conflict with their beliefs."

In particular, the Amish parents objected to the purported emphasis

---

23. *Wisconsin v. Yoder,* 406 U.S. 205 (1972). No reader of the case could doubt that it is a communal rights case that cannot, without almost complete distortion, be reduced into the standard liberal paradigm of "the individual" versus "the state." Although *Yoder* involves religion-based litigation, it would be easy enough to imagine an almost identical lawsuit arising in the context of American (or Canadian) Indians, whose claims we would presumably more easily recognize as "nationalist" than those of the Amish. Even the Amish, though, can easily enough be compared with more standard "nationalist" groups if one emphasizes, e.g., the use of a distinctive language. Although American Amish learn how to speak English, it is as a "second language"; the primary language of the community is so-called Pennsylvania Dutch (or German). See John A. Hostetter, *Amish Society* (2d ed., 1968). Perhaps one should say of the Amish that they are a micronation that, given their theology, has no desire at all for a political state.

placed by Wisconsin on "intellectual and scientific accomplishments, self-distinction, competitiveness, worldly success, and social life with other students." In contrast, according to the Supreme Court majority, "Amish society emphasizes informal learning-through-doing; a life of 'goodness,' rather than a life of intellect; wisdom, rather than technical knowledge; community welfare, rather than competition; and separation from, rather than integration with, contemporary worldly society." The majority also gave sympathetic attention to the claim that additional formal education would take the children "away from their community, physically and emotionally, during the crucial and formative adolescent period of life. . . . At this time in life, the Amish child must also grow in his faith and his relationship to the Amish community if he is to be prepared to accept the heavy obligations imposed by adult baptism." To remove the child from the guidance of his parents and other elders of the community would interpose "a serious barrier to the integration of the Amish child into the Amish religious community."

Whatever one might think of Amish society in particular, or integral faith communities in general, it is hard to think of many cultures that are less enamored of the relevance of Socrates and Mill — or, one suspects, even Tamir — to the lives of their members, except, of course, as Mill is invoked to justify the duty of the rest of us to tolerate their presence in our midst. But can anyone who asserts her commitment to liberal values, as Tamir most certainly does, be comfortable with a set of constitutional principles that seemingly requires the state to remain on the sidelines while the next generation of a particular subgroup is socialized into a given totalistic (and some might even say totalitarian) community? One need not have any interest at all in whether *Yoder* was "correctly decided," in terms of the jurisprudence of the U.S. Constitution, in order to regard it as a profoundly important test case concerning what constitutive principles ought to be adopted by someone devoted to the value of the examined life in all of its dimensions.

In any event, I presume that one can nonparadoxically answer affirmatively as to the right of the Amish parents and elders to control the education of their young if (but I should think only if) one believes that such cultures are sufficiently marginal within the overall self-reflective social order as to constitute no real threat to its maintenance. This, presumably, is the importance of Walzer's "harmlessness" criterion. Indeed, one can further defend the presense of the Amish community precisely in the name of our own self-reflection, inasmuch as that presence forces us to confront the value of our commitments to Caesar and mammon. But it should be noted — and emphasized — that those who inadvertently serve our own Socratic purposes engage in no significant self-scrutiny themselves, and acceptance of their right to perpetuate themselves involves the sacrifice of future generations to a worldview that most liberals, including Tamir, must view as seriously inferior to the self-reflective life celebrated by anyone for whom autonomy is a real value.

It is also important to note that toleration of strong parental control of education, such as that manifested in *Yoder,* is wholly different from what might be termed celebration. The freedom accorded the Amish seems to be based on the empirical claim that that freedom is in fact instrumentally useful to attaining non-Amish values (such as the appreciation that there are in fact multiple acceptable ways of living one's life), and not because of any belief in the intrinsic importance of Amish flourishing. Indeed, part of the "alienation" that Tamir writes about might follow precisely from the knowledge that one's own culture is not being celebrated, but only tolerated by a liberal community that acknowledges that even unattractive people (or cultures) ought to be protected in their way of life, at least if the cost is not too great to the wider polity.

Furthermore, it might be relevant that the Amish, as a "withdrawn" community, make no effort to participate in the decision-making structure of the polity. Like Jehovah's Witnesses, they want — in an adaptation of Louis Brandeis's definition of the "most fundamental right" — to be left alone. In sum, then, tolerating their communal existence within our larger, and quite different, national community costs us extremely little even as it provides the value of presenting us with an enacted alternative to our own life choices and, therefore, the possibility of living drastically different lives ourselves.

One can easily relax a number of these assumptions; at that point the question posed becomes considerably more difficult to resolve. Consider, for example, the particular subgroup of Satmar Chassidic Jews, recently described by the United States Supreme Court as "vigorously religious people who make few concessions to the modern world and go to great lengths to avoid assimilation into it."[24] The Satmars, though contemptuous of the modern world, are scarcely so withdrawn from it as the Amish. They vote (in line with the views expressed by the rabbi who leads the entire community), and it is undoubtedly their political skills that explain the concern of

---

24. *Board of Education, Kiryas Joel Village School District v. Grumet,* 114 S. Ct. 2481 (1994).

the governor and legislature of New York State to accommodate some of
their professed needs. Indeed, the possession of similar skills undoubtedly
explains the extensive aid given by the Israeli state, formally dominated by
secular Jews, to ultra-Orthodox sects that despise the ostensibly Jewish state
almost as much as does the Palestinian Liberation Organization.[25]

The Satmars make almost no attempt to recruit new members, but it
requires little effort to imagine groups that actively recruit and, through
political activity, attempt to move the general society far closer to its preferred, non-self-reflective vision of life. At that point one can certainly ask
why a liberal-nationalist state would be required to accept parental claims
to control the cultural development of their children, particularly if the state
is as concerned with the maintenance of a liberal (albeit nationalist as well)
political order as the groups with which the parents are affiliated are concerned to supplant that order with something considerably less liberal (and
committed to a very different version of nationalism as well). By stipulation,
we would then have good reason to believe that such control would take us
further from the general culture of self-reflection and autonomous choice
seemingly endorsed by Tamir. At this point Walzer's "in part" shows its
teeth, forcing us to decide between the various claimants.

Perhaps the central question here is something like the following: Is there
some given percentage of the citizenry that should (must) be suitably self-
reflective and committed to Tamir's notions of liberal nationalism before we
can feel entirely comfortable accepting the existence, and maintenance
through time, of more integrally national, illiberal, groups who do not at all
share her views? This question raises, I believe, an important theoretical
point: although one can imagine a structurally just society, in terms of distributive outcomes, without the presence of a single just individual—isn't
this, after all, the basic claim of a Mandevillian society where public virtue
(or at least benefit) magically comes from the homeostatic equilibrium of
private vices?—I find it extremely difficult to imagine that what Fishkin
describes as a "*self-reflective* society" or Tamir as a choice-enhancing na-

25. See, e.g., Clyde Haberman, "Hailed in Zion, Anti-Zionist 'King' from the U.S.," *New York
Times,* 7 June 1994, at 1, which describes the visit of the Satmar spiritual leader, Rabbi Moses
Teitelbaum, to Israel, where he was hailed by tens of thousands of his followers. Teitelbaum
emphasized the necessity to remain faithful to traditional Satmar beliefs, which include, as
described by the *New York Times,* "total opposition to the Zionist entity whose soil they tread,
for they believe it is a sin to create a Jewish state until after the Messiah comes."

tionalist one could exist absent some significant number of "self-reflective citizens." For the whole point of emphasizing internal states of mind like reflection or awareness of alternative possibilities is to avoid the kind of rationalist contractarianism that assesses the legitimacy of the society simply on the basis of its producing decisional outcomes that could be justified on the basis of some abstract theory. For certain kinds of liberals — and Tamir seems to be one of them — the intellectual processes on the way to decision seem important in their own right, incapable, therefore, of being reduced to the outcomes in which they eventuate.

Thus any theory that is based on notions of autonomy seems to require some minimal percentage of actual "self-reflective citizens" who in turn are crucial to constituting the culture that is endorsed by Tamir. One need not embrace a strong theory of methodological individualism; Tamir is clearly right in noting that "self-reflective citizens" are themselves constituted by their cultural norms, and our primary focus must be on the groups that in turn constitute the liberal (multi-)nationalist state. Still, our pragmatic language can scarcely allow us to focus exclusively on the character of a collective culture and to ignore entirely the importance of the concrete individuals who comprise it at any given point.

Presumably only the most foolish of utopians would demand that a self-reflective culture requires that all of its members meet the criteria for self-reflection and, concomitantly, that illiberal groups be prevented, as much as possible, from reproducing themselves through the process of educating their young. As a purely practical matter, one can even imagine that the number of reflective members required might be quite small under some specified conditions. For example, perhaps it might be as small as 10 percent if the rest of the society was sufficiently divided among a variety of non-self-reflective communities so that the self-reflective minority in fact enjoyed the decisive role in the scheme of public decision making. In a political democracy, though, formally committed to something approaching a one person — one vote principle, I would think that we would need to raise the number of self-reflective citizens to a fairly high level if one were to have any confidence that the results of one or two elections would not in fact wipe out any of the political policies seemingly necessary to the promotion of self-reflection. The only alternative to limiting the ballot to the suitably self-reflective would be to adopt a strong version of liberal constitutionalism that would in fact remove a variety of important decisions from the ambit of the legislature. I do not wish to explore this well-trod topic, though I assume that all of us are aware of some of its ramifications. At any rate, the "liberal" can all too easily devour the "democrat" (or the "nationalist").

IV

Liberalism has always had special difficulties dealing with children and education. Liberals are always happier talking about adults, precisely because it is they who can most easily be envisioned as possessing autonomy and giving consent. But adults die, to be replaced by the children they bear. Those committed to nationalist movements are usually fully aware of this point, which is one reason why so many pitched battles are fought over the "canon" that will be dispensed in the schoolroom.

One most often thinks of canonicity debates in terms of the titles of the books assigned. But one must also decide what language the books are to be taught in. Perhaps because of her immersion in a culture defined in part by its ideological commitment to Hebrew as its constitutive language, Tamir writes some especially interesting paragraphs about language (see, e.g., pp. 88–89) and the importance often placed by cultural nationalists on the perpetuation of their languages even (or especially) in an environment where the majority uses a different language.[26] Indeed, almost anyone who examines nationalism must address the issue of language. As David Miller writes, "National identity needs linguistic expression (in speeches, histories, and so forth) and the form of the expression, on most theories of language, modifies what is expressed."[27] And Will Kymlicka argues that "people should have, as part of the respect owed them as members of a cultural community, the opportunity to have a public education in the language of their community."[28]

More concretely, Michael Ignatieff notes, when analyzing the ferocity of the Québécois commitment to maintaining the use of French within their

---

26. Recall that she offered as one of the "objective characteristics" of a nation a shared language (p. 66). Spinner, in *The Boundaries of Citizenship*, supra note 18, at 140–66 devotes a chapter to "Language and Nationality." He offers the shrewd observation that "because liberal citizenship breaks down [traditional] boundaries, liberalism enhances the importance of language as a marker of identity, increasing the likelihood that some nationalist movements based on language will emerge." Id. at 153.

27. Miller, "The Ethical Significance of Nationality," supra note 3, at 657.

28. Kymlicka, supra note 3, at 195.

portion of a dominantly Anglophone Canada (and North America), that "Quebecois think of their language as a kind of invisible shield protecting their cultural integrity from the North American norm. The French language allows Quebecois a degree of cultural self-assurance toward the Americans that English Canadians can only envy."[29] In order to protect the language and the culture it signifies, the Quebec provincial government prohibits the education of the children of Francophones (and, indeed, all non-Anglophones) in English-language schools. And, as Mordecai Richler has noted, it is now the case that "the vast majority" of the new members of the Canadian parliament from Quebec elected in the October 1993 elections speak only French.[30] Yet, according to Ignatieff, "Quebecers insist that theirs is not an ethnic but a *liberal nationalism,* based on equal citizenship"; in support, they point to the fact that Anglophones are allowed to educate their children in English.[31] Non-Anglophone parents can presumably be forced to have their children learn French rather than English precisely because it is only economic — and not cultural — imperatives that make English the more "sensible" language to learn for anyone who contemplates the possibility of exiting from Quebec.

Tamir notes that Mill had argued "that linguistic homogeneity is a necessary condition for democratic politics to work, since it is only through this homogeneity that citizens can take part in the same political debate" (p. 128). This is obviously untrue in a fairly trivial sense, if "homogeneity" is defined as everyone speaking only the same language. The cogent question, both theoretically and practically, is whether everyone must speak at least one language in common, to be chosen, presumably, by the dominant national group within the state. There is a profound difference between a specific kind of cultural bilingualism, on the one hand, where everyone speaks at least language X in common, as well as any other language(s) personally meaningful to each given citizen and the national group with which he or she identifies and, on the other hand, what might be termed multimonolingualism, where there is no political commitment to assuring

29. Ignatieff, supra note 2, at 155. His entire chapter on Quebec, pp. 143–77, is especially interesting.

30. Mordecai Richler, "O Quebec," *The New Yorker,* 30 May 1994, at 52. Similarly, the majority of new members elected from the Western provinces of Canada are unilingually English-speaking. One suspects that more members of the governing elites of contemporary Western Europe can speak a common language — almost certainly English — than is now the case in Canada.

31. Ignatieff, supra note 2, at 169 (emphasis added).

that every member of the polity in fact shares a given language with everyone else. Instead, as in Switzerland, perhaps the most notable Western example of a multimonolingual polity, one group of citizens may speak only Italian while another speaks German or French. Canada may be following this same path, though the future existence of Canada, in its present territorial form, is considerably more open to doubt than is the case with Switzerland.

Although Tamir seems to endorse the creation, within the European Community, of an office for "languages in lesser use, to encourage the preservation and revival of ethnic languages" (quoted at p. 152), she is also quick to limit such endorsement by the condition that "the respect and recognition . . . for particularistic sentiments . . . do not threaten the union" (p. 152). Thus she appears to accept the legitimacy of Estonia's limitation of citizenship in the new nation-state to those who are proficient in Estonian (p. 159) even as she is critical of "the decision to allow Estonians living in Sweden to vote in a referendum on the nature of the emerging Estonian state while excluding inhabitants of Russian origin" (p. 158). The linguistic precondition for citizenship is compared by Tamir to the requirement in the United States that naturalized citizens demonstrate similar proficiency in English.

It scarcely seems a great leap from endorsement of such conditions on naturalization to acceptance of the propriety of states such as the United States and France, which offer birthright citizenship, requiring that these "automatic" citizens be introduced to the basics of the hegemonic culture, including most certainly its language. This does not, of course, preclude allowing the deviant culture to flourish as well within a public space that features use of its own language; rather, it establishes what Rawls might call a lexical ordering, whereby the conditions for the flourishing of a liberal nationalist democracy take priority over the claims, or "rights," of a group whose flourishing, at least in its own terms, would present any kind of threat to the overall political structure. English- (or Hebrew-) only is easy enough for any liberal to denounce. However, what about at least English (or Hebrew), at a high level of skill, even if, practically speaking, this makes it considerably more difficult to master other languages and, thus, to preserve a minority culture?[32] Or perhaps, as an intermediate position, one might

---

32. See Jacob T. Levy, "Language Rights, Literacy, and the Modern State," in *Language Rights and Political Theory* (Will Kymlicka and Alan Patten, eds., 2003).

limit full citizenship, including voting and other participation rights, only to those who had demonstrated facility in the "proper" language.

V

Yael Tamir has made an important theoretical contribution to a crucial debate that should interest anyone trying to come to terms with contemporary politics. It is a mark of her achievement that one finishes the book willing to credit the non-oxymoronic nature of the term "liberal nationalism" and, thus, to accept the possibility as well that Judith Shklar, for all of her justified wariness, was nonetheless wrong in suggesting that one was forced to choose between these (and that liberalism ought in fact be the choice). That being said, "possibility" does not equal certainty, and one now wants Tamir to flesh out her argument much more extensively, with much more attention to the specifics of some of the actual struggles waged by nationalists unwilling to accept the destiny of social marginality and alienation that her theory seems to condemn them to. Her account of political possibility may be plausible only because it refuses to come to terms with the fact that all too many people share none of her own liberal vision even as she calls upon her fellow liberals to be more sympathetic with the perspective of (at least some) nationalists. Were the world divided only between Tamirian liberal nationalists and Shklarian antinationalists, it would be far easier to award the victory to Tamir. But, of course, that is not the actual world we live in, and it is unclear that Tamir offers much real guidance as to how to respond to the actual nationalists who are most often found on the front pages of our newspapers and in the forefront of our consciousness.

9

"Culture," "Religion," and the Law

WITH RACHEL LEVINSON

Introduction

In 1993, Congress passed the Religious Freedom Restoration Act (RFRA),[1] which limited the ability of governments — national, state, and local — to enforce otherwise legitimate laws in circumstances where those laws placed a "burden" on a person's free exercise of her religious commitments. Any person proving the presence of such a burden would gain an exemption from enforcement of the law unless the state could demonstrate that "application of the burden to the person (1) is in furtherance of a compelling governmental interest; and (2) is the least restrictive means of furthering that compelling governmental interest."[2] The passage of RFRA came as a direct response to a 1990 Supreme Court decision holding that the First Amendment's Free Exercise Clause did not protect a Native American from liability for violating state law by engaging in the church sacrament of peyote.[3] In passing RFRA, Congress — and, by extension, the public, in-

This essay began as a paper written by Rachel Levinson for a seminar taught by Professor Mary Ann Case at the University of Chicago Law School. Both Levinsons are immensely grateful to Professor Case for her advice and counsel in the course of preparing that paper.

1. 42 U.S.C. 2000bb (1994).

2. 42 U.S.C. 2000bb(1)(a), (b).

3. *Dept. of Human Resources of Oregon v. Smith,* 494 U.S. 872 (1990). As a matter of fact, *Smith* was an extraordinarily convoluted case, and the litigants were not in fact being threatened with criminal prosecution. Rather, the case arose because they had been fired from their jobs as drug counselors (for violating the organization's prohibition of any and all drug use) and they claimed a right to unemployment compensation from Oregon. The United States Supreme Court, for its own reasons, believed that Oregon's duty to provide such benefits turned on whether the state could prohibit the drug use in question (rather than merely whether it was a

asmuch as the Congress was responding to massive lobbying by groups across the political and social spectrum — signaled that free exercise of religion is an especially cherished aspect of American liberty and that the Supreme Court's test articulated in *Smith* did not sufficiently protect it.[4]

As a matter of fact, RFRA was struck down in substantial respects by the Court in the 1997 case *City of Boerne v. Flores*,[5] at least with respect to its application to the states.[6] Congress's enactment of RFRA is still, however, highly significant. First, as already suggested, RFRA signals Congress's — and presumably the public's — commitment to protecting religious freedom absent a "compelling" governmental interest, a standard that often (though not invariably) restricts what government can do. Moreover, as a practical matter, it may be, and several cases have so held, that RFRA can legitimately be applied to the *national* government, even if not to state governments. In addition, there exist a number of "state RFRA" or state-constitution Free

---

reasonable job condition imposed by the drug rehabilitation center that had employed the litigants). In holding that Oregon could criminalize the conduct in question, *Smith* sharply restricted the reach of the previous compelling governmental interest tests developed in *Sherbert v. Verner,* 374 U.S. 398 (1963), and instead held that "an individual's religious beliefs do not excuse him from compliance with an otherwise [neutral law of general application] prohibiting conduct that the state is free to regulate." Id. at 888–89. Congress essentially used RFRA to reinstate the strict scrutiny standard.

4. It is also worth mentioning in this context the International Religious Freedom Act, Pub. L. 105–292, 27 October 1998, 112 Stat. 2787, which, among other things, establishes a commission charged with monitoring religious freedom around the world and requires that the State Department issue annual reports on religious freedom practices globally. It also authorizes the imposition of various measures, including sanctions, on countries who are deemed the worst violators of religious freedom. Congress declared that "[f]reedom of religious belief *and practice* is a universal human right and fundamental freedom articulated in numerous international instruments," which "should never be arbitrarily abridged by any government." 22 U.S.C. §§ 6401(a)(2) and (3) (emphasis added). One notes, incidentally, the word "arbitrarily" in the last sentence. Does this suggest that Congress was implicitly accepting the legitimacy of abridging "freedom of religion" if founded on a "reasonable" (but not necessarily "compelling") basis?

5. 521 U.S. 507 (1997).

6. Congress claimed to be exercising the power granted in Section 5 of the Fourteenth Amendment to "enforce" the rights protected by the substantive sections. The most important section is Section 1, which not only requires that states "provide equal protection of the laws," but also has been read by the Supreme Court to "incorporate" almost all of the Bill of Rights as protections against illegitimate state infringement. One of these protections, of course, is the Free Exercise Clause of the First Amendment. The Court, however, as has been its recent wont, declared that it possessed a monopoly over constitutional interpretation and that Congress was basically without authority to protect a constitutional right more vigorously than the Court itself deemed fit. Discussion of the (de)merits of the Court's position is well beyond the scope of this essay.

Exercise clauses that are being interpreted by state courts to include compelling-interest tests, which would, as a practical matter, diminish the significance of *Boerne* in at least those states.[7]

But the second reason for RFRA's significance, and far more important within the context of the issues examined in this book, is its specification that it is *religious* freedom — and the commitment to multiculturalism that is signified by exhibiting legal respect for at least some religious observances, even if they are in tension with general legal norms — that is being protected. Whatever may be the country's avowed commitments to *cultural* diversity, there is no analogous Cultural Freedom Restoration Act. One might quickly respond that there is nothing to be "restored" insofar as, in contrast with religion, there is no great tradition reflected in legal cases that protects what might be termed the "free exercise of one's culture" when that would conflict with general legal norms to the contrary. In any event, at no time during the years of debate about RFRA was there a similar broadly based social movement or political leader advocating that it be broadened to establish a more general right of "cultural freedom."

The cogency of this distinction is the topic of this essay. Why should practices rooted in religious belief be treated differently than "cultural norms," whether for good (as by receiving additional protection, as through RFRA) or potentially even for ill (if one reads the Establishment Clause to prohibit "special benefits" for the religious that would be otherwise tolerable if given to adherents of a secular subculture)? As to this latter point, it is worth noting an important paradox illustrated in the discussion in chapter 1 about the ability of members of religious groups to receive "diversity preferences." Generally, as we saw, "diversity" is just another name for multi*culturalism,* but few enthusiasts for "diversity" seem to be willing to take into account the religious backgrounds (or cultures) of job or university applicants into account. And the usual basis proffered for this failure, especially by public universities, is precisely the Establishment Clause inasmuch as it is interpreted as prohibiting the giving of special benefits to members of certain religious groups. More to the point, no public university has dared to bite this particular bullet.

Although this essay focuses on certain areas of the law that *do* seem to prefer religious to secular sensibilities, the overall reality with regard to the

---

7. See Daniel A. Crane, "Beyond RFRA: Free Exercise of Religion Comes of Age in the State Courts," 10 *St. Thomas L. Rev.* 235 (1998).

interplay of "religion" and "culture" is remarkably complex. Indeed, three possible reactions to the central question raised by this chapter are: (1) "religion" and "culture" should be treated identically, for good or for ill, whatever the specific issue in dispute; (2) explicitly "religious" claims should be treated better than (merely?) "cultural" claims; or (3) "cultural" claims should receive more favorable treatment than "religious" ones.[8] A fourth possibility, of course, is to say that "it all depends," that there is no algorithm that tells us which, if either, of the claims to favor in any given situation.

One rationale for preferring religious to nonreligious claims is straightforwardly legalist and, for anyone other than the lawyer, not very interesting. One might justify the distinction by simply pointing to the text of the Constitution and its seeming establishment of some kind of protected space for the "free exercise of religion." One might even be critical of any such protection but, nonetheless, concede that the Constitution does indeed offer it. For the positivist, who accepts the Constitution as it is[9] and is relatively uninterested in any counterfactual Constitution that might be, the brute force of the Free Exercise Clause is thought to halt further discussion at least until an appropriate Article V amendment erases it.

Our purpose in this essay, however, is far less that of positivist constitutional analysis than of normative (and analytic) inquiry. Imagine, for example, that an American lawyer is asked to advise a multicultural society elsewhere in the world how it should draft a new constitution. What lessons might she draw from the American experience by way of giving her answer?

We could, of course, spend the rest of this essay (and, indeed, the entire book) analyzing the protean term "culture." Clifford Geertz famously defined culture, however imperfectly, as a "historically transmitted pattern of meanings embodied in symbols, a system of inherited conceptions expressed in symbolic forms by means of which men communicate, perpetuate, and develop their knowledge about and attitudes toward life."[10] To adopt Mi-

8. This paragraph is deeply indebted to Robert Post's response to an earlier draft of this chapter.
9. Assuming, of course, that we can agree on interpretive approaches to giving meaning to the Constitution, another topic beyond the scope of this essay.
10. Clifford Geertz, *The Interpretation of Cultures* 89 (1973). A similar definition is offered by Bhikhu Parekh, *Rethinking Multiculturalism: Cultural Diversity and Political Theory* 143 (2000): "Culture is a historically created system of meaning and significance or, what comes to the same thing, a system of beliefs and practices in terms of which a group of human beings understand, regulate and structure their individual and collective lives." There are some obvious

chael Sandel's almost equally famous notion, to fully be part of a culture is to feel embedded in it—indeed, according to Sandel, "encumbered" by its demands. This, Sandel insists, is often not a matter of choice; rather, an individual recognizes its preexisting status as constituting her very identity. Thus, he has written that protecting the free exercise of religion has almost nothing to do with protecting the liberal value of choosing whether or not to affiliate with particular religious groups and everything to do with protecting the deeply felt obligations of "encumbered selves, claimed by duties they cannot renounce."[11] For Sandel, one no more "chooses" one's culture (or religion) than one chooses one's parents. Instead, the newborn is thrust into a family, and that family (and the surrounding "culture") will transform the infant into an identifiable "German," Croat," "Aleut," or whatever.

It is obvious that "religion" constitutes an important example (or subset) of "culture," as most easily illustrated by the fact that we can also speak of the transformation of the infant into an identifiable "Jew," "Muslim," or "Catholic." But, obviously, as demonstrated by Sandel's conception of culture, nonreligious aspects of culture clearly may grip an individual just as forcefully as does religion.[12] We turn now to more concrete demonstrations of this point.

---

problems with such definitions, beginning with the fact that these "inherited conceptions" "or historically created system[s]" are in fact dynamic, so that grandparents often can barely recognize their descendants. As Alasdair MacIntyre has written, "a living tradition . . . is an historically extended, socially embodied argument, and an argument precisely in part about the goods which constitute that tradition." Alasdair MacIntyre, *After Virtue* 207 (1981). It is difficult to disagree with Stephen Greenblatt's comment that "[l]ike 'ideology' . . . 'culture' is a term that is repeatedly used without meaning much of anything at all, a vague gesture toward a dimly perceived ethos." Stephen Greenblatt, "Culture," in *Critical Terms for Literary Study* 225 (Frank Lentricchia and Thomas McLaughlin, eds., 1990). Still, like James Clifford, we find that "culture is a deeply compromised idea [we] cannot yet do without." James Clifford, *The Predicament of Culture* 10 (1988). We owe these references to Robert C. Post, "Law and Cultural Conflict" (unpublished manuscript). Adam Kuper, *Culture: The Anthropologists' Account* (1999) presents an excellent recent account of the problems attached to various conceptions of the term.

11. Michael J. Sandel, "Religious Liberty: Freedom of Conscience or Freedom of Choice?" (unpublished paper), quoted in Yael Tamir, *Liberal Nationalism* 38 (1993).

12. It is important to recognize that one might not be able to understand the concept "Aleut" without including reference to traditional religious conceptions linked with "Aleutness," and, of course, much blood has been spilled over many centuries regarding ostensible linkages between membership in political communities and particular religions.

Exemplary Cases

"TRADITIONAL" MEDICINE

In 1990, Juliet Cheng, a Chinese American woman, battled with doctors and judges over the case of her seven-year-old daughter Shirley, who suffered from severe rheumatoid arthritis; Juliet wanted to use traditional Chinese therapies, at least in addition to and possibly in place of more Western remedies.[13] Shirley was diagnosed with the degenerative disease at the age of eleven months, and was already in a wheelchair by the time of Juliet's fight to treat her with traditional therapies. In the first few years of Shirley's illness, Juliet treated her with aspirin at the advice of her American doctors but discontinued that regimen when it made Shirley nauseous. This discontinuation was not without significant legal and personal consequence, as Juliet actually temporarily lost legal custody of Shirley. Upon regaining custody, Juliet started taking Shirley regularly to China, where Shirley was afforded some relief through a combination of Chinese and Western treatments. When the student revolution occurred in China in 1989, however, Juliet suspended her trips to China and instead began taking Shirley to see Lawrence Zemel, a conventionally trained Western doctor who prescribed drugs for Shirley. Juliet terminated the therapy when the drugs seemed to be giving Shirley nosebleeds and exacerbating her joint pain. Zemel then proposed that Shirley undergo surgery on her knees, hips, and left ankle; when Juliet refused and proposed instead to take Shirley to China for less extensive surgery combined with traditional Chinese therapy, the Connecticut Department of Children and Youth Services took Shirley into custody. Shirley was held at a children's hospital, Juliet was charged with neglect, and a superior court judge approved the operation requested by Zemel.

Further litigation ensued, and a United States district judge ultimately allowed Juliet two months to demonstrate that Chinese remedies could help Shirley's condition; if she could not demonstrate the efficacy of non-Western treatment in that time, then doctors would be allowed to operate on Shirley

13. Geoffrey Cowley with Lauren Picker, "Does Doctor Know Best?" *Newsweek,* 24 September 1990, at 84. All facts reported below come from this article, except as otherwise cited. One should, incidentally, recognize that Western medicine might well be described as "traditional" (or, at least, "conventional") within a society like the United States, which is one reason we place a significant burden on those who would deviate from it.

against Juliet's wishes.[14] At the end of that period, Juliet successfully persuaded two out of the three doctors appointed by the federal judge to examine Shirley that Shirley did not need to undergo immediate surgery.[15] One of the doctors emphasized that while "Shirley will probably ultimately require surgery . . . an important part of the child's doing well is [her family's] commitment to the therapeutic regimen. If you do something where you need the cooperation of the entire family for the child to get better, when it's against the family's wishes your probability of success is vastly reduced."[16]

The dispute among Juliet, the hospital, and the legal system represented a microcosm of a more general debate taking place in the United States with regard to the use of non-religiously-based alternative remedies. On the doctors' side, one practitioner — who did not treat Shirley but was asked for his medical opinion — said that while Chinese therapies could be effective in the initial phase of rheumatoid arthritis, a child with anatomical damage could be helped only by surgery.[17] Some observers also felt that if any treatment was available that might help — as surgery surely might — it was unacceptable for a parent to deprive his or her child of that care.[18] Cheng's supporters, however, were outraged by the obstacles to her using remedies rooted in her Chinese culture.[19] Cheng was obviously committed to helping her daughter, and she even seemed willing to try Western therapies; she said explicitly that her opposition to surgery stemmed from her belief that the inflammation needed to be controlled before surgery commenced in order for Shirley's body to be able to reap the benefits of surgery, and that recourse to traditional Chinese methods of healing in which she had great faith (albeit nonreligious) would be helpful in that regard.[20]

14. "Faith in Ancestors' Medicine Faces Test; Health: Chinese Woman Turns to Traditional Treatments for Daughter's Arthritis," *Los Angeles Times,* 25 November 1990, at A22.

15. James Feron, "Mother Apparently Wins Bid to Block Surgery," *New York Times,* 13 December 1990, at B5.

16. Id.

17. "Faith in Ancestors' Medicine Faces Test," supra note 14, at A22.

18. Cowley, supra note 13, at 84.

19. The Asian-American Council of Connecticut, for example, said that the American doctors' insistence that only surgery would work was equivalent to "[s]aying that Chinese medicine is no good" and argued that the focus on Western medicine displayed "absolute arrogance. . . . A lot of what [Western doctors] do is as shaky as traditional medicine." Id. at 84.

20. Interview by Paula Zahn with Juliet Cheng and George Athanson, *CBS This Morning* (24 September 1990).

Lest there be any doubt about the basis of Ms. Cheng's claims, her lawyer took care to dissociate her from religious denominations who oppose conventional medical treatment, emphasizing that "this is not a Jehovah's Witness case. This is not a case where she doesn't want anything done for the child predicated on religious principles. She wants a combination of Western and Oriental medicine, which is the best thing for the child. . . ."[21] Unlike cases we will see later, in which doctors battle parents who want to do nothing at all (insofar as prayer treatment is properly described as "doing nothing"), therefore, this fight was between doctors trained in the primacy of Western medicine and a mother who had been sufficiently socialized in traditional cultural notions to believe that her child could benefit from non-Western "traditional" medicine. Yet, as noted, she faced the possibility not only that her own choices would be overridden by a court, but also, and presumably more ominously, that she would lose custody of her daughter, who would likely become a ward of the state separated from embrace of an obviously caring (albeit possibly culturally deluded) mother.

TREATING ILLNESS THROUGH CHRISTIAN SCIENCE
Consider what might have been Juliet's and Shirley's fates had they (or at least Juliet) been a Christian Scientist following Mary Baker Eddy's teachings. A number of Christian Science parents have also been brought to court for denying their children medically recommended care; they, however, have a religious text to point to that supports their beliefs. According to Eddy, the founder of Christian Science and the author of its primary text, matter is "false" and only the mind is "true";[22] pain therefore arises only if the mind believes it exists: "You say a boil is painful; but that is impossible, for matter without mind is not painful. The boil simply manifests, through inflammation and swelling, a belief in pain, and this belief is called a boil. Now administer mentally to your patient a high attenuation of truth, and it will soon cure the boil."[23] As a caution to those adherents attracted by pharmacology, Eddy also teaches that even those drugs that seem to have positive effects are bad, as they "rob man of reliance on God, omnipotent Mind, and . . . poison[] the human system";[24] the positive results occur only be-

21. Id. Jehovah's Witnesses do not consent to blood transfusions, believing that they violate the religion's proscription against the eating of blood. *In re E.G.,* 133 Ill. 2d 98, 102 (Ill. 1989).

22. Mary Baker Eddy, *Science and Health with Key to the Scriptures* 108 (1994).

23. Id. at 153.

24. Id. at 169–70.

cause the "false human consciousness is educated to feel" those results.[25] Moreover, even ostensible positive belief of the patient, family, and physician may not suffice. If the patient still dies from some physical toxin, the death offers evidence of neither the objective danger of the material world nor the possibility that belief in God is not enough to save the patient. Rather, it testifies to the insufficient spiritual beliefs of others in the world:

> If a dose of poison is swallowed through mistake, and the patient dies even though physician and patient are expecting favorable results, does human belief, you ask, cause this death? Even so, and as directly as if the poison had been intentionally taken. In such cases a few persons believe the potion swallowed by the patient to be harmless, but the vast majority of mankind, though they know nothing of this particular case and this special person, believe the arsenic . . . to be poisonous, for it is set down as a poison by mortal mind. Consequently, the result is controlled by the majority of opinions, not by the infinitesimal minority of opinions in the sick-chamber.[26]

The detrimental and potentially fatal effects of the mortal mind may be conquered by an understanding in truth: "Fevers are errors of various types. . . . Unless the fever-picture . . . is destroyed through Science, it may rest at length on some receptive thought, and become a fever case, which ends in a belief called death, which belief must be finally conquered by eternal Life. Truth is always the victor."[27] The mind can thus conquer death itself: "The dream of death must be mastered by Mind here or hereafter. Thought will waken from its own material declaration, 'I am dead,' to catch this trumpet-word of Truth, 'There is no death . . .' "[28]

Christian Scientists are not committed to what might be termed "self-help" healing by parents or friends themselves. Instead, when Christian Scientists believe that a family member needs care, they are encouraged to obtain the services of a professional Christian Science practitioner or a nurse. Christian Science practitioners are "individuals who devote their full time to healing through prayer, or spiritual treatment. These individuals are . . . [listed] in *The Christian Science Journal*, after having given evidence of moral character and healing ability. . . . The practitioner's work . . . is a

25. Id. at 484.
26. Id. at 177–78.
27. Id. at 379–80.
28. Id. at 427–28.

religious vocation, a ministry of spiritual healing in its broadest sense."[29] Christian Science nurses provide somewhat more practical care, such as "dressing of wounds for those having spiritual treatment."[30]

In response to those who believe that children, who are likely not in a position to make fully rational choices about their own medical care, should perhaps receive more traditional (i.e., conventional Western medical) care until they are at an age of majority, the church reassures us that the benefits of spiritual healing are not limited to adults. "Spiritual healing," the church proclaims, "does not depend on age or experience. Little children respond naturally to God's love and to the mental environment surrounding them. As parents pray, their thoughts are freed from fear and filled with a sense of God's loving care. Both parent and child are benefited. Infants and children are often healed more readily than adults."[31] Needless to say, a rich array of legal cases have arisen from attempts at "spiritual healing" that have apparently gone awry.

As a matter of legal fact, most states offer some degree of immunity from legal liability for parents who treat their children with faith healing according to good faith religious beliefs.[32] The exemptions appear primarily in three kinds of statutes: those adjudicating a child's status (i.e., as a neglected or dependent child); child abuse and neglect reporting statutes; and criminal laws that prohibit harm to children (i.e., prohibit endangering a child's

29. *Walker v. Superior Court,* 47 Cal. 3d 112, 119 (Cal. 1988) (quoting Church of Christian Scientist's amicus curiae brief).

30. Should Christian Scientists failing to follow Eddy's admonitions fear that they will be punished in the afterlife, the Church asserts that heaven and hell are not "specific destinations one reaches after death, but [are] states of thought, experienced in varying degrees here and now, as well as after death." First Church of Christ, Scientist, Questions and Answers (accessed 30 January 2002), ⟨http://www.tfccs.com/gv/qanda/csq12.jhtml⟩. Moreover, if an adherent does choose to utilize traditional medical care, "he or she is neither condemned by the Church nor dropped from membership." First Church of Christ, Scientist, Questions and Answers (accessed 30 January 2002), ⟨http://www.tfccs.com/gv/qanda/csq6.jhtml⟩. Regardless, however, there are those who believe that use of medical remedies is akin to destroying the religion. See, e.g., *People v. Rippberger,* 231 Cal. App. 3d 1667, 1678 (1991).

31. First Church of Christ, Scientist, Questions and Answers (accessed 30 January 2002), ⟨http://www.tfccs.com/gv/qanda/csq9.jhtml⟩.

32. Jennifer L. Rosato, "Putting Square Pegs in a Round Hole: Procedural Due Process and the Effect of Faith Healing Exemptions on the Prosecution of Faith Healing Parents," 29 *U.S.F. L. Rev.* 43, 51 (1994). See also Cassandra Terhune, "Comment, Current International and Domestic Issues Affecting Children: Cultural and Religious Defenses to Child Abuse and Neglect," 14 *J. Am. Acad. Matrimonial Law* 152, 176–89 (1997), for a state-by-state canvass of the statutory exemptions.

welfare or engaging in criminal nonsupport).[33] The eagerness of states to protect Christian Scientists cannot, unlike RFRA, necessarily be interpreted as a manifestation of local commitment to safeguarding the religious practices of a small minority with odd views about medical treatment. Instead the exemptions originally arose because the predecessor of the current Department of Health and Human Services, prompted by the extremely active lobbying efforts of the Christian Science church, required states to enact such regulations in order to receive federal funding for child protection programs.[34] The DHHS currently "requires that abuse or neglect must be reported if there is harm or substantial risk of harm to the child, and that medical treatment must be ordered if such harm or substantial risk of harm exists. However, a faith healing parent still may be exempt from the court's finding neglect for failure to provide medical care."[35] It appears from the statutes that even in a circumstance where the law intervenes and orders medical treatment against a parent's wishes, the parent does not necessarily run the additional risk of being deemed an unfit parent and losing custody. Those statutory exemptions do not extend to the homocide statutes; failure to provide medical care may be protected, but the potentially fatal results of that failure are open to prosecution.[36] The exemptions do, though, help to explain why parents might claim in court that their failure to procure medical care for their children is protected.

It may be telling that most of the reported cases involving Christian Scientists seem to involve the death of the child in question. This suggests that the state has been far less willing to get involved in "spiritual treatment" that leads to less dire consequences, even if conventional medical personnel might contend that the child would be far better off receiving medical treatment. It might also suggest, of course, that cases don't come to the state's attention unless the child dies and that cases with less dire consequences remain invisible, as it were, to the state's gaze. This does not seem to describe the situation with Shirley Cheng, however, inasmuch as there was apparently no reason to believe that her life was in danger (nor, of course, did she in fact die) because of her being deprived of the benefits of conventional Western medicine.

33. Rosato, supra note 32, at 51–53.

34. Id. at 59.

35. Id.

36. Whether that confusion results in a denial of due process to the parents, due to the lack of notice, is outside the scope of this paper, but is thoroughly covered by Rosato, supra note 32.

Consider *Walker v. Superior Court*,[37] which involved the death from meningitis of the four-year-old daughter of Christian Scientists. During the seventeen days that the child was ill, the mother retained the services of an accredited Christian Science prayer practitioner and a Christian Science nurse.[38] As a result of the child's death, the mother was charged by the state of California with both involuntary manslaughter and felony child endangerment.[39] She cited the following provision from California's neglect law in claiming legal immunity for her actions:

> If a parent of a minor child willfully omits, without lawful excuse, to furnish necessary . . . medical attendance or other remedial care . . . for his or her child, he or she is guilty of a misdemeanor. . . . If a parent provides a minor with treatment by *spiritual means through prayer alone* in accordance with the tenets and practices of a recognized church or religious denomination, by a duly accredited practitioner thereof, such treatment *shall constitute 'other remedial care,'* as used in this section.[40]

The court concluded that the above section afforded parents who used prayer treatment to treat their children an exemption from the statutory requirement to provide them with adequate medical care.[41] It did not, however, construe the provision to apply to the quite different statutes involving involuntary manslaughter and felony child endangerment statutes. The court opined that the language providing that treatment by prayer would not *alone* constitute abuse or neglect indicated that "a child receiving prayer treatment can still fall within the reach of the statutory definitions if the provision of such treatment, coupled with a grave medical condition, combine to pose a serious threat to the physical well-being of the child."[42]

While the court acknowledged that the prayer treatment was "an article

---

37. 47 Cal. 3d 112 (Cal. 1988).

38. Id. at 118–19.

39. Id. at 119.

40. Id. at 120; Cal. Pen. Code (1st ed. 1872) §270 (emphasis added).

41. 47 Cal. 3d at 123.

42. Id. at 130. The language of the child welfare section is also instructive in this regard: "Cultural and religious child-rearing practices and beliefs which differ from general community standards shall not in themselves create a need for child welfare services *unless the practices present a specific danger to the physical or emotional safety of the child.*" Id. at 131; Cal. Welf. & Inst. Code, § 16509 (emphasis added). One should note, of course, that the California statute does indeed appear to protect both deviant "cultural *and* religious" practices, though we are not aware of any "cultural" cases that have been able to take advantage of the statute.

of genuine faith," and that its restriction would "seriously impinge on the practice of her religion," the court also pointed out that, according to the Church's amicus brief, using actual medicine would not have subjected the mother to stigmatization, would not have constituted "sin," would not have aroused "divine retribution," and was "not a matter of church compulsion."[43] The court attested to the strong justification behind the state's interest in safeguarding children's lives, and its weight as against the defendant's interest in her religious practice.[44] Finally, the court determined that the "imposition of felony liability for failure to seek medical care for a seriously ill child" was in fact the least restrictive alternative at the state's disposal; while the Church argued that state dependency proceedings would represent a less intrusive option, the court concluded that requiring a parent to face the loss of his or her child in a "disruptive and invasive judicial inquiry" might be more intrusive than privately facing an inquiry into criminal liability.[45] Moreover, because the state might frequently learn of a deprivation of medical care only after the child had fallen victim to extreme sickness or death, it was simply impractical to rely solely on dependency proceedings.[46] The court ultimately held that the mother's prosecution for involuntary manslaughter and felony child endangerment did not constitute a violation of statutory law or of the federal or state constitutions.[47]

In *Newmark v. Williams*,[48] however, the Supreme Court of Delaware concluded that when a child of Christian Science parents had only a low chance of recovering even with full medical treatment, the state was not

43. Id. It is worth noting that in an earlier case in a Pennsylvania superior court, the parents' pastor took a different view of the effects of straying from belief in spiritual healing, explaining: "We would consider going to a doctor and trusting in medicine doing greater harm [than trusting God to heal] because it would be harmful[,] as we believe . . . it would be harming the spiritual and eternal interest of the child and the parents as well in doing so." *Commonwealth v. Barnhart*, 345 Pa. Super. 10, 20 (Pa. Super. Ct. 1985). The court still determined, however, that given the state's role as *parens patriae*, its interest in the child's life outweighed the parents' considerable interest in religious freedom. Id. at 25–26.

44. 47 Cal. 3d at 139–40 (citing *Prince v. Massachusetts*, 321 U.S. 158, 170 (1944)) ("Parents may be free to become martyrs themselves. But it does not follow they are free, in identical circumstances, to make martyrs of their children before they have reached the age of full legal discretion when they can make that choice for themselves.").

45. Id.

46. Id. at 141.

47. Id. at 144. See also *People v. Rippberger*, 231 Cal. App. 3d 1667 (1991), for a similar case also involving meningitis.

48. 588 A.2d 1108 (Del. 1990).

justified in obtaining custody of the child in order to force him to undergo extensive treatment. At the time of the case, the Newmarks[49] had a three-year-old son, Colin, who was quite ill with a very aggressive and advanced type of pediatric cancer.[50] When the Newmarks first began to notice that Colin was ill, they took him to a children's hospital to have him examined; they acknowledged that this decision violated their Christian Science beliefs, but said that they did so in order to mitigate their potential criminal liability.[51] When a surgeon at the hospital examined Colin, he suggested that the Newmarks leave Colin at the hospital to have further testing done.[52] The Newmarks refused and took Colin back home to receive treatments from a Christian Science practitioner; within a week, however, Colin's symptoms manifested themselves again, and the Newmarks took him back to the hospital.[53] The surgeon discovered a tumor in Colin's intestines, and the Newmarks consented to surgery to remove it, believing that because the procedure was "mechanical" it did not violate their religious faith.[54] Although Colin originally showed signs of recovering well, the doctors subsequently determined that Colin had non-Hodgkins lymphoma, and that it had spread through his body.[55] An oncologist recommended to the Newmarks that they initiate a heavy course of chemotherapy, and told them that the treatment would offer about a 40 percent chance of curing the cancer; without the chemotherapy, Colin would die within six to eight months.[56] The Newmarks refused to subject Colin to chemotherapy and told the doctors that they would be procuring care for Colin from a Christian Science practitioner rather than utilize any medical treatment.[57]

---

49. Interestingly, the court explicitly noted that the Newmarks were "well educated and economically prosperous." Id. at 1109. Whether that fact helped settle the court's own doubts about leaving the child in their care or was meant as a signal that the court would favor leaving children with parents who seemed better able to meet the child's needs in other realms is unclear. It is somewhat ironic, however, that the fact seemed to have impressed the court; one could imagine a situation in which a court might be more sympathetic to less educated or well-off parents, concluding that their failure to provide their child with medical care demonstrated a lack of knowledge about modern medical practice rather than an explicit rejection of medical treatment.

50. Id.

51. Id. at 1110.

52. Id.

53. Id.

54. Id. at 1110–11.

55. Id. at 1111.

56. Id.

57. Id.

The court first reviewed the Delaware exemption to the child neglect statute,[58] which, though general in its phrasing, is obviously targeted toward Christian Scientists, given its reference to an "accredited practitioner," a term peculiar to Christian Science. The panel noted that the exception reflected the Delaware legislature's intent "to provide a 'safe harbor' for parents . . . to pursue *their own religious beliefs*."[59] After specifically declining to address the constitutionality of the statutory exceptions,[60] the court declared that the family court that had initially heard the case (and ruled against the Newmarks) had failed to properly weigh the parents' interests in their relationship with Colin and the severity of Colin's illness against the invasiveness of the treatment and the high likelihood of failure.[61] The court opined that "the parental right is sacred"[62] and that "the only party capable of authorizing medical treatment for a minor in 'normal' circumstances is usually his parent or guardian";[63] the court also recognized, however, that "parental autonomy over minor children is not an absolute right," and that the state, in its role as *parens patriae*,[64] "can intervene in the parent-child relationship where the health and safety of the child and the public at large are in jeopardy."[65]

The court determined that where a child was unable to make a decision about his own medical care — as was clearly the case with a three-year-old — the court had to use its own judgment, weighing the effectiveness and risk of the proposed treatment against the child's likelihood of survival with and without the treatment.[66] The court felt that the "[s]tate's interest in forcing a minor to undergo medical care diminishes as the risks of treatment increase and its benefits decrease."[67] Given the extremely invasive nature and dan-

---

58. "No child who in good faith is under treatment solely by spiritual means through prayer in accordance with the tenets and practices of a recognized church or religious denomination by a duly accredited practitioner thereof shall for that reason alone be considered a neglected child for purposes of this chapter." 10 Del. C. § 901(11) & 16 Del. C. § 907.

59. 588 A.2d at 1111 (emphasis added).

60. Id. at 1114.

61. Id. at 1115.

62. Id.

63. Id. at 1116.

64. *Parens patriae* is "[t]he principle that the state must care for those who cannot take care of themselves, such as minors who lack proper care and custody from their parents." (*Black's Law Dictionary 769* (6th ed., 1991)).

65. 588 A.2d at 1116.

66. Id. at 1116–17.

67. Id. at 1117.

gerous side effects of chemotherapy, coupled with a low chance of recovery, and a chance that in fact the chemotherapy itself would hasten Colin's death, the court concluded that the state was not entitled to take Colin into its custody.[68] It is, of course, unclear what the court would have done had the parents not been Christian Scientists and, relying only on traditional legal notions of parental rights over the treatment of children, had instead simply argued that they chose in effect to doom their child rather than subject him to the ravages of chemotherapy where there was "only" a 40 percent chance of some kind of cure. (One can only wonder what the court might have done had the medical professionals testified that the chemotherapy had, say, a 51 percent cure rate.) One must presume that the Delaware judges believed that the religion-specific exemption statute was relevant to the case.

Juxtaposing Religion and Culture

Because religion is obviously only one aspect of culture, one might wonder if the deference granted to religion would be reflected in similar respect for nonreligious forms of cultural "encumbrance." One should note—indeed emphasize—that putting the question this way is very different from asking if behavior motivated by nonreligious convictions (or, in the vernacular, private "conscience") should receive the same protection as religion. This latter question became especially important during the Vietnam Era with regard to granting potential draftees the status of "conscientious objectors." As Justice Clark put it, writing for the Supreme Court in the leading case of *United States v. Seeger,* "These cases involve claims of conscientious objectors under § 6(j) of the Universal Military Training and Service Act, which exempts from combatant training and service in the armed forces of the United States those persons who *by reason of their religious training and belief* are conscientiously opposed to participation in war in any form."[69] The Court in *Seeger* defined "religious belief" to include "[a] sincere and meaningful belief which occupies in the life of its possessor a place parallel to that filled by the God of those admittedly qualifying for the exemption."[70]

---

68. Id. at 1118.

69. *United States v. Seeger,* 380 U.S. 163, 164–165 (1965) (emphasis added).

70. Id. at 76. The Court stated that its new "test is simple of application. It is essentially an objective one, namely, does the claimed belief occupy the same place in the life of the objector as an orthodox belief in God holds in the life of one clearly qualified for exemption?" Id. at 184.

This seems to accept theologian Paul Tillich's functional definition of faith as one's "ultimate concern" and, therefore, to treat all such concerns, whether traditionally religious or not, as protected by the congressional statute being construed. And writers such as Rodney K. Smith have powerfully made the case, whether or not one is ultimately convinced, for offering greater protection to the claims of "conscience."[71] Such an approach reflects at least in part the deeply Protestant culture of the United States and its image of the lonely individual confronting God (or, if secular, determining the Meaning of Life) directly, without the mediating institutions that constitute culture (or Culture). The respect due "conscience" is an important topic, but it is not the central topic of *this* essay or, more to the point, of this book. Although the individuals we are discussing would certainly describe themselves (and be described by many others) as "conscientious," we are interested far less in "private conscience" than in the extent to which their (and others') views of the world, formed by immersion in—rather than active choice of—their own particular cultures, make claims about the importance of preserving their distinct cultures as social entities.

The importance of this point is underlined in what is surely one of the most famous "religion" cases, *Wisconsin v. Yoder,*[72] in which the Supreme Court recognized a right of Amish parents to defy the Wisconsin law that would have required them to send their children to school for at least ten years. The parents argued that Amish culture required only eight years of schooling and that preservation of the particular (and peculiar) Amish culture required that children leave school and begin their lives as working members of the community. Chief Justice Burger, writing for the majority, accepted this argument. Interestingly enough, however, he explicitly rejected its applicability to, say, followers of Henry David Thoreau or other secular opponents of mainstream culture: "A way of life, however virtuous and admirable, may not be interposed as a barrier to reasonable state regulation of education if it is based on purely secular considerations; to have the protection of the Religion Clauses, the claims must be rooted in religious belief." However, "delicate" it may be to determine what constitutes such a " 'religious' belief or practice," the Court attempted the task, for it is apparently unthinkable that "every person," or, presumably, every subculture, come to deviant conclusions

71. See Rodney K. Smith, "Converting the Religious Equality Amendment into a Statute with a Little 'Conscience,' " 1996 *Brigham Young U.L. Rev.* 645.
72. 406 U.S. 205 (1972).

on matters of conduct in which society as a whole has important interests. Thus, if the Amish asserted their claims because of their subjective evaluation and rejection of the contemporary secular values accepted by the majority, much as Thoreau rejected the social values of his time and isolated himself at Walden Pond, their claims would not rest on a religious basis. Thoreau's choice was philosophical and personal rather than religious, and such belief does not rise to the demands of the Religion Clauses.[73]

It was, therefore, absolutely crucial that the Amish were a long-established religion whose members had demonstrated over many years — indeed centuries — not only their deep commitment to the tenets ("encumbrances") of their sect but also the fact that, however different Amish culture might be from its mainstream counterpart, it was capable of surviving even in the late-twentieth-century United States (at least with certain accommodations). Moreover, it is surely significant that the Court appeared to view Amish culture with some benevolence, as it noted evidence "show[ing] that the Amish have an excellent record as law-abiding and generally self-sufficient members of society,"[74] though, of course, there is no reason to believe that law-abidingness and self-sufficiency are attributes uniquely linked to being religious. Henry David Thoreau might not have been particularly law-abiding due to his opposition to slavery — but, then, neither could the Reverend Martin Luther King be said to score very high in "law-abidingness," for much the same reason — though few could lay greater claim to self-sufficiency than Thoreau (and, presumably, his latter-day followers).

It is important, we believe, to note a potential difference between Thoreau and what might be called "Thoreauvians." The former is a discrete individual asserting claims of "conscience." As we have said earlier, however interesting and important such claims may be, they are not centrally relevant to the "multiculturalism" debate. But "Thoreauvians" might well be recognized as a distinct "subculture" organized around the beliefs and model set by Thoreau in much the same way that "Christians" organize themselves around the beliefs and model set by Jesus or "Buddhists" by the beliefs and model set by Buddha. Our central question is whether it is legiti-

73. Id. at 215–16.
74. Id. at 213.

mate to give only the latter two, and not the Thoreauvians, a measure of protection against majoritarian control.

Like the medical-care cases discussed above, therefore, *Yoder* requires us to confront the distinctions between our treatment, on the one hand, of behavior that is (correctly) interpreted as the outcome of religious beliefs, and, on the other hand, of quite similar behavior that is motivated by other "cultural" imperatives even if we (correctly) do not label them "religious." Given the disparate legal attitudes towards religion and culture, and given that religion and culture do not stand apart as distinctive aspects of people's lives, what might explain the different treatment that the two receive beyond wooden emphasis on the relevant text of the First Amendment? Does religion have important characteristics that the nonreligious side of culture is lacking, and does any such differential help to justify the difference in legal treatment? Pointing to the wording of the First Amendment might, of course, help to explain the difference in *constitutional* treatment, but, as suggested earlier, it does not explain why legislators trying to determine simply what kind of legislation is in the public interest would necessarily wish to protect "religious" as against "cultural" freedom.

DEFINITIONS OF RELIGION AND CULTURE

Religion and culture are both notoriously difficult concepts to define.[75] Do they constitute, at bottom, systems of *behavior* or of ideas and structures of *belief* (or, as is obvious, a complex blend of behavior coupled with beliefs as to why the behavior is significant or, indeed, obligatory)? Can one meaningfully distinguish between "core" aspects of a culture or religion and more "peripheral" aspects? How does one adjudicate among "local informants" who differ on what is "core" and what is "peripheral" in defining one as a member of a given religion or culture?

The Supreme Court, for example, has explicitly rejected its own capacity to make certain key judgments, pointing out that "[i]ntrafaith differences . . . are not uncommon among followers of a particular creed, and the judicial process is singularly ill equipped to resolve such differences. . . . [T]he guarantee of free exercise is not limited to beliefs which are shared by all of the members of a religious sect. . . . [I]t is not within the judicial*

---

75. See supra note 10. On religion, see Douglas Laycock, "Religious Liberty as Liberty," 7 *J. Contemp. Leg. Iss.* 313, 326–37 (1996) for an excellent brief overview of the problems presented in defining religion. See also Rebecca Redwood French, "From Yoder to Yoda: Models of Traditional, Modern, and Postmodern Religion in the United States," 4 *Ariz. L. Rev.* 49 (1999).

function and judicial competence to inquire [who] more correctly per-
ceive[s] the commands of their common faith."[76] As matter of fact, the
Supreme Court has proved to be inept in defining what constitutes a "religion" or a "faith" that is then presumptively protected by the Free Exercise
Clause. While it once notably referred to "an asserted claim so bizarre, so
clearly nonreligious in motivation, as not to be entitled to protection under
the Free Exercise Clause,"[77] the Court did not grace the opinion with concrete examples of such bizarre claims or delineate the criteria, beyond a
certain social tact, that saved, say, the beliefs quoted earlier from Mary
Baker Eddy's foundational book on Christian Science from any such desig-
nation. Indeed, in that same case the Court held that "religious beliefs need
not be acceptable, logical, consistent, or comprehensible to others in order
to merit First Amendment protection."[78] As a matter of fact, the Court has
said nothing that is useful to anyone looking for a serious analysis of the
concept of "religion."

Nor is one particularly enlightened when looking at other American
courts that have wrestled with the problem. We might begin with a 1975
case in which a United States court of appeals held that an "atheist" could
assert the legal benefits offered the "religious"[79] because his tenets were, in
the words of a Supreme Court decision, "held with the strength of religious
convictions."[80] Or consider the response of a Wyoming district court faced
with the task of assessing whether someone who styled himself the "Reverend" of his "Church of Marijuana" could claim the protection of RFRA
when charged with marijuana possession and trafficking. The judge com-
piled an exhaustive list of factors that courts have used in assessing whether
beliefs qualify as "religious" for First Amendment purposes.[81] The "factors"
have overtones of a laundry list, but they accurately capture what one or
another judge includes within his definitions. Thus some place emphasis on
certain structures of ideas, including metaphysical beliefs, moral or ethical
systems, and their degree of comprehensiveness as applied to various aspects
of life. Others focus on the presence of explicitly "sacred" figures, including

76. *Thomas v. Review Board of the Indiana Employment Security Division*, 450 U.S. 707, 715–
716 (1981) (emphasis added).
77. Id. at 715.
78. Id. at 714.
79. *United States v. Bush*, 509 F.2d 776 (7th Cir. 1975) (en banc).
80. *Welsh v. United States*, 398 U.S. 333, 339–40 (1970).
81. *United States v. Meyers*, 906 F. Supp. 1494, 1501–03 (D. Wyo. 1995), aff'd, 95 F.3d 1475
(1996).

founders, prophets, or teachers; important writings; gathering places; keepers of knowledge; ceremonies and rituals; organizational structures; holidays; diet (including fasting); appearance and clothing; and education of the young. Although the judge cautioned that the marijuana-using defendant did not have to establish a tight fit between his beliefs and the factors it listed — indeed, it stated that the "threshold for inclusion is low"[82] — the court ultimately determined that while "Meyers may sincerely believe that his beliefs are religious[,] . . . his beliefs do not constitute a 'religion' as that term is uneasily defined by law. . . ."[83] It is hard to believe that the particular claim asserted — i.e., the freedom to use otherwise prohibited drugs — did not have something to do with the reluctance to accept the litigant's claim to be "religious" and therefore enjoy the protections of RFRA.

A recent case arising out of Wisconsin not only offers an especially rich example of a court's struggling with defining "religion," but also demonstrates the legal importance of distinguishing "culture" from religion." Christopher Lee Peterson is an adherent of the World Church of the Creator, which promotes a system of beliefs, termed "Creativity," that teaches an especially virulent form of white supremacy.[84] Adherents of "Creativity" describe as "nonsense" beliefs in "angels and devils and gods and . . . silly spook craft" in favor of "the Eternal Laws of Nature."[85] As described by Judge Adelman, "Creativity considers itself to be a religion, but it does not espouse a belief in a God, afterlife or any sort of supreme being."[86] Why does it matter if we accept Creativity's self-description instead of viewing Peterson's immersion in the group and his devotion to white supremacy as evidence of the "culture" (or "subculture") that defines his core identity? The reason lies in the law.

The case arose under Title VII of the Civil Rights Act of 1964, which, among other things, prohibits employers from "discriminating" against their employees because of the latters' *religious,* but not, presumably, their nonreligious, "beliefs." The communications company for whom Peterson worked dismissed him from his job as dayroom supervisor after he had been pictured in the *Milwaukee Journal Sentinel* wearing a T-shirt with the picture of Benjamin Smith, a follower of Creativity who had shot several Afri-

82. Id. at 1501.
83. Id. at 1508.
84. 205 F. Supp. 2d 1014 (E. D. Wisc. 2002).
85. Id. at 1015, quoting from the website maintained by the World Church of the Creator.
86. Id.

can American, Jewish, and Asian persons. In that job Peterson had supervisory authority over several nonwhite employees, who were described by the company as expressing a lack of "confidence" in Peterson's fairness. He was transferred to the job of "telephone solicitor," which paid less and left him without any supervisory responsibility.

Judge Edelman interpreted Title VII as flatly prohibiting employers from using the religious "beliefs" of their employees as the basis for negative treatment. Peterson had not in fact been cited for negative "behavior" on the job, only for the repugnant beliefs that he held, which the company, of course, argued would make it presumptively difficult to serve in a supervisory role. So the key question is whether "Creativity" counted as a "religion" in Judge Edelman's eyes as well as Peterson's, and the answer was yes. "Creativity plays a central role in [Peterson's] life. [He] has been a minister of the World Church of the Creator for more than three years." Moreover, the judge noted that Peterson was committed to "putting [the teachings of Creativity] into practice every day." All of this led Judge Edelman to conclude that "the teachings of Creativity are 'religious' in plaintiff's 'own scheme of things.' These beliefs occupy for plaintiff a place in his life parallel to that held by a belief in God for believers in more mainstream theistic religions." The consequence, of course, is that the egregious Peterson was protected in his supervisory job because his beliefs were ostensibly *religiously* based rather than a matter of "merely" being ideologically committed to preserving the supremacy of his "white culture" by keeping members in a distinctly subordinate position.

To put it mildly, then, courts have thus neither demanded strict definitions of religion nor mandated that religious adherents conform to a particular notion about what constitutes religious belief or practice. Whatever explains the greater protection of "religion" as against "culture," it is *not* that analysts can more readily agree on what constitutes the former as against the latter.

It is also scarcely irrelevant that American history is replete with examples of the United States' particular fecundity with regard to creating new religions.[87] Indeed, Christian Science and the Jehovah's Witnesses, both of whom have contributed to much litigation involving medical treatment of minors, are "made-in-the-USA" religions, as is also the case, most notably,

---

87. See, e.g., Sydney E. Ahlstrom, *A Religious History of the American People* (1972), or the more recent (and highly provocative) Harold Bloom, *The American Religion: The Emergence of the Post-Christian Nation* (1992).

of the Mormon Church, whose reach now extends far beyond its country of origin (and which, because of its early requirement of bigamy, generated some of the most important early cases testing the limits of the Free Exercise Clause).[88] It may be overdetermined, then, that political leaders, including members of the judiciary, are willing to accord a certain respect to religious claims, at least when they are not so far from the mainstream as to appear "bizarre" or otherwise to challenge fundamental American verities.

This still does not fully explain, however, why equally nonbizarre or nonthreatening, albeit somewhat deviant, nonreligious subcultures are not accorded similar degrees of legal respect. At the very least, it seems almost bizarre (and even a bit threatening) to protect Christopher Peterson if we would not be equally solicitous of, say, a member of the Ku Klux Klan who forthrightly asserts the centrality of preserving "white culture" as his dominant aim in life. Of course, a "smart Klansman" (or his lawyer) would presumably be sophisticated enough to portray Klan ideology as "religious," but the question is either why we would be fooled or why it should matter whether we portray the views as the product of "culture" or of "religion." The Boy Scouts of America, for example, did not have to establish their bona fides as a "religious" organization in order to prevail on their claim that the First Amendment protected their "right of expressive association" to exclude gays from participation in the Scouts.[89] It would be easy

---

88. Mormons were, with slaveholders, the central targets of the new Republican Party born in 1856, whose platform pledged to attack the "twin relics of barbarism," i.e., slavery and polygamy. See, e.g., Sarah Barringer Gordon, *The Mormon Question: Polygamy and Constitutional Conflict in Nineteenth-Century America* 55 (2002). Thus one consequence of the 1860 triumph of Lincoln and his party was the passage in 1862 of the Morrill Act criminalizing polygamy, a central tenet of the Mormon Church. Id. at 81. Its terms were quite remarkable, including, in addition to the criminalization, the disincorporation by the Utah territorial legislature of the Church of Jesus Christ of Latter Day Saints. *Reynolds v. United States,* 98 U.S. 145 (1878), upheld the jail sentence imposed on George Reynolds, a leader of the Utah Mormon community, for bigamy. See also *The Late Corporation of the Church of Jesus Christ of Latter-Day Saints v. United States,* 136 U.S. 1 (1890), as the Court upheld the 1887 Edmunds-Tucker Act, which required the seizure of church property as a means of destroying the "Mormon supremacy and power" that enabled the "propagation of polygamy" among "ignorant and degraded people." See Gordon, pp. 202–3 (quoting Edmunds and the House committee report supporting the Act). The "legitimation" of the church came only after its elders declared in 1890 that they had received a revelation that in fact changed the doctrine in question. Id. at 290. Needless to say, this being an endlessly diverse American society, there exist "unreformed" Mormons who continue to practice polygamy and who on occasion are the subjects of Utah prosecution.

89. *Boy Scouts of America v. Dale,* 530 U.S. 640 (2000).

enough to view the case as protecting the freedom of the Scouts to maintain their homophobic culture against the attempt of the State of New Jersey to intervene via that state's general antidiscrimination law.

NEGOTIATIONS AND CHOICES

Perhaps the most extensive discussion of "culture" has occurred within the context of so-called cultural defense cases, in which persons accused of crimes claim either immunity from liability or, at least, a right to a diminished sentence because their acts, however objectionable from the perspective of "mainstream" culture, made perfectly good sense — or so it was alleged — within the context of their "home" culture. As we will see, the facts of the cases do not generate particular sympathy for those asserting "cultural defenses," but, then, it is scarcely the case that religion-based claimants are necessarily more sympathetic (think once more of Mr. Peterson), so something else must still explain the differences in response.

"Marriage by Capture" among the Hmong. Perhaps the most notorious such case is *People v. Moua,*[90] often termed the Hmong "marriage by cap-

___

90. *People v. Moua,* No. 315972-0 (Cal. Sup. Ct. Feb. 17, 1985). See Choua Ly, Comment, "The Conflict between Law and Culture: The Case of the Hmong in America," 2001 *Wis. L. Rev.* 471, 479 (2001), which offers a detailed exposition of the facts in the case (on which the following paragraphs are based).

According to Kong Moua, the defendant, who was twenty-three at the time of the case, he had been involved romantically with Seng Xiong for several months, since December 1983, and had known her for over a year. They had mutually decided to elope, and Kong, along with a male friend, went to pick up Seng at work at the Fresno City College in April 1984 in order to elope. The trio returned to the home of a close relative of Kong's, where several of his kin collected money to give to Seng's uncle and father to confirm the marriage. Kong and Seng had sex that night to consummate the marriage. The couple was met by the police the next day, as they left the house to talk with a lawyer about another matter, and were questioned about whether Seng had been kidnapped, but Seng said that the two were married. Seng's parents, however, took issue with the marriage, because of Kong's status as an orphan; while Seng originally told Kong that she wanted to marry him anyway, she told him several days later that she no longer wanted to be his wife. Kong accepted her wishes, but refused to satisfy her family's demand that he compensate Seng for her damaged reputation, saying that because she was the one who called off the union, she owed him. Kong felt that his refusal to pay restitution prompted Seng to call the police and report the kidnapping and rape charges.

As one might expect, Seng's version of the events was dramatically different. According to her, the pair met for the first time in December 1983 and never had any romantic involvement. When she left work on the day of the crime, Kong and his friend met her and told her they were kidnapping her and that she would marry Kong. She protested that she did not plan to marry

ture" case.[91] The defendant had been charged with rape and kidnapping, to which he offered the defense that the putative victim was actually a willing participant in the activities that led to the indictment, and that the proceedings, including her protests, followed a Hmong marriage ritual. Hmong marriage customs were thus an integral part of his defense.

Hmong culture apparently allows a young man interested in marriage to instigate marriage negotiations in three ways.[92] First, the youth may ask the girl's father for her hand in marriage. Because this practice requires a great deal of money, however, it is quite rare. Second, a couple in love might decide to elope; the elopment proceedings, though consensual, would require a show of protest by the girl in order "to protect her virtue and to prevent disrespect to her family, even though, secretly, she was glad to be married."[93] The families would then have to agree, as otherwise the situation would be quite shameful for both the girl and her family, and marriage negotiations would begin three days later. This practice continues to be common in both Laos and the United States. Finally, a young man with an unrequited interest in marriage might abduct an unwilling girl, take her to his family's house, and force sexual intercourse.[94] Here, obviously, the protests would be completely authentic, even if the young man might hope that they are merely formal, as is the purported case with "elopement."

The reader will not be surprised to learn that there were significant differences in the stories told by the defendant and the complainant. For her it was a rape, pure and simple. Yet not only did the judge allow the defense attorney to introduce a brochure detailing marriage by elopement, but the

---

Kong and tried unsuccessfully to call out for help. She was forced into sexual intercourse by Kong that evening, but told the police the next day that she had not been sexually molested and did not want to press charges on the kidnapping, in order both not to get Kong and his friend into trouble and not to miss the meeting with the lawyer. She subsequently tried to settle the matter through her family and get out of the marriage, but the families were not able to come to an agreement. She ultimately notified the police because the two men had said they might kidnap her again; she explained that she had not contacted the police immediately because she was trying to protect her reputation in the Hmong community, which had been sullied by her night with Kong.

91. See, e.g., Deirdre Evans-Pritchard and Alison Dundes Renteln, "The Interpretation and Distortion of Culture: A Hmong 'Marriage by Capture' Case in Fresno, California," 4 *S. Cal. Interdisciplinary L.J.* 1 (1994).

92. Ly, supra note 90.

93. Id.

94. Id.

state prosecutor also ultimately decided not to pursue charges either of kidnapping or rape and instead allowed the defendant to plead guilty to the far less serious offense of false imprisonment. The judge ultimately sentenced the defendant to 120 days in jail and required him to pay a fine of $1,000, with $900 of the money going to compensate the victim, a sentence far less severe than that available had the defendant been charged with the more serious offenses.

This case undoubtedly fits to some extent into the conventional criminal law category of mistake of fact. For example, a defendant is usually entitled to claim "self-defense" so long as it was "reasonable" to view the victim as presenting a threat, even if it turns out that the facts were completely otherwise. But it should be obvious that what constitutes a "reasonable" belief in such cases may be a function of wider cultural norms. In a culture that did not endorse or recognize marriage by capture, a woman's vigorous resistance to forcible intercourse simply could not be interpreted as a formal protest that should be understood in fact as a sign of consent. Any individual man might, of course, claim that "no means yes," and he might even find some support for that view in an extraordinarily macho American subculture, but it is unlikely that the community's cultural practices would explicitly sanction such a practice and "justify" a judge's determination that the legal cost of such behavior should be only four months in jail. What distinguishes the Hmong case is that the defendant could indeed invoke far deeper cultural norms and that the prosecutor and judge could believe that respect for other cultures justified a leniency that would no longer be available in all but the most benighted community to swaggering predatory males.

Oyako Shinju: Parent-Child Suicide. A second dramatic example of the cultural defense involves cultural evidence of *oyako shinju,* or parent-child suicide, a Japanese practice apparently imported to the United States by some Japanese immigrants. The best-known American case is that of Fumiko Kimura, who in 1985 drowned her two children off the California coast and then tried to drown herself because her husband had been having an affair.[95] Kimura told investigators that she "had not wanted to leave her children

95. Sharan Suri, Note, "A Matter of Principle and Consistency: Understanding the Battered Woman and Cultural Defenses," 7 *Mich. J. Gender & L.* 107, 119 (2000). See also Doriane Lambelet Coleman, "Individualizing Justice through Multiculturalism: The Liberals' Dilemma," 96 *Colum. L. Rev.* 1093, 1094 (1996) (noting that "no state has formally recognized the use of exonerating cultural evidence").

behind to suffer hardship or unhappiness. . . . [S]he feared they would be hurt like her, and she did not want anybody else to get them."[96] She also thought that she was "sending them to a better place."[97] Because the family name is extremely important in Japan, and because Japanese parents tend not to think of children as autonomous units, parent-child suicide is not infrequent in Japan, as a way to keep children from suffering the ignominy of being left behind by a suicidal parent.[98] In 1980, statistics revealed that 252 instances of *oyako shinju* initiated by the mother occurred that year.[99] Although Japanese law officially permits the death penalty for parents who survive *oyako shinju,* they are usually only lightly punished.[100] In Kimura's case, while she originally faced charges of first-degree murder, carrying a possible death sentence, she was allowed to plead no contest to two reduced counts of voluntary manslaughter.[101] Facing a maximum sentence of thirteen years in prison,[102] Kimura was ultimately sentenced to five years' probation, ordered to undergo psychiatric treatment, and credited fully for one year served in the county jail.[103] Again, an American judge was sufficiently persuaded by evidence that the practice was acceptable in the defendant's home culture to justify the imposition of a far lower sentence than might otherwise have been handed down.

A "Chinese" Response to Adultery. Finally, consider the judge's remarkable decision in *People v. Chen,*[104] in which a Chinese immigrant to the United States admitted killing his wife with a claw hammer following her admission of infidelity. The defense attorney was allowed to present an expert who testified that Chen's violent reaction was typical of a Chinese male confronted with infidelity and that "Chinese react in a much more violent way to those circumstances than someone from our own society," because the

96. Tamara Jones, "Cultural Shock: Crimes Split Legal Experts — U.S., Japan Views Differ on Mother-Child Suicide," *The Record,* 13 October 1985, at A29.

97. Coleman, supra note 95, at 1142.

98. Todd R. Eastham, "Family Suicide: A Tapestry of Love and Death," *United Press International,* 16 June 1985.

99. Id.

100. "Kids' Deaths: Japanese Mom Pleads No Contest," *The Record,* 20 October 1985, at A28.

101. Mary Ann Galante, "Mother Guilty in Drownings," *Nat'l L.J.,* 4 November 1985, at 10.

102. Id.

103. "Mother Placed on Probation in 2 Drownings," *Los Angeles Times,* 21 November 1985, at 1.

104. No. 87-774 slip op. (N.Y. Sup. Ct. Dec. 2, 1988).

adultery indicates that the man has lost "the most minimal standard of control over his wife."[105] The judge was sufficiently impressed by this testimony to acquit Chen of the murder charges; instead, he found Chen guilty only of second-degree manslaughter. "Were this crime . . . committed by the defendant as someone born and raised in America, or born elsewhere but primarily raised in America, even in the Chinese American community," the judge conceded, "the Court would have been constrained to find the defendant guilty of manslaughter in the first-degree." However, Chen was defined by the all-too-sympathetic judge as "someone who is essentially born in China, raised in China, and took all his Chinese culture with him except the community which would moderate his behavior," therefore justifying the reduction to manslaughter in the second degree.[106]

Ironically, this last reference to "the community which would moderate his behavior" was a reference to the expert's testimony that Chinese practice (in China) is not in fact to kill the betraying wife; instead, the surrounding community, while sanctioning certain actions (presumably including violence) against the wife, would nonetheless counsel against such extreme measures. So Chen benefitted from the fact that he had brought only the worst of his culture (at least according to the judge) and not the whole culture, which would have included norms of restraint as well as violence. In an important way, Chen was able to use the *absence* of his culture to get away with murdering his unfaithful partner. In any event, Chen was viewed, because of his culture, as lacking certain abilities to engage in self-control that would have been expected of any better-socialized American.

One might, of course, object to the judge's decision in the *Chen* case because it is so protective of male violence against women, not to mention the fact that there was no plausible claim that the defendant's culture included a "duty" to kill his wife, a claim that was arguably present in Kimura's killing her children as part of an attempt at parent-child suicide. Ayelet Shachar accurately describes the decision in cases like Chen's as demonstrating deference "to a group's *nomos,* even when a group's practices systematically expose certain categories of group members, such as women, to sanctioned intra-group maltreatment."[107] Such a policy of nonintervention is pursued

105. Cathy C. Cardillo, Note, "Violence against Chinese Women: Defining the Cultural Role," 19 *Women's Rights L. Rev.* 85, 92 (1997).

106. Id. at 93.

107. Ayelet Shachar, "Reshaping the Multicultural Model: Group Accommodation and Individual Rights," 8 *Windsor Rev. Leg. Soc. Issues* 83, 95 (1998).

on the assumption that it is the most neutral approach that the state can take to an ethnic or cultural group. Instead, however, it "inadvertently partakes in maintaining intra-group power relations, and in legitimizing the position of those already in power to speak as the authoritative interpreters of that culture."[108] Similarly, here — to the extent that it is even accurate to say that it is part of Chinese culture that men beat their wives, which is questionable[109] — an ostensibly noninterventionist policy has very concrete and nonneutral effects on the vulnerable members of that group.[110]

This helps to explain why political theorist Susan Okin has plausibly argued that multiculturalism is "bad for women"[111] and thus not worthy of the (unthinking) support often given it. Indeed, she has suggested that female members of a patriarchal culture — and should it matter whether patriarchy is derived from "religious" or more secular "cultural" norms? — might "be much better off if the culture into which they were born were either to become extinct (so that its members would become integrated into the less sexist surrounding culture) or, preferably, be encouraged to alter itself, so as to reinforce the equality of women — at least to the degree to which this value is upheld in the majority of culture."[112] A grim example supporting Okin's point is provided by the sentencing by a Pakistani tribal council, in June 2002, of a young woman to be gang-raped as retribution for a crime allegedly committed by her brother.[113] In an op-ed comment by a

---

108. Id. at 99–100.

109. Shortly after the *Chen* decision came down, the executive director of the Organization of Chinese American Women in New York said: "It's not the Chinese culture that says a husband can kill a wife. One's cultural background is not an excuse for murder." Judith Lyons, "Chinese Wife Killer Gets Probation," *Asian Week,* 19 May 1989 (quoted in Cardillo, supra note 105, at 93).

110. The New York Asian Women's Center received multiple phone calls and visits from women who were afraid of their husbands; one husband told his wife that "If this is the kind of sentence you get for killing your wife, I could do anything to you. I have the money for a good attorney." Alexis Jetter, "Fear Is Legacy of Wife Killing in Chinatown; Battered Asians Shocked by Husband's Probation," *New York Newsday,* 26 November 1989, at 4 (quoted in Holly Maguigan, "Cultural Evidence and Male Violence: Are Feminist and Multiculturalist Reformers on a Collision Course?" 70 *N.Y.U. L. Rev.* 36, 94 (1995)).

111. Susan Moller Okin, "Is Multiculturalism Bad for Women?" in *Is Multiculturalism Bad for Women?* (Josh Cohen et al., eds., 1999).

112. Id. at 22–23.

113. See Ian Fisher, "Account of Punjab Rape Tells of a Brutal Society," *New York Times,* 12 July 2002, at A3.

Pakistani journalist, Beena Sarwar, under the title "Brutality Cloaked as Tradition,"[114] she writes:

> In the tribal parts of Pakistan, local men are seizing more power via religion or tradition. . . . [Or consider] Zahid Shah, a mentally disturbed young man in another Punjabi village who was accused of blasphemy by a cleric and stoned to death by an enraged mob barely a week before the Jaranwala case [and its sentence of rape]. Blasphemy carries a death sentence in any case, but the accused are often killed by vigilantes. . . . Meanwhile, the government is gradually handing over the rights of women as citizens and indeed as human beings to tribal elders in a society that has, to a degree, long considered women as lesser beings, family property and repositories of the family honor. . . .

There is no good reason for one to tolerate such outrages. It is difficult, indeed, for one to believe that the world would not be better off if such cultures (or aspects of culture)[115] simply disappeared. If we share Okin's skepticism about the desirability of automatically accepting the virtues of "multiculturalism," there is no good reason to limit that skepticism to what might be called "secular" multiculturalism as against deviant cultures grounded on "religious" norms. Does any reader, for example, think that it makes a difference in the Pakistani case whether the local elders are enforcing their "cultural traditions" instead of what they conceive to be required by Islamic law?[116]

In any event, the implication of those who strongly defend accepting the

---

114. Beena Sarwar, "Brutality Cloaked as Tradition," *New York Times*, 6 August 2002, at A15.

115. Leti Volpp emphasizes that "[w]e sometimes assume culture to be static and insular, a fixed property of groups rather than an entity constantly created through relationships. This assumption is made much more frequently for outsider communities. . . . " Instead, we must always be aware of the "hybridity, fluidity, and complexity" of all cultures. See Volpp, "Blaming Culture for Bad Behavior," 12 *Yale J.L. & Human.* 89, 94 (2000). This is true enough, but, as a pragmatic matter, it is unsurprising that the victims of the Pakistani "traditional culture" are more impressed by the rigidity of the culture than of its potential flexibility. It does, however, remind us that one need not condemn an entire culture in order to believe that parts of it are terrible and merit elimination.

116. Douglas Laycock has reminded us that even under RFRA, religious burdens are permissible if justified by a "compelling state interest," and it is unthinkable that the United States would in fact allow analogous conduct. Indeed, RFRA was provoked, as indicated earlier, by the fact that many courts have been quite unwilling to require any significant accommodation of those whose religious observances put them at odds with secular (or even "mainstream religious") society.

priority of ostensible cultural imperatives, including those who defend the so-called cultural defenses discussed above, is that a person's behavior is simply ordained, or at least determined in large part, by his or her cultural dictates. In important senses it is the culture itself that is culpable, not the actor charged with the offense, who is "encumbered" within a given cultural "script"—what Yale professor Jack Balkin has termed "cultural software"[117]—that leads to individuals playing one set of roles rather than another in their enacted lives. Perhaps we might believe that persons have more choice of secular than of religious scripts, but it is not clear how one would prove any such assertion.

The issue of choice is one that plays a major part in our conceptions of both religion and culture as a whole. Martin Luther's claim that "Here I stand; I can do no other" can be read quite literally. That is, recognizing the authority of the Pope would so violate his sense of who he had become that he simply could not do it. As suggested earlier, to the extent that Luther was "the first Protestant," he can probably be viewed more accurately as making a claim of "conscience" than of culture. Once Protestantism is adopted by millions of people, however, it obviously starts looking far more like a "culture," in terms of its subscribers feeling compelled to act in accordance with its tenets, and later Lutherans could as easily be viewed as involving "cultural" norms that do indeed "compel" obedience. Once one recognizes that one can as easily feel compelled by "cultural" as by "religious" norms, we are still left with the problem of explaining what distinguishes our response to them.

Perhaps the central distinction involves our description of what compels the behavior in question. To say that one is "religiously" compelled instead of "culturally" compelled is not simply a difference in nomenclature. Rather, one may often be saying, in the former instance, that one is submitting to a divinely dictated command where disobedience would bring with it the threat of punishment, perhaps lasting for an eternity, in an afterlife, a fear that is presumably quite different from the standard-instance claim of cultural compulsion. Consider in this context the following comment by two ethicists discussing the willingness of society to require that the children of Jehovah's Witnesses get blood transfusions over their parents' objections:

> Lurking in this choice is the bias of a secular society that values the body over the spirit. If courts and bioethics scholars really believed that the

117. J. M. Balkin, *Cultural Software* (1998).

child's soul existed independently after death and would be condemned to eternal damnation, they might not order blood transfusions [or, presumably, engage in other parental regulation like that described above] over the objections of parents. . . . But in our secular society, judges have unanimously agreed to rank the danger of eternal damnation below the possibility of death.[118]

Two questions immediately arise, however. One, of course, involves the point that not all "religions" — especially as defined by American courts — include reference to supernatural divinities who issue ascertainable commands. All of the so-called Abrahamic religions — Judaism, Christianity, and Islam — do indeed ask us to picture a Sovereign God, but this is not true, for example, of Buddhism. Secondly, even religions that include reference to a supernatural divinity might not view its divinity as issuing commands whose disobedience will trigger punishment.[119]

It is illuminating to return to the example of Christian Scientist parents. They might indeed decline to obtain medical treatment for a child simply because that would constitute disobedience to divine will. There seems no doubt that this captures the phenomenological reality of many Christian Scientists. In this respect, they are identical to Jehovah's Witnesses, who claim to be following a divine command not to "drink blood" when they resist blood transfusions.

But there may be a vital difference between the Jehovah's Witnesses and the Christian Scientists. The Witnesses apparently believe that one is damned, presumably for an eternity, if one violates the divine commandment. The possible sacrifice of one's brief time on Earth is a cheap price to

118. Nancy Dubler and David Nimmons, *Ethics on Call* 272 (1992), quoted in April L. Cherry, "The Free Exercise Rights of Pregnant Women Who Refuse Medical Treatment," 69 *Tenn. L. Rev.* 563, 589 (2002).

119. Which is not to say, of course, that even claims of the threat of dire divine punishment necessarily compel acquiescence in the believers' claims, as revealed in the Jehovah's Witnesses cases. Such cases present the most dramatic conflict between secular and religious sensibilities precisely because anyone upholding the rejection of parental authority, as we do, must, as Professors Dubler and Nimmons suggest, also reject as ontologically and epistemologically meaningless the claims asserted by the parents as to the consequences of the transfusion. If *we* genuinely believed that the children would be faced with eternal damnation, it is hard to believe that we would not in fact stay the state's interventionist hand. But neither we nor, we suspect, those likely to read this book in fact find the Witnesses' assertions anything other than "bizarre" or, at the least, less immediately "compelling" than the "compelling interest" that law recognizes in saving a child's life.

pay if the cost of gaining a few added years is eternal damnation. It is not at all clear, however, whether Christian Science presents similarly dire options. On the one hand, some adherents clearly believe that a commitment to Christian Science simply does not permit resort to medical treatment,[120] and Eddy's teachings themselves caution that using a traditional medical remedy will only detract from the efficacy of the prayer treatment.[121] Yet the institutional church itself explicitly says that followers will suffer no punishment, such as excommunication or even condemnation,[122] should they seek ordinary medical treatment. The church's doctrines imply that whatever the results in this life of failing to adhere to the church's proscriptions against medical care, the tenets of the religion apparently include no threat of hell in the afterlife.[123] Christian Science appears to be about striving towards a closer relationship with God;[124] procuring medical treatment may lead to greater distance from the divine in this lifetime, but this is not the result of divine "punishment."

Things get even more complicated if one's adherence to religious observance is "habitual" rather than the felt fidelity to divine command. Both of us, for example, would define ourselves as "secular Jews," which means, among other things, that neither of us feels ourselves truly "bound" or "obligated" to the Halakhic covenant that Orthodox Jews trace back to the purported encounter between God and Moses at Sinai. Yet we follow a number of Jewish dietary restrictions, including the prohibitions against eating pork or shellfish, though neither of us fears the slightest "punishment," divine or otherwise, should we deviate.[125] Our behavior is, perhaps, little different from traditional Southerners who insist that one must eat black-eyed peas on New Year's Day in order to reaffirm traditional values

120. *Rippberger,* supra note 30, at 1678–79.

121. Eddy, supra note 22, at 169–70.

122. First Church of Christ, Scientist, Questions and Answers (accessed 30 January 2002), ⟨http://www.tfccs.com/gv/qanda/csq19.jhtml⟩. It may be worth noting that this information is gleaned from a distinctly "public" source available to anyone interested in gaining more information about Christian Science. Some religions have decidedly esoteric tenets that are revealed only to active adherents, though we have no particular reason to believe that Christian Science is like, say, Scientology in this respect.

123. Id.

124. Id.

125. Rachel Levinson writes, however, that "While I don't believe in God, if I did, I would believe in an angry God—so perhaps there's a little element of hedging my bets in adhering to certain traditional Jewish practices."

(and, one hopes, gain a measure of good luck for the coming year). That is, it reflects "only" our cultural heritage — and our continuing identification with a Jewish community that is defined, among other ways, by dietary customs. Does this matter?

Several years ago, before the Supreme Court invalidated RFRA, one of us (Sanford Levinson) was intensely involved in an Internet discussion group among constitutional law professors about what constituted a "burden" on the free exercise of religion. He proposed the following hypothetical: Levinson is incarcerated in a federal prison that served pork (and fried all of its food in lard). Would he have a right to be served other food?[126] Everyone on the list agreed that if he were an Orthodox Jew, phenomenologically involved in a covenant with God that included, among its demands, the eating only of kosher food, then it would be an easy case under RFRA. But, of course, Levinson is not such a Jew; he is, as already indicated, a "secular Jew" who happens to observe certain dietary restrictions out of a mixture of habit and a desire to maintain a cultural identification with the Jewish community. He does not, however, "keep kosher" in any general sense: He gladly eats nonkosher beef or chicken and would, for example, be completely happy, in the hypothetical, to be served nonkosher beef, even accompanied by cheese, in lieu of the forbidden pork.

At least one distinguished law professor, one of the leading authorities in the United States on the relationship between law and religion (and the potential meaning of RFRA), declared that Levinson should *not* prevail under RFRA. He could not, that is, posit the existence of a genuine "religious burden," which for this professor did indeed seem linked, at the very least, to a genuinely felt "obligation" to divine authority and, moreover, possibly to some fear of divine sanction for disobedience. For him, Levinson would be analogous to the traditional Southerner mentioned above, "demanding" black-eyed peas on New Year's Day, or an Albanian demanding some special food on some day special to that ethnic group. These latter are clearly "only" cultural customs entitled to no special recognition, and so, it was argued, was Levinson's distaste for lard-saturated food.[127]

Sanford Levinson confesses that he could think of no particularly good

---

126. There is no doubt, incidentally, that RFRA applied to prisons. Indeed, some of the most vigorous opposition to the Act came from prison wardens who objected to the possible "intervention" in their institutions.

127. For a view more supportive to Levinson's hypothetical claim, see Douglas Laycock, "Religious Liberty as Liberty," 7 *J. Contemp. Legal Issues* 313, 335 (1996).

reason why he *should* prevail in a RFRA claim even as our ethnic claimant would fail. Perhaps the best reason is that we would object to the state's making the kinds of specific inquiries into the nature of our religious beliefs necessary to ascertain the particular kinds of "commitments" or "obligations" one claims to possess. From this perspective, if it is the case that Jews historically do not eat certain foods because of what were communally shared beliefs that God prohibited them on pain of punishment, that is enough to protect anyone who today identifies him- or herself as "Jewish" even if one's "Judaism" is defined in secular terms. But consider the possible paradox if the secular Jew is protected while a committed (secular and non–religiously identified) vegetarian would not be, even if the vegetarian in question is a committed ("encumbered") member of a community that believes that killing sentient beings is the equivalent of murder and that eating them is the moral equivalent of cannibalism. Surely she feels the same kind of violation of self as, say, a conscientious objector sent to war.

The issue of *kashruth* underscores the important fact that there is no necessary connection between religious imperatives and what we ordinarily view as "morality." Sanford Levinson does not in the least regard the eating of pork as "immoral"; more importantly, neither does even the most Orthodox view of Judaism. The ban on eating pork (or any other unkosher food) is a *legal* requirement imposed by Jewish law on Jews, nothing more, nothing less. Non-Jews are not bound, which is an obvious clue to its basically amoral status if, at least, one links the concept of a "moral" point of view with some kind of universalization. Jewish doctrine does recognize seven "Noachide" laws that are indeed binding on all humans and that are clearly "moral" in their thrust, but a key point made by Maimonides and other analysts of Jewish law is that there is no necessary "rationale," including, of course, a moral rationale, for many Jewish laws binding only on members of the Jewish community. What makes them obligatory on those Jews who conform to Halakhic injunctions is that they are commanded. God, in effect, is like King Lear, who emphasized to his recalcitrant daughter that she should "reason not the need" when being presented with his rather arbitrary desires. One should simply behave as commanded. And if, like non-Jews, one has not accepted the yoke of Siniatic covenant, one obviously has no need to honor the "commands" purportedly issued at Sinai.

Whatever rationale might exist for "accommodating" a religious Jew by providing a pork-free diet, then, it has literally nothing to do with morality. And if, as we have seen, it is based on protecting the religious Jew from facing the prospect of divine punishment for violating divine command, that rationale makes no sense with regard not only to the "secular Jew," who is perhaps better analyzed as an adherent to "Jewish culture" than to "Jewish religion," but also to those religious traditions that do not include notions of divine punishment or even chastisement within their theologies.

SIGNIFICANCE OF GOOD-FAITH INTENTIONS

One could imagine viewing religiously based actions in terms of "good faith." The Newmarks, for instance, chose to forego treating their child not because they wished him ill, but precisely because they believed that God would step in and provide a cure. In the Chen case, in contrast, it is impossible to offer a "good-faith" rationale for murdering his wife with a claw hammer. Instead, he claimed that the law should excuse his horrendous action because of his particular cultural background. Still, the absence or presence of "sincere good intentions" scarcely serves to explain or to resolve the tension between the treatment of "religion" and the treatment of "culture."

Even if we believe that "good faith" is indeed worthy of automatic respect, itself a controversial premise, there is no reason to assume that those claiming religious grounds for their actions are any more "sincere" (or, more to the point, any less "strategic") in their presentation than those willing to rely simply on the importance of their cultural traditions. The Free Exercise Clause generates what economists would call an "incentive" to frame one's claims as "religious,"[128] since, as we have seen, the legal system, at least on occasion, looks with favor on such claims. And, of course, there is also an incentive to appear sincere in making such claims. But we have no good way to read a person's mind in order to determine the degree of good faith that underlies any particular claim, nor, of course, are we willing to assess the "truth" of religious claims.

In any event, there is no reason whatsoever to believe that Juliet Cheng was any less sincere or in good faith than the Christian Scientists. All of the parents provided care of a type that they genuinely believed would help heal their child; similar identity of good faith is presumably present with regard to Amish or hippie parents who want to protect their children from the ravages of what they perceive as sanctity- or life-destroying surrounding

128. As seen, perhaps, with regard to the "Church of Marijuana." One has to be very generous indeed not to be quite suspicious of the religious bona fides of its membership and to wonder if they would bother structuring themselves as members of a "church" if society provided strong protection to deviant nonreligious subcultures.

cultures. And Peterson and a typical Klansman are, no doubt, equally sincere in their desire to preserve a culture predicated on white supremacy and the subordination of other, "inferior," cultures. We might well, of course, want to emphasize one of the essential differences between the Amish and the Klansmen, which is that the latter, far from wanting simply to be "left alone" by the surrounding society, instead wish actively to engage with that society through acts of confrontation ranging from "in-your-face" marches to acts of horrendous violence. Note well, though, that this kind of defense suggests that the Klan might be allowed to educate their children in schools devoted to perpetuating the ideology of White Supremacy. This is, obviously, a controversial issue, but should it be any more controversial, say, than the right of Islamic fundamentalists in the United States to educate their children in *madrasses* that teach hatred of the United States and its secular culture and at least a measure of respect, if not outright support, for Osama bin Laden and his confederates?

Moreover, it is obvious that the presence of good faith does not guarantee the larger society's approval — or even "tolerance" — of a group's practices. The Christian Science parents who treated their children with prayer healing had nothing but good faith; the courts took careful notice of that fact, but determined nonetheless that the parents' actions had to be analyzed according to the objective reasonableness of their beliefs, not the subjective motivations behind them. Even if adherents to given cultures and religions could be further subdivided by reference to the presence of honorable and dishonorable intentions, that distinction in itself would not begin to explain the different legal treatment of the two.

Conclusion

It should be clear that religion and culture, even those aspects of culture that are separable from religion, are not easily distinguishable. They are not fully differentiable either in theory or in application. Religion often is but a part of culture; to claim that they are completely distinct would be logically incoherent. As we have seen, religion does not necessarily triumph over nonreligious culture in terms of being easily definable, nor do we seem to be helped by looking for different kinds of felt compulsion to conform to its precepts. The most important analytical difference appears to be the felt threat of divine punishment, but, as we have also seen with regard to the Christian Science cases, the law ultimately does not seem to turn on whether a particular church's theology includes the presence of such threats. And there is certainly no reason to believe that Seeger's and Peterson's "religion-like" ultimate concerns that brought them within the ambit of statutory protection included any notion that either faced punishment beyond his own bad conscience should he be forced to collaborate with inquity.

Might anything else (beyond, as mentioned at the outset, the happenstance of constitutional text) explain the general differences in treatment accorded "religious" as against "cultural" claims? Might it be relevant, for example, that many colonial Americans (including those we identify as "framers of the Constitution") were fleeing religious oppression in England, and therefore gave priority to protection of religion in this country? For a group fearful of tyranny of the majority, protecting religion more stringently than culture might make sense. The idea of a religion of one is coherent in a way that a culture of one is not (again, see Luther) — and the danger of tyranny is more real when it is practiced by a group against only one. One person can receive a revelation from God, and though we may disagree with the message, we may be willing to credit the sincerity of the belief that it happened. There is no culture, by contrast, without regularized norms and some sort of community. That community may dwindle, may come under attack, or may promote practices that we find undesirable, but without community, and shared practices, there is no culture. Perhaps, then, laws and constitutional provisions exist to protect religion because one person standing against the masses has little else with which to buttress himself, while a person sharing a common culture must by definition share it with someone else, and they as a group can protect themselves through ordinary political means against attackers.

All of this being said and (possibly) conceded, it is still difficult to explain why anyone who is genuinely "wrestling with diversity" should feel him- or herself more "pinned down," as it were, by religious as against "cultural" claims. Life in a "diverse" or a "multicultural" society surely requires that one genuinely learn to live with groups that are quite different from one another, whatever the sociological or metaphysical bases of their differences, at least until a given group presents genuine threats to "outsiders" (or to vulnerable "insiders" such as children). Lawyers may have to continue to emphasize the importance of religion-based "exercise," but it is not clear why the rest of us should be in thrall to the particular text of the United States Constitution in this way.[129]

This is not to argue, of course, that there is any necessarily correct answer to the dilemmas posed by "diversity." Though the essays in this book are, generally speaking, more sympathetic than not to claims made in behalf of "diversity," it should be clear that they also reflect some degree of skepticism about the ability to rely with any great confidence on the concept to provide specific answers. (This was the theme of the first essay in this collection.) Indeed, we are sympathetic with Stanley Fish's acerbic distinction between "boutique multiculturalism" and "strong multiculturalism."[130]

Boutique multiculturalists, he argues, "will always stop short of approving other cultures at a point where some value at their center generates an act that offends against the canons of civilized decency as they have been either declared or assumed" by the culture from which one is peering outward.[131] He offers as a challenge to those who consider themselves "multiculturalists" or devotees of what might be termed "strong diversity" the *fatwa* issued in Iran against Salman Rushdie for his blasphemy against Islam in *Satanic Verses;* obviously, the cases involving "cultural defenses" to crimes committed against women or children also present similar challenges, as does, even more dramatically, the punishment inflicted in Pakistan on the helpless young woman for her brother's alleged misdeeds.

Among other things this suggests once more the futility of looking for an abstract set of "principles" that will necessarily provide definitive answers to the kinds of questions raised throughout this book. As Robert Post has written, any discussion must be "relentlessly contextual" and "deeply dependent upon the particular substance and specific history" of the various claimants, including, of course, the state that claims the right to disrupt what are asserted to be cultural or religious rights.[132] Both political theorists and lawyers may be disturbed by the suggestion that there are few, if any, principles or legal concepts that offer solutions to our dilemmas and that,

---

129. Indeed, one could write a separate essay (which we shall not do) on how the Free Speech Clause of the First Amendment or the Equal Protection Clause of the Fourteenth Amendment (not to mention the Establishment Clause of the First Amendment) requires that "culture"-based exercises receive the same levels of protection as do religion-based ones.

130. Stanley Fish, "Boutique Multiculturalism," in *The Trouble with Principle* 56 (1999).

131. Id.

132. See Robert C. Post, "Law and Cultural Conflict" 26 (unpublished manuscript).

instead, one will almost necessarily respond to the exigencies of specific cases and their contexts. But if one could truly "pin" the dilemmas posed by "diversity" to the mat, then the duty to "wrestle with diversity" would come to an end and a winner could simply be declared. Instead, as with other basic existential questions, the wrestling is a permanent condition.

Bibliography

Adler, Nancy J. *International Dimensions of Organizational Behavior,* 2d ed. Boston: Kent, 1991.

Ahlstrom, Sydney E. *A Religious History of the American People.* New Haven: Yale University Press, 1972.

Aleinikoff, Thomas Alexander, et al. *Immigration and Citizenship: Process and Policy,* 4th ed. St. Paul, Minn.: West, 1998.

Allegretti, Joseph. "Christ and the Code: The Dilemma of the Christian Attorney." *Catholic Lawyer* 34 (1988): 131.

Anderson, Benedict. *Imagined Communities,* rev. ed. New York: Verso, 1991.

Asante, Molefi K. *The Afrocentric Idea.* Philadelphia: Temple University Press, 1987.

——. *Kemet, Afrocentricity, and Knowledge.* Trenton, N.J.: Africa World Press, 1990.

Audi, Robert. "Religion and the Ethics of Political Participation." Review of *Religious Convictions and Political Choice,* by Kent Greenawalt. *Ethics* 100 (1990): 386.

——. "The Separation of Church and State and the Obligations of Citizenship." *Philosophy and Public Affairs* 18 (1989): 259.

Auerbach, Jerold S. "Law and Lawyers." In *Jewish-American History and Culture: An Encyclopedia,* edited by Jack Fischel and Sanford Pinsker. New York: Garland, 1992.

——. *Rabbis and Lawyers: The Journey from Torah to Constitution.* Bloomington: Indiana University Press, 1990.

——. *Unequal Justice: Lawyers and Social Change in Modern America.* New York: Oxford University Press, 1976.

Avineri, Shlomo. *The Making of Modern Zionism: Intellectual Origins of the Jewish State.* New York: Basic Books, 1981.

Baker, Liva. *Felix Frankfurter.* New York: Coward-McCann, 1969.

Balkin, J. M. *Cultural Software.* New Haven: Yale University Press, 1998.

Barnes, Fred. "Rev. Bill." *The New Republic,* 3 January 1994.

Bates, Stephen. *Battleground: One Mother's Crusade, the Religious Right, and the Struggle for Control of Our Classrooms.* New York: Poseidon Press, 1993.

Bellah, Robert, et al. *Habits of the Heart.* Berkeley: University of California Press, 1985.

Beschle, Donald L. "The Establishment Clause and Religion in Child Custody Disputes: Factoring Religion into the Best Interest Equation." *Michigan Law Review* 82 (1984): 1701.

——. "God Bless the Child? The Use of Religion as a Factor in Child Custody and Adoption Proceedings." *Fordham Law Review* 58 (1989): 383.

Bickel, Alexander M. *The Morality of Consent.* New Haven: Yale University Press, 1975.

Bigongiari, Dino, ed. "First Part of the Second Part of the Summa Theologicam." In *The Political Ideas of St. Thomas Aquinas.* New York: Hafner, 1953.

Bleich, J. David. "Jewish Law and the State's Authority to Punish Crime." *Cardozo Law Review* 12 (1991): 829.

Bloom, Harold. *The American Religion: The Emergence of the Post-Christian Nation.* New York: Simon and Schuster, 1992.

Borden, Morton. *Jews, Turks and Infidels.* Chapel Hill: University of North Carolina Press, 1984.

Bork, Robert. *The Tempting of America: The Political Seduction of the Law.* New York: Free Press, 1980.

Bowen, William G., and Derek Bok. *The Shape of the River: Long-Term Consequences of Considering Race in College and University Admissions.* Princeton: Princeton University Press, 1998.

Bradley, Gerard. "Dogmatomachy: A 'Privatization' Theory of the Religion Clause Cases." *St. Louis University Law Journal* 30 (1986): 275.

——. "No Religious Test Clause and the Constitution of Religious Liberty: A Machine That Would Go of Itself." *Case Western Reserve Law Review* 37 (1987): 673.

Bressler, Dov. "Arbitration and the Courts in Jewish Law." *Journal of Halacha and Contemporary Society* 9 (1985): 105.

Brest, Paul, et al., eds. *Processes of Constitutional Decisionmaking: Cases and Materials,* 4th ed. Gaithersburg, N.Y.: Aspen Publishing, 2000.

Brewer, Scott. "Figuring the Law: Holism and Tropological Inference in Legal Interpretation." *Yale Law Journal* 97 (1988): 823.

Brighouse, Harry. "Is There Any Such Thing As Political Liberalism?" *Pacific Philosophical Quarterly* 75 (1994): 318.

Brimelow, Peter. *Alien Nation: Common Sense about America's Immigration Disaster.* New York: Random House, 1995.

Bronner, Ethan. *Battle for Justice: How the Bork Nomination Shook America.* New York: Norton, 1989.

Brown, Kevin. "Do African-Americans Need Immersion Schools? The Paradox Created by Legal Conceptualization of Race and Public Education." *Iowa Law Review* 78 (1993): 813.

Broyde, Michael J. "On the Practice of Law According to Halacha." *Journal of Halacha and Contemporary Society* 20 (1990): 5.

Brubaker, Rogers. *Citizenship and Nationhood in France and Germany.* Cambridge: Harvard University Press, 1992.

Burt, Robert. *Two Jewish Justices: Outcasts in the Promised Land.* Berkeley: University of California Press, 1987.

Bushnell, Horace. *American Writing on Popular Education: The Nineteenth Century,* edited by Rush Welter. New York: Bobbs-Merrill, 1971.

Buss, Emily. "The Adolescent's Stake in the Allocation of Educational Control Between Parent and State." *University of Chicago Law Review* 67 (2000): 1233.

Callan, Eamonn. *Creating Citizens.* Oxford: Oxford University Press, 1997.

Cardillo, Cathy C. "Violence against Chinese Women: Defining the Cultural Role." *Women's Rights Law Review* 19 (1997): 85.

Cardozo, Benjamin. *The Nature of the Judicial Process.* New Haven: Yale University Press, 1921.

Carens, Joseph. "Immigration and the Welfare State." In *Democracy and the Welfare State,* edited by Amy Gutmann. Princeton: Princeton University Press, 1988.

Carrington, Paul. "The Theme of Early American Law Teaching: The Political Ethics of Francis Lieber." *Journal of Legal Education* 42 (1992): 339.

Carter, Stephen L. *The Culture of Disbelief: How American Law and Politics Trivialize Religious Devotion.* New York: Basic Books, 1993.

——. "Strife's Dominion." Review of *Life's Dominion,* by Ronald Dworkin. *The New Yorker,* 9 August 1993.

——. "The Religiously Devout Judge." *Notre Dame Law Review* 64 (1989): 932.

Chávez, Lydia. *The Color Bind: California's Battle to End Affirmative Action.* Berkeley: University of California Press, 1998.

Cherry, April L. "The Free Exercise Rights of Pregnant Women Who Refuse Medical Treatment." *Tennessee Law Review* 69 (2002): 563.

Clark, David S. "Transnational Legal Practice: The Need for Global Law Schools." *American Journal of Comparative Law* 46 (1998): 261.

Clifford, James. *The Predicament of Culture.* Cambridge: Harvard University Press, 1988.

Cohen, Alfred S. "On Maintaining a Professional Confidence." *Journal of Halacha and Contemporary Society* 7 (1984): 84.

Cohen, Haim H. "Attorney." In *The Principles of Jewish Law,* edited by Menachem Elon. Jerusalem: Encyclopedia Judaica, 1975.

Cohen, Steven M. *American Modernity and Jewish Identity.* Bloomington: Indiana University Press, 1983.

Coleman, Doriane Lambelet. "Individualizing Justice through Multiculturalism: The Liberals' Dilemma." *Columbia Law Review* 96 (1996): 1093.

Coleman, Ron. "A Lawyer and His Sabbath." *Student Lawyer,* December 1987.

Connolly, William E. *The Terms of Political Discourse,* 2d ed. Princeton: Princeton University Press, 1983.

Coser, Lewis A. *Greedy Institutions: Patterns of Undivided Commitment.* New York: Free Press, 1974.

Cover, Robert. *Justice Accused.* New Haven: Yale University Press, 1975.

Cowley, Geoffrey, and Lauren Picker. "Does Doctor Know Best?" *Newsweek,* 24 September 1990.

Crane, Daniel A. "Beyond RFRA: Free Exercise of Religion Comes of Age in the State Courts." *St. Thomas Law Review* 10 (1998): 235.

Crosson, Frederick J. "Religion and Natural Law." *CCIA Annual: Liberty and Law: Civil and Religious* 8 (1989): 75.

Culler, Jonathan. "Political Criticism: Confronting Religion." In *Framing the Sign: Criticism and Its Institutions.* Norman: University of Oklahoma Press, 1988.

Cuomo, Mario. "Religious Belief and Public Morality: A Catholic Governor's Perspective," 13 September 1984 (unpublished manuscript).

Curry, Thomas J. *The First Freedoms: Church and State in America to the Passage of the First Amendment.* New York: Oxford University Press, 1986.

D'Amato, Anthony, and Arthur J. Jacobson. *Justice and the Legal System: A Coursebook.* Cincinnati: Anderson, 1992.

Dalin, David G., ed. *American Jews and the Separationist Faith: The New Debate on Religion in Public Life.* Washington, D.C.: Ethics and Public Policy Center, 1993.

Danelski, David. *A Supreme Court Justice Is Appointed.* New York: Random House, 1964.

Dauer, Edward A., and Arthur Allen Leff. "Correspondence: The Lawyer as Friend." *Yale Law Journal* 86 (1977): 573.

De Crèvecoeur, J. Hector St. John. *Letters from an American Farmer.* New York: Fox, Duffield, 1904 (1782).

Dershowitz, Alan M. *Chutzpah.* Boston: Little Brown, 1991.

DeVille, Kenneth. "Defending Diversity: Affirmative Action and Medical Education." *American Journal of Public Health* 89 (1999): 1256.

Dworkin, Ronald. *Taking Rights Seriously.* Cambridge: Harvard University Press, 1978.

Eddy, Mary Baker. *Science and Health with Key to the Scriptures.* Boston: Writings of Mary Baker Eddy, 1994.

Ely, John Hart. *Democracy and Distrust.* Cambridge: Harvard University Press, 1980.

Epstein, Richard. "The Supreme Court, 1987 Term — Foreword: Unconstitutional Conditions, State Power, and the Limits of Consent." *Harvard Law Review* 102 (1988): 4.

Estlund, Cynthia L. *Working Together: How Workplace Bonds Strengthen a Diverse Democracy.* Oxford: Oxford University Press, 2003.

Evans-Pritchard, Deirdre, and Alison Dundes Renteln. "The Interpretation and Distortion of Culture: A Hmong 'Marriage by Capture' Case in Fresno, California." *Southern California Interdisciplinary Law Journal* 4 (1994): 1.

Finley, Lucinda. "Transcending Equality Theory: A Way Out of the Maternity and the Workplace Debate." *Columbia Law Review* 86 (1986): 1118.

Finnis, John. *Natural Law and Natural Right.* New York: Oxford University Press, 1980.

Fish, Stanley. "Boutique Multiculturalism." In *The Trouble with Principle.* Cambridge: Harvard University Press, 1999.

——. *The Trouble with Principle.* Cambridge: Harvard University Press, 1999.

Fishkin, James. *The Dialogue of Justice.* New Haven: Yale University Press, 1991.

Foner, Eric. *The Story of American Freedom.* New York: Norton, 1998.

Fort, Timothy L. *Law and Religion.* Jefferson, N.C.: McFarland, 1987.

Freedman, Monroe H. "Legal Ethics from a Jewish Perspective." *Texas Tech Law Review* 27 (1996): 1131.

——. "Professional Responsibility of the Criminal Defense Lawyer: The Three Hardest Questions." *Michigan Law Review* 34 (1996): 1469.

French, Rebecca Redwood. "From Yoder to Yoda: Models of Traditional, Modern, and Postmodern Religion in the United States." *Arizona Law Review* 4 (1999): 49.

Fried, Charles. "The Lawyer as Friend: The Moral Foundations of the Lawyer-Client Relation." *Yale Law Journal* 85 (1976): 1060.

Frimer, Dov I. "The Role of the Lawyer in Jewish Law." *Journal of Law and Religion* 1 (1983): 297.

Galinski, Myer. *Pursue Justice: The Administration of Justice in Ancient Israel*. London: Nechdim Press, 1983.

Galston, William. *Liberal Purposes: Goods, Virtues, and Duties in the Liberal State*. Cambridge: Cambridge University Press, 1991.

Geertz, Clifford. *The Interpretation of Cultures*. New York: Basic Books, 1973.

George, Robert. "Moral Particularism, Thomism, and Traditions." *Review of Metaphysics* 42 (1989): 593.

———. "Recent Criticism of Natural Law Theory." Review in *University of Chicago Law Review* 55 (1988): 1371.

Gilligan, Carol. *In a Different Voice*. Cambridge: Harvard University Press: 1982.

Glendon, Mary Ann. *Rights Talk: The Impoverishment of Political Discourse*. New York: Free Press, 1991.

Goffman, Erving. *The Presentation of Self in Everyday Life*. Garden City, N.Y.: Doubleday, 1959.

Goldscheider, Calvin. *Jewish Continuity and Change: Emerging Patterns in America*. Bloomington: Indiana University Press, 1986.

Gordon, Robert W. "Corporate Law Practice as a Public Calling." *Maryland Law Review* 49 (1990): 255.

———. "The Independence of Lawyers." *Boston University Law Review* 68 (1988): 1.

Gordon, Sarah Barringer. *The Mormon Question: Polygamy and Constitutional Conflict in Nineteenth-Century America*. Chapel Hill: University of North Carolina Press, 2002.

Gore, Al. *Earth in the Balance: Ecology and the Human Spirit*. Boston: Houghton Mifflin, 1992.

Greeley, Andrew. "Protestant and Catholic: Is the Analogical Imagination Extinct?" *American Social Review* 54 (1989): 485.

Greenawalt, Kent. *Private Consciences and Public Reasons*. New York: Oxford University Press, 1995.

———. *Religious Convictions and Political Choice*. New York: Oxford University Press, 1988.

———. "Religious Convictions and Political Choice: Some Further Thoughts." *DePaul Law Review* 39 (1990): 1019.

Greenblatt, Stephen. "Culture." In *Critical Terms for Literary Study,* edited by Frank Lentricchia and Thomas McLaughlin. Chicago: University of Chicago Press, 1990.

Greene, Jay. "Why School Choice Can Promote Integration." *Education Week,* 12 April 2000.

———. "Civic Values in Public and Private Schools." In *Learning from School Choice,* edited by Paul E. Peterson and Bryan C. Hassel. Washington, D.C.: Brookings Institution, 1998.

Gutmann, Amy. "Civic Education and Social Diversity." *Ethics* 105, no. 3 (April 1995): 516.

———. *Democratic Education*. Princeton: Princeton University Press, 1987.

Halberstam, Malvina. "Interest Analysis and *Dina De-Malkhuta Dina,* A Comment on Aaron Kirschenbaum, The Sovereign Power of the State: A Proposed Theory of Accommodation in Jewish Law." *Cardozo Law Review* 12 (1991): 951.

Halivni, David Weiss. "Can a Religious Law Be Immoral?" In *Perspectives on Jews and Judaism: Essays in Honor of Wolfe Kelman,* edited by Arthur A. Chiel. New York: Rabbinical Assembly, 1978.

Hall, Timothy L. "Education Diversity: Viewpoints and Proxies." *Ohio State Law Journal* 59 (1998): 551.

Hauerwas, Stanley. "Freedom of Religion: A Subtle Temptation" (unpublished manuscript).

Helmreich, William B. *The World of the Yeshiva: An Intimate Portrait of Orthodox Jewry.* New Haven: Yale University Press, 1986.

Henry, Sue Ellen, and Abe Feuerstein. "Now We Go to Their School: Desegregation and Its Contemporary Legacy." *Journal of Negro Education* 68, no. 2 (Spring 1999): 164.

Herring, Basil F. *Jewish Ethics and Halakha for Our Time: Sources and Commentary.* New York: Ktav, 1984.

Hessler, Peter. "A Rat in My Soup." *The New Yorker,* 24 July 2000.

Hollenbach, David. "The Common Good Revisited." *Theological Studies* 50 (1989): 70.

Hollinger, David. *Postethnic America: Beyond Multiculturalism.* New York: Basic Books, 1995.

Holmes, Oliver Wendell. *Collected Legal Papers.* New York: Harcourt Brace, 1920.

———. *The Common Law.* Boston: Little Brown, 1881.

———. "The Path of the Law." *Harvard Law Review* 10 (1897): 457.

Hostetter, John A. *Amish Society,* 2d ed. Baltimore: Johns Hopkins University Press, 1968.

Hughes, Robert. *The Culture of Complaint.* New York: Oxford University Press, 1993.

Hunter, James D. *Culture Wars.* New York: Basic Books, 1991.

———. *Before the Shooting Begins: Searching for Democracy in America's Culture War.* New York: Free Press, 1994.

Idleman, Scott C. "The Role of Religious Values in Judicial Decision Making." *Indiana Law Review* 27 (1993): 433.

Ignatieff, Michael. *Blood and Belonging: Journeys into the New Nationalism.* New York: Farrar, Straus and Giroux, 1993.

Issacharoff, Samuel. "*Bakke* in the Admissions Office and the Courts: Can Affirmative Action Be Defended?" *Ohio State Law Journal* 59 (1998): 669.

Jeffries, John. *Lewis Powell.* New York: Charles Scribner's Sons, 1994.

Judt, Tony. "The New Old Nationalism." *The New York Review of Books,* 25 May 1994.

Kannar, George. "The Constitutional Catechism of Antonin Scalia." *Yale Law Journal* 99 (1990): 1927.

Kaplan, Justin, ed. *Barlett's Quotations,* 16th ed. Boston: Little, Brown, 1992.

Kirschenbaum, Aaron. "Representation in Litigation in Jewish Law." In *Diné Israel,* 6th ed., edited by Zéev W. Falk and Aaron Kirschenbaum. Tel Aviv: Tel Aviv University, 1975.

Kirschenbaum, Aaron, and John Trafimow. "The Sovereign Power of the State: A Proposed Theory of Accommodation in Jewish Law." *Cardozo Law Review* 12 (1991): 925.

Klingenstein, Susanne. *Jews in the American Academy 1900–1940: The Dynamics of Intellectual Assimilation.* New Haven: Yale University Press, 1991.

Koufax, Sandy. *Koufax.* New York: Viking, 1966.

Kronman, Anthony T. *The Lost Lawyer: Failing Ideals of the Legal Profession.* Cambridge: Harvard University Press, 1993.

Kuper, Adam. *Culture: The Anthropologists' Account.* Cambridge: Harvard University Press, 1999.

Kymlicka, Will. *Liberalism, Community and Culture.* Oxford: Clarendon, 1989.

Kymlicka, Will, and Wayne Norman. "Return of the Citizen: A Survey of Recent Work on Citizenship Theory." *Ethics* 105 (1994): 352.

Lasch, Christopher. "The Revolt of the Elites: Have They Canceled Their Allegiance to America?" *Harper's,* November 1994.

Law, Anna O. "The Diversity Visa Lottery: A Cycle of Unintended Consequences in United States Immigration Policy." *Journal of American Ethnic History* 21, no. 4 (summer 2002): 3–29.

Laycock, Douglas. "Religious Liberty as Liberty." *Journal of Contemporary Legal Issues* 7 (1996): 313.

———. "The Remnants of Free Exercise." *Supreme Court Law Review* (1990): 1.

———. "A Survey of Religious Liberty in the United States." *Ohio State Law Review* 47 (1986): 409.

———. "Towards a General Theory of the Religion Clauses: The Case of Church Labor Relations and the Right to Church Autonomy." *Columbia Law Review* 81 (1981): 1373.

Levine, Peter. *Ellis Island to Ebbets Field: Sport and the Jewish American Experience.* New York: Oxford University Press, 1992.

Levinson, Meira. *The Demands of Liberal Education.* New York: Oxford University Press, 1999.

Levinson, Sanford. *Constitutional Faith.* Princeton: Princeton University Press, 1988.

———. "Constitutional Rhetoric and the Ninth Amendment." *Chicago-Kent Law Review* 64 (1985): 131.

———. "*Hopwood:* Some Reflections on Constitutional Interpretation by an Inferior Court." *Texas Forum on Civil Liberties and Civil Rights* 2 (1996): 113.

———. "The Multicultures of Belief and Disbelief." Review of *The Culture of Disbelief: How American Law and Politics Trivialize Religious Devotion,* by Stephen L. Carter. *Michigan Law Review* 92 (1994): 1873.

———. "On Positivism and Potted Plants: 'Inferior' Judges and the Task of Constitutional Interpretation." *Connecticut Law Review* 25 (1993): 843.

———. "Religious Language and the Public Square." Review of *Love and Power: the Role of Religion and Morality in American Politics,* by Michael J. Perry. *Harvard Law Review* 105 (1992): 2061.

———. "Suffrage and Community: Who Should Vote?" *Florida Law Review* 41 (1989): 545.

———. "Unnatural Law." Review of *The Partial Constitution,* by Cass Sunstein. *The New Republic,* 19–26 July 1993.

———. "Who Is a Jew(ish Justice)?" *Cardozo Law Review* 10 (1989): 2359.

Levinson, Sanford, and J. M. Balkin. "Constitutional Grammar." *Texas Law Review* 72 (1991): 1771.

Levy, Jacob T. "Liberalism's Divide: After Socialism and Before." *Social Philosophy and Policy* 20, no. 1 (2003).

———. "Language Rights, Literacy, and the Modern State." In *Language Rights and Political Theory,* edited by Will Kymlicka and Alan Patten. Oxford: Oxford University Press, 2003.

Lichtenstein, Aharon. "Does Jewish Tradition Recognize an Ethic Independent of Halakha?" In *Modern Jewish Ethics,* edited by Marvin Fox. Columbus: Ohio State University Press, 1975.

Loewy, Arnold H. "Taking *Bakke* Seriously: Distinguishing Diversity from Affirmative Action in the Law School Admissions Process." *North Carolina Law Review* 77 (1999): 1479.

Lowe Jr., Eugene Y., ed. *Promise and Dilemma: Perspectives on Racial Diversity and Higher Education.* Princeton: Princeton University Press, 1999.

Luban, David. *Lawyers and Justice.* Princeton: Princeton University Press, 1988.

Luckey, William. "The Role of Religion in Modern Democracy in the Political Thought of John Courtney Murray, S.J. 3." August–September 1989 (unpublished manuscript).

Lukács, Georg. *History and Class Consciousness.* Cambridge: MIT Press, 1971.

Ly, Choua. "The Conflict between Law and Culture: The Case of the Hmong in America." *Wisconsin Law Review* (2001): 471.

Lyons, Judith. "Chinese Wife Killer Gets Probation." *Asian Week,* 19 May 1989.

Macedo, Stephen. *Diversity and Distrust: Civic Education in a Multicultural Democracy.* Cambridge: Harvard University Press, 1999.

MacIntire, Alasdair. *After Virtue.* Notre Dame, Ind.: Notre Dame University Press, 1981.

Maguigan, Holly. "Cultural Evidence and Male Violence: Are Feminist and Multiculturalist Reformers on a Collision Course?" *New York University Law Review* 70 (1995): 36.

Malamud, Deborah C. "Affirmative Action, Diversity, and the Black Middle Class." *University of Colorado Law Review* 68 (1997): 939.

——. "Values, Symbols, and the Facts in the Affirmative Action Debate." *Michigan Law Review* 95 (1997): 1668.

Massaro, Toni Marie. *Constitutional Literacy: A Core Curriculum for a Multicultural Nation.* Durham: Duke University Press, 1993.

Mauro, Tony. "Brennan Gets an Education in 'Intolerance.'" *Legal Times,* 29 May 1989.

McConnell, Michael W. "Christ, Culture, and Courts: A Niebuhrian Examination of First Amendment Jurisprudence." *DePaul Law Review* 42 (1992): 191.

——. "Multiculturalism, Majoritarianism, and Educational Choice: What Does Our Constitutional Tradition Have to Say?" *University of Chicago Legal Forum* (1991): 123.

——. "The Selective Funding Problem: Abortions and Religious Schools." *Harvard Law Review* 104 (1991): 989.

McGowan, Miranda Oshige. "Diversity of What?" In *Race And Representation: Affirmative Action,* edited by Robert Post and Michael Rogin. Berkeley: University of California Press, 1998.

Menkel-Meadow, Carrie. "Portia in a Different Voice: Speculations on a Woman's Lawyering Process." *Berkeley Women's Law Journal* 1 (1985): 39.

Miller, David. "The Ethical Significance of Nationality." *Ethics* 98 (1988): 547.

——. "In Defense of Nationality." *Journal of Applied Philosophy* 10 (1993): 3.

Minow, Martha. *Making All the Difference: Inclusion, Exclusion, and American Law.* Ithaca, N.Y.: Cornell University Press, 1990.

Mintz, Alan. "Manners, Morals, and the Academy." Review of *Jews in the American Academy,* by Susanne Klingenstein. *The New Republic,* 9 March 1992.

Monk, Ray. *Ludwig Wittgenstein: The Duty of Genius.* New York: Free Press, 1990.

Moore, Michael. "Moral Reality." *Wisconsin Law Review* (1982): 1062.

——. "A Natural Law Theory of Interpretation." *Southern California Law Review* 58 (1985): 278.

Morgan, Edmund S. *Inventing the People: The Rise of Popular Sovereignty in England and America.* New York: Norton, 1988.

Moskos, Charles C., and John Sibley Butler. *All That We Can Be: Black Leadership and Racial Integration the Army Way.* New York: Basic Books, 1996.

Moynihan, Daniel Patrick. *Pandaemonium: Ethnicity in International Politics.* New York: Oxford University Press, 1993.

Murray, John Courtney. "Governmental Repression of Heresy." *Proceedings of the Catholic Theological Society of America,* 1948.

——. *We Hold These Truths: Catholic Reflections on the American Proposition.* New York: Sheed and Ward, 1960.

Nagel, Thomas. "Moral Conflict and Political Legitimacy." *Philosophy and Public Affairs* 16 (1987): 215.

Nederhood, Joel. "Doing Christian Law." *The Christian Lawyer* 3 (1971): 3.

Noonan, John. "The Catholic Justices of the United States Supreme Court." *Catholic Historical Review* 67 (1981): 369.

——. "The Purposes of Advocacy and the Limits of Confidentiality." *Michigan Law Review* 64 (1966): 1485.

Nussbaum, Martha. "The Future of Feminist Liberalism." Presidential Address to the American Philosophical Association Central Division, 22 April 2003.

Okin, Susan Moller. "Is Multiculturalism Bad for Women?" In *Is Multiculturalism Bad for Women?* edited by Josh Cohen, et al. Princeton: Princeton University Press, 1999.

Orfield, Gary, and Susan E. Eaton and The Harvard Project on School Desegregation. *Dismantling Desegregation: The Quiet Reversal of* Brown v. Board of Education. New York: New Press, 1996.

Parekh, Bhikhu. *Rethinking Multiculturalism: Cultural Diversity and Political Theory.* Cambridge: Harvard University Press, 2000.

Parrish, Michael E. "Cold War Justice: The Supreme Court and the Rosenbergs." *American Historical Review* 82 (1977): 805.

Patterson, James. Brown v. Board of Education: *A Civil Rights Milestone and Its Troubled Legacy.* New York: Oxford University Press, 2001.

Patterson, Orlando. "Race Over." *The New Republic,* 10 January 2000.

Perry, Barbara. "The Life and Death of the 'Catholic Seat' on the United States Supreme Court." *Journal of Law and Politics* 6 (1989): 55.

Perry, Michael. *Morality, Politics and Law: A Bicentennial Essay.* New York: Oxford University Press, 1988.

Plato. *Gorgias.* Translated by Walter Hamilton. Harmondsworth, U.K.: Penguin, 1971.

Post, Robert C. *Constitutional Domains: Democracy, Community, Management.* Cambridge: Harvard University Press, 1998.

——. "Law and Cultural Conflict" (unpublished manuscript).

Povarsky, Chaim. "Jewish Law v. the Law of the State: Theories of Accommodation." *Cardozo Law Review* 12 (1991): 941.

Powe, Lucas A. "The Senate and the Court: Questioning a Nominee." Review in *Texas Law Review* 54 (1976): 891.

Price, Monroe E. "Text and Intellect." *Buffalo Law Review* 33 (1984): 562.

Quint, Emanuel. *A Restatement of Rabbinic Civil Law,* vol. 1. Northvale, N.J.: J. Aronson, 1990.

Radosh, Ronald. *The Rosenberg File: A Search for the Truth.* New York: Holt, Rinehart, and Winston, 1983.

Rae, Douglas, et al. *Equalities.* Cambridge: Harvard University Press, 1981.

Rawls, John. *A Theory of Justice.* Cambridge: Harvard University Press, 1971.

Raz, Joseph. "Facing Diversity: The Case of Epistemic Abstinence." *Philosophy and Public Affairs* 19 (1990): 3.

Rees III, Grover. "Questions for Supreme Court Nominees at Confirmation Hearings: Excluding the Constitution." *Georgia Law Review* 17 (1983): 913.

Richards, David A. J. Review of *Conflicts of Law* and *Morality and Religious Convictions and Political Choice,* by Kent Greenawalt. *Georgia Law Review* 23 (1989): 1189.

Richler, Mordecai. "O Quebec." *The New Yorker,* 30 May 1994.

Rieland, Randy, and Michael J. Weiss. "God, Gibbs, and the Redskins." *The Washingtonian,* September 1992.

Ritter, Lawrence S. *The Glory of Their Times: The Story of the Early Days of Baseball Told by the Men Who Played It.* New York: Morrow, 1984.

Rodell, Fred. "The Joker of Judicial Experience." *The Progressive,* January 1957.

Rosato, Jennifer L. "Putting Square Pegs in a Round Hole: Procedural Due Process and the Effect of Faith Healing Exemptions on the Prosecution of Faith Healing Parents." *University of San Francisco Law Review* 29 (1994): 43.

Rosen, Robert E. "Jews and Corporate Legal Practice." Paper presented at a conference on Jews and the Law, Madison, Wisconsin, November 1991.

Rosenberg, Gerald N. *The Hollow Hope: Can Courts Bring About Social Change?* Chicago: University of Chicago Press, 1991.

Rosenblum, Nancy. *Another Liberalism: Romanticism and Reconstruction of Liberal Thought.* Cambridge: Harvard University Press, 1987.

———. "Separating the Siamese Twins: 'Pluralism' and 'School Choice.'" In *School Choice: The Moral Debate,* edited by Alan Wolfe. Princeton: Princeton University Press, 2002.

Rousseau, Jean-Jacques. *Emile, or On Education.* Translated by Allan Bloom. Ithaca, N.Y.: Cornell University Press, 1979.

Rudenstein, Neil L. "The Uses of Diversity." *Harvard Magazine,* March–April 1996.

Sandel, Michael. *Liberalism and the Limits of Justice.* Cambridge: Cambridge University Press, 1982.

———. "Religious Liberty: Freedom of Conscience or Freedom of Choice?" (unpublished manuscript).

———. "Political Liberalism." *Harvard Law Review* 107 (1994): 1765.

Scalia, Antonin. "God's Justice and Ours." *First Things,* May 2002.

Schachter, Herschel. " 'Dina De-Malchusa Dina': Secular Law as a Religious Obligation." In *Halacha and Contemporary Society,* edited by Alfred S. Cohen. New York: Ktav, 1983.

Schauer, Frederick. "May Officials Think Religiously?" *William and Mary Law Review* 27 (1986): 1075.

Schorske, Carl E. *Fin-de-Siècle Vienna: Politics and Culture.* New York: Knopf, 1979.

Shachar, Ayelet. "Reshaping the Multicultural Model: Group Accommodation and Individual Rights." *Windsor Review of Legal and Social Issues* 8 (1998): 83.

Shaffer, Thomas L. *American Legal Ethics: Text, Readings, and Discussion Topics.* New York: Matthew Bender, 1985.

——. *On Being a Christian and a Lawyer.* Provo, Utah: Brigham Young University Press, 1981.

——. *American Lawyers and Their Communities.* Notre Dame, Ind.: Notre Dame University Press, 1991.

Sherry, Suzanna. "Outlaw Blues." Review of *Red, White, and Blue,* by Mark V. Tushnet. *Michigan Law Review* 87 (1989): 1418.

Siegel, Reva B. "The Racial Rhetorics of Colorblind Constitutionalism: The Case of *Hopwood v. Texas.*" In *Race and Representation: Affirmative Action,* edited by Robert Post and Michael Rogin. Berkeley: University of California Press, 1998.

Sigelman, Lee, et al. "Making Contact? Black-White Social Interaction in an Urban Setting." *American Journal of Sociology* 101 (1996): 1306.

Smith, Rodney K. "Converting the Religious Equality Amendment into a Statute with a Little 'Conscience.'" *Brigham Young Law Review* (1996): 645.

Spinner, Jeff. *The Boundaries of Citizenship: Race, Ethnicity, and Nationality in the Liberal State.* Baltimore: Johns Hopkins University Press, 1994.

Spinner-Halev, Jeff. "Extending Diversity: Religion in Public and Private Education." In *Citizenship in Diverse Societies,* edited by Will Kymlicka and Wayne Norman. New York: Oxford University Press, 2000.

Stampp, Kenneth. *America in 1857: A Nation on the Brink.* New York: Oxford University Press, 1980.

Stolzenberg, Nomi Maya. "'He Drew a Circle that Shut Me Out': Assimilation, Indoctrination, and the Paradox of a Liberal Education." *Harvard Law Review* 106 (1993): 581.

Sugrue, Thomas J. *The Origins of the Urban Crisis: Race and Inequality in Postwar Detroit.* Princeton: Princeton University Press, 1996.

Sullivan, Kathleen M. "Sins of Discrimination: Last Term's Affirmative Action Cases." *Harvard Law Review* 100 (1986): 78.

——. "Religion and Liberal Democracy." In *The Bill of Rights in the Modern State,* edited by Geoffrey R. Stone, et al. Chicago: University of Chicago Press, 1992.

——. "Unconstitutional Conditions." *Harvard Law Review* 102 (1989): 1413.

Sunstein, Cass. *The Partial Constitution.* Cambridge: Harvard University Press, 1993.

Suri, Sharan. "A Matter of Principle and Consistency: Understanding the Battered Woman and Cultural Defenses." *Michigan Journal of Gender and Law* 7 (2000): 107.

Swisher, Carl Brent. *Roger B. Taney.* New York: Macmillan, 1935.

Tamir, Yael. *Liberal Nationalism.* Princeton: Princeton University Press, 1993.

Taylor Jr., Stuart. "Inside the Whirlwind: How Zoë Baird Was Monstrously Caricatured for the Smallest of Sins, Pounded by Press and Popular Righteousness, and Crucified by Prejudice and Hypocrisy." *American Lawyer,* March 1993.

Terhune, Cassandra. "Current International and Domestic Issues Affecting Children: Cultural and Religious Defenses to Child Abuse and Neglect." *Journal of the American Academy of Matrimonial Law* 14 (1997): 152.

Thernstrom, Stephen, ed. *Harvard Encyclopedia of American Ethnic Groups.* Cambridge: Harvard University Press, 1980.

Thomas, David A., and Robin J. Ely. "Making Differences Matter: A New Paradigm for Managing Diversity." *Harvard Business Review* (September–October 1996): 79.

Tierney, Brian. "The Crisis of Church and State, 1050–1300." Engelwood Cliffs, N.J.: Prentice-Hall, 1964.

Tucker, Gordon. "The Confidentiality Role: A Philosophical Perspective with Reference to Jewish Law and Ethics." *Fordham Urban Law Journal* 13 (1985): 99.

Tushnet, Mark. V. Review of *Religious Convictions and Political Choice,* by Kent Greenawalt. *Columbia Law Review* 89 (1989): 1131.

Underkuffler, Laura. " 'Discrimination' on the Basis of Religion: An Examination of Attempted Value Neutrality in Employment." *William and Mary Law Review* 30 (1989): 581.

U.S. Department of Education, National Center for Education Statistics. *Private Schools in the United States: A Statistical Profile,* NCES 97–495. Washington, D.C., 2000.

——. *Private School Universe Study, 1997–98,* NCES 1999–319. Washington, D.C., 1999.

Volokh, Eugene. "Diversity, Race as Proxy, and Religion as Proxy." *UCLA Law Review* 43 (1996): 2059.

Volpp, Leti. "Blaming Culture for Bad Behavior." *Yale Journal of Law and Humanities* 12 (2000): 89.

Waldron, Jeremy. "One Law for All? The Logic of Cultural Accommodation." *Washington and Lee Law Review* 59 (2002): 3.

Walzer, Michael. *Obligations: Essays on Disobedience, War, and Citizenship.* Cambridge: Harvard University Press, 1970.

Wanderer, Nancy A., and Catherine R. Connors. "Culture and Crime: *Kargar* and the Existing Framework for a Cultural Defense." *Buffalo Law Review* 47 (1999): 829.

Westen, Peter. *Speaking of Equality: An Analysis of the Rhetorical Force of "Equality" in Moral and Legal Discourse.* Cambridge: Harvard University Press, 1990.

Williams, Katherine Y. and Charles A. O'Reilly III. "Demography and Diversity in Organizations: A Review of 40 Years of Research." *Research in Organizational Behavior* 20 (1998): 77.

Wittgenstein, Ludwig. *Philosophical Investigations,* 3d ed. New York: Macmillan, 1958.

Wolfe, Alan. *One Nation after All: What Middle-Class Americans Really Think about God, Country, Family, Racism, Welfare, Immigration, Homosexuality, Work, the Right, the Left, and Each Other.* New York: Viking, 1998.

Wright, George. "Legal Obligation and the Natural Law." *Georgia Law Review* 23 (1989): 997.

Yovel, Yirmiahu. *Spinoza and Other Heretics: The Marrano of Reason.* Princeton: Princeton University Press, 1989.

Yudof, Mark G. *When Government Speaks.* Berkeley: University of California Press, 1983.

——. *Educational Policy and the Law,* 3d ed. St. Paul, Minn.: West, 1992.

Index

Sanford Levinson is the W. St. John Garwood and W. St. John Garwood Jr. Centennial Chair in Law and Professor of Government at the University of Texas at Austin. His previous books include *Written in Stone: Public Monuments in Changing Societies* (1998); *Constitutional Faith* (1988) and the edited collections *Legal Canons* (1999); *Constitutional Stupidities, Constitutional Tragedies* (1998); *Responding to Imperfection: The Theory and Practice of Constitutional Amendment* (1985); and *Interpreting Law and Literature: A Hermeneutic Reader* (1988).

Library of Congress Cataloging-in-Publication Data

Levinson, Sanford.

Wrestling with diversity / Sanford Levinson.

p. cm.   Includes bibliographical references and index.

ISBN 0-8223-3226-4 (cloth : alk. paper)

ISBN 0-8223-3239-6 (pbk. : alk. paper)

1. Multiculturalism — Law and legislation — United States. 2. Multiculturalism — Religious aspects. 3. Human rights. I. Title.

KF4755.L48 2003   342.73'0873 — dc21   2003007676